Time in Action

This book explores the role of time in rational agency and practical reasoning. Agents are finite and often operate under severe time constraints. Action takes time and unfolds in time. While time is an ineliminable constituent of our experience of agency, it is both a theoretical and a practical problem to explain whether and how time shapes rational agency and practical thought.

The essays in this book are divided into three parts. Part I is devoted to the temporal structure of action and agency, from metaphysical and metaethical perspectives. Part II features essays about the temporal structure of rational deliberation from the perspective of action theory and theories of practical reasoning. Part III includes essays about the temporal aspects of failures of practical rationality. Taken together, the essays in this book shed new light on our understanding of the temporality of agency that coheres with our subjective sense of finitude and explains rational agency both in time and over time.

Time in Action will be of interest to advanced students and researchers working on the philosophy of time, metaphysics of action, action theory, practical reasoning, ethical theory, moral psychology, and rational justification.

Carla Bagnoli is Professor of Philosophy at the University of Modena and Reggio Emilia, and Visiting Fellow at All Souls College, University of Oxford. She has written extensively on Kantian ethics, the theory of practical reasoning, moral emotions, and responsibility. She is the author of *Ethical Constructivism* (Cambridge UP 2021), and the editor of *Constructivism in Ethics* (Cambridge UP 2013) and *Morality and the Emotions* (Oxford UP 2011).

Routledge Studies in Contemporary Philosophy

Epistemic Uses of Imagination
Edited by Christopher Badura and Amy Kind

Political Philosophy from an Intercultural Perspective
Power Relations in a Global World
Edited by Blanca Boteva-Richter, Sarhan Dhouib, and James Garrison

The Single-Minded Animal
Shared Intentionality, Normativity, and the Foundations of Discursive Cognition
Preston Stovall

Autonomy and Equality
Relational Approaches
Edited by Natalie Stoljar and Kristin Voigt

Contractarianism, Role Obligations, and Political Morality
Benjamin Sachs

Force, Content, and the Unity of the Proposition
Edited by Gabriele M. Mras and Michael Schmitz

John Rawls and the Common Good
Edited by Roberto Luppi

Philosophy of Love in the Past, Present, and Future
Edited by André Grahle, Natasha McKeever, and Joe Saunders

Time in Action
The Temporal Structure of Rational Agency and Practical Thought
Edited by Carla Bagnoli

For more information about this series, please visit: www.routledge.com/Routledge-Studies-in-Contemporary-Philosophy/book-series/SE0720

Time in Action
The Temporal Structure of Rational Agency and Practical Thought

Edited by Carla Bagnoli

NEW YORK AND LONDON

First published 2022
by Routledge
605 Third Avenue, New York, NY 10158

and by Routledge
4 Park Square, Milton Park, Abingdon, Oxon, OX14 4RN

Routledge is an imprint of the Taylor & Francis Group, an informa business

© 2022 Taylor & Francis

The right of Carla Bagnoli to be identified as the author of the editorial material, and of the authors for their individual chapters, has been asserted in accordance with sections 77 and 78 of the Copyright, Designs and Patents Act 1988.

All rights reserved. No part of this book may be reprinted or reproduced or utilised in any form or by any electronic, mechanical, or other means, now known or hereafter invented, including photocopying and recording, or in any information storage or retrieval system, without permission in writing from the publishers.

Trademark notice: Product or corporate names may be trademarks or registered trademarks, and are used only for identification and explanation without intent to infringe.

Library of Congress Cataloging-in-Publication Data
A catalog record for this book has been requested

ISBN: 978-0-367-20158-6 (hbk)
ISBN: 978-1-032-24686-4 (pbk)
ISBN: 978-0-429-25984-5 (ebk)

DOI: 10.4324/9780429259845

Typeset in Sabon
by Apex CoVantage, LLC

Contents

Credits	vii
Introduction CARLA BAGNOLI	1

PART I
Acting in Time — 13

1. **Verbs of Action and Acting in Time** — 15
   JENNIFER HORNSBY

2. **Action Cubes and Traces** — 32
   CONSTANTINE SANDIS

3. **Normative Powers, Agency, and Time** — 52
   ARTO LAITINEN

PART II
Diachronic Self-Governance — 73

4. **A Planning Agent's Self-Governance Over Time** — 75

   Appendix: Acting Together With Oneself Over Time — 95
   MICHAEL E. BRATMAN

5. **The Structures of Temporally Extended Agents** — 108
   LUCA FERRERO

Contents

6 Agency and Time   133
ABRAHAM SESSHU ROTH

7 Sticking to It and Settling: Commitments, Normativity, and the Future   149
CAROLINE T. ARRUDA

8 Extended Agency and the Problem of Diachronic Autonomy   173
JULIA NEFSKY AND SERGIO TENENBAUM

9 Hard Times: Self-governance, Freedom to Change, and Normative Adjustment   196
CARLA BAGNOLI

PART III
Failures of Temporal Agency   219

10 Weakness and the Memory of Resolutions   221
LAURENT JAFFRO

11 Inverse Akrasia: A Case for Meta-Reasoning About One's Emotions   243
MONIKA BETZLER

12 Individual Time-Bias and Social Discounting   264
BRIAN HEDDEN

List of Contributors   284
Index   285

Credits

All these chapters are original contributions to this volume, except Chapter 4, "A Planning Agent's Self-Governance Over Time", by Michael E. Bratman, which was presented at the workshop on *Time in Action* held at the *Center for the Study of Mind in Nature*, at the University of Oslo, in 2017, and first appeared in his *Planning, Time, and Self-Governance: Essays in Practical Rationality* (Oxford University Press, 2018, pp. 224–249). We would like to thank Oxford University Press for granting permission to reprint this material. Bratman's "Appendix" to this chapter has been especially written for this volume and appears here for the first time.

Introduction

Carla Bagnoli

While time is an ineliminable constituent of our ordinary experience of agency, explaining how time shapes rational agency and practical thought has proven to be a daunting philosophical task.[1] This volume brings together philosophers of different fields who have joined forces to undertake this endeavor. The implications and consequences of the temporality of agency are explored from various philosophical perspectives, ranging from the metaphysics of agency, to the theory of practical rationality, to moral and political philosophy.

Philosophers interested in the metaphysics of action have predominantly focused on the explanation of action as situated in time, by engaging in discussions regarding the causal role of agents.[2] A central problem is how to account for the place of agents in a world whose operations are supposed to be physical if the phenomenon of agency is not merely an aspect of the phenomenon of mentality. By contrast, practical philosophy has approached time as a distinctive source of constraints on human agency, often described in contrast to idealized accounts of rational agency.[3] Debates about practical reasoning typically focus on the fact that finitude is a source of severe limitations on rational agency and practical thought, insofar as it curtails the opportunities of action, limits cognitive capacities and information and restricts the horizon within which choice is envisioned. Finite agents deliberate under the pressure of time.[4] Moral philosophers have paid special attention to the relation between finitude and embodiment, which has been traditionally regarded as the main obstacle to the full display of rationality. On this view, embodiment is the origin of various sorts of vulnerabilities, and temporal bias is nothing but one manifestation of the fragility of the will.[5] Normative theories of practical rationality in moral and in political philosophy search for principles that allow finite rational agents to decide when it is rationally best to act, how to decide between goods that are located at different times, or how to deliberate effectively under temporal pressure.

The essays included in this collection hope to make some progress in both formulating and addressing these large questions about how time affects rational agency and practical thought. They share the assumptions

DOI: 10.4324/9780429259845-1

that the metaphysics of agency is shaped by time, that our subjective awareness of finitude and temporal extendedness plays a significant role in our practical thought, and that this awareness should be a driving consideration in designing a normative account of practical rationality. From this perspective, temporality is not only a source of predicaments but also (and more importantly) a constitutive feature of human agency that gives rise to distinctive philosophical problems regarding the shape of action and the forms of rational deliberation.

The volume is organized into three inter-related parts. Part I is titled *Acting in Time* and concerns a set of issues that arise when we consider time as a feature of agency rather than as an abstract dimension in which action happens. This part includes three essays dedicated to the metaphysical construal of acting in time, the temporal structure of action, and its impact on the philosophy of language, moral philosophy, and metaethics. In Chapter 1, **Jennifer Hornsby** discusses the impact of the standard theory of action on the metaphysics of time. She notices that the philosophy of action has been concerned primarily with human agency, and that within this domain, current debates have been predominantly organized around the causal theory of action defended by Donald Davidson (1978). The main reason for such a wide endorsement is that the event-causal framework appeals to anyone committed to a naturalistic account of rational action based on a parsimonious ontology, including non-reductivist accounts that make room for agential phenomena. A theory of human action aims to identify the core features of human agency and explain how they cohere with the possibility that we are fully embedded in an event-causal order. Hornsby is well known for her powerful critique of the "standard story", according to which actions are caused by the combination of beliefs and desires (Hornsby 2004, 2010). In this chapter, she takes as her target the event-causal framework, going back to Davidson's arguments regarding the ontology of events with an eye to the general implications that such arguments have for the language of action and the metaphysics of time. As for repercussions in the philosophy of language, Hornsby focuses on the treatment of the progressive tense in semantics and the so-called "imperfective paradox", engaging with the solutions envisaged by Zoltán Gendler Szabó (2004). Her more general aim is to show that the rejection of the causal account of action raises important metaphysical questions, some of which are anticipated by G.E.M. Anscombe (1957, §23), and that these questions are carried forward by a number of philosophers that distance themselves from and provide alternatives to the causal theory of action (e.g., Thompson 2008).

In Chapter 2, **Constantine Sandis** contributes to reinforcing some of the points pressed by Hornsby, by appropriating Paul Ricoeur's "philosophy of the trace", which deeply resonates with various attempts to distinguish between "doings" and "things done" in analytic philosophy of action (e.g., John Macmurray, G.H. von Wright, and Anscombe). Ultimately, this approach reclaims models of action inspired by Hegel as a preferable alternative to Davidson's causal theory (Taylor 1983; Laitinen and Sandis 2010; Brandom 2019), Following Ricoeur, Sandis understands the "things we do" as marks left on time by the events of our acting, thereby uncovering a tight relation between the philosophy of action and the philosophy of history (Ricoeur 2000). Such marks are somehow more permanent than passing events and can be represented with regard to different dimensions (e.g., inner/outer, surface/foundation, and foreground/background). Furthermore, Sandis' proposal improves upon Ricoeur's understanding of action in terms of cubes and traces by offering a more coherent general conceptual framework that takes actions as processes rather than events. This conceptual and metaphysical apparatus enables us to correctly approach "acting rightly" as opposed to "doing the right thing", hence correcting some serious misunderstandings that mar normative ethics insofar as it conflates these notions (Sandis 2017). This novel approach promises to make progress in various interrelated debates about reasons, intentions, and consequences, as well as in the ethics of memory, cultural heritage, and the right to be forgotten. This argument establishes a direct connection between the philosophy of action, moral philosophy, and the philosophy of history.

In Chapter 3, **Arto Laitinen** addresses the problem of temporality by examining the metaphysical status of the evaluative standards of action, which is a central topic in moral philosophy and metaethics. Laitinen compares and assesses the prospects of three metaethical theories regarding truths that are situation-specific and sensitive to time. First, realism defends the existence of situation-specific truths, independently of whether the situation actually obtains and whether any actual judgment is made concerning the situation. Second, and by contrast, constructivism denies the existence of situation-specific truths prior to and independently of practical reasoning. Third, progressive historicism ties determinate truths to a progressively justified evaluative framework and to this extent brings to the fore the problem of normative and evaluative change. Laitinen finds the third theoretical option promising, reclaiming the Hegelian lineage from Charles Taylor and Alastair MacIntyre to John Dewey, already highlighted by Sandis in Chapter 2 (and Laitinen and Sandis 2010). These philosophers approach change not only as a metaphysical quandary but also (and more importantly), as a practical (moral, legal, and political) issue. This perspective allows us to fruitfully approach foundational issues such as whether there are pre-institutional normative powers, whether the exercise of normative power is transformative, and whether and how history matters for the metaphysics of supervenience. Laitinen considers and rejects several proposals modeled on positive law: e.g., that of the authority of positive law, and civil disobedience. In contrast to these proposals, he argues for a distinctive progressivist model that vindicates the role of general principles in generating truths, while recognizing the importance of their sensitivity to time.

Part II is titled *Diachronic Self-Governance* includes six essays about the features of diachronic agency, which are central topics in the philosophy of action and in the theory of practical rationality. The essays address problems that affect rational agents insofar as they are temporally extended and discuss the rationale, justification, and scope of the norms of diachronic practical rationality, such as diachronic self-governance, coherence, and stability over time. In Chapter 4, **Michael Bratman** asks how diachronically self-governing planning agency secures stability over time. In his previous works, Bratman has argued that human agency is to be understood in terms of three core features: reflectiveness, planfulness, and the conception of life as temporally extended. The capacity for planning is a distinctive form of purposiveness and comes with commitments to various norms of practical rationality. In this chapter, Bratman further investigates the specific dimension of diachronic self-governance and argues that it responds to some common threats that undermine our organization and stability over time. Thus, to understand how self-governance works, it is important to understand what these threats are. Importantly, Bratman's aim is to identify a model of self-governance that is not merely apt for managing ourselves over time but is also expressive of the relevant sort of cross-temporal connections. Thus, for instance, the way that Ulysses binds himself to overcome temptation does not qualify as the sort of rational self-governance that secures diachronic stability over time (Elster 1998, 2000). By contrast, Bratman seeks the relevant sort of inter-connections that will support the planning agent's (synchronic and diachronic) stability. The plan theoretic model promises to be fertile for a number of different decisions problems, such as the famous dilemma faced by Sartre's student. Why should the student avoid going back and forth between the two options, settle on a course of action, and stick with it? The answer builds upon the argument that establishes an analogy between a planning agent's diachronic self-governance and shared agency. According to Bratman, certain structural features of socially shared agency have intrapersonal, cross-temporal analogues that are an important aspect of diachronic self-governance. The analogy should not be understood in terms of an interpersonal bargain between temporal selves at different times. To attribute diachronic self-governance to a planning agent is to say that she is not merely managing herself, by governing her relevant actions at each relevant time along the way. More to the point, her thought and action at these times along the way are interconnected in ways that support the metaphor of shared agency: at these different times, she is thinking and acting "together" with herself. To sustain this conception, Bratman proposes a diachronicalized view of the practical standpoints on action. This proposal bears important implications for other widely discussed cases, such as brute shuffling, temptation, and the toxin puzzle.

In the *Appendix* to this chapter, Bratman further develops the structural analogy between planning diachronic agency and shared agency that arises from the interlocking intentions of individuals. The analogy is helpful in accounting for decision problems, in an alternative to models of practical reasoning that accept the "myth of the unstructured weighing of reasons". According to Bratman, plans provide the background against which deliberative problems are framed, and options are filtered (Bratman 1987, pp. 33–34). In fulfilling this role, plans involve and commit to norms of practical rationality, such as consistency, means-ends coherence, and diachronic stability. His argument is that the norm of diachronic stability tracks the conditions of self-governance over time. Planning agents have a *pro tanto* reason to govern their lives, and in virtue of this tracking relation, they also have a *pro tanto* normative reason to favor conformity in particular cases.

All the chapters in Part II are ideally in dialogue with the work of Michael Bratman, either developing or critically engaging with some aspects or presuppositions of his planning theory. In Chapter 5, **Luca Ferrero** investigates the relationships between the different possible temporal structures of extended actions, their ends, and the lives of agents. Ferrero distinguishes two basic ways in which a single activity extends over time: the mere continuity of its momentary stages and temporal extension in the mode of "temporal unity", which is the form of genuinely diachronic intentional agency. Though extended, human agency is finite, and the operations of psychological and executive powers are temporally constrained. To capture these local features of human agency, Ferrero talks of "temporal selves", which are neither assimilated to instantaneous "time-slice selves" – terminology used in the metaphysics of transtemporal identity – nor do they imply that the agent's stance is momentary. In fact, Ferrero agrees with Bratman (2018, and Chapter 4 of this volume) that very little sense can be given to a momentary practical standpoint. However, he argues that the passage of time tends to generate by itself forms of alienation from distant temporal selves. To fend off this disruptive tendency and sustain a genuine form of temporally extended agency, the separate temporal selves must share a temporally extended and integrated practical standpoint in the distinctive mode of unity and integration. Ferrero argues that this form of identity does not precede temporal identification but is co-constituted with it and takes the form of interselves cooperation (cf. Dorsey 2018; Bratman, Appendix). His account of the complexities of the modes of integration is meant to counter those current accounts, which are confined to simpler and highly idealized models of identification. The comparative advantage of this view is that it makes sense of the goods that can be achieved only by agents capable of strong modes of integration (Ferrero 2009).

In Chapter 6, **Abraham Sesshu Roth** elucidates the distinctive attitude that an agent takes toward her prospective action when she decides and intends it. Philosophers often deploy the term "settling" to refer to decisions or intentions in contrast to other attitudes regarding a prospective action, such as entertaining the possibility of it, expecting it, finding it attractive, valuing it as worth doing, etc. (Bratman 1987). Roth notices that the term is used ambiguously and distinguishes between two senses. The intransitive sense of settling concerns the agent being settled on a goal and entails that the agent has ruled out alternative courses of action and takes the necessary steps and means to do what she intends to do. The transitive sense of settling some prospective matter is more robust and involves a distinctive committal to acting as intended. Once this distinction is introduced, a problem arises about deciding future action. How do decisions have a direct impact on action at some temporal remove? Ordinary agents seem to adopt a robust sense of intending, which settles matters beforehand. But this intuitive notion seems to hold a commitment to the implausible thought that one can directly settle a future state and thus raises thorny philosophical issues about the coherence of a transcendent yet practical standpoint. After examining various solutions to this problem, Roth concludes that the robust notion of settling that is implicit in deciding requires that the non-transcendent temporal and causal process through which temporal rational agents exercise their influence must be conceived of in a certain way by the agent. The governance of future actions is secured through a process that involves an immediate and rational uptake of the intention by the agent at subsequent times.

In Chapter 7, **Caroline T. Arruda** considers whether and how commitments secure diachronic stability. At first sight, they seem apt to the task insofar as they share some features of the mechanisms that are generally thought to provide stability. They are means to settle on a decision, seem to possess a forward-looking normative force like plans, are self-directed like promises, and express virtues such as strength of will, stability, and perseverance. Because of these apparent features, commitments seem to qualify as indirect sources of agential stability, where stability is understood in terms of our capacity for "stick-to-it-ness". Arruda discusses some scenarios in which the capacity of commitments to support agential stability just in virtue of making them is called into question. To make progress on this issue, conceptual refinement and case-driven argumentation are provided. Arruda distinguishes four specific kinds of stability that the concept of agential stability comprises and reconsiders whether commitments help with any of these dimensions of agential stability. Thus framed, the question of how commitments support and contribute to agential stability is shown to be interestingly connected to more substantive views of normativity. While commitments do not provide agential stability in the direct way in which they do generally thought to work, they do in fact indirectly support agential stability. They do so in virtue of their relationship to what is important for us or what we value. Thus, commitments are means for but not the sources of normative agential stability. A tenet of Arruda's work is that our evaluative commitments play a large role in the exercise of the capacities that pertain to a full-blown agent. To this extent, one has only a hypothetical reason for being an agent.

In Chapter 8, **Julia Nefsky and Sergio Tenenbaum** propose a novel approach to the problem of agential autonomy over time, which is a central theme in current debates. If one is simply acting according to prior decisions, does one ever act autonomously? This problem is typically framed in terms of temporal selves. The past self seems to be in charge of the present self's action. If the present self is just acting according to the past selves' prior deliberation, without any further reasoning or mechanism of endorsement, then it is unclear how present action is the result of present autonomous agency. On the contrary, it appears that the present self is fulfilling the wishes of the past self, carrying on its plans, realizing its purposes, and performing its commands. The present self might refuse to go through with the former self's orders. However, refusal to carry on the past self's plan and reconsideration cannot be the way in which the self systemically operates, otherwise there will be no genuine ability to make effective future-directed decisions. Such an ability requires being able to settle on a decision in a way that blocks systematic reconsideration. The problem of diachronic autonomy is to explain how the present self can act autonomously while carrying on the decisions of its former self. There is wide agreement that diachronic autonomy is a problem that distinctively affects extended agents. In contrast, Nefsky and Tenenbaum argue that current formulations of the problem of diachronic autonomy are incoherent because they implicitly presuppose two inconsistent conceptions of human agency: that is, the time-slice conception and the temporally extended conception of agency. In fact, there is no special problem of diachronic autonomy and no disanalogy between synchronic and diachronic exercises of autonomous agency.

In Chapter 9, **Carla Bagnoli** investigates some examples of temporal dissonance, which she takes to be paradigmatic of temporally structured agency. Despite the heavy weight of past deliberations and decisions, temporally structured agents such as we are conceive of themselves as free to change their plans, free to come to terms with the claims of the past, and free to question whether past commitments still provide compelling reasons for action. Indeed, preserving such freedom is an ethical and political priority, related to the right to develop one's own conception of the flourishing life. Bagnoli argues that to fully understand the freedom to change and develop, we have to take into account temporal constraints on rational agency in ways that have largely escaped current debates. Such debates construe the challenge posited by temporal constraints on rational choice as a threat to diachronic coherence and self-governance. By contrast, Bagnoli brings into sharp relief rational practices of "normative adjustment" as the key modes of dynamic self-governance, arguing that the temporal agents' deliberative powers are directly invested in this endeavor. She points toward a dynamic conception of practical rationality that draws on a plastic network of normative and cognitive capacities and competences, such as temporally oriented emotional attitudes and meta-cognitive capacities. The dynamic view of self-governance promises a better understanding of cross-temporal conflicts of value, in contrast to the analogy with shuffling and conversion.

Part III of the volume is titled *Failures of Temporal Agency* and includes three essays about varieties of practical irrationality which are of moral and political significance. Time constrains agency in many ways, as it limits the range of options that are open to agents, impacts on the ends that they can achieve, limits the means available to them, and severely affects their cognitive capacities and practical resources. In Chapter 10, **Laurent Jaffro** discusses the temporal aspects of the relations between evaluative judgments and choices. According to a widespread view, a value judgment cannot have any authority on our current preference set without being co-present with it or part of it. This view plays a crucial role in a common understanding of diachronic control and weakness of the will. In the first part of the chapter, Jaffro offers reasons to doubt that this view is credible, based on considerations that resonate with the theory of bounded rationality and the debate on the organizing role of pre-commitments (cf. Morton 2012; Elster 2000). In the second part of the chapter, Jaffro argues that there is an important difference between the memory of past practical judgments and the memory of past reasoning. Moral judgment involves a sort of commitment to act upon the judgment when action is required. Contrary to a claim defended by Leibniz, Jaffro argues that the memory of practical evaluations is ultimately normative and not reducible to the factual memory of the operations of reasoning. Correspondingly, weakness of the will basically depends on defective normative memory, combined with other circumstantial factors. To compensate for such a problematic condition, human agents avail themselves of normative tools of self-management, such as the anticipatory self-commands identified by Thomas Schelling (1984). The normative memory of our past evaluations importantly shapes the context of choice, in a manner that contrasts with the claim that practical reasoning deals with normative reasons in a vacuum, as if the deliberative domain is unstructured (cf. Bratman's Appendix). According to Jaffro, the normative memory of the past influences choice in a manner analogous to pre-commitments: that is, by imposing diachronic constraints on the self. In the case of weak agents, this influence is more effective than the appeal to the norm of coherence.

In Chapter 11, **Monika Betzler** addresses the problem of "inverse akrasia": that is, the case in which an agent acts against her best judgment on account of an emotion, and the resulting action ultimately proves to be the reasonable thing to do. Cases of inverse akrasia seem to show that akrasia is not irrational when akratic agents are guided by emotions toward their good. On the basis of this claim, some philosophers have further held that best judgments are beliefs (e.g., Arpaly 2000), that emotions can track reasons (e.g., Brady 2013), and qualify as forms of moral discernment, at least when a kind of regulative control is in place (e.g., Jones 2003). In contrast to these proposals, Betzler argues that cases of inverse akrasia are not necessarily cases of rational agency, although they are instructive about reasons' sensitivity to time and the temporal structure of rational agency. For temporally extended agents, reasons can expire over time, and best judgments generate only pro tanto reasons. Thus, rational agency requires more than synchronic coherence and conformity to the authority of one's best judgment. Temporally extended rational agents whose reasons are sensitive to time are also required to monitor the reasoning that led to their best judgment and likewise check the appropriateness of their attitudes in light of changing reasons. Betzler argues that this function is only partially fulfilled by appropriate emotions. Insofar as emotions are reason-tracking, agents can revise their best judgment on the basis of their reasoned emotions so as to maintain their rational agency over time. Thus, Betzler proposes a reasoning pattern that progresses from appropriate emotions to the reconsideration of best judgment, thereby making room for emotions in self-correcting and self-monitoring practices of practical reasoning.

In Chapter 12, **Brian Hedden** considers the issue of how appropriate attitudes to time within a life relate to appropriate attitudes to time across lives. An individual is time-biased if she weights the interests of her near-future selves more heavily than those of her far-future selves. A society employs a discount rate if it weights the interests of near-future people more heavily than those of far-future people. Many economists and philosophers assume that the two issues are independent, so that the permissibility of individual time-bias does not entail the permissibility of social discounting, or *vice versa*. In contrast, Hedden argues that the two issues should be approached together, as they exhibit significant structural similarity. First, in his view, there are strong analogies between individuals and groups. On the one hand, a temporally extended agent can be represented as a group consisting of her various time-slices; on the other hand, certain groups that display a unified and coherent pattern of behavior can be represented as group agents. This representation encourages the view that there are structural analogies between norms for individuals and norms for groups. However, the analogy is based on different considerations than those pertinent to temporally extended agency. In fact, in previous works, Hedden (2015) has argued for the radical claim that the locus of rationality is the time-slice rather than the temporally extended agent. On his impersonal, time-slice-centric approach, what rationality demands of agents is determined by evidence, and thus past beliefs or actions have no special place and apply no legitimate normative pressure. The purported advantage of this view is that it grounds normative reasons about what one ought to do on one's current perspective on the world and avoids any metaphysical commitments about temporal extendedness.

The relationship between different time-slices of the same person is no different from the relationship between different people. Second, Hedden argues that nearly all major arguments for and against the permissibility of individual time-bias apply equally for or against social discounting, and *vice versa*. He concludes that individual time-bias is permissible if and only if social discounting is permissible.

The authors hope that this collection of innovative essays on the temporality of agency will spark interest and encourage further research on topics that are central to intertwined debates in metaphysics, action theory, the theory of practical reason, and moral and political philosophy.[6]

Notes

1 See, e.g., Bratman (2010, 2018), Holly (2013), Altshuler and Sigrist (2016), and Ferrero (2022, part 7).
2 On the causal theory of action, see Davidson (1963, 2001), Mele (1992), and Aguilar and Buckareff (2010). On the critical assessment of the standard story of action, see Hornsby (2004, 2008, 2010), Schlosser (2010), Stout (1996, 2018), Clark (2017, 2019), and cf. Smith (2012).
3 See, e.g., Gigerenzer and Goldstein (1996), Morton (2012), and Millgram (2014) and (2022).
4 Examples of this line of inquiry include Loewenstein and Elster (1992), Elster (1998, 2000), Andreou and White (2010), Tenenbaum (2014), Andreou and Tenenbaum (2016), and Andreou (2020).
5 Classical readings include Nagel (1970) and Parfit (1984). For some representative examples of recent literature, see Wallace (2013), Hare (2008), Hedden (2015), Dougherty (2015), Dorsey (2018), and Ferrero (2022, part 7).
6 Most of these chapters were presented at two workshops of the European Network of Practical Reasoning and Normative Psychology, held at the *Center for the Study of Mind in Nature*, at the University of Oslo, which I organized as part of the activities of my Professorial Fellowship at the Department of Classics, History of Arts and Ideas, respectively in 2016 and 2017, respectively. I would like to thank my colleagues Christel Fricke, Olav Gjelsvik, and Caj Strandberg for their unfailing support on these occasions, as well as the audiences, and participants, and in particular those who are not present in this volume, Edward Harcourt, Matthias Haase, Douglas Lavin, Sarah Paul, and Christophe Salvat.

References

Aguilar, Jesús H. and Buckareff, Andrei A. eds. 2010. *Causing Human Actions: New Perspectives on the Causal Theory of Action*. London: Bradford Books.
Altshuler, Roman and Sigrist, Michael J. eds. 2016. *Time and the Philosophy of Action*. London: Routledge.
Andersen, Holly. 2013. "The Representation of Time in Agency." In Adrian Bardon and Heather Dyke eds. *Blackwell Companion to Philosophy of Time*. Hoboken, New Jersey: Wiley-Blackwell.
Andreou, Chrisoula. 2020. "Dynamic Choice." In Edward N. Zalta ed. *The Stanford Encyclopedia of Philosophy* (Winter 2020 Edition). URL = <https://plato.stanford.edu/archives/win2020/entries/dynamic-choice/>.

Andreou, Chrisoula and Tenenbaum, Sergio. eds. 2016. *Belief, Action and Rationality Over Time*. London: Routledge.
Andreou, Chrisoula and White, Mark D. eds. 2010. *The Thief of Time: Philosophical Essays on Procrastination*. Oxford: Oxford University Press.
Anscombe, G.E.M. 1957. *Intention*. Oxford: Basil Blackwell and Cambridge, MA: Harvard University Press.
Arpaly, Nomy. 2000. "On Acting Rationally against One's Best Judgment." *Ethics*, 110(3): 488–513.
Brady, Michael S. 2013. *Emotional Insight: The Epistemic Role of Emotional Experience*. Oxford: Oxford University Press
Brandom, Robert B. 2019. *A Spirit of Trust: A Reading of Hegel's Phenomenology*. Cambridge, MA: Harvard University Press.
Bratman, Michael E. 1987. *Intention, Plans, and Practical Reason*. Cambridge, MA: Harvard University Press.
Bratman, Michael E. 2010. "Agency, Time, and Sociality." *Proceedings of the American Philosophical Association*, 84(2): 7–26.
Bratman, Michael E. 2018. *Planning, Time, and Self-Governance: Essays in Practical Rationality*. New York: Oxford University Press.
Clarke, Randolph. 2017. "Free Will, Agent Causation, and 'Disappearing Agents'." *Noûs*, 76–96.
Clarke, Randolph. 2019. "Agent Causation and the Phenomenology of Agency." *Pacific Philosophical Quarterly*, 100(3): 747–764.
Davidson, Donald. 1963. "Actions, Reasons, and Causes." *Journal of Philosophy*, 60(23): 685.
Davidson, Donald. 1978. "Intending." *Philosophy of History and Action*, 11:41–60.
Davidson, Donald. 2001. *Essays on Actions and Events*. Oxford: Clarendon Press.
Dorsey, Dale. 2018. "Prudence and Past Selves." *Philosophical Studies*, 175(8): 1901–1925.
Dougherty, Tom. 2015. "Future-Bias and Practical Reason." *Philosophers' Imprint*, 15(30): 1–16.
Elster, Jon. 1998. *Ulysses and the Sirens: Studies in Rationality and Irrationality*. Cambridge, MA: Cambridge University Press.
Elster, Jon. 2000. *Ulysses Unbound: Studies in Rationality, Precommitment, and Constraints*. Cambridge, MA: Cambridge University Press.
Ferrero, Luca. 2009. "What Good is a Diachronic Will?" *Philosophical Studies*, 144(3): 403–430.
Ferrero, Luca. ed. 2022. *The Routledge Handbook of Philosophy of Agency*. Milton Park Abingdon: Routledge.
Gigerenzer, Gerd and Goldstein, Daniel G. 1996. "Reasoning the Fast and Frugal Way: Models of Bounded Rationality." *Psychological Review*, 103(4): 650–669.
Hare, Caspar. 2008. "A Puzzle about Other-Directed Time-Bias." *Australasian Journal of Philosophy* 86: 269–277.
Hedden, Brian. 2015. *Reasons Without Persons: Rationality, Identity, and Time*. Oxford: Oxford University Press.
Hornsby, Jennifer. 2004. "Agency and Actions." In Helen Steward and John Hyman eds. *Agency and Action*. Cambridge: Cambridge University Press, 1–23.

Hornsby, Jennifer. 2008. "Agency and Alienation." In Mario De Caro and David MacArthur (eds.), *Naturalism in Question*. Cambridge, MA: Harvard University Press, 173–187.
Hornsby, Jennifer. 2010. "The Standard Story of Action: An Exchange." In Jesús H. Aguilar and Andrei A. Buckareff eds. *Causing Human Actions: New Perspectives on the Causal Theory of Action*. Cambridge, MA: MIT Press, 57–68.
Jones, Karen. 2003. "Emotion, Weakness of Will, and the Normative Conception of Agency." In Anthony Hatzimoysis ed. *Philosophy and the Emotions*. Cambridge: Cambridge University Press, 181–200.
Laitinen, Arto and Sandis, Constantine. eds. 2010. *Hegel on Action*. London: Palgrave Macmillan.
Loewenstein, George and Elster, Jon. 1992. *Choice Over Time*. New York: Russell Sage Foundation.
Mele, Alfred R. 1992. *Springs of Action: Understanding Intentional Behavior*. Oxford: Oxford University Press.
Millgram, Elijah. 2014. "Segmented Agency." In Manuel Vargas and Gideon Yaffe (eds.), *Rational and Social Agency: The Philosophy of Michael Bratman*. Oxford: Oxford University Press, 152–189.
Millgram, Elijah. 2022. "Bounded Agency." In Ferrero, The Routledge Handbook of Philosophy of
Agency. New York: Routledge. 68–75.
Morton, Adam 2012. *Bounded Thinking: Intellectual Virtues for Limited Agents*. Oxford: Oxford University Press.
Nagel, Thomas. 1970. *The Possibility of Altruism*. Oxford: Clarendon Press.
Parfit, Derek. 1984. *Reasons and Persons*. Oxford: Oxford University Press.
Ricoeur, Paul. 2000. *La Mémoire, l'Histoire, l'Oubli* [Memory, History, Forgetting]. Chicago: University of Chicago Press.
Sandis, Constantine. 2017. "The Doing and the Deed: Action in Normative Ethics." *Royal Institute of Philosophy Supplement*, 80: 105–126.
Schelling, Thomas. 1984. "Self-Command in Practice, in Policy, and in a Theory of Rational Choice." *The American Economic Review*, 74(2): 1–11.
Schlosser, Markus E. 2010. "Agency, Ownership, and the Standard Theory." In A. Buckareff, J. Aguilar and K. Frankish eds. *New Waves in Philosophy of Action*. London: Palgrave-Macmillan, 13–31.
Smith, Michael. 2012. "Four Objections to the Standard Story of Action (and Four Replies)." *Philosophical Issues*, 22(1): 387–401.
Stout, Rowland. 1996. *Things That Happen Because They Should: A Teleological Approach to Action*. Oxford: Oxford University Press.
Stout, Rowland. ed. 2018. *Process, Action, and Experience*. Oxford: Oxford University Press.
Szabó, Zoltán Gendler. 2004. "On the Progressive and the Perfective." *Noûs*, 38(1): 29–59.
Taylor, Charles. 1983. "Hegel and the Philosophy of Action." In Laitinen and Sandis eds. Hegel on Action. Palgrave-Macmillan. 2010: 22–41.
Tenenbaum, Sergio. 2014. Choice Over Time. Special issue of *Inquiry*, 57(3).
Thompson, Michael. 2008. *Life and Action*. Cambridge, MA: Harvard University Press.
Wallace, R. Jay. 2013. *The View from Here: On Affirmation, Attachment, and the Limits of Regret*. New York: Oxford University Press.

Part I
Acting in Time

1 Verbs of Action and Acting in Time

Jennifer Hornsby

Overview

This chapter is intended to alert philosophers who take no account of it to the fact that agents live and act in time, and that time passes as they act. It is critical of Davidson who, in taking teleological explanation to be reducible to causal explanation, introduced an ontological reduction. Davidson thus provided a treatment of actions as events which failed to allow for the fact that so long as someone is (or was) acting, something is (or was) ongoing. It is also critical of attempts to introduce an ontology of "events in progress" alongside the Davidsonian event ontology. More generally, it argues that in much philosophy of action, there is a failure to recognize that verbs of action, whether they occur with perfect or with imperfect aspect, are predicated of agents. And it suggests that it is endemic to much analytic philosophy, which settles for imagining that all predication can be treated along Fregean lines, to fail to register any difference between, for example, "Φ-d" [perfect] and "was Φing" [imperfect]. The consequence is that philosophers whose work takes place against a background of the field as Davidson introduced it treat agency from an abstracted perspective so that they rule out any proper understanding of agency from the perspective of the agent herself.

1. Time as a Topic in Metaphysics

Time being a topic in metaphysics, one might think that questions about time in action would concern how such accounts of time as there are in the literature would play out in the philosophy of action or would concern connections between the idea of agency and ideas of persistence, continuity, and change. Such overarching questions in metaphysics have not been addressed in the philosophy of action as it has developed, however. Philosophy of action as we know it has been confined more or less to human action, with the result that questions about specifically human agency have assumed priority over questions about agency that a metaphysician might see fit to ask.

DOI: 10.4324/9780429259845-3

Michael Bratman isolates "our reflectiveness, our planfulness, and our conception of our agency as temporally extended as among the *core* features of human agency", and he says that "a theory of human action . . . needs to clarify the relation between these core features . . . and the possibility that we are fully embedded in an event causal order". One could hardly disagree with Bratman that understanding these features may have "great significance for the kinds of lives we can live".[1] But one could have questions about the causal order and about what our being fully embedded in it amounts to.

Bratman has said of his own work that it "has taken place against a background of field-defining work by Donald Davidson".[2] At one point, Bratman mentioned what has been thought to be a difficulty for Davidson's causal theory of action, a difficulty about knowing "how to say what counts as an appropriate explanatory relation between intention and action" – what it is "for the intention to issue in the action 'in the right way'".[3] Bratman set the difficulty aside, indicating that it might go away if one settles for "a kind of conceptual non-reducibility of individual intentionality of action", and he cites Davidson in support.[4] Davidson had suggested that his account of the concept of acting with an intention should be taken to provide "not a definitional, but an ontological, reduction". Davidson had high hopes for his ontological reduction. "If it succeeds", he said, "it is enough to answer many puzzles . . . , and to explain the possibility of autonomous action in a world of causality" (p. 88 [1978]).[5] Ontological reduction was achieved by introducing events, the relata of *cause*, with actions among them.

I have come to disagree profoundly with the sort of story of human action told by Davidson. A very long time ago, I accused Davidson of using "action" ambiguously, thinking that he sometimes used it so that its application was confined to things of the past and at other times applied it to things that might or might not be past. Still in my book *Actions*,[6] although I didn't accept Davidson's story, I went along with it insofar as I supposed that a relation "cause" between events was fundamental to an account of agency. That is something I stopped believing a good few years ago. But it is only quite recently that I have looked again specifically at the arguments that Davidson gave, in papers of more than 50 years ago, in which he introduced his ontology of events. I find that, although the papers have been much referred to, those arguments have never received much detailed scrutiny. I shall revisit them here.

I shall come to argue that in appreciating what is wrong with the theory of action to which Davidson's ontology leads, one learns something more general about the repercussions for thinking about *time* in a manner got from treating predication as analytic philosophers are apt to treat it. I'll return at the end to more about what I mean in saying this, when I come to suggest that broad metaphysical questions are raised when Davidson's story of action is put in question (§7).

2. Events as Introduced by Davidson

Since I'm going to focus on the predication of action verbs in connection with Davidson's conception of actions, let me start by quoting some sentences in which Davidson made a series of predications of verbs. The sentences come near the start of his well-known paper "Actions, Reasons and Causes".

> I flip the switch, turn on the light and illuminate the room . . . and also alert the prowler. . . . Here I do not do four things, but only one, of which four descriptions have been given. I flipped the switch because I wanted to turn on the light.
>
> (p. 4 [1963])

Two things might strike one about this. First, when Davidson says he does "only one" thing, he appears to come close to contradicting himself: he explicitly denies that he does three of the things that only a moment previously he said he does. Second, there is a switch of tense: Davidson starts with: "I flip the switch" and proceeds to "I flipped the switch". It can seem as if the four things which Davidson said he *does* need to be thought of as just one (the "only one"), when they are thought of as *done* things, as things he *did*.[7]

Davidson's claim that he did only one thing of which he gave four descriptions is an effect of his treatment of actions as individuals, as "*bona fide* entities to be described and redescribed" (p. 165 [1969]. Davidson had already settled on the view that actions are reported with past tense predications: his question was "What is the relation between a reason and an action when the reason explains the action by giving the agent's reason for doing what he *did*?" (p. 3, my italics [1963]). Perhaps he ought really to have started off in the past tense saying "I flipped the switch, I turned on the light, . . .". But perhaps one should think of Davidson as having used his present tense – "I flip", "I turn on", "I illuminate" – in setting up an example of something he did, the reasons for which can be enquired into. In that case, his present tense at the time of its use would say what was then going on. At any rate "I flip the switch" could not be meant as what is called habitual such as is found in "I flip the switch every time I go into my office". Nor could it be meant to generalize across time – to convey something to be taken to apply in the past, the present, and future.[8] If Davidson really meant to employ a present tense, then his "flip", "turn on", "illuminate" would have been used to say what he was doing. He would have used them in something like the way in which someone giving radio commentary on a tennis match uses the simple present when he says: "He serves at 108 miles per hour and it comes back at 130". The commentator's "serves" and "comes back" don't speak either of what regularly happens or of what is such as always to happen but of what *is happening* even as he speaks. In order to speak unambiguously of what *is happening* even as one speaks, the progressive seems to be needed.[9] If so, then Davidson might better have said "I am flipping the switch", "I am turning on the light".

Given that flipping a switch takes no more than a few picoseconds, we are not likely to think of it as something that Davidson was doing. It is easier to think about the action which Davidson took the sentence "I flipped the switch" to refer to. About this, Davidson said it was an entity of which he had given four descriptions. Would he say this also of his flipping the switch – of what, as I've put it, was happening? Well, I'm going to suggest that no answer to such a question can be found in Davidson – that Davidson gave an account of action whose effect was to rule out the use of the progressive. The absence of a progressive predication of "flip the switch", such as occurs in "Davidson is (/was) flipping the switch, could hardly seem to matter very much". But an understanding of the progressive can be of importance when it comes to things we do which it takes a bit longer to do than it takes to flip a switch.[10] And it is the progressive we use if ever we say what we are doing.

3. "Action Sentences"

When Davidson said "'I turned on the light' ... clearly refers to a particular event" (p. 5 [1963]), he thought that the same particular event could be referred to by different sentences. But Davidson soon came to deny that it was the office of a whole sentence to refer. When he introduced events in his paper on the logical form of action sentences, he relied on our having "a clear semantics for first-order quantificational languages" (p. 144 [1967a]), and he claimed that sentences containing what are superficially two-place predicates, such as "turned on", "flipped", "buttered", and "climbed", should be seen as containing three-place predicates, with a place occupied by an event variable. Thus, "Jones buttered the toast" should be construed as having quantificational form: "($\exists x$) (Buttered (Jones, the toast, x)". Davidson's assigning it such a form was at the service of explaining certain inferences – from "Jones buttered the toast in the bathroom" to "Jones buttered the toast", for example. By treating "in the bathroom" "slowly", "at midnight", and some other adverbs as predicates of events, Davidson made available a way of explaining a range of inferences – Adverb Deletion as they might be called. At the same time, he provided himself with an understanding of actions as *relata* of the relation "cause".

One sees here the intrusion of a certain conception of predication – of predication as it is treated in such languages as those for which Davidson relied on our having a clear semantics. There is simply no place for adverbs in such languages. If a place is to be found for adverbs in sentences of predicate calculus, it may seem that they must themselves be treated as predicates (as instances of "F" in "F*a*" or "F*x*"), and then a domain of items of which they make predications will be needed.

Davidson gave the name of action sentences to those whose logical forms he gave. These sentences contain "verbs of action", verbs defined by Davidson as saying "what someone *did*" (p. 118, my italics [1967a]). But, of course, the verbs that occur in "buttered the toast", "climbed the mountain", etc., do not occur only in the simple past tense, and Davidson must have appreciated this when he spoke of "actions that take much time" (p. 88 [1978]). Indeed, he once said that "All actions take some time to perform" (Davidson 1985a, p. 215). Well, if it takes time to butter the toast, then there must have been a time when Jones, who buttered the toast, *was buttering* the toast. (And if Jones buttered the toast slowly, then one assumes that the toast had been being buttered by Jones for longer than it might have been.) Davidson, however, nowhere spoke to the understanding of "was buttering" or "was being buttered". True, he had something to say about tense.[11] But "buttered" and "was buttering" are alike in tense, both being past tense. The difference between "buttered" and "was buttering" is a difference not of tense but of aspect: "buttered" has perfect aspect and "was buttering" imperfect.

Davidson spoke of actions as "often referred to or defined partly in terms of some terminal stage, outcome, or consequence" (p. 4 at n. 2 [1963]). Thereby he characterized what have been called *accomplishments*. An accomplishment verb (more accurately verb phrase), when used to say what someone did, conveys that the relevant terminal stage, outcome, or consequence has eventuated. (Buttered toast, one might say, was the outcome of Jones's buttering the toast; Meyer's presence at the peak of Kibo was the terminal stage of his climb of Kibo.) Given his concern with intentional action and teleological explanation, it is not surprising that Davidson should have focused on accomplishments. For someone's intention is fulfilled only when her intended goal or *telos* (marked by a terminal stage, outcome, or consequence) has been reached.[12] One who had intended to do something may have been doing it, but only when she had come to have done it could it be said that she *did* it. Whereas Davidson's account of action sentences was designed to explain inferences from "She V-d F-ly" to "She V-d" (inferences of Adverb Deletion), he lacked any resources for explaining another easily recognizable inference, from "X V-d" to "X was V-ing" – from the simple past which is perfect to the past progressive which is imperfect. (The instances of "V" here are accomplishment verbs.)

Anyone who pays attention to the progressive of Davidson's verbs of action will find something else that needs to be explained. Whatever X did, X was doing, but X might have been doing something yet never have done it. Someone might be doing something but be stopped in their tracks or otherwise prevented from finishing, and it might be that even while someone was doing something, they changed their mind about the wisdom of finishing. The question, then, must be not only how to account for the inference that Davidson manifestly left out of account – from "X V_A-d" to "X was V_A-ing" – but also how to avoid the converse inference which is invalid – from "X was V_A-ing Y" to "X V_A-d Y". If Davidson could have acknowledged that his action verbs can occur in the imperfect, then he would surely have wanted an explanation of how it could be that someone could be (/have been) doing something which she never will do (/did). And given that his action verbs can occur in the imperfect, it must be a question for those who follow Davidson how their imperfect occurrences might be accommodated.

The invalidity of the inference from "X was V_A-ing Y" to "X V_A-d Y" is known as the imperfective paradox. Of course, there is nothing strictly *paradoxical* about this – about the fact that it can be true that X was doing something that she never actually did. The linguistic phenomenon was given the name of a paradox by virtue of there being tense logicians who at one time assumed the equivalence of "X was A-ing" and "X A-d" and then were led to a contradiction. The so-called paradox has been discussed by linguists and philosophers of language for 50 years. The example that has endured is the example of Mary who was crossing the street but didn't get across. (In the story as it is usually told what prevented Mary from getting across was her being hit by a truck when she was part of the way across.)

4. Treatments of the Progressive

Some philosophers of language have wanted to "solve" the imperfective paradox in furtherance of Davidson's treatment of action sentences. As Zoltan Gendler Szabo said:

> Davidson's suggestion that the logical form of action sentences contains existential quantification over underlying events has turned into a thriving research program in the last forty years yielding satisfying accounts of the semantics of manner adverbs, perception reports, the progressive aspect, plurals, causatives, . . ., and much else.
>
> (Szabo 2011)

Szabo for his own part engaged in this research program. And I think it will be instructive to look at the account he gave of the progressive.

Szabo's idea was to introduce underlying events into the logical form of sentences containing verbs used to say what someone *was doing*. These now are the verbs that are to be construed as containing a place for variables that superficially they do not appear to. They are to be treated using a predicate modifier whose semantic value is a function that maps A events onto what Szabo calls A events-in-progress. In the particular example I shall look at, Szabo was concerned with the inference from (1) to (2).

(1) John melted the butter (2) John was melting the butter

Szabo gave (1LF) and (2LF) as the respective logical forms of these sentences, using "IP" – which is short for "in progress" – for the modifier.[13] And Szabo provided informal versions of what his statements of logical form recorded.

> (1LF) $\exists e\ ((IP\{Melting\}\ e) \wedge \text{agent}\ (e, John) \wedge \text{theme}\ (e, \text{the butter}_i) \wedge \exists s\ (\text{being molten}, s) \wedge \text{theme}\ (s, \text{the butter}_i) \wedge \text{CAUSE}\ (e, s)).$
>
> INFORMALLY: "There was a melting of the butter in progress by John and it causally led to a state of the butter being molten".
>
> (2LF) $\exists e\ ((IP\{Melting\}\ e) \wedge \text{agent}\ (e, John) \wedge \text{theme}\ (e, \text{the butter})).$
>
> INFORMALLY: "There was a melting of the butter in progress by John".

(2LF) can be derived from (1LF) by simple conjunction elimination. At the same time, (2LF) being, as it were, self-standing, there could be no reason to think that it might imply (1LF). The imperfective paradox then appears to be "solved". But I think that Szabo's informal versions hide complexities in his official (LF) versions and that they cover up problems with them. So I shall argue now.

In (1LF), Szabo places the subscript "i" on two occurrences of the word "butter". This is in order that the same butter should be assigned both as theme of a melting in progress and as theme of the state which the melting in progress CAUSE. Could it really be necessary to go to such lengths to ensure that John should have come to have melted the very butter that he started off melting? If John intended to melt *this* butter, one would have thought that he was doing something in fulfillment of his intention only so long as *this* butter was melting, and to have fulfilled his intention when *it* had melted.

The "CAUSE" of (1LF) appears to be untensed. But given that the sentence subject to treatment contains "melted", we must be entitled to think of if at least implicitly past tensed. Szabo says that "It is crucial that 'CAUSE' is not the relation expressed by the English verb 'cause'" (p. 513). And sure enough: when the sentence is put into a sort of English and paraphrased, this "CAUSE" is glossed "causally *led* to". But in whatever manner the state there (of the butter_i, of being molten) might have been led to in the case that John melted the butter, one might have thought that it was being led *toward* while he was melting the butter. That is exactly what has to be ruled out, however. The fact that "X A-d" cannot be inferred from "X was A-ing" ensures that what it is for X to have been A-ing must not be thought of in such a way as to presuppose that X *has* A-d. Yet if the state that exists when John *has* melted the butter is taken to be something toward which John's melting of the butter had been leading, then its existence surely *is* presupposed to his melting the butter.

What sort of a thing is this led-to state anyway? It must be a purely momentary thing. For if there were a sudden freeze the moment John had melted the butter, then John would still have melted the butter, but the butter would not have participated in any continuing state of moltenness. Probably anyone who sees fit to quantify over such momentary states will be attracted to a certain view of the butter's progressing toward the state of which Szabo predicates "being molten": they will be likely to think of the butter as passing through a series of states. If there is a momentary state when the butter is molten, then must there not be a new momentary state at any time during the time when it is coming to be molten? If so, one will need to think of John's melting of the butter as consisting in a sequence of static items. Such thinking appears to eliminate anything dynamic from what was happening even as the butter was melting.

A more revealing gloss of Szabo's (1LF) than Szabo's own informal version might have it start: "A causal relation holds between an in-progress-melting-to-which-John-stands-in-the-relation-*agent*-and-the-butter-stands-in-the relation-*theme*". This gloss draws attention to a further feature of Szabo's account: the introduction of "agent" and "theme", so-called thematic relations.[14] (The introduction of "theme" is what gave rise to the need to place the subscripts on "the butter".) One might wonder why a number of different relational predications should be thought to underlie such a relatively simple sentence as "John melted the butter". And one might be troubled by what could seem to be implied by thinking that John, in order to have melted the butter, must bear to an event a relational tie, "Agent". If bearing this relation to an event were really required of John, might John not also be required to bear a further relation to the event, namely, the relation to it which is borne by one who bears to it this relation?[15]

There is another point to notice about Szabo's treatment of the paradox. He accounts for perfectives and imperfectives alike in terms of his events in progress. His imperfective modifier is applied to "melting" to yield a past-tense imperfective ("was melting"), which is used in turn to give the form of the perfective ("melted"). It can seem to follow from this that someone might have a range of verbs in her vocabulary but have no understanding of those verbs excepting as they occur in progressive predications: she understands "was melting" (and the like) but doesn't understand "melted" (and the like). It is then as if someone might know what she was doing but lack any reason ever to stop, never knowing that she had finished.[16]

I should acknowledge that Szabo has much more to say about the progressive than I have attended to here. I have extracted just a part of his account, in order to bring to light the problems there are about handling progressives in a manner that may come naturally to philosophers today, especially to those who take Davidson to have initiated a research program. I should also acknowledge that there are other accounts of the imperfective paradox than those inspired by Davidson. These, found now in the linguistic literature, provide *modal* analyses of "X was A-ing"; they speak of continuation branches of events in possible worlds. In an earlier paper, Szabo was rightly dismissive of such modal accounts as he considered (see Szabo 2004). New analyses have been provided. These have led to new counterexamples, which have led to new analyses – which have led to new counterexamples, etc. One seems bound to wonder how much complexity it *could* be right to attempt to uncover in an analysis of something that we readily understand.

5. Compositionality in Semantics

Someone who had been taught a little predicate calculus would treat the sentence 'John melted the butter' as saying that the two-place relation 'melted' obtains between John and the butter. Their treatment of the sentence would place it in the first-order quantification theory on which Davidson said he relied, but very evidently would give no hint as to what it could amount to that Jones was melting the butter. Szabo stuck to quantification theory but saw the need to decompose "melted" and other simple past tense verbs. They are to be broken down into a number of relations – "agent", "theme", "state", and "CAUSE" – relations in which things of one or another sort may stand to an in-progress event. Might Davidson, who acknowledged that it takes time to do something, have turned to semantics for a treatment of "was melting" and the like?

In philosophy of language, Davidson is well known for what is sometimes called the principle of compositionality. In his view, "The work of a theory [of meaning] is in relating the known truth-conditions of each sentence to those aspects of the sentence that recur in other sentences, and can be assigned identical roles in other sentences" (Davidson 1967b, pp. 319–320). Davidson reiterated this view when he was talking specifically about action, saying then that "to know the logical form of a sentence is to know, in the context of a comprehensive theory, the semantic roles of the significant features of the sentence" (p. 146 [1970]). One might suppose that Davidson would have thought that "butter" (the transitive verb) retains a significant semantic role in sentences containing "buttered", "was buttering", "will be buttering", and "to butter" and that he would have thought that "-ed" (the past tense morpheme) recurs in "melted", "climbed", "turned on", etc. But the behavior of verbs, as they may occur with different tense and aspect (and indeed in infinitives), was never of concern to Davidson. Davidson confined himself to certain verbs as they are used when inflected so as to be past and perfect. It was in those terms that he launched an ontology for the philosophy of action, leaving out great tracts of what anyone would naturally think of as the language of action.

It might be objected that Davidson really must have allowed that it is possible to talk about someone who is going to do something or who is or was doing something. Indeed in a couple of places, Davidson can be found to have spoken in such a way as to acknowledge that this is possible. He spoke of "the action . . . entirely in the future" (p. 92 [1970]) and of "completed actions" (p. 110 [1967a]). And of course, we know what he meant. But my claim is that in these places, he used "action" in a manner at odds with his official view of actions – of entities that exist when someone has done something. Given that Davidson's actions exist by virtue of what has occurred, he was not entitled to think either of *an action* as a future entity or of *actions* as things that might or might not be completed. On Davidson's account of what an action is, unless and until an agent reaches her end, so that her intended "terminal stage, outcome, or consequence" is in place, there is as yet no action.

There is another, more telling, example in which Davidson talked in a manner which, given his views about actions and quantification, he could not officially have authorized. Davidson produced a series of sentences in which present tense progressives are predicated, saying that these sentences "are made true by the same action" (p. 110 [1967a]). But can that which does not yet exist be something that now makes a sentence true? Davidson's sentences were "I am writing my name on a piece of paper", "I am . . . writing a cheque", and "I am paying my gambling debt", and they are joined with "with the intention of". A reader of G.E.M. Anscombe's *Intention* will be struck by the fact that when Davidson gave this example, he took over a formula from her. Anscombe, however, issued a general reminder that "a man can *be doing* something which he nevertheless does not *do*, if it is some process or enterprise which it takes time to complete and of which, therefore, if it is cut short at any time, we may say that he *was doing* it, but *did not do* it".[17] Anscombe could not possibly have treated an action as something which exists when something has been done. (Anscombe's is of course a reminder of what is known as the imperfective paradox.)

6. The Nature of Events

Having paid attention to matters of the tense and aspect of verbs, I have drawn attention to some of the consequences of thinking of actions as belonging in the domain of events as this was understood by Davidson. But one can broach questions about the ontology that Davidson introduced by asking, more straightforwardly perhaps, what the nature is of events as Davidson would have had us conceive them.

Those who accept Davidson's causal theory of action take an action to be "an event caused in the right way". But there is then some disagreement among them as to how more exactly one should think of actions. Some think of an action as the outcome of a process and thus as something that occurs *at* the time an agent first had acted; some think of an action as constituted by, or identical with, a process and thus as occurring *over an interval* of time beginning when the agent started to act and ending when she was done. The latter, processual view appears to be the majority view among Davidson's followers. But Davidson himself can seem to have been in two minds about this.

When he first introduced actions as a species of event, Davidson said "If I turned on the light, then I must have done it at a precise moment, in a particular way – every detail is fixed" (p. 6 [1963]). Here it is made to seem as if there had been only one particular way in which Davidson could have turned on the light. If so, it isn't possible that Davidson should (say) have exerted a force on the light switch very slightly different from the force he actually exerted. (The point is more obvious if one considers something which it takes somewhat longer to do than it takes to turn a light on, of which it will be more obvious that it could have been done in a variety of ways.) Davidson's claim about his action's "fixedness" appears wrong as it stands, then. And it also appears to be inconsistent with his saying that "any one of an indefinitely large number of actions would satisfy a want" (p. 6 [1963]). That makes it seem that someone might have satisfied a want in particular ways very different from the way in which actually she did.

Why should Davidson ever have thought of actions as fixed in every detail? I surmise that having taken an action's existence to require a past tense verb to have application, he needed then to think of actions as members of a domain whose members are not merely not such as to change but are also past entities to which further temporal concepts have no application. Consider, for example, Davidson's analysis of the action sentence "Meyer climbed Kibo": "There exists an event which is a climbing of Kibo by Meyer" (p. 183 [1970]). The pastness conveyed by "climb*ed*" is expressed with "there exist an event". Perhaps Davidson thought of "is a climbing" as lacking any tense. In that case, even if Meyer's climbing of Kibo could be taken to have been constituted of processes, still it will have the character of an immutable object.

However this may be, there is a difficulty about knowing what it might be for Davidson's actions to be "concrete particulars". It may be hard to think of them so when it is allowed that an agent had been doing whatever she did. When criticizing Szabo, I said that what it is for X to *have been* A-ing must not be thought of in such a way as to presuppose that X *has* A-d: only when someone has reached her intended end is there an event such as Davidson would call her action. Is her action then to be thought of as something that did not exist until she had A-d? Only when she had A-d had her action come to be. The existential quantifier seems unfitted to convey the sort of *being* in which actions may be supposed to participate.

7. Lessons in Metaphysics

Davidson's work informs analytic philosophy today very much less than it did 30 or 40 years ago, and I have attended here only to his early papers. But I want to suggest that my criticisms of Davidson impact upon how we must think about acting in time even now. (1) Davidson's causal theory of action still finds favor with many. (2) Even those who have abandoned Davidson's theory of action may fail to appreciate the problems with Davidson's ontology. (3) The predicate calculus as we know it, and as it provides a foundation for semantics, has no way to treat imperfect predication. I shall say a little under each of these three heads before I conclude.

(1) The field which Bratman took Davidson to have defined is one in which many continue to work. We are told:

> The event-causal framework is by far the most widely accepted view in the contemporary philosophy of mind and action. One reason for this is that the commitment to the event-causal framework is tantamount to a commitment to a very minimal and widely endorsed kind of naturalism.
>
> (Schlosser 2019)

If this is so, then a story of action such as Davidson told lives on. No doubt some writers have thought that Davidson's own causal theory needs considerable modification. Others may think that we are bound to treat causal concepts by invoking relations in which events find a place even if we need a theory of action quite different from Davidson's. Treatments of the imperfective paradox such as I looked at will be thought to belong in such a theory and will be taken to be fitted to the event-causal framework. If that is indeed a framework to which naturalism of a widely endorsed kind is committed, then very much more has been at issue in my discussion of Davidson than anything taught by Davidson himself.

(2) Davidson thought of events as comprising one category in an overall ontology, the other category being objects. He wrote:

> One is an object which remains the same object through changes, the other a change in an object or objects. Spatiotemporal areas do not distinguish them, but our predicates, our basic grammar, our ways

of sorting do. Given my interest in the metaphysics implicit in our language, this is a distinction I do not want to give up.

(p. 311 [1985b])

Davidson took the difference between objects and events to be a difference in the manner in which they relate to locations in space and time. "It may be that events occur at a time in a place while objects occupy places at times", he said (p. 301 [1985b]). Well, I have suggested that an idea of things that occurs *at* times cannot exhaust an understanding of what might be taken to be the occupants of the temporal world. "An object remains the same through changes", Davidson says.[18] Are we not bound to allow that an object persists even while it is changing or is being changed?

I traced Davidson's introduction of an ontology of events to the need he saw to absorb adverbs into sentences of the predicate calculus: he treated adverbs as predicates of events. But Davidson used the word "occurred" as a predicate of events. He said, for instance, "Eve's eating of the apple occurred", taking this sentence to entail ("($\exists x$) (Ate, Eve, the apple)"). But, of course, the word "occur" is not only found in "occurred". It is possible to speak of what is *occurring*. And, certainly, we often enough can say what is occurring, or happening, or going on, whether in our immediate surroundings or further afield. Use of the progressive is indispensable. Davidson can seem to have been intent upon obliterating it. And it seems we must rethink the premises of Davidson's ontology. (We might even wonder whether everything in the spatial world deserves to be reckoned simply an "object".)

(3) There are questions about verbs themselves, not only about adverbs, in relation to the semantics of predication. I find that analytic philosophers who attend to the idea of predication treat verbs as just any old predicates. So they treat "flies", "swims", and "runs" (for instance) alongside "is wise", "is brave", and "is Austrian-born" (for instance).[19] It is recognized that verbs, like other predicates, carry tense, so that just as "*was* wise" may be predicated of Gildas, and "*was* Austrian-born" of Wittgenstein, so "*flew*" may be predicated of Tweety and "*ran*" of Pheidippides. But when tense is brought in, something is left out. For not only are "flies" and "flew" predicable of Tweety so also is "is flying"; not only are "runs" and "ran" predicable to Pheidippides, so also is "was running". The point is that many predications of verbs carry aspect: they differ in respect of whether they are perfect or imperfect not only in respect of their tense. I have argued already that aspect goes missing from a theory of action like Davidson's. The present point is that it also goes missing from what is usually taught about predication. It can then seem to be endemic to analytic philosophy to forget about aspect. (And, although this is another matter, verb aspect generally goes missing in the metaphysics literature on

time, where a leading question is whether *tense* should be reckoned "an irreducible feature of the world".)

Bratman spoke of "the possibility that we are fully embedded in the causal order". I have taken exception to the idea that the causal order might be the order of Davidson's events, thinking that our conception of causality could not be confined to a relation between events. But what did Bratman mean in speaking of the possibility of our being "fully embedded"? Perhaps he meant to suggest that we can conceive of our agency only in the world in which we find ourselves. That is surely right. But "embedded"? It is not as if we are implanted, or inserted into, a temporal reality. For we live and act in time. And it is in time that we understand ourselves, using the progressive in saying what we are doing.

This is what I said when I spoke of Davidson's use of tense when he first embarked on a theory of action. I distinguished then between the use of the present tense to generalize across times and to speak of what is present – actually present, as one might put it. It could be a habit of some philosophers always to abstract from what first they know in order that they should be able to come up with generalizations. But what first they know, they could only know by virtue of their living in time.

***

Work in the philosophy of action by those who are influenced by philosophers of the past, whether by Aristotle, say, or by Kant, will not be infected by any of the presumptions introduced in the last century of analytic philosophy. Much that is written in philosophy of action pays no attention to questions in metaphysics or semantics. Some work does address metaphysical questions but without paying any particular attention to what contemporary metaphysicians and semanticists have to say. Yet I think that there can be a danger for present-day philosophers of distracting themselves from the phenomena of the first concern, by working always from an abstracted perspective. That is why I've thought it worthwhile to expose what I see as the pitfalls of the causal theory of action. And that is why it is very good that we have been given an account of the form of sentences about action which provides a corrective to the causal theory.[20]

Notes

1 See pp. 22–23 of Bratman (2007) from Chapter 2: "Reflection, Planning, and Temporally Extended Agency".
2 See n. 2, p. 18 of Bratman (2018) from Chapter 1: "Introduction: The Planning Theory".
3 The difficulty here has been called the problem of deviant causal chains, first so-called as a problem for the "belief desire theory" in which intentions as such are not ascribed a role in action explanation. An enormous amount has

been written about the problem; but obviously this can only be of interest to those who have been brought to believe that it is such as to be solved.
4 See Bratman (2014), "Building Blocks: part 1", Chapter 2, at p. 46, with the quotation from Davidson at footnote 9.
5 Here and elsewhere in referring to an essay reprinted in Davidson (2001a), I give a page reference to the reprinted version, and, in parentheses, a reference to the particular essay from which I have quoted.
6 Hornsby (1980b). The earlier paper I mentioned, I gave as a talk at the 4th International Wittgenstein Symposium in 1979: see Hornsby (1980a).
7 Davidson distinguished *alert the prowler* from the other things on his list of four, this being something he did but not intentionally. This is a consequence of Davidson's privileging the adverbial use of "intention", and thus setting off with the assumption that it must be philosophy of action's first task is to find conditions for the correct application of "intentionally". Davidson's was a piecemeal approach to the concept of intention, as G.E.M. Anscombe once put it.
8 The use of the present tense to generalize across time is exceedingly common, inside and outside philosophy. To illustrate with a single example from philosophy: a philosopher who claims "If A intentionally Φ-s, then A knows how to Φ" commits herself to past and future versions of the claim.
9 Needed by speakers of English at least. It can be different in other languages where use of verb inflection on its own is not enough to communicate what I take to be communicated with "am – ing" and "is – ing".
10 Davidson set off with the assumption that philosophy of action's first task is to find conditions for the correct application of "intentionally", so that he distinguished *alert the prowler* from the other things on his list of four, this being something he did but not intentionally. And probably we're less apt to think that in Davidson's example, he was ever alerting the prowler than we are to think that he was flipping the switch.
11 In Davidson (1967b), he took tense to be a demonstrative element in a sentence. This is the paper in which Davidson defended a principle of compositionality in semantics, of which more in §5.
12 Davidson spoke of action explanation as *teleological* at p. xvi [2001b] and at p. 9 [1963]. He took his ontological reduction to enable the reduction of teleological connections to causal relations.
13 See Szabo (2008). I have given the labels (1LF) and (2LF) to Szabo's (30″) and (32′) (both at p. 512), Szabo having spoken of these as giving the logical form. Szabo sometimes speaks of analyses, and he says that he takes analyses to be precursors of compositional semantic theories.
14 Those in Szabo's line of work make use of thematic relations beyond "Agent" and "Theme": they introduce all of "Experiencer", "Goal", "Instrument", "Location", and "Benefactive" as relations to events in purporting to spell out the structure of a great range of sentences.
15 My concern here is that those who introduce thematic relations can appear to take a first step from which a regress could be generated – a regress akin to that of the famous argument of Bradley's (1897, Chapter 3).
16 Szabo's idea of an event in progress is bound to call up an idea of *process*. (Szabo himself thinks of processes as not such as to culminate, so he might not wish to think of John's melting the butter and the like as processes. Much might be said about process even aside from wanting to make connections between processes and events in Davidson's sense. But several philosophers have wanted to introduce one or another *ontology* of process either making use of processes as playing a role hand in hand with Davidsonian events or having processes play the very role that Davidson's events

are supposed to play. I mention this in §6. Here I need to acknowledge that an account I once gave myself cannot be right. In that account, events were to be treated as composed of *processual stuff* somewhat in the way that space-occupying objects are composed of matter. This cannot be right for the reason, as I can crudely put it now, that it fails to allow for what might be called the intrinsic directionality of time—for an attribute of time not shared with space.
17 Anscombe (1957); I have quoted from §23, p. 39. A resurgence of interest in *Intention* led to its reprinting by Harvard University Press in 2000, which in turn has led to a sustained interest.
18 Davidson avoids Quine's four dimensionalism and thereby avoids the various kinds of "four-dimensionalism" found in much contemporary analytic metaphysics. In the present context, I can only say that I trust it is clear that I think he is right to do so.
19 I can only substantiate this by adverting to the literature on "the concept horse paradox" where Frege's conception of predication is much discussed. What goes for Frege (who took it to be the semantic function of a predicates to stand for concepts [or properties]) goes also for Davidson (who took predicates to be true or false of objects).

"Fly", "swim", and "run" are sometimes said to be activity verbs. In predicate calculus, they will be treated as one-place predicates. For simplicity's sake, I confine myself here to what are taken to one-place predicates. When it comes to accomplishment verbs, two-place predicates may be introduced and may be taken to stand for relations. For the failure of understanding – the distortions of what we actually think – to which such a treatment leads, see Ford (2014). One might put one of Ford's main points by saying that when an object is being changed by an agent, the object's being changed is not dissociable from the agent's changing it.
20 I mean the account found in Michael Thompson 2008. One of the aims of this book is "to convince [its] reader that certain classes of complete contentful thoughts share forms not found on a list like Frege's" (p. 19). Thoughts having non-Fregean forms of predication exhibit types of generality and temporality unrecognized by Frege or by Davidson. For the purposes of understanding agency, Thompson has us appreciate what he calls process- or event forms.

As well as Thompson, I should mention here others I have talked with who have helped me to get past such ways of thinking as have come to be standard in much philosophy of action. They include Anton Ford, Adrian Haddock, Jesse Mulder, Will Small, and Rachael Wiseman. And there are many others whose work illustrates the importance of Anscombe's work (mentioned earlier where n. 17 is flagged) and who see that there is all the difference in the world between Davidson's philosophical outlook and Anscombe's.

References

Anscombe G.E.M. 1957. *Intention*. Oxford: Basil Blackwell. Reprinted by Harvard University Press, Cambridge, MA, 2000.
Bradley F.H. 1897. *Appearance and Reality*. New York: Macmillan. (https://archive.org/details/appearanceandrea00braduoft/page/26/mode/2up)
Bratman Michael. 2007. *Structures of Agency*. New York: Oxford University Press.
Bratman Michael. 2014. *Shared Agency: A Planning Theory of Acting Together*. New York: Oxford University Press.

Bratman Michael. 2018. *Planning, Time and Self Governance: Essays in Practical Rationality*. New York: Oxford University Press.
Davidson, Donald. 1963. "Actions, Reasons, and Causes". In Davidson 2001a.
Davidson, Donald. 1967a. "The Logical Form of Action Sentences". In Davidson 2001a.
Davidson, Donald. 1967b. "Truth and Meaning". *Synthèse*, 17(3): 304–323.
Davidson, Donald. 1969. "The Individuation of Events". In Davidson 2001a.
Davidson, Donald. 1970. "Events as Particulars". In Davidson 2001a.
Davidson, Donald. 1978. "Intending". In Davidson 2001a.
Davidson, Donald. 1985a. "Appendix B. Reply to Quine on Events". In Davidson 2001a.
Davidson, Donald. 1985b. "Replies to Essays I-X". In *Essays on Davidson: Actions and Events*, eds. B. Vermazen and J. Hintikka. Oxford: Oxford University Press.
Davidson, Donald. 2001a. *Essays on Actions and Events*. Oxford: Clarendon Press.
Davidson, Donald. 2001b. "Introduction". In Davidson 2001a.
Ford, Anton. 2014. "Action and Passion". *Philosophical Topics*, 42(1): 13–42.
Hornsby, Jennifer. 1980a. "Actions and Abilities". In *Language, Logic and Philosophy*, ed. R. Haller. Wien: Hölder-Pichler-Tempsky, 387–391.
Hornsby, Jennifer. 1980b. *Actions*. London: Routledge and Kegan Paul.
Schlosser Markus. 2019. "Agency". In *The Stanford Encyclopedia of Philosophy (Winter 2019 edition)*, ed. Edward N. Zalta. <https://plato.stanford.edu/archives/win2019/entries/agency/>
Szabo, Zoltan Gendler. 2004. "On the Progressive and the Perfective". *Noûs*, 38(1): 29–59.
Szabo, Zoltan Gendler. 2008. "Things in Progress". *Philosophical Perspectives* 22(Philosophy of Language): 499–525.
Szabo, Zoltan Gendler. 2011. "*Review* of Scott Soames' *Philosophy of Language* (2010)". *Notre Dame Philosophical Reviews*, 17 February 2011.
Thompson, Michael. 2008. *Life and Action*. Cambridge MA: Harvard University Press.

2 Action Cubes and Traces

Constantine Sandis

> To what extent may we say that what is *done* is inscribed? . . . We say that such and such an event *left its mark* on its time . . . in a metaphorical way, some actions are events that imprint their mark on their time. But on what did they imprint their mark? Is it not in something spatial that discourse is inscribed? How could an event be printed on something temporal? . . . Could we not say that history is itself the record of human action? History is the quasi "thing" on which human action leaves a "trace", puts its mark. Hence the possibility of "archives" . . . like a text, human action is an open work, the meaning of which is "in suspense" . . . the text may be reached from different sides. Like a cube, or a volume in space, the text presents a "relief". Its different topics are not on the same altitude.
>
> Paul Ricoeur (1986: 142–9)[1]

Prologue

"True love leaves no traces", sang Leonard Cohen, and in Mary Torjussen's first novel, the narrator's boyfriend is said to be *Gone Without a Trace*. As the novel reveals, however, all actions involve the leaving of a trace of *some* kind, if only in one's mind. Indeed, we might go as far as saying that to act *is* to leave some kind of trace in the world. In time, the material, psychological, or digital traces that our actions result in may be faded, lost, forgotten, covered up, or altogether vanished.[2] But they can also endure, remaining open to re-discovery at any moment. Like a moth-ridden bundle of letters discovered in an abandoned attic, some will only ever be of parochial interest, while others stand as marks on the history of the world (see §2).

With the notable exception of Paul Ricoeur, the philosophy of the trace exists entirely independently from the concerns of mainstream philosophy of action, and vice versa. This is partly an effect of the so-called analytic/continental divide, variations of which stubbornly persist despite the popularity of protestations against it. But it is equally due to the unfortunate way in which contemporary moral theory has divorced itself from the

DOI: 10.4324/9780429259845-4

philosophy of action which has in term long abandoned the philosophy of history. This essay attempts to undo some of this damage by presenting a three-dimensional approach to action that is as much informed by Hegel, Levinas, and Ricoeur as it is by Anscombe and Hornsby.

1. Aspects of Action

On Hegel's worldview, "the self-consciousness of heroes (like that of Oedipus and others in Greek tragedy) had not advanced out of its primitive simplicity either to reflection on the distinction between deed and action, between the external event and the purpose and knowledge of the circumstances, or to the subdivision of consequences" (PR 1821: § 118A). The Greeks thus

> "accepted responsibility for the whole compass of the deed" (*ibid*), despite the fact that "the right of the will to recognise as its action, and to accept responsibility for, only those aspects of its deed which it knew to be presupposed within its end, and which were present in its purpose.
>
> (PR 1821: §117)

While current action theory distinguishes between willful, deliberate, intended, foreseen, and unforeseen harm, as well as between different motives and mitigating circumstances, in some ways not much has changed since the Greeks. We (perhaps cannot help but to) confront action through some particular aspect, such as trace, consequence, motive, purpose, or intention, but never all of them at once. Yet we continue to take people to be responsible for actions as a *whole*, whatever the mitigation.

The mereology of action suggests that there is no such thing as knowledge or responsibility of action *tout court*. This is because the various "inner" and "outer" aspects of any given action are arranged in such a way that one may have knowledge of – or be responsible for – what one is doing *qua* one of them but not *qua* another. If action didn't contain divisions such as that between "what is purposed and what is accomplished" (PR 1821: 114A), then the relation between practical knowledge and what actually happens would not have presented such a challenge for philosophers, such as Anscombe, who wish to emphasize our non-observational knowledge of action.[3]

To keep to Hegel's own example, Oedipus is responsible for patricide *qua* external deed but only for striking an old man in self-defense *qua* intended action. The former constitutes one of the act's "outer" aspects (such as its traces and consequences) and the latter one of its "inner" ones.[4] Hegel thus distinguishes between the ancient ethical concern with objective deed (*Tat*) and our additional modern interest in subjective elements of action, including those of foresight, knowledge, motive, intention, and purpose (*Handlung*).⁵ These "inner" and "outer" aspects should not be understood as ontologically separable components. Indeed, in stating that "[t]he laurels of mere willing are dry leaves which have never been green" (PR 1821: §124A), Hegel reveals himself to be an early enactivist for whom volition, intention, and other psychological predicates only gain meaning insofar as they are made flesh in action. Charles Taylor summarizes this aspect of Hegel well when we write that "[i] n order to understand mental life as something we have to achieve understanding of . . . we have to abandon the view of it as constituted of data. We have to understand it as action" (Taylor 1979: 85, cf. Taylor 1983: 24–25).

Robert Brandom also distinguishes between an externalist strand in Hegel (according to which actions are identified and individuated "according to what is actually done") and an internalist one (according to which they are identified and individuated "by the agent's intention or purpose") (Brandom 2019: 384). He next suggests that it is on the first of these two views "that the inner can be understood only in terms of its outer expression" (*ibid*). But Brandom dissolves the apparent tension between the two views by declaring them to be two sides of the *same* concept of action (Brandom 2019: 374), despite the fact that Hegel clearly distinguishes between three concepts of action: *Tun* (act), *Tat* (deed), and *Handlung* (action).

It is telling that Brandom completely ignores the first of these, despite its function as a *tertium quid* that deals with conflicts between *Tat* and *Handlung*. Brandom takes "*Tat*" to refer to "the deed done, with all of its accordioned descriptions" and "*Handlung*" to "that same deed *as* the agent's doing", further characterizing the latter "*as* specifiable by the restricted set of descriptions under which it is intentional, and hence something *done* at all" (Brandom 2019: 389).⁶ In so doing, he confuses Hegel's threefold understanding of action with a one-dimensional Davidsonian schema according to which "[w]hat makes an event, performance, or process an *action*, something *done*, is that it is *intentional* under *some* description" (Brandom 2019: 368).⁷

Hegel distinguishes between the notion of an act (*Tun*) from the "internal" standpoint of the agent (behavior in so far as it relates to one's own foreknowledge, purpose, intention, and knowledge) and that from "external" standpoints (e.g., legal, scientific, cultural, etc.). He terms the former *Handlung* (action) and the latter *Tat* (deed). This distinction should not be confused with the contemporary one between actions and mere bodily movements. For one, both *Handlung* and *Tat* are aspects of conduct that results from the will, *viz.*, *Tun* (*LA* 1835: 1160ff.). Moreover, Hegel's taxonomy is motivated by concerns relating to modes of perception. So, whereas theorists such as Davidson (and, following him, Brandom) assert that all actions are events that are intentional under some description, Hegel reserves the term "*Handlung*" for just those aspects of behavior that are highlighted by a specific set of agent-related descriptions. This is

Action Cubes and Traces 35

not an ontological category, for there are no such objects as actions under specific descriptions (see Anscombe 1979).

What thus first appear as two distinct one-dimensional views of one event are, for Hegel, two different sides or aspects of a single *three-dimensional* account comprised of the inner, outer, and extended (or environmental) aspects of acts. His enactivism thus consists in a holistic understanding of mind and behavior as two different aspects of one thing that is both embedded within (but also indefinitely extended throughout) the agent's environment. This dynamic interaction between agent and world renders us hostage to luck: a stone thrown is the devil's (PR 1821: §119A).[8] To act is to leave traces that stand in a fundamentally different relation to time from the ephemeral events of our producing them, viz., that of being left *on* time rather than occurring *in* it.[9] Any trace left will be imputable to us from *some* perspective, but not from others.

Hegel's writings on action form the roots from which Ricoeur's picture of actions as cubical volumes with inner/outer, surface/foundation, and foreground/background perspectives grow (as illustrated in Figure 2.1). Ricoeur models actions on texts whose "different topics are not on the same altitude". Accordingly, "the reconstruction of the whole has a perspectivist aspect similar to that of perception" and "a specific kind of one-sidedness is implied in the act of reading ... what we want to understand is not something hidden behind the text, but something disclosed in front of it" (Ricoeur 1986: 160).[10]

When we observe someone acting, we typically don't see any one of the previously mentioned ("inner" or "outer") aspects in isolation. What

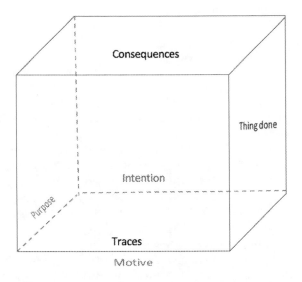

Figure 2.1 Action Necker Cube (Abstract)

we typically see (and react to) is an action *qua* some aspect(s) of it, not the aspect(s) in isolation. Some of these aspects will be at the forefront and others in the background, if not altogether unnoticed. On any given occasion, we may see some action as the expression of a particular intention, the means to achieving a specific goal, the cause of some grave consequence, or the result of some identifiable motive. The motives "behind" any given action may be all-too-obvious or an utter mystery. Zooming in, we might view this action (e.g., someone's running a particular stretch) as the moving of one's body or even some specific physiological aspect of this ("she's panting!"). Stepping back, we see the same act as the bringing about of a certain consequence ("she's raising money for a good cause"). When the consequence is intended, the latter description can also give us the agent's reason. When not, it serves to highlight something that the agent is unaware of ("she's left shoe marks").

Taylor (1983: §2) puts forth an interpretation of Hegel as a proponent of a "qualitative conception of action" shared by Anscombe (1957). This is to be contrasted with the more familiar causal one defended by Donald Davidson (1963) but associated with Hegel by Knowles (2010) and Brandom (2019). On the latter view, actions are famously seen as "external" events with an "internal" cause. According to the qualitative conception, by contrast, agential knowledge is non-observational because "the agent is the being responsible for the direction of action, the being for whom and through whom action is directed as it is" (Taylor 1983: 25). Since "as agents we already have some sense, however dim, inarticulate, or subliminal, of what we are doing", knowledge of our own actions action differs from that of external events for it is "a matter of making articulate what we already have an inarticulate sense of" (*ibid*). But this misses a key part of Hegel's account; as already noted, actions for Hegel are neither "internal" nor "external", but are knowable via either aspect.

In the ideal case, the objective reality of our actions as performed in time will match up to what we set out to do. But things often go wrong, and not just in ways that we couldn't have foreseen.[11] So while agents have non-observational knowledge of their doings *qua* purpose and intention, ignorance of the external reality of their deeds *cannot* be remedied by making articulate what they already have some inarticulate sense of. Here we also find a crucial gulf between Hegelian and Freudian approaches to Greek tragedy. According to the latter, there are no mistakes and all actions performed "in ignorance" are revelatory of unconscious desire. On the former, by contrast, "unconsciously committed crimes" (LA 1219) do not entail subconscious knowledge, intention, or desire, though they must nonetheless be accepted as the fruits of one's wider purpose.[12]

Anscombe approximates Hegel's view in allowing that there can be two ways of knowing one thing, *viz.*, action.[13] For Hegel, however, knowledge of action *qua* purpose is to be contrasted with knowledge of action *qua* objectivity. While he doesn't conceive of these as two distinct ontological categories any more than Anscombe would,[14] he denies that it makes sense to talk of knowledge of action *tout court*. As with a Necker cube, we may bring about an aspect shift in an observer by asking them to see the action one way rather than another, by attending to a particular aspect. This is the case not only with actions occurring before us but equally with any behavior we may recount and discuss, be it of a personal acquaintance, something reported in the papers, or a character in a novel. We find a layered illustration of this in Luke (23:33–34):

> And when they came to the place that is called Calvary, there they crucified him, and the criminals, one on his right and one on his left. And Jesus said, "Father, forgive them, for they know not what they do." And they cast lots to divide his garments.[15]

What *were* they doing? What did they *think* they were doing? And what did they ultimately *do*? Had they no practical knowledge whatsoever? And who were "they" anyhow? It's not my purpose to adjudicate over the historical accuracy of the report, let alone the question of whether "they" is here intended to refer to "the chief priests, the leaders, and the people" to whom Pilate has handed Jesus over, or to the Roman soldiers who divide his clothes among themselves.[16] How one answers it will affect which internal aspects of "what they are doing" are brought to the foreground.

In the former reading, "they" know that they are handing over Jesus to the Romans to be crucified and that, in so doing, they are condemning him to death. On the latter (illustrated in Figure 2.2), "they" know that

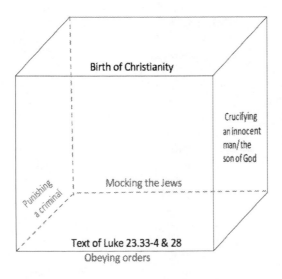

Figure 2.2 Action Necker Cube (Concrete)

they are following orders and putting this person (who is said to have claimed to be "The King of the Jews") to death by nailing him to a cross.

The "internal" aspects of motives, purpose, and intention will look rather different when considering the actions of the chief priests versus those of Roman soldiers, while the "external" ones may remain constant. This is not to say that the two are unrelated, but though *some* key aspects of our doings are an expression of our motives and intentions, many are not.[17] Either interpretation allows that "they" can be said to know that they are killing someone. For it would be no excuse to say "I only intended to nail him to the cross, the rest was up to fate or God".[18]

More to the point, "they" don't know that they are giving birth to Christianity and thereby also setting in motion a particular unfolding of history. From within a Christian outlook, they are also killing the innocent Son of God, fulfilling the book, accomplishing God's will, and creating the possibility for atonement. So understood, they might equally be forgiven *because* of what they unwittingly do, viz., performing the necessary evil required for the very reconciliation of God and mankind.

Whatever happened on Calvary left its mark on history, but its traces do not form a single track. Each new path gives rise to new ways of describing the original acts. To speak of action as having multiple descriptions and only being intentional under some of them camouflages the fact that this is only true about our doings and not the things we do. Indeed, in intentionally doing or not doing some given thing, one is invariably doing or not doing a number of other things (both intentionally and otherwise),[19] including the leaving or erasing of various traces. Two or more people may even act together with perfect coordination *and* practical success, despite a near-absolute lack of shared motive, purpose, or even (in highly comic or tragic scenarios) intention.

It is also commonplace nowadays to talk of acting as the (causal) bringing about of a bodily movement. But neither physical actions (such as holding a door shut by keeping one's arm pressed on it) nor mental ones (such as reciting a poem to oneself) need to involve bodily movements.[20] Moreover, even if we restrict ourselves to those that do, it is a moot point whether they are identical to the bringing about of the bodily movement in question is a moot point. The causal understanding of basic arm raisings as the bringing about of arm risings may be contrasted with a constitutive account according to which the agent, *in* raising her arm, makes it true that her arm rises in the sense that this occurs *in virtue of* her raising it. Such truth-making relations are constitutive rather than causal, for in the ordinary case of arm raising, there is nothing that the agent does in order to bring about her arm's rising; the agent's arm rises *in virtue of* her having raised it, much like a tablecloth is colored in virtue of its being red.[21] Whenever we act, we make any number of things true and, by the same token, a number of other things false. If to act *is* to leave a trace of some kind, then in acting we make it true that we have left a trace. As we shall see, this is so even when we are engaged in the act of eliminating traces.

2. Traces on Time

While the philosophical concept of the trace can be traced at least as far back as Plato's memory impressions [σημεῖα ἐνσημαινομένους] (T191d) and their analogue in writing [γραφῆς] (P 1995: 275a), the history of its historiographical incarnation arguably begins with Hegel's 1822–23 lectures (see Hegel 1837) and is followed shortly thereafter by Neander (1826) and Macaulay (1828).[22] These foundations are built upon by Dilthey (1860), Edmunds (1869), Nietzsche (1874), Heidegger (1927), and Arendt (1958), although accounts of "the trace" don't fully emerge until Levinas (1963, 1972), Derrida (1967a & b), and Ricoeur (1985, 1986, 2000).[23]

The question of what makes any given trace a *historical* goes hand in hand with that of what makes demarcates some particular fact as historical. E.H. Carr famously pronounced that "not all facts about the past are historical facts, or are treated as such by the historian" (Carr 1961: 4). The claim is plausible, but there are no fixed criteria for determining which facts are of historical significance. Carr's own take was that past facts are transformed into historical ones by a process of selection that begins with a proposal for membership, after which they only become established as such if the nomination has been seconded and sponsored by other historians.[24] The view would come under the fire of Geoffrey Elton, who mocks Carr's distinction between facts of the past and historical facts.[25] In its place, Elton puts forward a trace theory of historical facts according to which any past event may count as a historical fact if it has left traces for historians to discover. The study of history is thereby considered to be dependent on the provision of such traces:

> Historical study is not the study of the past but the study of present traces of the past; if men have said, thought, done or suffered anything of which nothing any longer exists, those things are as though they had never been. The crucial element is the present evidence, not the fact of past existence . . . the surviving traces of the past are not confined to material survivals; evidence can to some extent be discovered where it appeared not to exist, and the historian's techniques at times enable him to reconstruct that which is lost from that which is still around.
>
> (Elton 1967: 20; cf. 81)

This outlook has more recently been defended by Richard Evans who writes that "a historical fact is something that happened in history and can be verified as such through the traces history has left behind. Whether or not a historian has actually carried out the act of verification is irrelevant to its factuality: it really is there independently of the historian" (Evans 1997: 76).

It is not factuality that is up for dispute here, however, but what makes any given past fact *historical*. Even Elton must allow that the fact that I just put the kettle on is not (at least for now) a historical fact, no matter what traces I may have left behind. Like past facts, the present traces that provide evidence for them (be they buildings, documents, objects, carpet stains, etc.) can themselves become historical. But what makes them so surely comes down to degrees of interest rather than club membership. To complicate things, the very act of leaving a trace can itself be deemed historical and independently so of whether the trace in question remains present; it is sufficient that there exist traces of the traces.

Despite this vast historiographical concern with traces and the rise of action theory from the ashes of philosophy of history, the connection between kinds of everyday action and the leaving of traces has been little explored outside the work of Levinas, Ricoeur, and their followers. Levinas writes:

> [T]he trace . . . signifies outside of all intention of making a sign and outside of any project that would sight it. When one "pays by check" in a commercial transaction so as to leave a trace of payment, the trace is inscribed in the very order of the world. However, the authentic trace disturbs the world's order. It is "superimposed" . . . the imprint left by the one who wanted to erase his traces in an attempt, for example, to accomplish the perfect crime. The one who left traces while erasing his traces didn't want to say or do anything by the traces he leaves . . . His trace does not *signify* his past, as it does not *signify* his labor, or his enjoyment in the world, it *is* disturbance itself (one is tempted to say *engraving*) with irrefutable gravity.
> (Levinas 1972: 41–44)

Action traces can be far removed from a person's intention and yet stand as firm evidence of their purpose and, at times, even motive. In Claude Lanzmann's monumental documentary *Shoah*, Holocaust survivor Abraham Bomba recollects that "they told us to clean the whole place . . . And in no time this was as clean as though people had never been on that place. There was no trace, none at all, like a magic thing, everything disappeared".[26] Lanzmann explains that when he started the film he had to deal with the disappearance of the traces and "make a film on the basis of this nothingness". He describes the result as an "originary event" constructed with "traces of traces".[27] These include the traces of Nazi attempts to "obliterate all traces"[28] of what they had done, e.g., by plating pines that were 3–4 years old "to camouflage all the traces" Lanzmann (1985: 10).[29]

Action Cubes and Traces   41

So, what is it for a person to leave a trace by acting or, indeed, suffering?[30] And how do traces differ from consequences? We might begin to answer by noting that we *leave* traces but not consequences and that we bring about or *cause* consequences but not traces, though consequences can leave behind traces of their own.[31] To act is, in effect, to leave a trace, even when the action is one of attempting to remove one's former traces. The foot- or fingerprint, stain, smoke, ink mark, etc., that we leave is a trace of our action but not a consequence.[32] Traces are fragments of the past that have "not yet passed away" (Ricoeur 1985: 77), hence Heidegger's (characteristically overdone) puzzlement over how it is that fragments of the past (e.g., a Greek temple) can remain present-at-hand (BT §§72–77). These traces, be they physical or otherwise, are the vehicles through which that which is no longer may continue to have effects through time.

However, Ricoeur mistakenly identifies the trace with *what* is done and actions as the events of inscribing traces on time. This is because he understands the things we do as marks left on time by the events of our acting, much as the things written are the residual trace of the writing event. I quote from lines surrounding the text of this essay's epigraph:

> What in effect does writing fix? Not the event of speaking but the "said" of speaking . . . what we write, what we inscribe, is the noema of the speaking . . . It is not the speech *event*, it is speech itself insofar as it is *said* . . . the detachment of the *meaning* of the action from the *event* of the action . . . We speak of marking events. Are there not "marks" on time, the kind of thing that calls for a reading rather than for a hearing? . . . In the same way that a text is detached from its author, an action is detached from its agent and develops consequences of its own . . . our deeds escape us and have effects we did not intend . . . Social time, however, is not only something that flees; it is also a place of durable effects, of persisting patterns. An action leaves a "trace", it makes its "mark" when it contributes to the emergence of such patterns, which become the documents of human action.
> (Ricoeur 1986: 142–149)

On this analogy, the things we do are in some (admittedly metaphorical) sense more permanent than the fleeting events that come and go. In the case of writing, the distinction comes closer to that between a process and its resulting product. The suggestion is that we might, by extension, hold the same to be true of the act of speaking what is spoken and, *a fortiori*, that of the doing and the deed.[33] He is aware, however, of the difficulty that, when all is said and done, things imprinted on time itself do remain in the world in the literal way that a text can; even audio-video recordings are souvenirs of the event itself and not its traces.

Ricoeur thus identifies deeds with action traces, when what we actually do in acting is to *leave* traces. While his characterization of doings as the leaving of traces is an insightful one, he conflates the traces we leave with what we do when we act, viz., leave a trace. The error is fueled by the fact that the French verb "faire" is used to denote both making and doing.[34] Crucially, this failure leads to further confusions about the relation of actions to their location and effects in space and time. Inspired by Ricoeur, I have previously stated that "our deeds are but the ashes of our acts in time".[35] But this isn't quite right, for what we do in acting is *to leave* traces. The ashes of one's life, then, are not one's deeds *per se* but only their results.

Ricœur's ontology of action connects with Jennifer Hornsby's way of framing the distinction as one between (i) the spatiotemporally located events of our doing things and (ii) the things we do, the latter admitting to being done by different agents across more than one location or occasion, including the possible future (as in Lenin's *What is to be Done?*). Hornsby writes:

> The word "action" is ambiguous. Where it has a plural: in ordinary usage what it denotes, nearly always, are the things people do; in philosophical usage, what it denotes, very often, are events, each one of them some person's doing something.
>
> (Hornsby 1997: 142)

And, before here, John Macmurray:

> The term "action" is involved in the same ambiguity [as] terms like "perception" or "conception". It may refer either to what is done or to the doing of it . . . either "doing" or "deed". When we talk of an action we are normally referring to what is done.
>
> (Macmurray 1938: 74–76)

My own two cents is that in everyday English, the locution "thing done" is ambiguous between the two senses of action that the previously mentioned philosophers distinguish. The context is usually sufficient for us to know what was meant; we understand expressions such as "the hardest thing I ever did", "look what you did", and "see what I did there?" as easily as we understand assertions like "the soup is always great at Gino's", "tonight's soup is very good", and "your soup looks nicer than mine, I wonder if you got a fresher batch".

Whatever the linguistic facts, there is conceptual space for Hornsby's (1997) distinction between particular doings and repeatable things that you and I might both do.[36] Unsurprisingly, we find competing ontologies of doings and things done in the literature, with little consensus on whether the former are particulars, events, processes, instances of relations, etc., and the latter universals, types, results, products, etc. For example, Prichard (1932), von Wright (1963: 39), and Charles (2018) conceive of the thing done as the bodily event that action results in. But one does not "do" any bodily movements that one's actions may result in. Rather, *in* acting, one makes it the case that any such bodily movements occur.[37] *What* we do when we act, then, is make certain things true. Leaving traces is making it the case that traces are left, even if we don't typically do so knowingly. While we can act with the specific purpose of leaving certain traces if we so please, our control of them diminishes over time, if not always quite as rapidly as it did for poor Hansel and Gretel.[38]

When we deliberate about any given course of action, we typically consider it from the point of view of our purpose and, should we go forward with it, intention. This directedness does not preclude us from considering what the likely consequences might be or from pondering about the motive we'd be acting from, but it is our purpose that ultimately keeps everything else in check. In the present moment, by contrast, actions are typically encountered from the point of view of what one is doing and its immediate consequences. We often can't help but to see the action as motivated by certain concerns, but at other times, we make an inference to the same effect. In acting, we move from considering things we *could do* to engaging ourselves in the process of doing them. After the fact, we can look back at the events (or incomplete processes) of our acting from the point of view of not just their consequences but their more general spatiotemporal situation. The further past an action is, the wider this context becomes, and the more likely we are to begin from distant traces and work backward. While we can *try* to consider action from as many points of view as possible, we cannot simultaneously do so from all of them. Instead, we switch our attention from one aspect to another and try to form a fuller picture. Actions contain multitudes, but there is no view outside of space and time from which we can encounter any given act through all its different aspects. That is the paradox of action.

3. Rightness and Responsibility

The epistemic perspectivism (or lack of absolute standpoint) of action has implications for moral worth, luck, and responsibility. We have already seen that a person may have knowledge of action *qua* some things and not *qua* others. *Pari passu*, they can be held responsible for them from, say, the point of view of intention without being responsible from the point of view of knowledge, let alone objectivity. Arto Laitinen and I have defended the view that this is the best way to make sense of the tension between Hegel's claims that (i) agents have the right to be held responsible *only* for those aspects of their deed that were in fact included in their conscious purpose, intention, or foresight (aka their actions) and yet (ii) are responsible not only for what such actions but also for what *should* have been foreseen in the circumstances (viz., what *would have* been by a thinking agent).[39]

On this interpretation, the various aspects of right are the conceptual apparatus through which Hegel is able to make fine-grained moral judgments. As such, they mirror various combinations of subjective and/or objective aspects of action. Accordingly, the accountability of one who is guilty of failing to foresee certain consequences may be mitigated by their right of knowledge, and that of one who foresees (but does not intend) certain unfortunate consequences, by their right of intention. Such rights are real but not absolute; the full picture is determined by their interplay with other rights.

While Hegel's primary concern is to mark out different scopes of responsibility, he allows that one's action may be wrong *qua* deed but morally worthy *qua* intended action. For example, Oedipus acts rightly but (through bad luck) does the wrong thing. This preserves both the Kantian intuition that moral worth is not a matter of incident or resultant luck and the opposing view that what we end up doing is a matter of luck to the extent that it wasn't intended or rationally foreseeable.[40] Bernard Williams is thus only half right when he states that "the aim of making morality immune to luck is bound to be disappointed" for the reason that it is "deeply and disquietingly subject to luck".[41] The objective aspects of action are not the whole story. As E.R. Dodds puts it in his masterpiece, *The Greeks and the Irrational*:

> Suppose a motorist runs down a man and kills him, I think he ought to feel that he has done a terrible thing, even if the accident is no fault of his: he has destroyed a human life, which nothing can restore. In the objective order it is his acts that count, not intentions. A man who has violated that order may well feel a sense of guilt, however blameless his driving.
>
> (Dodds 1966: 183–184)[42]

To kill an innocent man is a terrible thing to do, but the unlucky motorist has not acted terribly in doing so. What about the inverse scenario in which the motorist is imprudent but doesn't run anybody over? The worst thing that this second driver does (viz., risk killing somebody with his reckless driving) is, in the objective order of things, not nearly as bad as the worst thing that the prudent but unlucky motorist does (kill an innocent man). Yet it is the second driver who acts wrongly. The wrongness here is not simply a matter of what she does (as in the case of an otherwise prudent driver who has unwittingly ingested a drug) but of his very doing of it.[43] The problem of moral luck as traditionally conceived is thus a product of the confused standard line that "[w]hen we say that *what he did* was wrong we mean that *he acted wrongly*".[44] Steven Sverdlik tries to improve the latter by suggesting that the moral properties (or at least deontic ones) of the things we do are dependent on our motives for doing them:

> There is an action X such that if X were performed from one motive it would fall into one deontic category and if X were performed from another motive it would fall into a second deontic category in virtue of these differences in motives.
>
> (Sverdlik 2011: 4)

But if a deed can be performed from different motives, it cannot be that deed itself that ever belongs to a deontic category, only the performing of it from a certain motive.[45] The same is true for many cases of intention. Moreover, one can act wrongly with the best of intentions, even if the doing isn't intentional under the infraction-highlighting description. For instance, a white person's styling their hair as dreadlocks or cornrows may count as an instance of cultural appropriation, however benevolent their intention. To condemn them straight out for this would be to ignore the more virtuous aspects of their action, e.g., they were seeking pay tribute to another culture or express solidarity with a specific group of people. But this does not *in itself* expunge them from the accusation that they could have and should have known better.

It might be objected, at this point, that moral and legal philosophy already has at their disposal all the tools they need to deal with such cases. After all, they have a long history of distinguishing between intention and (mere) foresight, motive and consequence, recklessness and negligence, and so on. The problem is not with the distinctions themselves but with uses they are put to. It is asked whether the rightness of "an action depends on the motive or its consequences"; it is asked whether or not morality is a matter of luck; and it is asked what the conditions for moral responsibility are, and how they differ from those of causal responsibility. These are all symptoms of an absolutist approach to action that fails to do justice to the proper mereology of all its aspects. At the very least, normative theories owe us more detail about the sort of thing actions must be if they are to have the kinds of moral properties ascribed to them. It is no good to simply say that they are events that are intentional under some description or processes that progress across time.

4. Epilogue

To praise or blame people solely on the grounds of what they did or didn't do is to give in to what we might call the obituary view of moral appraisal.[46] Obituaries typically provide embellished lists of successes and failures, e.g., she founded a charity, directed two Oscar-winning documentaries, wrote an influential book, etc. Indeed, the very chronology of peoples' lives is typically offered as a sort of list of things done at various moments in time. This is the action event as fact[47]: she was born at t1, went to school A at t2–t5, studied subject X at university B graduating at t6, took a job working for firm C at t7, and so on. There is no attempt to reveal actions as three-dimensional objects whose "inner" and "outer" aspects unfold in time and whose traces persist long after the fleeting event has come and gone. Ronald Dworkin writes:

> The final value of our lives is adverbial, not adjectival. It's the value of the performance, not anything that is left when the performance is subtracted.
>
> (Dworkin 2011: 197)[48]

Dworkin's view is the mirror contrast of that which Parfit would end up offering across *On What Matters*, in which all that ultimately matters is what you achieve and not how we come to do so. I have tried to show both doings and deeds matter in different objective and subjective respects. There is no competition between them, nor is there any sense in which it makes sense to ask whether someone was responsible for an action *tout court*. This is the hardest lesson to learn because the impetus comes to us so naturally.[49]

Notes

1. Ricoeur (1986: 148ff).
2. See Ricoeur (2000: 13ff.); cf. Changeux and Ricoeur (2000: 427).
3. Anscombe (1957: §45); cf. Powell (1967)
4. PR (1821: §114); see also §119; cf. Williams (1993: 69–70).
5. See Sandis (2010).
6. All emphasis in the original.
7. Emphasis in the original. The precedence of "intentional" over "voluntary" and "purposeful" here is telling.
8. For the Aristotelian origins of Hegel's outlook, see Speight (2001: 46ff.).
9. [See Hornsby, Chapter 1, this volume.]
10. Cf. Wittgenstein (PI §89).
11. See Laitinen and Sandis (2019).
12. See Sandis (2010: 44–45).
13. See Frey (2019: 1128).
14. See Anscombe (1979).
15. English Standard Version (I have replaced "the Skull" with "Calvary"). Some translations (e.g., the New Revised International Version) have "what they are doing". This present continuous parsing of "what they do" suggests a single action that has yet to be completed, as opposed to a series of ongoing actions that fall under the same kind (see Sandis 2016).
16. In John (19: 16ff.), it is the Roman soldiers who take charge of Jesus, but the "forgive them for . . ." line is absent, as it is from the parallel passages in Matthew and Mark (in which "they" remains opaque).
17. Purpose is more complicated, insofar as one's purpose may include "external" aspects of one's deed that go beyond intention or even foresight, e.g., consequences that one ought to have foreseen (see Laitinen & Sandis 2019).

18 Admittedly this sort of line has a little more mileage if one's victim claims to be the son of God.
19 See Sandis (2021).
20 See Sandis (2012: 6ff.).
21 See Sandis (forthcoming).
22 I don't mean to suggest that there were no earlier uses of the word "trace" to denote an earlier event. The *Oxford English Dictionary* offers Cowley (1656: I.iii), Whiston (1696: II 1722]186), and Pope (1713: 372) [misprinted by the OED as "1710"], but the philosophical concept of a historiographical trace as we know it today is not yet quite at work in these texts. Hume mainly uses it as a verb (see the subsequent note), though in Vol. V of his *History of England*, he tells the reader that "though parity may seem at first to have had place among Christian pastors, the period, during which it prevailed, was so short, that few disputed traces of it remained in history" (HE V.54.2).
23 Most of the authors mentioned earlier use "trace" as both a noun [*Spur, la trace*] and a verb [*verfolgen, tracer*].
24 It's unclear whether he took such appointment by community (if not quite committee) to be equally capable of downgrading what was previously taken to be a historical fact into a more commonplace one.
25 Elton (1967: 76ff.) and Elton (1991: 27 and 65). Cf. Evans (1997: 75ff.). I return briefly to the relation of facts to events in this essay's Epilogue.
26 Bomba, in Lanzmann (1985: 45).
27 Lanzmann, as quoted in Liebman (2007: 3–4).
28 Beauvoir (1985: vii).
29 See also Lanzmann (1985: 13, 45–46).
30 See Crampton (1974).
31 Levinas insists that only living beings can leave traces, but his point is ultimately a semantic one: "things . . . in themselves do not leave a trace but produce effects, that is to say, remain in the world. One stone scratched another. The scratch can of course be taken for a trace: in reality, without the man who held the stone, the scratch is nothing but an effect. It is no more a trace than a brush fire is the trace of thunder" (Levinas 1972: 43).
32 When online traces are removed, e.g., under the "right to be forgotten" act, what happens to the traces left by the removers? Should these be removed too? And then what? Ricoeur writes that "when there are no formal 'records' (like those which are kept by institutions like employment offices, schools, banks, and the police), there is still an informal analogue of these formal records which we call reputation and which constitutes a basis for blaming" (Ricoeur 1989: 154). This social imprint partly constitutes what Angela Merkel has called "the currency of trust". How does trust relate to data, and its traces and lack thereof? And what of the traces on search engines of those looking for traces that have been removed? Detectives leave fingerprints too.
33 Ricoeur has speech act theory in his sights but is more interested in the things we say through action than in the things we do with words. For "the disclosure of the agent in speech and action", see Arendt (1958: 175–181).
34 Cf. Arendt (1958: 19, n. 19) who relates the contrast between these activities to that between works and deeds, the differentiation of which ultimately informs her own distinction between work and action.
35 Sandis (2017: 126).
36 We don't do our own doings any more than we fear our own fearings or suspect our own suspectings (cf. A.R. White 1972). Matthew Hanser (2008) thinks of all such distinctions as type/token ones (cf. Clark 1989; Harman 2000), but there is good reason to be suspicious of this, because the things we do

are *instances* of types and it accordingly makes sense to think of one's doing something as one's instantiating the type that their deed falls under (cf. Steward 1997: 120–134 and Dancy 2009: 401). Davidson (1967) tries to demonstrate that *all* sentences that mention things done are replaceable by ones that only quantify over events without loss of meaning. His position, however, cannot adequately deal with normative statements (see Sandis 2012: 145ff.).
37 Cf. Charles (2018: 38).
38 The Egyptian pharaohs have arguably done betters in terms of the intended marks their burial preparations have left on time, though they were ultimately aiming for an afterlife that didn't take the form of Boris Karloff movies. The traces one leaves do not necessarily point to anything resembling truth, as illustrated by Timothy-Garton Ash's description of what he found in his Staci file, which he in turn uses to trace and confront the German friends and acquaintances who had informed on him (Ash 1997).
39 Laitinen and Sandis (2019).
40 See Nagel (1976) and Williams (1976). Constitutive luck is tricker, because who we are is only partly determined by our deeds and doings.
41 Williams (1976: 21 and 36).
42 The example originates in Bowra (1944: 168–170).
43 If this approach to moral luck is broadly right, then it should also help us with the old debate between subjectivism and objectivism about our duties when acting under uncertainty (see Zimmerman 2008).
44 Bennett (1995: 46), my emphasis. See also Dancy (2009: 400ff).
45 Derek Parfit similarly writes that "our acts are merely events in time" but proceeds to conflate these with things done (Parfit 2011: 270).
46 See Sandis (2015: §3).
47 See Austin, Strawson, and Cousin (1950). Cf. Vendler (1967: 31–32, and 122–146), H. White (1995), and Evans (1997: 78–90).
48 Note the allusion to Wittgenstein's famous rhetorical question, "what is left over if I subtract the fact that my arm goes up from the fact that I raise my arm?", *Philosophical Investigations*, trans. G.E.M. Anscombe (Oxford: Blackwell, 1953), §621. Dworkin models his distinction between having a good life and living well to that between art products and artistic acts of creation, without committing himself to any views about what art *is*; cf. Sandis (2017).
49 Many thanks to Katja Behrens for helping me design the Necker cubes. A much earlier version of this essay was presented at the *Hegel and the Philosophy of Action* conference which took place at the University of Valencia, November 9–11, 2016, (just after Leonard Cohen died and Donald Trump was elected President of the USA). Thanks to all who somehow still managed to listen and participate in discussion. I'm pleased to be able to finally complete the essay on the 250th anniversary of the greatest philosopher of action. This would not have been possible without Carla Bagnoli, without whose help this paper would be a lot worse.

References

Anscombe, G.E.M. (1957), *Intention* (Oxford: Basil Blackwell).
Anscombe, G.E.M. (1979), 'Under a Description'; as reprinted in her *Collected Philosophical Papers Volume II* (Oxford: Blackwell), 2018–2019.
Arendt, H. (1958), *The Human Condition*, 2nd edition [1998] (Chicago, IL: The University of Chicago Press).
Ash, T.-G. (1997), *The File* (London: Random House).

Austin, J.L., Strawson, P.F., & Cousin, D.R. (1950), 'Truth', *Aristotelian Society Supplementary*, Vol. 24, No. 1, 111–172.
Beauvoir, S. de (1985), 'Preface' to Lanzmann (1985).
Bennett, J. (1995), *The Act Itself* (Oxford: Oxford University Press).
Bowra, M. (1944), *Sophoclean Tragedy* (Oxford: Clarendon Press).
Brandom, R.B. (2019), *A Spirit of Trust: A Reading of Hegel's Phenomenology* (Boston, MA: Harvard University Press).
Carr, E.H. (1961), *What Is History?* (London: Macmillan).
Changeux, J.-P. & Ricoeur, P. (2000), *What Makes Us Think?: A Neuroscientist and a Philosopher Argue about Ethics, Human Nature, and the Brain* (Princeton, NJ: Princeton University Press).
Charles D. (2018), 'Processes, Activities and Actions', in R. Stout (ed.), *Process, Action and Experience* (Oxford: Oxford University Press).
Clark, R. (1989), 'Deeds, Doings and What is Done', *Noûs*, Vol. 23, No. 2, 199–210.
Cowley, A. (1656), *Pindarique Odes* (London: Humphrey Mofeley).
Crampton, G.R. (1974), *The Condition of Creatures: Suffering and Action in Chaucer and Spenser* (New Haven, CT: Yale University Press).
Dancy, J. (2009), 'Action in Moral Metaphysics', in C. Sandis (ed.), *New Essays on the Explanation of Action* (London: Palgrave Macmillan), 396–415.
Davidson, D. (1963), 'Actions, Reasons, and Causes', *Journal of Philosophy*, Vol. 60, 685–700; as reprinted in Davidson (2001: 3–19), to which any page numbers given refer.
Davidson, D. (1967), 'The Logical Form of Action Sentences' (1967); as reprinted in Davidson (2001: 105–121), to which any page numbers refer.
Davidson, D. (2001), *Essays on Actions & Events*, 2nd ed. (Oxford: Clarendon Press).
Derrida, J. (1967a), *L'écriture et la différence* (Paris: Éditions du Seuil).
Derrida, J. (1967b), *De la grammatologie* (Paris: Les Éditions de Minuit).
Dilthey, W. (1860), 'Schleiermacher's Hermeneutical System in Relation to Earlier Protestant Hermeneutics', eds. R. A. Makkreel & F. Rodi, trans. T Nordenhaug, *Wilhelm Dilthey: Selected Works* (Princeton, NJ: Princeton University Press), Vol. IV.
Dodds, E.R. (1966), *The Greeks and the Irrational* (Berkeley, CA: University of California Press).
Dworkin, R. (2011), *Justice for Hedgehogs* (Boston, NJ: Harvard University Press).
Edmunds, F. (1869), *Traces of History in the Names of Places* (London: Longmans, Green, and Co.).
Elton, G.R. (1967), *The Practice of History* (Sydney: University of Sydney Press).
Elton, G.R. (1991), *Return to Essentials: Some Reflections on the Present State of Historical Study* (Cambridge: Cambridge University Press).
Evans, R.J. (1997), *In Defence of History* (London: Granta Books).
Frey, J. (2019), 'Anscombe on Practical Knowledge and the Good', *Ergo*, Vol. 6, No. 39, 1121–1151.
Hanser, M. (2008), 'Actions, Acting, and Acting Well', in Russ Shafer-Landau (ed.), *Oxford Studies in Metaethics* (Oxford: Oxford University Press), Vol. 3, 272–273.

Harman, G. (2000), *Explaining Value and Other Essays in Moral Philosophy* (Oxford: Oxford University Press).

Hegel, G.W.F. (1821), *Grundlinien der Philosophie des Rechts* [*Elements of the Philosophy of Right* – PR], ed. A.W. Wood, trans. H.B. Nisbet (Cambridge: Cambridge University Press), 1991.

Hegel, G.W.F. (1835), *Vorlesungen über die Ästhetik* [*Aesthetics: Lectures on Fine Art* – LA], trans. T.M. Knox. 2 vols. (Oxford: Clarendon Press), 1988.

Hegel, G.W.F. (1837), *Vorlesungen über die Philosophie der Weltgeschichte* [*Lectures on the Philosophy of World History* – LPH], *Vol. I: Manuscripts of the Introduction and the Lectures of 1822–3*, eds. & trans. R.F. Brown & P.C. Hodgson (Oxford: Clarendon Press), 2011.

Heidegger, M. (1927), *Sein und Zeit* [*Being and Time* – BT], trans. H. B. Nisbet (Cambridge: Cambridge University Press), 1991.

Hornsby, J. (1997), *Simple Mindedness: In Defense of Naive Naturalism in the Philosophy of Mind* (Cambridge, MA: Harvard University Press).

Hume, D. (1754), *The History of England [HE], Vol. V: From the Invasion of Julius Caesar to The Revolution in 1688* (London: George Bell).

Knowles, D. (2010), 'Hegel on Actions, Reasons, and Causes', in Laitinen & Sandis (2010: 42–58).

Laitinen, A. & Sandis, C. (eds.) (2010), *Hegel on Action* (London: Palgrave Macmillan).

Laitinen, A. & Sandis, C. (2019), 'Hegel on Purpose' (with Arto Laitinen), *Hegel Bulletin*, Vol. 40, No. 3 (Dec), 444–463.

Lanzmann, C. (1985), *Shoah* – extensively corrected and revised 1995 edition (New York, NY: Da Capo Press).

Levinas, E. (1963), 'La trace de l'autre', *Tidischrift voor filosofie* Vol. 25, No. 3 (Sep), 605–623.

Levinas, E. (1972), *Humanism of the Other* [*Humanisme de l'autre homme*], trans. N. Poller (Champaign, IL: University of Illinois Press).

Liebman, S. (ed.) (2007), *Claude Lanzmann's Shoah: Key Essays* (Oxford: Oxford University Press).

Macaulay, T.B. (1828), 'History' [Review of *The Romance of History* by Henry Neele], *Edinburgh Review*, Vol. 47, No. XCIV (May), 331–367.

Macmurray, J. (1938), 'What is Action?', *Proceedings of the Aristotelian Society*, Supp. Vol. XVII.

Nagel, T. (1976), 'Moral Luck'; as reprinted in his *Mortal Questions* (Cambridge: Cambridge University Press, 1979).

Neander, J.A.W. (1826), *Allgemeine Geschichte Der Christlichen Religion Und Kirche* [*General History of the Christian Religion and Church*], Vol. 1 (Hamburg: Friedrich Pertches), trans. J. Torrey (Boston, MA: Crocker & Brewster), 1854.

Nietzsche, F. (1874), *Vom Nutzen und Nachteil der Historie für das Leben* (Leipzig: Verlag von E.W. Fritzsch).

Parfit, D. (2011), *On What Matters* (Oxford: Oxford University Press).

Plato, *Phaedrus* [P], trans. A. Nehamas & P. Woodruff (Indianapolis, IN: Hackett Publishing), 1995.

Plato, *Theaetetus* [T], trans. J. McDowell (Oxford: Clarendon Press), 1973.

Pope, A. (1713), *Windsor-Forest* (London: Bernard Lintott).

Powell, B. (1967), *Knowledge of Actions* (London: George Allen & Unwin).

Prichard, H.A. (1932), 'Duty and Ignorance of Fact', as reprinted in his *Moral Writings*, (ed.) J. MacAdam (Oxford: Clarendon Press), 2004, 85.
Ricoeur, P. (1985), *Temps et récit* [*Time and Narrative*], Vol. 3, trans. K. Blamey & D. Pellauer (Chicago, IL: University of Chicago Press), 1988.
Ricoeur, P. (1986), *Du texte à l'action. Essais d'herméneutique II* [*From Text to Action: Essays in Hermeneutics, II*], trans. K. Blamey & J. Evanston (London: Bloomsbury), 2008.
Ricoeur, P. (2000), *La Mémoire, l'Histoire, l'Oubli* [*Memory, History, Forgetting*] (Chicago, IL: University of Chicago Press), 2004.
Sandis, C. (2010), 'The Man Who Mistook his Handlung for a Tat: Hegel on Oedipus and Other Tragic Thebans', *Bulletin of the Hegel Society of Great Britain*, No. 62, 35–60.
Sandis, C. (2012), *The Things We Do and Why We Do Them* (London: Palgrave Macmillan).
Sandis, C. (2015), 'Motivated by the Gods', in A. Buckareff, C. Moya, & S. Rosell (eds.), *Agency and Responsibility* (London: Palgrave Macmillan), 209–225.
Sandis, C. (2016), 'He Buttered the Toast While Baking a Fresh Loaf', *Philosophy and Public Issues*, Suppl. Vol. 5, No. 3, 27–42.
Sandis, C. (2017), 'The Doing and the Deed: Action in Normative Ethics', *Royal Institute of Philosophy Supplement*, 80(ed. A. O'Hear), 105–126.
Sandis, C. (2021), 'What Is It to Do Nothing?', in V. Rodriguez-Blanco & G. Pavlakos (eds.), *Negligence, Omissions and Responsibility: Reflecting on Philosophy of Action* (Cambridge: Cambridge University Press)
Sandis, C. (forthcoming), 'Agents as Truth-makers', forthcoming in my book *From Action to Ethics: A Pluralistic Approach to Reasons and Responsibility* (London: Bloomsbury).
Speight, A. (2001), *Hegel, Literature and the Problem of Agency* (Cambridge: Cambridge University Press).
Sverdlik, S. (2011), *Motive and Rightness* (Oxford: Oxford University Press).
Taylor, C. (1979), 'Action as Expression', in C. Diamond & J. Teichman (eds.), *Intention and Intentionality* (Sussex: Harvester Press).
Taylor, C. (1983), 'Hegel and the Philosophy of Action'; as reprinted in Laitinen & Sandis (2010: 22–41).
Vendler, Z. (1967), *Linguistics in Philosophy* (Ithaca, NY: Cornell University Press).
Von Wright, G.H. (1963), *Norm and Action* (London: Routledge & Kegan Paul).
Whiston, W. (1696), *A New Theory of the Earth* (London: Benjamin Tooke).
White, Alan R. (1972), 'What We Believe', in N. Rescher (ed.), *Studies in the Philosophy of Mind* (Oxford: Blackwell), 69–84.
White, H. (1995), 'Response to Arthur Marwick', *Journal of Contemporary History*, Vol. 30, No. 2 (Apr), 233–246.
Williams, B.A.O. (1976), 'Moral Luck'; as reprinted in his *Moral Luck* (Cambridge: Cambridge University Press).
Williams, B.A.O. (1993), *Shame and Necessity* (Berkeley, CA: University of California Press).
Zimmerman, M. (2008), *Living with Uncertainty* (Cambridge: Cambridge University Press).

3 Normative Powers, Agency, and Time

Arto Laitinen

Agency and time are intimately related. Agency is often defined as the power to bring about and prevent change, and change takes time. Agents do not merely persist in time like stones or other typical three-dimensional objects; they have active abilities or capacities to alter their circumstances. That is central to what it is to be an agent. Not all changes are agentially caused, some are just impersonal events, and not all theories of action pay attention to agency, but to the extent that agency is thematized, it is linked to their power to change the world.[1]

What is less often discussed is the relevance of different kinds of change to agency. This article focuses on non-causal normative change and on the question of whether agents have *normative powers*, i.e., power to bring about normative change directly. Such normative change proper can be distinguished from descriptive changes in the worldly circumstances (which naturally may be normatively significant) on the one hand and from institutional change (which equally may be normatively significant) on the other hand. Normative powers can be said to be "capacities to create normative reasons by our willing or say-so" (Chang 2020, 275).[2] If there are such powers, they are to be included in a theory of agency as well. Are there such powers?

To get the question in focus, it will prove helpful to characterize the three kinds of changes (1.1) and the relevant kind of normativity: the "normativity proper" of oughts and normative reasons, rather than that of social norms and institutional decrees (see Section 1.2). This distinction is relevant for separating normative change proper from institutional change. Sections 1.3–1.4. explain how descriptive and institutional change are normatively significant, without direct exercises of proper normative powers. The contrast to them puts the exercise of normative powers in sharper relief. Section 1 thus carves the conceptual space for normative powers.

Is there something that occupies that conceptual space? Do we have such (proper) normative powers, to bring about normative change directly, and not merely by changing the reason-giving descriptive features of the circumstances and in some pre-institutional (as opposed to post-institutional

DOI: 10.4324/9780429259845-5

as it were) way? This paper argues, by answering some challenges to the view, that we do. Section 2 responds to two challenges, one arguing that *all normativity is institutional* (2.1) and a *Challenge from Supervenience*, claiming that exercises of normative powers would violate considerations of supervenience (2.2).

Section 3 responds to a challenge – generalizing Kent Hurtig's (2020) challenge about consent – which states that exercises of normative powers are valid only in cases when they do not matter – they never bring about a "normative transformation" at the level of what the agent overall ought to do. Discussing this challenge is illuminating in showing that consent – and thus at least some normative powers – is normatively transformative in some cases. It also locates the main contribution of exercises of normative powers at a different level than that of overall oughts. It also suggests further conditions for consent being relevant and valid – sometimes normative powers are invalid and thus void of normative effects.

Section 4 concludes that rational agents as possessors of normative powers are not merely responsive to pre-existing normative reasons, they can also create normative reasons (Chang 2020; Laitinen 2020b). A "responsive" view of rational agency sees us as being able to track existing normative reasons and bring about at least descriptive changes (on which normative changes supervene). The "constructive" or "creative" view of rational agency sees us as being able to construct at least an institutional world but if we have also properly normative powers to create normative reasons.[3] This chapter argues we are both responsive and creative.

1. Carving the Conceptual Space for Normative Powers

1.1. *Descriptive, Institutional, and Normative Change*

Descriptive change is an alteration in the descriptive features of the situation: before closing the door, the door was open, and afterward, it is closed, and it was the agent who closed it. It is relatively clear that agents can do such things.

Institutional change takes place in pre-existing (or as a borderline case, emerging) institutional setting, positive law being one primary example. In that setting, the institutional standing or status of individuals can change. Say, Joe Biden can become the president of the U.S. With social roles, individuals acquire rights, obligations, tasks, and prerogatives. Institutional reality is ripe with different roles that come with defined further institutional powers: priests are able to perform marriages, and presidents are able to declare wars, etc. Acquisition and exercise of such pre-defined institutional powers (what John Searle (2010) dubbed "deontic powers") will also bring about institutional changes. Now all of institutional reality seems to depend on the brute capacity of humans (together) to institute such task-role systems (Tuomela 2013). To avoid infinite regress, it must be the case that such brute capacity is not institutionally created. So *qua* human agents, we have the power to institute, to create institutional reality, and *qua* role holders within the existing institutional reality, we have the extra powers that come with whatever role one happens to hold. Both the institutional reality and one's place in it are historically contingent (cf. Ásta 2018), but the brute human capacity to create institutions is pre-institutional and not dependent on such historical contingencies.

Both descriptive changes and institutional changes *can be normatively significant*. That a forest is on fire is a strong reason not to go to the forest. Legislating a valid law forbidding entrance to forests creates a different reason against going to the forest. In these cases, a normative change results from descriptive or institutional change and exercise of "descriptive" or institutional agential powers, respectively.

Is there additionally such a thing as *direct normative change* via exercise of normative powers, which would be separate from the normative alterations resulting from exercises of descriptive or institutional powers? Can we, for example, will reasons for action into existence, merely by promising, consenting, giving a word, committing, by our say so?

1.2. Normativity Proper: Reasons and Oughts

The chapter will adopt the view that the normativity of reasons and oughts, which is here called *normativity*1, or normativity proper, is central.[4] It is an open question whether all de facto requirements or expectations or socially constructed norms are normative in that sense. Arguably it depends on the contents of the norms and the authority of the legislative process, whether we have good reasons, or ought, to meet the requirements, to obey the law, or to follow the etiquette, or to conform to others' interpersonal expectations, requests, demands, or prescriptions. Whether and when positive norms generate such normative1 reasons is a difficult and important substantive question (that will be touched in Section 3.4).[5]

In another sense, social norms are trivially and constitutively normative, or by definition normative in another sense, normativity2: some forms of behavior are ruled as acceptable (e.g., driving on the right) and others as unacceptable (e.g., driving on the left) in light of the norm. Even a morally bad norm (that we have no reason to follow, and which ought to be changed, and ought not to prevail) classifies behaviors as acceptable or unacceptable in light of that norm or standard.[6] So surely social norms are then by definition normative? Call this conformity to social norms and actual expectations *normativity*2. It is *not* an open question whether social norms are normative in *that* sense – they are by definition normative2. But importantly, it is an open question whether one has good reasons, or sufficient reason, or ought, to follow any social norm – that is, whether the norm in question is normative1 (they are meant to be, but may fail). An unjust social norm might give us opposite

Normative Powers, Agency, and Time 55

reasons – we might have reasons to oppose existing social norms because they are unjust.

In this chapter, "normativity" is used only in the sense of normativity1. It is in that sense that it is an open question whether social norms, positive law, interpersonal expectations, and so on are normative.[7] This chapter focuses on the question of whether we have normative powers and can bring about normative change in that sense. By contrast, this chapter takes for granted that we have powers to bring about institutional change, and while it is an open philosophical question in social ontology to make sense of that, there are no urgent skeptical challenges: it is more or less a platitude that humans can create an institutional world. While institutional change is also normative2 change, I will merely call it institutional change for clarity.[8]

1.3. The Normative Significance of Descriptive Change

Normatively significant descriptive facts are ubiquitous. The fact that the trash bin is full is a reason for me to empty the trash bin. The fact that my tooth is aching is a reason to take a painkiller. That a boulder falls is a reason for the driver to swerve. The fact that I'm tired is a reason to postpone a decision. That I dropped into a well is a reason for others to help me out. That a taxation system is unjust is a reason to try to change it. That current industrial arrangements pose a threat of catastrophic climate change is a reason to collectively transform them. That a comment would be a grave insult is a reason against making the comment,[9] and so on and so forth.

Facts or considerations that speak in favor (or against) certain acts are normative reasons. In any situation, there are several reasons, and what the agent ought to do overall depends on the overall balance of reasons. Each of the facts or considerations can be called a "contributory" reason, as they contribute to the overall balance. What one has most reason to do, or ought to do, results from the balance of the contributory reasons and can be called the "overall" balance of reasons (Dancy 2004).

In a helpful terminology, an ordinary, descriptive fact (e.g., that a boulder falls) is a *normatively significant* fact, when it functions as a contributory reason (Parfit 1997). So, for example,

> Fact 1: The trash bin is full.
> Fact 2: Fact 1 is a reason for agent A to empty the trash bin.

Fact 2 is a *normative fact*, which involves a reason. Fact 1 is a *normatively significant* fact, because it figures in the normative fact. There can be meaningful disagreement about descriptive features (is the trash bin really full?) and about their normative significance (even if it is, is it really a reason?).

Suppose then that there is a descriptive fact that is not a reason for anyone to do anything: let us assume it is not relevant to anyone's duties, practical goals, or relevant for promoting value of any kind.

> Fact 1*: the average wind speed at the measuring station at Somewheresville on Tuesday the 24th was a bit less than on Monday the 23rd.
> Fact 2*: Fact 1* is not a reason for anyone to do anything.

We can say that in this case Fact 1* is normatively insignificant. One interesting class of insignificant descriptive differences consists of irrelevant details of otherwise significant facts: the more finely individuated details do not show up on the normative radar, as they were. If the trash bin is full, one has a reason to empty it, and it often does not matter much what kind of trash is in it, or what the detailed spatial arrangement between different pieces of trash is. Or if one sees that someone is about to go and walk on thin ice, one has reason to warn them independently of whether it is Monday or Tuesday, morning or afternoon, if they are wearing green or pink, etc. And if someone insists they have human rights, almost any particular features from age and gender to shoe size and number of siblings do not matter. Or, in another way, as organisms are multiply realizable as atom-level arrangements, it does not matter which exact atoms currently compose the rights-bearing organism or organism in need. Such variations show that there are a number of further insignificant descriptive facts even in cases that contain normatively significant descriptive facts. Understanding normativity includes understanding which descriptive facts are normatively significant and which are not, and in virtue ethics the virtue of *phronesis*, practical wisdom is the name for that ability to discern normative significance.

Ordinary "descriptive" worldly change concerns those facts (Fact 1 and 1* in the schema) that are not themselves normative. In case they are normatively significant, they make a difference to normative facts or considerations (Fact 2 in the schema), but if they are normatively insignificant, no normative change occurs.

The ordinary agential powers are powers to bring about changes in the descriptive situations (Fact 1 and Fact 1*). The power to change normative facts (e.g., Fact 2 in the schema) is here called a normative power. It is helpful to formulate a conditional *normative principle:* "If Fact 1, then . . .". For any normative fact (Fact 2, 2*, . . .), there is a similar principle. The only difference between a fact and a principle is that the principle leaves it open whether there is an obtaining state of affairs or not; that is, whether Fact 1 really is a fact or not. By contrast, as formulated, the normative fact (Fact 2) entails Fact 1. It may well be that there are two types of candidate normative powers – the power to create a valid principle which holds over situations (and are non-committal to whether the principle applies in the situation here and now) and the power to create a token normative fact (with or without implications for similar cases elsewhere) (Shafer-Landau 2003).

1.4. The Normative Significance of Institutional Change

The human institutional reality is in its entirety the making of human agents, past and present. It is clear that humans have the requisite capacities and powers to create an institutional reality, and the institutional roles may contain new powers. Institutions can also adopt policies, for example, in recruitment or student admission. In Michael Bratman's (2007, 283–310) example, a university decides, for example, to give legacy considerations weight in their practical reasoning. Adopting such criteria means that something is a reason to the admission committee that wasn't before it. It is relatively clear that institutions can bring it about that some feature is a reason to accept a candidate.

Are such institutional powers normative powers in the relevant sense? The distinction between what social norms require (normativity2) and what the agent ought to do (normativity1) is accepted by virtually all moral theories, in different vocabularies. If the social norms require of an agent (typically a role holder) to Phi, it is an open question whether the agent thereby ought to Phi. Sometimes the answer is positive, while sometimes the agent ought to disregard the norms, and sometimes the agent ought to do exactly the opposite in the spirit of disobedience.

A simple moral argument can be given: if the social norms are morally horrendous, moral agents should follow their own conscience rather than the social norms, and to the best of their ability, try to change the social norms. In a typical variety of cases, however, when the social norms are not horrendous, but yet far from ideal, the agent both ought to obey the social norms in force (despite their imperfections they may play important coordinating roles, for example, and have been legislated in legitimate way) and try to work to get the social norms improved.

Nonetheless, social norms and declarations are *supposed to* be good enough, so that they do provide agents with reasons for action. That is the point of social norms, after all. In the cases when they succeed, a normative change is brought about via the exercise of institutional powers. It is a different kind of normative change from one which directly results from descriptive change in the situation. That a road is blocked by boulders is a reason to find another route. But even in the absence of boulders, a law can make it impermissible to use a route.

Thus, social norms seem to be able to bring about normative change, in a different way: in two descriptively similar situations, the agent has reason to Phi in one but not in the other, in virtue of the institutional change.[10]

2. Is the Conceptual Space Empty? Two Challenges

2.1. Are There Pre-Institutional Normative Powers?

Direct normative change differs, then, both from descriptive change and from institutional change. Both of these may be normatively significant, and indeed institutional change is typically supposed to bring about normative change.

Do human agents have a more direct normative power, for example, to promise, to give their consent, or in other ways bind their wills, that does not derive from, for example, collectively accepted institutions or norms? If human agents do have such powers, they are either original powers or derive from contingent institutions. But human agents have in any case the original power to create the contingent institutions, so original powers need to be postulated in either case. The question is merely whether a better theory of promising sees it as a contingent institutional practice or a non-contingent human power to bind one's will.

Thus, one argument against "original" normative powers is that the only normative powers derive from contingent institutions. Call this *the challenge from institutional powers*. It would hold there are no direct normative changes – only institutional ones.

Here's a case that suggests that there could be normative powers in the absence of institutional setting.

> DESERT: Suppose two strangers meet in a desert, outside of the reach of any institution. They are tired and have some shelter but need water from the oasis that is still some distance away. Both would have enough energy to walk that distance. A volunteers to go and get water for both, and B gladly accepts. A visits the oasis and comes back without bringing water to B. B is by now significantly more tired and is not sure whether he has enough energy to walk the distance and come back to the shelter.

A does not violate any institutional norms, as there are none at play. A would have had independent reasons to bring water to B, even without having given his word: B needs water. But the promise certainly adds an extra reason, and indeed without it, B would have gone to get water himself. If there is a new reason, then the exercise of normative power, promise, directly adds a reason that was not there independently in virtues of the descriptive facts of the situation and in the absence of institutional settings.

Thus, there is reason to think that at least some normative powers are direct and pre-institutional, not in need of institutional standing. Note that even if it would turn out that all normative powers do presuppose institutional roles, human agents would still have institutionally mediated normative powers.

2.2 A Challenge From Supervenience

An opposite challenge to normative powers can be posed, the *Challenge from Supervenience*. It captures the sense that it should be the world that fixes normative reasons and oughts, and not our thoughts.

Here's the challenge: It is widely agreed that how things are normatively supervene globally on the descriptive features. In an exact descriptive duplicate of the world, the reasons would be the same, for the counterpart agents in that world. The descriptive features of the world fix what we have reason to do, and there is no other way to change the normative shape of the situation, than by changing the descriptive shape of the situation. There is no room for exercises of normative powers if supervenience holds; or so the challenge claims.

How to assess the challenge? The question is twofold: how do past exercises of normative powers figure in the situation here and now, and what does supervenience look like at the time of exercising normative powers?

First, past commitments, promises, and other exercises of normative powers must of course be taken into account, in describing the situation the agent faces. Two descriptively otherwise similar situations, where in one I have previously promised to water my neighbor's flowers while they are away, and in another, there is no such promise, are normatively different. Promises by their very nature are meant to be in force over time: if they would cease to be relevant when the act of promising is over, they would be pointless. Thus, to find the relevant base for describing the situation "here and now", one must take the past into account.

Past exercises of normative powers are merely one example of how the past matters: a history of oppression and injustice, or reasons of gratitude for past favors, or history of interpersonal relationships naturally affect the situation here and now. So global supervenience must be formulated in a way that takes the past into account, to capture the normatively significant features in the present. Past exercises of normative powers are among the events in the past that shape the current situation. The interesting point that this reveals is that discussions of supervenience must be sensitive to history.

What does supervenience look like at the time of exercising normative powers? A dualism that would locate agents with normative powers somehow outside the world would have to reject supervenience. A change in the agent's mind would directly change the normative shape of the situation, without anything changing in the descriptive state of the world. A view that holds agents as certain kinds of embodied, worldly creatures, i.e., as organisms or animals with agential capabilities, would have to draw a difference between those aspects of the world that the agent encounters as the circumstance or situation for action and those aspects of the world (the agent's brain, body, living organism, *etc.*) in which the agent herself is embodied – which in one sense *are* the agent and in another sense are the *agent's* body (roughly, those aspects of the world that cease to function when one commits suicide and that one cares about when one cares about one's health and capabilities, etc.).[11] For supervenience to hold, the exercises of normative powers by embodied agents must supervene on physical features: changes in willing and commitment presumably are changes in brain states, etc., and expressions like spoken promises presumably supervene on movements of air, etc. Global supervenience merely tells us that an exact copy of the physical features, including subpersonal brain states and movements of air, will result in an exact copy in the normative features. So at least global supervenience between physical states and normative states can be preserved. The lesson is that supervenience must take into account not only the descriptive state of the situation that the agent encounters but also the states of the agent.

So it turns out that global supervenience can hold even if we accept normative powers. The supervenience base must be historically extended in including the normatively significant facts from the past and it must be extended to include relevant states of the embodied agent.

3. Is Exercise of Normative Powers Ever Transformative? The Case of Consent

This section discusses an argument that exercises of normative powers are not normatively transformative. Given that the sole function of normative powers is to bring about normative change (which may or may not be "transformation" in the technical sense defined later), it would be bad news for normative powers if they are never transformative. The discussion focuses on the case of consent, but similar arguments can be made concerning other powers, such as promising. If the question is whether the exercise of normative powers is *ever* transformative, it suffices to show that it is in the case of one specific normative power, the power to give consent.

3.1. The Challenge

It is widely accepted that consent can be normatively transformative. There are things that without B's consent, A ought not to do to B, but with B's consent, it is OK to do to B. It is up to B; it is B's call to consent to the treatment.[12] Standard examples vary from medical treatments to sexual intercourse.

Kent Hurtig (2020) argues for a surprising view that consent is not normatively transformative, it cannot change what we have overall decisive reason to do, that is, ought to do. He defines normative transformation in a clear and precise way, but I think ultimately too narrowly. He focuses on change at the level of overall oughts. A transformation takes place

Normative Powers, Agency, and Time 61

if before the consent B has a decisive reason – understood as the total balance of reasons – against Phi-ing, and after the consent, B no longer has a decisive reason against Phi-ing. Hurtig argues against a strong thesis, which claims that such transformation necessarily takes place with consent:

The Transformation Thesis (T):

Necessarily, A's validly consenting to B's Phi-ing changes the situation from there being decisive reason for B not to Phi before A consents, to its not being the case that there is decisive reason for B not to Phi after A consents. (There is decisive reason for someone to Phi just in case the balance of total reasons for and/or against Phi-ing favours Phi-ing).

(Hurtig 2020, 106)

A weaker form would say that consent typically, or sometimes, brings about normative transformation in the overall oughts (decisive reasons, balance of reasons). Hurtig (ibid., 98) argues against such weak forms as well, in claiming that "*consent is necessarily not normatively transformative*". In the next sections, I will try to show that the weaker view – consent sometimes is normatively transformative – is correct. This will require analyzing the kinds of normative change that consent primarily does (removing one moral wrong-making feature, and thereby one strong and important reason against, and so typically tipping the balance at the overall level), which explains its effect on the overall ought.

Hurtig first rightly notes that typical analyses of consent take it that certain conditions need to be met: competence condition, knowledge condition, and voluntariness condition. He argues that when these conditions are met, consent is never transformative. The conditions are in more detail:

The Competence Condition

A's general cognitive and emotional capacities at the time of consenting are "sufficiently mature" and they are not at the time of consenting impaired by conditions like being depressed, seriously intoxicated, in excruciating pain, agitated, and irritable, etc.

The Knowledge Condition

A has sufficient knowledge of all the facts that are relevant to B's Phi-ing. (What is the purpose of B's Phi-ing? How is B's Phi-ing related to that purpose? What are the potential payoffs and risks of B's Phi-ing?)

The Voluntariness Condition

A is not being coerced, unduly persuaded, or manipulated. (A's assenting to B's Phi-ing must be above the threshold of voluntariness.)

(ibid., 105)

Hurtig also notes that the type of action in question must not be such that it is impermissible with or without consent to do it: If B's Phi-ing is consent-independently impermissible, then A's consenting to B's Phi-ing cannot make it permissible, such as A becoming B's slave, or A allowing B to "kill him for some trivial reason"*(ibid.,* 106). Consent is relevant only in a range of cases that are "consentable".

Hurtig gives a nice example, *Tattoo*, which I will rename *Ugly Tattoo with Consent* later (to contrast it with three other cases: a *Nice Tattoo with/without consent* and *Ugly Tattoo without Consent*).[13]

Here is the case, *Tattoo*, aka *Ugly Tattoo with Consent* in my terminology:

> B approaches A and asks if A is interested in getting a large facial tattoo. A is made aware of all the following salient facts about the procedure and outcome: 1. The procedure will be very expensive. 2. It will be very painful. 3. The tattoo will be ugly and permanent. 4. The tattoo will cause friends and family serious discomfort. 5. A will enjoy wearing it for only a very short period. 6. B will be slightly better off financially by tattooing A. A consents.
>
> *(ibid.,* 106)

Hurtig argues that for the knowledge condition to be met, A should know all the relevant facts. They include the fact that the combined normative weight of 1–4 is far greater than the combined weight of 5–6. If the agent does not know them, then plausibly the knowledge condition is not satisfied and the consent is not valid. But, Hurtig argues, if A does know there is a decisive reason against consenting, he is not fully practically rational in consenting. Hurtig argues that A is actually practically irrational, weak-willed, in such a way that his consent is not valid. In this way, Hurtig builds a case for thinking that consent is valid only in cases where it is done in accordance with the balance of independent reasons for or against Phi-ing, and in these cases, it is not normatively transformative.

How should this challenge be assessed? There are several aspects: first, examining what is the normative effect that consent has, and second, reassessing the claim that B's consent is valid and not normatively void only in cases where it does not make a difference at the level of overall oughts. This takes us to a closer discussion on conditions when consent is valid and on a range of cases where it is valid and makes a normative difference.

3.2. The Primary Normative Function of Consent

To see the normative effect of consent, let us focus first on cases (like tattooing) that would be violations of bodily integrity without consent but are not violations of bodily integrity with consent.[14] If something is a violation of bodily integrity, it is *prima facie* morally impermissible in virtue of being a violation of bodily integrity, and moral impermissibility is a strong reason against an action. Whether it is sufficiently strong to tip the balance of reasons depends on other reasons present in a situation, and as there is an endless variety of situations, these need to be addressed case by case. Furthermore, whether it is morally impermissible depends on the presence of other morally relevant factors that affect its permissibility.

Thus, the normative effect of consent can be captured in the principle (further explainable in terms of rights): "Phi-ing without consent is a violation of bodily integrity, whereas Phi-ing with consent is not a violation of bodily integrity". Such violations are morally wrong-making, and on their own make Phi-ing *prima facie* wrong. Whether they make Phi-ing (in the situation) morally wrong without the qualification "prima facie, depends on other morally relevant features present in the situation: perhaps Phi-ing would have enormous beneficial consequences, etc. That Phi-ing is morally wrong is a strong reason against Phi-ing, whereas "that Phi-ing is morally permissible" is as such no reason in favor of Phi-ing. Whether it is sufficiently strong to tip the balance of reasons depends on other reasons present in a situation.

Another aspect of consent is similar: it would be a paternalistic violation of autonomy to do to B beneficial deeds without B's consent. "Phi-ing without B's consent is a violation of B's autonomy, whereas Phi-ing with B's consent is not a violation of B's autonomy". Again, such violations are morally wrong-making and make Phi-ing *prima facie* wrong and together with the other morally relevant considerations can suffice to make Phi-ing wrong (without the qualification "prima facie"), and such that one ought not Phi.

Thus, the normative effect of consent, or normative powers more broadly, is not directly at the level of overall oughts; the effect at that level can be countered by other features. Let us have this route via moral wrong-making in mind in discussing the challenge. Thus, whether or not consent is morally transformative at the level of overall oughts, it can be normatively significant in altering the reasons at play. Let us first consider some cases, assuming consent is possible, and then return to Hurtig's point that the conditions for consent are not met in *Tattoo* or other potentially transformative cases.

A change in "the moral relations between A and B" (Hurtig 2020, 101 and passim.) thus need not be a transformation at the level of the overall balance of reasons against Phi-ing; it can be a change at the level of contributory reasons, before and after consent. Terminologically, we can agree

64   Arto Laitinen

to use "normative transformation" for changes at the overall balance of reasons and call "normative change" also other changes, for example, changes at the level of contributory reasons for or against Phi-ing.

3.3. Variations in Which Consent Is Normatively Transformative

Even though the case, *Ugly Tattoo with Consent*, would manage to show that there are cases in which consent (assuming for now that it is possible) does not bring about transformation in the overall balance of reasons, this leaves it open whether there are also cases in which consent *does* bring about a transformation in the overall recommendation whether to Phi.

Hurtig seems to think not. He writes, "since there is nothing special about *[Ugly] Tattoo [With Consent]*, the point generalizes" (107). But what is true about ugly tattoos may not generalize to nice tattoos, and what is true about cases with consent may not generalize to cases without consent. There are four kinds of cases that we need to discuss one by one. One class consists of cases, where there are strong independent reasons against Phi-ing but A consents (Hurtig's example belongs here). Another consists of cases, where there are strong independent reasons against Phi-ing and A does not consent. In a third class, there are no strong independent reasons against Phi-ing, but A does not consent. In a fourth class, there are cases where there are no strong independent reasons against Phi-ing and A consents.

Consider first *Nice Tattoo without Consent*.

> B approaches A and asks if A is interested in getting a wonderful tattoo. A is made aware of the following salient facts about the procedure and outcome: 1. Having the tattoo would enhance the quality of A's life; 2. B is willing to do this as a favour to A, hoping at the same time to enhance the warm relation between A and B, which matters to both A and B, 3. Making the tattoo without A's consent would be paternalistic and violate A's bodily integrity, 4. Making the tattoo with A's consent will not be violating A's autonomy or bodily integrity. Yet, A does not consent, and B is made aware of this.

In this case, there is a sharp contrast between A's reasons to consent and B's reasons to make the tattoo. A's consent or lack of it will be very relevant to whether B ought or ought not to make the tattoo. A's consent is not of course relevant to whether A should consent or not – that would be unintelligible bootstrapping. Before A has given or denied their consent, the overall ought is indeterminate: on the one hand, there are reasons that speak in favor of having the tattoo (and these reasons at the same time speak in favor of giving the consent), but on the other hand, the moral permissibility of tattooing is not yet determinate. The decision *not* to

Normative Powers, Agency, and Time   65

consent thus has at least the effect that despite these reasons for making the tattoo, it is now established that it would be morally impermissible to do it. There now is a decisive reason against tattooing, and so a moral transformation has taken place. On an alternative reading, it was morally impermissible all along, and what would have made it a case of moral transformation would have been actual consent. That is the case in the next case:

> *Nice Tattoo with Consent* B approaches A and asks if A is interested in getting a wonderful tattoo. A is made aware of the following salient facts about the procedure and outcome: 1. Having the tattoo would enhance the quality of A's life; 2. B is willing to do this as a favour to A, hoping at the same time to enhance the warm relation between A and B, which matters to both A and B, 3. Making the tattoo without A's consent would be paternalistic and violate A's bodily integrity, 4. Making the tattoo with A's consent will not be violating A's autonomy or bodily integrity. A consents, and B is made aware of this.

The consent removes a weighty reason against tattooing. Without consent, B has a decisive reason against tattooing, but with consent, B does not have a decisive reason against tattooing. A normative transformation, as defined by Hurtig, takes place. In the case, *Nice Tattoo and Consent*, there is a normative change at the contributory level, and given 3–5, the change is sufficient to transform the overall balance of reasons.

The remaining type of case, *Ugly Tattoo without Consent*, is similar to Hurtig's case, but A does not give his consent. This denial of consent *adds* to the stock of reasons against tattooing. It does not make a transformation in overall recommendation but affects the strength of the case against Phi-ing. In *Ugly Tattoo without Consent*, there is an independent decisive reason against tattooing and explicit denial of consent. The normative case against tattooing is stronger than in *Ugly Tattoo with Consent*. The fact that it would be a violation of bodily integrity is a further reason against making the tattoo. This shows how the normative shape of a situation can change in different ways – transformation in the overall recommendation is not the only way (and indeed the overall balance of reasons can be transformed only if there is a change at the level of contributory reasons).

But at least if consent is ever possible in these four kinds of cases, they attest to the normative changes and transformations that consent can bring about.

3.4. Is Consent Valid in These Cases?

Hurtig's challenge puts special weight on it being irrational to give consent when the balance of reasons favors not consenting. But let's take the third case, *Nice Tattoo with Consent*. Here, A has reasons to consent and does so. There is no reason to think A is incompetent or uninformed. Nonetheless, consent is normatively transformative.

It is also clear that there are cases where A has reasons to consent but does not, and yet the withholding of consent is valid. Take a variation of the *Nice Tattoo* – case, where A is approached by several tattoo artists simultaneously but has reasons to only take one tattoo. He would have reasons to consent to C's tattooing or D's tattooing but for no further reason chooses E's tattooing – it is A's call and needs no further reasons. The case, in relation to C and D, is that of *Nice Tattoo without Consent*.

So, the commonsense view that A can validly, competently, well-informedly, and voluntarily deny consent even in cases where A has reasons to consent is vindicated. A's reasons to give or withhold consent are different from B's reasons to Phi, in that the latter are sensitive to A's actual consent, especially in cases where the decision is A's call.

Are there are other conditions for the exercise of normative powers, in addition to *Competence, Knowledge,* and *Voluntariness*?

One condition concerns the contents. As the case of slavery suggests, some contents are "committable", "eligible", and "consent-able" and some are not. The "committable", optional one can be as such worthwhile goals, but if not adopted as (possibly long-term) goals, they do not really figure as reasons at all nor provide grounds for instrumental means-ends-reasons. They need to be activated as it were, via adoption as ends. Some features, by contrast, are reasons giving even without such "adoption as a purpose", and the responsive view is right that there are such reasons (typical moral reasons for example) and, further, that there are contents which remain ones we have no reason to pursue (see Laitinen 2020b; MacCormick 1972, on "obediential" vs. "voluntary" obligations).

Or alternatively, the optional "committable" goals can provide required, compulsory, mandatory reasons once committed to. Some goals are in themselves mandatory ends, some are optional, and some are forbidden. The optional goals are ones that one is permitted to pursue. Pursuing the optional goals does not necessarily turn the optional goals into required ones. But as autonomous agents have the power to commit themselves, to promise to others or to themselves, such commitments may "upgrade" the contents from merely optional to obligatory. Commitments make a difference only concerning committable goals: some contents are already obligatory, and some remain forbidden. The optional, committable aims can take the form of a "must" or a requirement once the agent has exercised the autonomous power to commit themselves.[15]

Another variation on this idea that only some contents are "committable", "eligible" whereas others are in any case compulsory and others are forbidden, is to say that that the "committable", "eligible" goals are incommensurable or roughly on a par. This is Ruth Chang's (2020) view. There is room for a choice when none of the options is better than another.

Already the difference between consenting to a treatment by others and committing oneself autonomously to a long-term goal shows that different normative powers are indeed different, so the ways in which the "eligible" content makes a difference can be expected to be varied.

A further way in which an exercise of normative power may be invalid is that breaches the limits of the authority in question. Typically the agent who exercises normative power has a say in the matter, and so is an authority, whose decision matters relatively content independently. In Joseph Raz's (1990) example, a superior in the military has the power to command, and even if in one's judgment the command is suboptimal one ought to obey: it is nonetheless the superior's call – and the command is an authoritative reason. Similarly, democratic decision-making has authority, and even those who voted against a proposal are bound to the result, even if they explicitly thought that a better candidate proposal was on the table. Such authority has limits though, as all military ethics and theories of civil disobedience agree. The rights of everyone affected are relevant to such limits of the authority (Christiano 2008). Overstepping the bounds of one's authority is thus a further way in which the exercise of the normative power can be invalid and fails to provide genuine reasons for action.

This brief list of conditions (Competence, Knowledge, Voluntariness; Eligible contents; Bounds of Authority in the rights of affected parties) for exercises of normative powers is not exhaustive but shows that the exercise of normative powers is normatively transformative only within limits.

4. Agency

There are a number of features of agency that would be seriously truncated if we did not have normative powers (Section 4.1). If rational agents have normative powers, they are not merely responsive but also creative (Section 4.2).

4.1. Features of Agency That Entail Normative Powers

A number of features of agency presuppose or entail normative powers. Without normative powers, those features of agency would be significantly truncated.

One is *interpersonal coordination*. In a *Desert*, two people coordinate the efforts to fetch water. In the absence of authority to command, it is a clearly useful device that one of them can create an obligation for oneself and create a corresponding right for the other. It is a good idea, that agents can create reasons, obligations, and rights, that they afterward can respond to and live up to.[16] Without such a normative power, the range of reasons would lack any reasons deriving from voluntary decisions or their expressions.

There have been attempts to redescribe such reasons as deriving, for example, from the reliance in question (Scanlon 1998, cf., however, Gilbert 2004). There seems to be a great normative difference between a case where B relies on A on the basis of B's own private uncommunicated anticipations on what will happen, and a case where A informs B of A's intention to do the anticipated thing. But further, there is a normative difference between A informing B of A's intention and A giving their word *in order to* get B to rely on A. Any plausible theory of interpersonal coordination must take into account such promises, oaths, and so on, which differ from mere communication of intention. Putting them aside gives a truncated image of what agents can do.

Another is *cross-temporal coordination and the power to commit*. Mutatis mutandis, the same points can be given concerning the power of an agent to commit themselves over time. Deciding to run a marathon, to have oneself tied to a post in order to hear the sirens sing, to have a degree in Social Policy, to run for president, to build a house, *etc.*, are examples that show that it is important to have plans, long-term intentions or commitments (see, e.g., Bratman 1999; Liebermann 1998). A form of human agency without such capacities would be truncated. Exercise of such capacities affects the reasons that agents have in future situations: having decided to run a marathon gives one reason to do a certain kind of workout and to buy certain kinds of shoes, whereas a decision to start playing floorball or doing yoga gives one different reason.

Further, can *personal autonomy* be made sense of without assuming it involves exercise of normative powers? The long-term decisions are at the same time realizations of the value of personal autonomy. If such commitments involve exercise of normative powers, then realizations of personal autonomy do. The concept of personal autonomy helps us to see the value in leading a life in pursuit of such commitments. Successful pursuit of worthwhile commitments contributes not only to a good life but also to an autonomous good life. To the extent that personal autonomy is valuable, exercises of normative powers in leading one's life are valuable; and paternalistic violations of autonomy may show why some good deeds are wrong without consent. Without exercises of normative powers, one's life would not only be truncated in lacking cross-temporal and interpersonal coordination – but it would also be lacking in terms of personal autonomy.

4.2. *Responsive, Creative, or Both?*

On a view that can be called Responsiveness Only, the supposed effects of exercises of normative powers seem suspect:

> If there is no reason for A to withhold consent, it's difficult to see how A's withholding consent can *create* a decisive reason for B not to Phi.

Normative Powers, Agency, and Time 69

Such a creation of a decisive reason would involve an objectionable kind of voluntarism about the normative: it would involve bootstrapping a decisive reason into existence *ex nihilo*.

(Hurtig 2020, 110)

This objection nicely voices the responsive view of rational agency: rational agents respond to reasons; they do not create them at will. Ruth Chang provides the exact mirror image to this view; she insists that we do not exercise our normative powers *for reasons*. She calls the responsive view "passive" as in it agents do not create reasons – I prefer the title "responsiveness" as that is in no way passive:

> Crucially, our willing in the exercise of robust powers is not itself a choice governed by reasons. It is just something we do. This is perhaps the deepest difference between "passive" and "active" accounts of rational agency. On the passive view, everything we do as an intentional exercise of rational agency is guided by reasons. On the active view, some intentional exercises of rational agency are things we do as matter of will, and are not themselves guided by reasons. It is this freedom to have an active role in determining the reasons we have that is the hallmark of the rational agency that underwrites robust normative powers. Robust normative powers put the agent back in rational agency. By exercising such powers, we have a fundamental say in determining how we should live. In so far as this is an attractive view of rational agency, we have reason to take robust normative powers seriously.
>
> (Chang 2020, 298)

If the view that I have tried to defend in this chapter is right, rational agents are responsive to reasons, and that responsiveness is of course active.[17] Further, the exercises of normative powers are themselves responsive to reasons (reasons to decide this way rather than that way). Even if the reasons would be incommensurable, we are nonetheless responding to reasons. In Jonathan Dancy's (2000) example, when choosing whether to wear this shirt rather than that shirt, we are still responsive to all the reasons for wearing some shirt. But, despite being responsive, exercises of normative powers are also transformative and creative. We live in a normative reality, some aspects of which are not of human making, some result from previous exercises of normative powers, and with fresh exercise of normative powers we can add to that reality.

Notes

1. On the role of agency in theory of action, see Hornsby (2004) and Ricoeur (1992).
2. On normative powers, see Raz (1972), MacCormick (1972), Raz (1990), Owens (2012), Raz (2019 ms), Chang (2013), and Chang (2020). Hurd

(1996) rightly notes that the "moral magic" in normative powers is a matter of creating rights and obligations: "We regularly wield powers that, upon close scrutiny, appear remarkably magical. By sheer exercise of will, we bring into existence things that have never existed before. . . . What is the nature of these things that we create and destroy by our mere decision to do so? The answer: the rights and obligations of others. And by what seemingly magical means do we alter these rights and obligations? By making promises and issuing or revoking consent." Cf. also Hohfeld (1919) on powers and Thomson (1990) on rights.

3 On constructivism, see Bagnoli (2011, 2013, 2021).
4 See, e.g., Broome (2013), Dancy (2000), Parfit (1997), and Raz (1999).
5 See Raz (1999), Christiano (2008), and also Searle (2010) for whom institutional statuses can generate desire-independent reasons for action.
6 Bicchieri (2006), Copp (1995).
7 Accordingly, *moral rights* belong to normativity1, whereas *legal rights* belong to normativity2. Moral rights and directed moral obligations differ from reasons and oughts in having a dyadic (interpersonal) structure. For more on dyadic normativity, see Laitinen and Särkelä (2020).
8 Laitinen (2020a) discusses up to eight candidate usages of normativity, arguing that four of them are indeed different senses of "normativity" (normativity of reasons; of social norms; wide-scope oughts; and ought-to-be's), whereas four others are cases of the previous senses of normativity, or not normative at all (related to linguistic meaning; the "direction of fit" of desires; subjective authority of intentions and motivations; and interpersonal requests and demands).
9 See, e.g., Dancy (2000), Raz (1990), Chang (2020), and McNaughton and Rawling (2004).
10 Thus, the supervenience basis of the reasons includes the instituting of the social norms—if an exact copy of the world history is made, also the same institutional decisions are made.
11 Like any organism, the agent's body is a self-sustaining and self-regulating entity, so there is a principled answer to what aspects of the world constitute the agent: the organism that has the agential capabilities.
12 Hurtig (2020), 97.
13 Hurtig (2020) goes through similar four cases in the context of asking when is consent valid.
14 This can be further elucidated with appeal to moral *rights*, but for our purposes, we do not need a full analysis of rights.
15 See Lilian O'Brien (2019) on must thoughts.
16 For a theory like Joseph Raz's, which holds that normative powers exist if they are justified, the very existence of normative powers hangs on them "being a good idea" or as I put it, "a useful device": "a person's act is an exercise of a normative power if it brings about or prevents a normative change because it is, all things considered, desirable that that person should be able to bring the change about or prevent it by performing that act" (Raz, 2019 ms, 2).
17 See, e.g., Ricoeur (1992) and Raz (1999) on our being active and passive. Raz argues that we are also active when responsive.

References

Ásta (2018) *Categories We Live By*. Oxford: Oxford University Press.
Bagnoli, Carla (2011) "Constructivism in Metaethics". In *The Stanford Encyclopedia of Philosophy* (Winter 2011 Edition), ed. E. N. Zalta, http://plato.stanford.edu/archives/win2011/entries/constructivism-metaethics/;

Bagnoli, Carla (ed.) (2013) *Constructivism in Ethics*. Cambridge: Cambridge University Press.
Bagnoli, Carla (2021) *Ethical Constructivism*. Cambridge: Cambridge University Press.
Bicchieri, Carla (2006) *The Grammar of Society: The Nature and Dynamics of Social Norms*. Cambridge: Cambridge University Press.
Bratman, Michael E. (1999) *Faces of Intention: Selected Essays on Intention and Agency*. Cambridge: Cambridge University Press.
Bratman, Michael E. (2007) *Structures of Agency: Essays*. Oxford: Oxford University Press.
Broome, John (2013) *Rationality through Reasoning*. Oxford: Wiley Blackwell.
Chang, Ruth (2013) "Commitments, Reasons, and the Will". In Russ Shafer-Landau (ed.), *Oxford Studies in Metaethics*. Oxford: Oxford University Press, Vol. 8, pp. 74–113.
Chang, Ruth (2020) "Do We Have Normative Powers?". *Aristotelian Society Supplementary Volume*, 94(1), pp. 275–300. https://doi.org/10.1093/arisup/akaa012
Christiano, Thomas (2008) *The Constitution of Equality: Democratic Authority and its Limits*. Oxford: Oxford University Press.
Copp, David (1995) *Morality, Normativity, and Society*. Oxford: Oxford University Press.
Dancy, Jonathan (2000) *Practical Reality*. Oxford: Oxford University Press.
Dancy, Jonathan (2004) *Ethics without Principles*. Oxford: Oxford University Press.
Gilbert, Margaret (2004) "Scanlon on Promissory Obligation: The Problem of Promisees' Rights". *Journal of Philosophy*, 101(2), pp. 83–109.
Hohfeld, W. N. (1919) *Fundamental Legal Conceptions*. New Haven: Yale University Press.
Hornsby, Jennifer (2004) "Agency and Actions". In H. Steward & J. Hyman (eds.), *Agency and Action*. Cambridge: Cambridge University Press, 1–23.
Hurd, Heidi (1996) "The Moral Magic of Consent". *Legal Theory*, 2(2), pp. 121–146.
Kent, Hurtig (2020) "Consent and Normativity". In M. Garcia-Godinez, R. Mellin & R. Tuomela (eds.), *Social Ontology, Normativity and Law*. Berlin: De Gruyter, 97–114.
Laitinen, Arto (2020a) "Varieties of Normativity: Reasons, Expectations, Wide-Scope Oughts, and Ought-to-be's". In Miguel Garcia-Godinez, Rachael Mellin & Raimo Tuomela (eds.), *Social Ontology, Normativity and Law*. Berlin: De Gruyter, 133–157.
Laitinen, Arto (2020b) "Finding by Making: The Mediating Role of Social Constructions, Commitments, and Resonance in Hegelian Normative Realism". In James Gledhill & Sebastian Stein (eds.), *Hegel and Contemporary Practical Philosophy: Beyond Kantian Constructivism*. New York: Routledge, ch. 8.
Laitinen, Arto & Särkelä, Arvi (2020) "Social Wrongs". *Critical Review of International Social and Political Philosophy*. https://doi.org/10.1080/13698230.2020.1853435
Liebermann, Marcel (1998) *Commitment, Value and Moral Realism*. Cambridge: Cambridge University Press.
MacCormick, Neil (1972) "Voluntary Obligations and Normative Powers I". *Proceedings of the Aristotelian Society Supplementary Volume*, 46, pp. 59–78.
McNaughton, David & Rawling, Piers (2004) "Duty, Rationality, and Practical Reasons." In Alfred R. Mele & Piers Rawling (eds.), *Oxford Handbook of Rationality*. Oxford: Oxford University Press.

O'Brien, Lilian (2019) "The Subjective Authority of Intention". *Philosophical Quarterly*, 69(275), pp. 354–373.
Owens, David (2012) *Shaping the Normative Landscape*. Oxford: Oxford University Press.
Parfit, Derek (1997) "Reasons and Motivation". *The Aristotelian Society Supplementary Volume*, 77, pp. 99–130.
Raz, Joseph (1972) "Voluntary Obligations and Normative Powers II". *Proceedings of the Aristotelian Society Supplementary Volume*, 46, pp. 79–102.
Raz, Joseph (1990) *Practical Reason and Norms*. Princeton: Princeton University Press.
Raz, Joseph (1999) "When Are We Active?" In *Engaging Reason*. Oxford: Oxford University Press.
Raz, Joseph (2019 ms) "Normative Powers (revised) (July 1 2019)". Oxford Legal Studies Research Paper No. 36/2019; Columbia Public Law Research Paper No. 14–629; King's College London Law School Research Paper 26–2019. Available at SSRN: https://ssrn.com/abstract"3379368 or http://doi.org/10.2139/ssrn.3379368.
Ricoeur, Paul (1992) *Oneself as Another*. Chicago: The University of Chicago Press.
Scanlon, Thomas (1998) *What We Owe to Each Other*. Cambridge, MA: Belknap Press.
Searle, John (2010) *Making the Social World*. Oxford: Oxford University Press.
Shafer-Landau, Russ (2003) *Moral Realism: A Defence*. Oxford: Oxford University Press.
Thomson, Judith Jarvis (1990) *The Realm of Rights*. Cambridge, MA: Harvard University Press.
Tuomela, Raimo (2013) *Social Ontology*. Oxford: Oxford University Press.

Part II
Diachronic Self-Governance

4 A Planning Agent's Self-Governance Over Time

Michael E. Bratman

What is it to govern your thought and action not only at a time but also over time? Let's focus the question a bit. We are planning agents. Almost all of our intentional activity is embedded in planned temporally extended activity that is structured by prior partial plans. These plans settle practical issues, pose problems of means and the like, filter solutions to those problems, and guide action. These structures of planning support important forms of cross-temporal and social organization in ways that are compatible with our cognitive and epistemic limits. Given their basic role in cross-temporal organization, we can expect these planning structures to play a central role in diachronic self-governance. So let's ask, more specifically, what is it for a planning agent to govern her thought and action over time?[1]

In the background are two ideas. The first is that self-governance over time involves, in part, responding to certain common threats to important forms of cross-temporal organization and stability. Our account of a planning agent's diachronic self-governance needs to say more about those threats and the response characteristic of diachronic self-governance. Second, we do not want to see such self-governance as, at bottom, the workings of a self who is separate from the psychic economy and stands back and pulls the strings. We want a model of a kind of cross-temporal psychic functioning that ensures a planning agent's relevant self-governance over time. So let's see.

1. Self-Governance at a Time and over Time

An initial idea is that for a planning agent to govern her action over time she needs at the least to be synchronically self-governing at relevant times (or small temporal intervals) along the way. But what is such synchronic self-governance? Here we can draw from Harry Frankfurt's appeal to "where (if anywhere) the person himself stands."[2] Self-governance involves guidance of thought and action by the agent's relevant practical standpoint. The standpoint needs to guide choice that is in accord with that standpoint; and the standpoint itself needs to be sufficiently coherent

DOI: 10.4324/9780429259845-7

to constitute a clear place where the agent stands on relevant practical issues. In this way we understand synchronic self-governance without an irreducible appeal to a little person in the head who is pulling the strings.

A planning agent's self-governance over time involves, then, such synchronic self-governance at relevant times or during small temporal intervals along the way.[3] On this model, not all cases of successful self-management over time will constitute such diachronic self-governance. Ulysses has a strategy of self-management over time by tying himself to the mast, thereby blocking his self-governance when the sirens call; but his successful diachronic self-management is not diachronic self-governance.[4]

There is a partial parallel here with rational planning agency quite generally. In rationally planning my actions over a stretch of time, I at least implicitly suppose that, given my plan, when the times of action arrive it will be rationally permissible for me to carry out my plan then. Rational planning for a temporally extended stretch of activity needs to accommodate the supposed rational execution of the plan at times along the way. This is a norm of rational planning. In the case of diachronic self-governance what we have is not a rationality norm but a metaphysical constraint: an individual's self-governance over time needs to accommodate her self-governance at each relevant time (or relevant temporal interval) along the way. In each case we have a principle of over-time/at-a-time coordination.

I think we should retain such over-time/at-a-time coordination of diachronic and synchronic self-governance.[5] But I also take it that diachronic self-governance is not merely a concatenation of self-governance of the same person at various times along the way.[6] It involves, as well, appropriate *interconnections* across time. What interconnections?

2. Interconnections: The Plan-Theoretic Model

As I see it, the basic context in which the issue of a planning agent's diachronic self-governance arises is one in which the agent is engaged in plan-shaped temporally extended activity.[7] This suggests that a planning agent's diachronic self-governance involves synchronically self-governed choices at the relevant times along the way of a relevant planned temporally extended activity, where these choices over time are tied together by the interconnections characteristic of planned temporally extended activity.

What interconnections are these? Well, the plans that guide such temporally extended activity will settle relevant practical questions and will normally at least implicitly cross-refer to each other: one's plan for today will typically involve a reference to one's earlier and later plans; and vice versa. These issue-settling, cross-referring plans will frame much of one's practical thought and action over time: they will pose problems of means and preliminary steps in filling in one's so-far partial plans as time goes by and in ways that, taken together, mesh; and they will filter options that are potential solutions to those problems. In playing these roles these plans will induce forms of psychological connectedness and continuity of intention and plan that are in the spirit of broadly Lockean models of personal identity over time.[8]

Given these roles of plans in structuring the agent's temporally extended practical thought and action, we can expect that her standpoints at times along the way will be plan-infused.[9] These standpoints will involve both plans for temporally extended activities and relevant general policies, including policies about weights for deliberation.[10] In planned temporally extended activity these plan-infused standpoints will be interconnected in the cited ways. And this leads to the proposal that the cross-temporal interconnections that are characteristic of a planning agent's self-governance over time, given self-governance at times along the way, involve the interconnections that are characteristic of relevant planned temporally extended activity. This is the *plan-theoretic model* of these interconnections.

A complexity is that, given the hierarchical structure of plans, these cross-temporal interconnections can be at different levels. In particular, there can be such interconnections at the level of an overarching plan despite a breakdown in interconnection at a more specific level of sub-plans. Perhaps I continue with my overall plan to earn a law degree but change my sub-plan from one focusing on criminal law to one focusing on tort law. There are relevant cross-temporal continuities of intention at the level of the overall plan; but there is a breakdown in continuity in my sub-plans concerning area of concentration. Such upper-level continuities would help support my diachronic self-governance. And it may well be that I now sensibly believe, perhaps in light of new information, that I have conclusive reason to make the change in my lower-level plans. So sticking with my prior plan in favor of criminal law would be stubbornness, not synchronic self-governance. However, if, in contrast, there were available a way of continuing with my lower-level plans so that there would be self-governance at times along the way and relevant cross-temporal interconnections at *both* lower and higher levels of the hierarchy, then the plan-theoretic model will say that a breakdown in plan continuity at the lower level would to some extent diminish the extent of diachronic self-governance.

This plan-theoretic model has an important implication. Consider Sartre's young man. He must choose between staying with his mother and fighting with the Free French.[11] Suppose at t_1 he chooses to stay with his mother. At t_2, however, he reconsiders and changes his mind and decides to fight with the Free French. Both at t_1 and at t_2 he sees the conflict as a conflict of non-comparable values. So it seems that at each time in acting on his choice he is synchronically self-governing, since his choice and action at each time cohere with and are guided by a basic value of his, one that he supposes is not outweighed or overridden in the circumstance. However, in shuffling from his decision at t_1 to his decision at t_2[12] he is breaking the cross-temporal interconnections characteristic of planned temporally extended activity. If, in contrast, he had stuck with his initial decision to stay with his mother, his intentions over time would have been connected in these ways. In shuffling from one decision to another, though he is self-governing at each time, he does not satisfy the plan-theoretic model of the interconnections involved in self-governance over time. In contrast, he would satisfy that model were he to stick with his prior decision.

Granted (and to return to the complexity noted earlier), even if he shuffles in this way he might satisfy the plan-theoretic model, of the interconnections involved in self-governance over time, at the level of some persisting, higher-level plan—for example, a plan to give due regard to duties of loyalty. Nevertheless, there was available to him a way of resisting shuffling and continuing with his lower-level plans so that there would be self-governance at times along the way *and* relevant interconnections at both lower and higher levels of the hierarchy of his plans. So, on the model, his shuffling diminishes the extent to which he is diachronically self-governing.

But why accept this plan-theoretic model of relevant interconnections?

3. The Argument from Settling Function

I begin by considering an argument that is in the spirit of an earlier essay.[13] This argument is not, however, conclusive. So I will turn to a second argument.

This first argument draws from the settling function of intentions and plans, and can be articulated by way of a pair of premises. The first premise concerns a functional role that is characteristic of intention:

(i) The functional roles of prior intentions and plans include settling relevant practical matters in a way that supports the cross-temporal intention-interconnections that are characteristic of planned temporally extended activity.

The second premise draws on an insight from Sydney Shoemaker. Shoemaker noted that the psychological continuity that plays a basic role in Lockean theories of personal identity over time "is just the playing out over time of the functional natures of the mental states characteristic of persons."[14] And an analogous idea seems apt here:

(ii) The cross-temporal interconnections that are characteristic of a planning agent's self-governance over time involve the "playing out over time of the functional natures of the" relevant plan states.

When we put (i) and (ii) together we get

(iii) The cross-temporal interconnections that are characteristic of a planning agent's self-governance over time involve those interconnections that are characteristic of planned temporally extended activity.

And that is the plan-theoretic model of the relevant interconnections.

On reflection, however, one might challenge premise (i).[15] Why not instead say only that the relevant functional role of plan states is to support the cross-temporal intention-interconnections that are characteristic of planned temporally extended activity so long as the agent continues to judge that considerations on balance strongly favor the plan? And Sartre's young man does not judge that considerations on balance strongly favor his plan to stay with his mother, though he does judge that these considerations weakly favor that plan.

So if we are going to defend the plan-theoretic model we need to see if there is a further argument in its defense. And I think that there is. The argument I think I see[16] appeals to a version of a parallel that has struck many philosophers—a parallel between the cross-temporal organization of an individual's activity and interpersonal, social organization.

4. Acting "Together" with Oneself at Different Times: the Shared Agency Model of Diachronic Self-Governance

The idea is that in diachronic self-governance one and the same person's agency at different times is drawn together in ways that to some extent parallel the ways in which different agents are interconnected when they act together. I do not say that in diachronic self-governance there are, literally, multiple agents acting together. I retain the commonsense thought that there is one agent who acts at different times; and this contrasts with interpersonal shared agency involving multiple agents. Nevertheless, there is a revealing, if partial, parallel between an individual's diachronic self-governance and interpersonal shared agency. And this parallel helps explain the significance to us of such diachronic self-governance. In diachronic self-governance I am not just governing my relevant actions at each relevant time along the way. In addition, my thought and action at the times along the way are, at least implicitly, interwoven and interconnected in ways that support the helpful metaphor that "we"—that is, me at these different times—are thinking and acting "together".

Now, others have explored the idea of a bargain between the agent at t_1 and the agent at t_2.[17] Edward McClennen, for example, seeks "a theory of what constitutes a fair bargain between one's different, time-defined selves."[18] The agent at t_1 strikes a bargain with his later t_2-self, a bargain that enjoins his t_2-self to stick with the agent's decision at t_1. The idea of a bargain, however, seems to involve a kind of reciprocal interrelation that is not possible here. After all, the person-stage at t_1 will not be around when the person-stage at t_2 acts, and will not be in a position to respond to whether that later person-stage keeps up her end of the bargain.[19]

My proposal that a planning agent's diachronic self-governance involves an intrapersonal analogue of shared agency is not the proposal of a bargain between the person at t_1 and the person at t_2. Instead, the proposal is that certain structural features of socially shared agency have intrapersonal, cross-temporal analogues,[20] and that this helps support the idea that these intrapersonal analogues are an aspect of a planning agent's diachronic self-governance.

How then should we understand relevant forms of shared agency? In other work[21] I argue that a basic idea here is that of a shared intention: a shared intention of the participants to J is central to a shared intentional activity of J-ing together. And I argue that this shared intention is, in basic cases, constituted by a web of interconnected intentions of each of the participants in favor of their J-ing, together with associated cognitive attitudes of those participants. This web of attitudes of the participants is constituted as follows:

(A) The participants each have intentions in favor of J, intentions that interlock in the sense that each intends that they J in part by way of the intentions of each that they J.[22]
(B) Each intends that they J in part by way of mutual responsiveness of each to each in the execution of these intentions of each, and so by way of relevant sub-plans of each that mesh with each other.
(C) Each believes correctly that there is persistence interdependence between the intentions of each that they J.
(D) Each believes that if these intentions do persist, they will indeed J.[23]
(E) All this is out in the open among the participants.

When such a structure of interconnected attitudes leads to the joint J-ing by way of the intended mutual responsiveness and mesh, there is shared intentional action.

And now my proposal is that the cross-temporal, intrapersonal "glue" characteristic of a planning agent's diachronic self-governance involves intrapersonal analogues of the interpersonal connections characteristic of shared intention and shared intentional agency. These intrapersonal analogues of conditions of shared intention and shared intentional agency support the metaphor that in diachronic self-governance the synchronically self-governing agent at each time is acting "together" with the synchronically self-governing agent—namely, herself—at other times, in a sense of "together" that comes from our theory of shared agency.[24] And an idea in the background of this *shared agency model* of the cross-temporal interconnections involved in a planning agent's diachronic self-governance is that it helps explain the significance to us of such diachronic self-governance.[25]

In thinking about a planning agent's self-governance over time it is tempting to appeal to a kind of cross-temporal narrative unity: there is a "story" that ties together the different elements over time. Depending on what counts as such narrative unity, this idea may apply to many cases. But according to the shared agency model, the more basic cross-temporal unity at work in diachronic self-governance is the unity involved when the agent is acting "together" with herself over time, in a sense of "together" that comes from the theory of shared agency.

5. Planned Temporally Extended Agency and Shared Agency

The next step is to argue that planned temporally extended agency does indeed involve intrapersonal, cross-temporal analogues of conditions of socially shared intention. In this way the shared agency model helps support the plan-theoretic model of the cross-temporal connections that are characteristic of a planning agent's diachronic self-governance.

There will, of course, be important differences between my planned temporally extended agency and our acting together. In particular, our acting together will normally involve two-way causal interactions: what I think and do affects what you think and do, which affects what I think and do. In contrast, there will be a causal asymmetry in the case of my planning agency over time: what I think and do now can causally influence what I think and do later, in a way in which what I think and do later cannot causally influence what I think and do now. (Though my present anticipation of what I will think and do later can of course affect what I think and do now.) So the analogies between planned temporally extended agency and shared intentional agency will at most only be partial. But we can still ask whether these partial analogues, if such there are, shed light on diachronic self-governance.

So let's consider conditions (A)—(E) of shared intention and see what their analogues would be in a case of an individual's planned temporally extended activity. To do this, let's work with an example. Suppose that, given expected time pressures at this evening's interview, I decide at t_1 on strategy A for responding to certain anticipated questions at t_2. At t_1 I form an intention to engage in A at t_2. I also fill in this plan a bit: I develop at t_1 a partial sub-plan for A-ing at t_2. Later, t_2 arrives, conditions are as I had at t_1 anticipated, and I proceed to fill in my sub-plans further and follow through with A then, at t_2. Let's see if there are, in this temporally extended activity, analogues of conditions (A)—(E) of shared intention.

To keep track, let's use *italics* to indicate a relevant analogue condition. Begin with (A), the interlocking condition. And consider the relation between my intention at t_1 to A at t_2 and my intention at t_2 to A at t_2. An initial point is that in so intending at t_1 I do not think my intention will simply reach its ghostly hand over time and shape my action at t_2.[26] Instead, I will normally suppose that my intention at t_1 will persist between t_1 and t_2, shape associated thought and action along the way, and thereby issue at t_2 in my updated intention to A then.[27] It is this updated intention to A that I expect will issue in my A-ing: I certainly do not expect some unrelated intention at t_2 to do this work. And this is, at least implicitly, how I intend this process to work its way through. So, at least implicitly, my intention at t_1 to A at t_2 *interlocks* with my intention at t_2 to A then: at t_1 I intend, at least implicitly, that I A at t_2 by way of my intention at t_2 to A at t_2; and at t_2, at least implicitly, I intend to A then as a way of following through with my intention at t_1 to A at t_2.[28] So we have this intrapersonal analogue of condition (A) of shared intention.

Consider now the first part of condition (B), the intended mutual responsiveness condition. In the intrapersonal case, at t_1 I intend, at least implicitly, that my intention at t_2 to A at t_2 work its way through to action in ways compatible with my present intentions (at t_1) concerning how to A at t_2. Further, at t_2 I intend, at least implicitly, to A in a way that fits with my intentions at t1 concerning how to A. So there is a kind of *intended mutual responsiveness* (though not mutual causal interaction) between my intentions at t_1 and at t_2. So, there is this intrapersonal analogue of the first part of condition (B) of shared intention.

Consider now the second part of (B), the intended mesh condition. In the intrapersonal case, at t_1 I intend, at least implicitly, that the sub-plans I have so far constructed for A-ing at t_2 mesh with the sub-plans I will construct and act on at t_2, and at t_1 I intend, at least implicitly, that I A at t_2 by way of those meshing sub-plans at t_2. Further, at t_2 I intend, at least implicitly, to A by way of sub-plans at t2 that mesh with the partial sub-plans I had formulated at t_1. So at t_1 and at t_2 I intend, at least implicitly, that my A-ing at t_2 go by way of sub-plans at t_2 that *mesh* with my sub-plans at t_1. So, there is this intrapersonal analogue of the second part of condition (B) of shared intention.

Consider now condition (C), the condition of correct belief in interdependence. In the intrapersonal case, my intention at t_1 to A at t_2 depends on my expectation that, if conditions at t_2 are as I at t_1 expect them to be, I will continue so to intend at t_2. Further, at least in some cases, at t_2 I know that if I had not intended at t1 to A at t_2 then I would not at t_2 be intending to A then.[29] So my intention at t1 is dependent on my expectation of my later intention. And my later intention may be accompanied by the knowledge that it depends on my earlier intention. So, there is at least a partial analogue of condition (C).

Consider now condition (D), an expectation of success condition. In the intrapersonal case, at t_1 I believe that, given that my intention does persist, I will A at t_2. And at t_2 I believe that, given that my intention to A has persisted, I will indeed A at t_2.[30] So there is, throughout t_1-t_2, conditional *expectation of success* in A-ing.

Finally, all of these analogues in the intrapersonal case will normally be *out in the open* for me throughout t_1-t_2. At each stage along the way I will be in a position to know that I have so far satisfied the cited conditions and justifiably to expect that I will continue to do so. So there is an analogue of condition (E) of shared intention.

So in my planned temporally extended activity there are intrapersonal analogues of interlocking intentions, intended mutual responsiveness and mesh in sub-plans, and expectations of success. There is at least a partial analogy with the condition of true beliefs about interdependence. And throughout there can be cognitive accessibility to all these elements, and so an analogue to the out-in-the-open condition. Appeal to these shared-agency-analogue conditions supports the metaphor that *I at t_1* and *I at t_2* are acting and thinking *together* in an intrapersonal *analogue* of shared intentional activity.

Indeed, there are kinds of shared intentional activity that are even closer to such cases of planned individual activity over time. For example, in the multigenerational shared activity of the building of a cathedral, the interrelations among the agents of different generations will involve causal asymmetries similar to those in the intrapersonal temporally extended case.[31] So in this respect there will be an even closer analogy between such social cases and the cited kind of temporally extended individual planned activity.

Of course, the cited cross-temporal structure in the case of my temporally extended planned activity may not be present in cases in which the world develops between t_1 and t_2 in ways that are counter to my relevant expectations at t_1 about conditions at t_2. But what matters for present purposes are cases in which these expectations are realized and one does indeed act over time in ways that involve carrying out one's prior plan. And in such cases, planned individual activity over time involves cross-temporal intrapersonal connections that are substantially analogous to the interpersonal connections characteristic of shared intention.

Recall now that according to the shared agency model, the cross-temporal connections that are characteristic of a planning agent's diachronic self-governance involve intrapersonal analogues of conditions of socially shared intention. What we have just seen is that such intrapersonal analogues are provided by the intention interconnections characteristic of planned temporally extended agency. Further, and as noted earlier, the issue of a planning agent's diachronic self-governance normally arises within the background of planned temporally extended agency. Taken together, these points support the conjecture that the interconnections characteristic of planned temporally extended agency are central to a planning agent's diachronic self-governance. And that is the plan-theoretic model of these cross-temporal interconnections. A striking fact at the

84   *Michael E. Bratman*

bottom of the plan-theoretic model of the cross-temporal, intrapersonal glue characteristic of diachronic self-governance is that the cross-temporal structure of planned temporally extended activity involves an intrapersonal analogue of acting together. We have sought a deeper rationale for that plan-theoretic model, and now we have it, one that draws on the shared agency model.

6. Willpower and an End of One's Diachronic Self-Governance

Let me turn now to a further question about a planning agent's self-governance over time. Suppose that you know you will be tempted to drink heavily tonight at the party.[32] You now think that, in light of what matters to you, this is a bad idea. However, you know that at the party your evaluation will shift in favor of drinking more. You also know that if you did drink heavily your evaluation would later shift back and you would regret that. So this morning you resolve to drink only one glass tonight. The problem is that, as you know, if you were to stick with your resolve at the party, you would act against what would then be your present evaluation. And we normally suppose that action contrary to one's present evaluation is a breakdown in self-governance.

What if you abandon your prior resolve and drink heavily at the party, given your present evaluation in favor of that? Well, in that case your intentions and plans over time will not conform to the plan-theoretic model of the connections involved in diachronic self-governance. And that will tend to block your diachronic self-governance.

So in neither case will you be, in a clear way, diachronically self-governing. But it also seems an important commonsense idea that willpower can be a central case of diachronic self-governance. What to say?

We sometimes avoid such problems by, prior to the party, changing the world outside our minds in a way that induces new reasons to stick with our prior resolve. One might, say, make a side bet. This is the snowball effect.[33] Again, we sometimes manage to resist reconsideration of our prior resolve, and this can many times be a good strategy, especially given the normal costs and risks of such reconsideration.[34] Both snowball effects and sensible resistance to reconsideration provide important support to the stability of our temporally extended agency. But cases of temptation and potential willpower seem sometimes to involve something further.[35] After all, it seems that there will be many cases of temptation in which we do in fact reconsider our prior resolution and we are not protected by some prior side bet or other snowball effect.[36]

A thought here is that we have available a form of theoretical reasoning that can support sticking with our prior resolve. After all, in such a case you will at the time of temptation know that your then-present evaluation diverges from your earlier and expected-later evaluation. This might lead you to adjust your then-present evaluation to be more in line with your different evaluations at these different times. This might be an aspect of a form of theoretical reasoning that aims at smoothing out differences in judgment across time.[37] Could we appeal to such theoretical reasoning to explain how willpower can comport with self-governance?

Well, at the time of temptation you will think that your earlier and later evaluations are mistaken, and so wonder why you should change your present evaluation in order to smooth out these cross-temporal differences in evaluation. And it is not clear why you should have any intrinsic concern with such diachronic theoretical constancy—why such a concern would not simply be an undefended concern with cross-temporal theoretical tidiness.[38] But in any case, what is central for present purposes is that such theoretical thinking is not directly concerned with or responsive to the presence of the prior resolution. Yet what we are trying to explore is the potential role of that prior resolution in diachronic self-governance. A related point is that we seek an account of willpower that also applies to resistance to shuffling in cases like that of Sartre's young man. But in such cases of persisting non-comparability there is already constancy of evaluation over time: the problem is that this constant evaluation underdetermines what to do. So appeal to cross-temporal theoretical smoothing will not explain what blocks shuffling.

Perhaps we should instead challenge the assumption that in the conflict, at the time of temptation, between prior resolution and present evaluation it is the present evaluation that speaks for the agent and shapes her then-present standpoint. Perhaps we should instead say that in some cases it is the prior resolution that speaks for the agent. That is why acting in accord with that prior resolution at the time of temptation can cohere with synchronic self-governance.[39] Further, given that the evaluation at the time of action is made in light of what matters to the agent, and given that what matters to the agent is shaped by her standpoint, this impact of the prior resolution on the agent's standpoint can then ground a re-shift in the evaluation so that it favors sticking with one drink.[40]

But given just these two elements—prior resolution and present evaluation—and given the normal status of the agent's evaluation, it is going to be difficult to explain why the prior resolution trumps the evaluation in shaping where the agent stands.[41] A more straightforward strategy would be instead to appeal explicitly to a third element, one that can explain this significance of the prior resolution to present standpoint. And a natural idea here would be to appeal to an end in the agent's standpoint that favors follow-through with the prior resolution and thereby potentially supports both a shift in standpoint and a re-shift in evaluation, both in the direction of willpower. In playing this dual practical role such an end could help explain how willpower can cohere with both synchronic and diachronic self-governance.

What is it to have an end? Well, to have X as an end is, roughly, to have a noninstrumental concern in favor of X. This is not the same as having an intention in favor of X. First, not all intentions are ends in this sense, since some intentions are solely instrumental. And, second, even for a planning agent not all ends are intentions, since—in contrast with intentions—it is common to have ends one knows are not co-realizable.

The proposal, then, is that a relevant end, in this sense of end, can, together with the cited prior resolution, play a dual role of supporting both a re-shift in evaluation and a re-shift in standpoint. But, how precisely should we conceptualize this proposed dual role of such an end? Should we say that this end, together with the prior resolution, directly supports a re-shift of evaluation in favor of willpower, and that given this re-shifted evaluation there is a corresponding shift in what the agent's standpoint supports? Or should we say that this end, together with the prior resolution, directly supports a shift in standpoint, and that given this shift in standpoint there can be a corresponding shift in evaluation (since this evaluation is made in light of what matters to the agent, and what matters to the agent is shaped by her standpoint)?

It seems to me that the second proposal—one that prioritizes the impact of the end on the agent's standpoint—fits best with our underlying model of self-governance. The idea is that what is fundamental is what is favored by the agent's standpoint. This shapes what matters to the agent. And the relevant evaluations are evaluations in light of what matters to the agent. What was wrong with the earlier, simple proposal that it is the prior resolution, rather than the present evaluation, which dominantly speaks for the agent was not that it focused primarily on the impact of these different elements on the agent's standpoint. The problem, rather, was that, in the absence of the sort of third element to which we are now appealing, it seemed difficult to defend this priority of the prior resolution in shaping the agent's standpoint. Once we introduce this third element, however, we potentially have a straightforward explanation of the impact of the resolution on the agent's standpoint. And we thereby potentially have a straightforward explanation of its impact on the agent's relevant evaluation.

But what end is this? One idea, due to Jordan Howard Sobel, would simply be that the agent as a matter of fact "puts a premium on steadfastness".[42] In a related proposal, Wlodek Rabinowicz highlights the idea that one's preferences may well be "influenced by [one's] previously chosen plan of action".[43] In each case the idea would be that the agent has an end of "steadfastness", or of fitting with a "previously chosen plan", and this end, together with the prior resolve, explains how her standpoint at the time of temptation gives independent significance to relevant cross-temporal interconnections in a way that potentially shifts her standpoint to favor willpower and thereby supports a corresponding re-shifting of evaluation in favor of willpower. So an end along the lines of Sobel's and

Rabinowicz's discussions would potentially play the cited dual role of shaping standpoint and thereby shaping evaluation.

But here the worry is that in appealing to such an end we are appealing simply to a concern in favor of mere cross-temporal psychic tidiness. And we do not want a central element in diachronic self-governance to involve such a brute concern with tidiness.[44]

What we need, then, is an end that, in tandem with the prior resolve, can play these two coordinated roles by favoring something that involves but goes beyond cross-temporal coherence. Here we might consider a proposal by Thomas Kelly, in the context of a discussion of sunk costs, that it can be sensible to have an end of redeeming one's own earlier actions, of preventing them from having been in vain.[45] And this end is not simply a concern with cross-temporal mental tidiness. But even if we agree with Kelly that such a backward-looking end can sometimes be sensible, its application will not be sufficiently general to solve our problem about willpower. Perhaps one's earlier resolve not to drink heavily at the party has already issued in actions that have themselves had significant costs, and so an end of preventing those costly actions from being in vain might support follow-through at the time of the party. But this is a special case. One may simply have decided in the morning not to drink heavily in the evening, and now the time—and the temptation—has arrived. There has been no significant prior, costly action that might be the target of redemption.

What we need is a more generally applicable end, but one that is not simply a concern with cross-temporal mental tidiness. And a natural proposal, based on a kind of inference to the best explanation, would appeal to a (perhaps implicit) end of one's diachronic self-governance itself—where that diachronic self-governance is understood along the lines we are currently developing.[46] This is not merely an end of diachronic coherence, though diachronic self-governance involves cross-temporal coherence. This end of one's diachronic self-governance would sometimes support willpower in the face of temptation, since such willpower would involve the cross-temporal continuity and interconnection of plan structures that is, I have argued, an element in diachronic self-governance. In this way this end of one's diachronic self-governance would be poised to help stabilize the agent's temporally extended, planned activities in the face of anticipated temptation.

Further, such cases of temptation—where these sometimes take the form of temptations to procrastinate—pervade our lives.[47] If the end of diachronic self-governance is part of the structure of a planning agent's response, in diachronic self-governance, to such pervasive sources of instability, we can plausibly see that end as a central element in a planning agent's self-governance, one that stands guard against such instability. A planning agent's self-governance over time involves coordination of two kinds of coherence within planned temporally extended activity: the synchronic coherence involved in self-governance at relevant times along the way, and the coherence involved in relevant cross-temporal continuities and interconnections of intentions over time. The proposal is that this coordination of these two forms of coherence is normally supported by standpoints that include the end of diachronic self-governance, and that the presence of this end stands guard to support this coordination in the face of pervasive potential threats to the needed stability over time.

So by modeling a planning agent's diachronic self-governance as involving this end of her diachronic self-governance we provide for the possibility of diachronically self-governing willpower. We help explain the potential robustness of diachronic self-governance in the face of certain characteristic threats of instability. And we do this by appeal to an end that—in contrast with mere mental tidiness—is, plausibly, worth wanting.

Is there an analogous argument that synchronic self-governance involves an end of synchronic self-governance? Well, what is needed for synchronic self-governance is guidance by the substantive concerns that constitute the agent's then-present standpoint. And it is not clear why these substantive concerns must include a concern specifically with self-governance. In contrast, when we turn to diachronic self-governance we face a distinctive, time-induced issue of coordination between present standpoint and cross-temporal continuity. The end of one's diachronic self-governance is a response to that issue. If this is right, there is an asymmetry here. However, insofar as synchronic self-governance is an element in diachronic self-governance, there will be an indirect argument for the need for an end of synchronic self-governance.

The next step is to see more precisely how the presence of this end of diachronic self-governance would help make possible a form of willpower that coheres with both synchronic and diachronic self-governance.

7. Diachronicalized Standpoints

The first step is to note that the relevant end will not simply be an end of maximizing the amount of one's diachronic self-governance—an end that would argue against taking a nap. It will, rather, be an end in favor of one's diachronic self-governance given that certain preconditions are met. In particular, this end will come to bear at a given time if the agent is engaged in a relevant planned temporally extended activity and her standpoint at that time—a standpoint that includes this very end—would support a choice that also satisfies the intention-interconnection conditions of diachronic self-governance. Since this conditional end concerns the role of a standpoint that itself includes this end, this is a reflexive (and conditional) end in favor of diachronic self-governance.

We can now distinguish two cases. In a simple case the support of the standpoint at that time for a choice that coheres with one's diachronic self-governance does not depend on the presence in that standpoint of the end of that diachronic self-governance. This may happen in a case of potential shuffling given ongoing non-comparability in which, even in the absence of the end of diachronic self-governance, the standpoint supports—albeit, weakly—refraining from such shuffling. In a second, more complex case, the support of the standpoint for a choice that coheres with one's diachronic self-governance depends on the way this end in favor of that diachronic self-governance—an end that is itself in that standpoint—favors that choice in part because that choice would satisfy the diachronic interconnection conditions on diachronic self-governance. As we have begun to see, this may happen in a case of potential willpower in the face of temptation. In either case, and this is the central idea, the agent's standpoint at that time—one that includes this conditional, reflexive end in favor of one's diachronic self-governance—would support the joint satisfaction of the conditions of both synchronic and diachronic self-governance.

Let's see in more detail how this works in a temptation case. In such a case the agent's conditional and reflexive end of her diachronic self-governance would support willpower if that end were brought to bear on that willpower; and, given her planned, ongoing temporally extended activity, it will be brought to bear if her standpoint at the time of temptation, *supplemented by the support this end would provide*, would support that willpower. If the agent's conditional and reflexive end of diachronic self-governance is sufficiently important to her to make it true that her standpoint at the time of temptation, supplemented by the support this end would provide, would support that willpower, then the agent satisfies the relevant preconditions, and her conditional end in favor of her diachronic self-governance does indeed support sticking with her prior resolve.

A complication is that this end in favor of her diachronic self-governance may not always be sufficiently important to the agent to re-shift her standpoint in this way in a temptation case. After all, that standpoint involves a complex web of elements, only one of which is this end. Other ends can in a given case trump the potential impact of this conditional end in favor of diachronic self-governance.[48] When other ends do trump, they block relevant diachronic self-governance (though they need not block synchronic self-governance), and so they block the satisfaction of the relevant precondition. This is what happens when the agent decisively rejects her earlier plan, despite her end in favor of her diachronic self-governance. But sometimes in a temptation case this end in favor of diachronic self-governance would have sufficient priority to support sticking with the prior resolve in a way that is sufficient to re-shift the agent's standpoint so that it now favors sticking with her prior resolve. In such a case the agent's sticking with her resolve can cohere with both synchronic and diachronic self-governance. The agent will thereby be in a position to re-shift her evaluation concerning further drinking: she can now favor abstaining since that would comport with her self-governance, both at the time and over time, and so—given her end of her diachronic self-governance—with where she now stands. We thereby explain how willpower can sometimes (though not always) cohere with self-governance.

So a way to ensure that at least some cases of willpower involve synchronic self-governance at the time of resisting temptation is to appeal to the cited conditional end in favor of one's diachronic self-governance. As noted, this end will be reflexive in the sense that it supports a choice insofar as that choice would comport with both diachronic and synchronic self-governance *given this very end* (and its impact on the agent's standpoint, and so on synchronic self-governance, and so on diachronic self-governance).

The next point is that once this conditional, reflexive end is on board it will also favor constancy of decision in the face of non-comparability. Sartre's young man, having chosen to stay with his mother, comes to a time when he reconsiders. At this time he satisfies the relevant precondition: he has a standpoint that (weakly) supports the choice to continue helping his mother, where that choice would thereby comport with synchronic self-governance and, given the history, with diachronic self-governance. So, this choice to continue with his mother—in contrast with a shuffled choice instead to fight with the Free French—would be supported by his conditional, reflexive end in favor of his diachronic self-governance.

Granted, there is no guarantee that this will result in his standpoint *strongly* favoring the option previously chosen. A basic feature of non-comparability is that if A and B are non-comparable, it is possible to add into the mix a further consideration, C, in favor of A, and yet it still be true that A together with C remains non-comparable with B.[49] Nevertheless, we have an explanation of why, even if the non-comparability remains, shuffling in such a case is a breakdown in diachronic self-governance, whereas resistance to shuffling can comport with diachronic self-governance and so be supported by the end of diachronic self-governance.

In supposing that the agent's standpoint includes the cited conditional, reflexive end in favor of her diachronic self-governance I am supposing that this standpoint is, as I will say, *diachronicalized*: it includes an element that can sometimes accord significance to relevant plan-infused cross-temporal interconnections, interconnections that are not merely cross-temporal mental tidiness. And the idea is that a planning agent's diachronic self-governance in the case of willpower involves a standpoint that is diachronicalized in this way, and that such a standpoint will also support a planning agent's diachronic self-governance in resisting brute shuffling.

8. Later Reflection and Plan-Induced Temporal Footprint

We need one further idea. Suppose that in Gregory Kavka's toxin case you decide at t1 to drink a disgusting toxin at t3.[50] You make this decision at t1 because you know that given that decision you will get a great reward at t2. You also know throughout that your reward at t2 depends on your decision at t1 but does not depend on your following through with that decision at t3. You decide at t1 to drink at t3, you get the reward at t2, and t3 arrives. At t3 you are faced with a choice of whether to stick with your intention to drink the toxin at t3. If you stick with it, your intentions during t1-t3 will satisfy the shared-agency-analogue conditions with respect to this time interval. But won't you nevertheless be acting contrary to your standpoint at t3? Well, on our way to a model of a planning agent's diachronic self-governance we have supposed that you have the conditional, reflexive end of your diachronic self-governance. So we need to ask whether, given this end, your standpoint at t3 may turn out to support drinking the toxin. If it does then your drinking the toxin at t3 may fully comport with both your synchronic and your diachronic self-governance. But that seems wrong.

In response we might try simply to say that in this toxin case at t3 your end of your diachronic self-governance will not outweigh your end of not getting very sick. But in discussing the temptation case we supposed that your end of your diachronic self-governance might sometimes in effect outweigh your end of drinking more wine. And it is not clear how we could defend in a principled way this purported, systematic difference between the cases.

I think there is a structural issue here, one distinct from the question of the relative weights an agent assigns to avoiding the discomfort of toxin-drinking in comparison with diachronic self-governance. We can articulate this structural issue by considering your relevant reflections at a later time, t4.[51] In particular, we consider your reflections at t4, on the basis of what you at t4 know were your relevant non-evaluative beliefs at t3, on your decision at t3. In the temptation case, if you did stick with your prior resolve to resist the temptation, such reflections at t4 would, we may assume, *not* issue in regret about your decision at t3. In the toxin case, in contrast, if you did at t3 stick with your prior resolve to drink toxin, such reflections *would*, we may assume, issue in a kind of regret at t4 about your decision at t3. Drinking toxin is, after all, awful. In the toxin case—in contrast with the temptation case—sticking at t3 with your prior intention would be something you would regret at t4 when reflecting in the cited way on that decision.

This suggests that sticking with your intention at t3 to drink the toxin does not fit into the kind of cross-temporal structure of plan-infused attitudes that is an element of diachronic self-governance. And this is a contrast with the kind of temptation case at issue here. The end of one's diachronic self-governance conditionally supports sticking with one's resolve in a temptation case in part because sticking with one's resolve fits together, in shared-agency-analogue ways, not just with one's earlier resolve but also with one's relevant, anticipated later attitude concerning one's exercise of willpower. In sticking with one's resolve one is acting "together" with oneself at both earlier and later times. It is this relevant anticipated later regret at abandoning one's resolve that distinguishes this temptation case from the toxin case in which what is anticipated is, rather, relevant later regret at having followed through with one's intention to drink the toxin. In drinking the toxin one would not be acting "together" with oneself at the later time, t4. This is what allows us to resist the idea that drinking the toxin would be an element in diachronic self-governance and so potentially be supported by the conditional, reflexive end of one's diachronic self-governance.

But why does this yet later time matter? The answer seems to be that appeal to such later times is at least implicitly built into the plans that frame the relevant temporally extended activity. The planned temporal shape of the activity will frequently extend to relevant later times—to, as I once said, plan's end.[52] In the temptation case we are thinking of the planned project of resisting temptation as extending beyond the moment of expected temptation and including one's relevant later reflections on earlier follow-through. And in the toxin case we are thinking of the plan for getting the money as extending beyond the time of drinking the toxin and including one's relevant later reflections on earlier follow-through. In each case, diachronic self-governance with respect to the planned temporally extended activity needs to involve relevant shared-agency-analogue plan-theoretic continuities that extend through to plan's end. And that is why the conditional, reflexive end of one's diachronic self-governance, while it will sometimes support willpower, will not (on current assumptions) support drinking the toxin. It will not support drinking the toxin because following through with the intention to drink will not fit appropriately with one's relevant, anticipated regret, at plan's end, concerning such follow-through.

9. A planning Agent's Diachronic Self-Governance

We now have in place the building blocks for a model of a robust form of a planning agent's self-governance over time:

First, the agent is engaged in *planned temporally extended activity*. Given the hierarchical structure of plans, this planned temporally extended activity can be shaped by a higher-level plan that remains in place even as lower level sub-plans are adjusted. And these plans specify a *temporal footprint*, one that will commonly include one's relevant later responses to one's then-earlier efforts.

Second, there is synchronic *self-governance at (during) relevant times (small temporal intervals) along the way* in the execution of the plan that frames the relevant temporally extended activity. This synchronic self-governance involves coherence of standpoint and coherence of choice with coherent standpoint.

Third, there are appropriate *cross-temporal interconnections* between relevant plan-infused attitudes. These interconnections involve cross-temporal interconnections of intention that are characteristic of planned temporally extended activity, all in the context of self-governance at times along the way. These plan-theoretic interconnections induce associated shared-agency-analogue interconnections. And these shared-agency-analogues support the metaphor that in the temporally extended activity involved in diachronic self-governance the agent at different times along the way is "acting together" with herself at the other relevant times along the way.

As noted, a complexity is that there can be these interconnections at a higher level of the hierarchy of plans despite breakdowns in interconnection at a lower level of sub-plans. Such higher-level interconnections can, together with other relevant elements, sometimes suffice for diachronic self-governance. However, if the breakdown at the lower level could have been avoided in a way that cohered with diachronic (and so, synchronic) self-governance at that level, then that lower-level breakdown diminishes the extent of diachronic self-governance even given the higher-level interconnections.

Fourth, the standpoints at times along the way are *diachronicalized*: they include a conditional, reflexive end in favor of one's diachronic self-governance. A precondition of this end is that the agent is engaged in a relevant, planned temporally extended activity, and his diachronicalized standpoint at the time at issue would support the joint satisfaction of conditions of both synchronic and diachronic self-governance. This conditional, reflexive end to some extent helps coordinate the coherent standpoints at each relevant time along the way with the cross-temporal interconnections involved in diachronic self-governance. It does this by sometimes inducing within the standpoint at a given time relevant significance of the cited connections across time. And the time frame that is relevant to this end of diachronic self-governance is specified by the plan that frames the underlying temporally extended activity.

In short, this model of a planning agent's self-governance over time highlights: (1) planned temporally extended activity, and an associated time frame; (2) self-governance at (during) relevant times along the way of that activity; (3) plan-infused cross-temporal interconnections that have a structure that is to some extent analogous with the interpersonal structure of interlocking intentions of individuals in shared agency; and (4) diachronicalized standpoints at (during) relevant times along the way. These diachronicalized standpoints help support the coordination between (2) and (3) in response to characteristic threats to stability.

Such diachronic self-governance on the part of a planning agent is responsive to common threats of instability within her temporally extended agency, namely: threats of potential shuffling and of temptation. These responses to these threats involve diachronicalized standpoints and go beyond snowball effects and sensible non-reconsideration. But these responses need not involve an implausible rigidity. We highlight the twin ideas that a planning agent's diachronic self-governance normally involves the end of her diachronic self-governance and can involve the stability of prior intentions in cases of resisting shuffling and in some cases of willpower. But we also acknowledge the Sartre-inspired thought that in some cases "the prior project collapses into the past in the light of a new project which rises on its ruins."[53]

Appendix
Acting Together With Oneself Over Time*

Michael E. Bratman

My discussion, in this present essay, of a planning agent's self-governance over time is part of a larger project that concerns the interrelations between, on the one hand, structures of human agency and, on the other hand, norms of practical rationality that are both supported by those structures and whose guidance helps constitute those structures. This larger project builds on the theory of rational planning agency in Bratman (1987) and is the focus of my essays in Bratman (2018a), from which the present essay is taken.[54] In this Appendix to my essay, "A Planning Agent's Self-Governance Over Time,"[55] I locate its discussion within this overall view and, along the way, address a pressing concern about the role in this overall view of the end of self-governance over time.

We – unlike some agents – are, and have reason to be, planning agents. Our practical thinking is shaped in fundamental ways by our prior, partial, future-directed plans. In particular, our prior, partial plans provide a background framework for our weighing of substantive reasons for and against various options. Given the normal partiality and stability of our prior plans, this background framework poses problems of means for further deliberation over time and filters potential solutions to those problems with an eye to their compatibility with one's system of plans. In these ways, our prior plans help answer the question "where do decision problems come from?" (Bratman 1987, p. 33) It is a mistake to think of our weighing of substantive reasons as taking place in an unstructured context: we might call this mistake *the myth of the unstructured weighing of reasons*. Instead, our weighing of reasons is structured by our background of prior, partial plans, a background that poses problems and filters options (Bratman 1987, pp. 33–34).

This framework-providing role of our plans involves distinctive norms of plan rationality. These include wide-scope norms of synchronic means-end coherence and consistency, as well as a diachronic norm of plan stability. This plan-rationality-shaped structuring of our practical thinking supports important forms of human practical organization, individual, cross-temporal, and social.

A planning agent who reflectively scrutinizes these plan-rationality-shaped aspects of her practical thinking has available two forms of justifying support for these norms. (A) Given basic features of our human minds – including the epistemic and cognitive limitations highlighted by Herbert Simon's reflections on bounded rationality – guidance by these norms generally conduces to our basic ends. (B) At least in a wide range of cases, a pro tanto normative reason of self-governance favors the application of these norms to the particular case. (B) in turn involves two ideas. First, the conditions of satisfaction of these norms are themselves conditions of corresponding forms of self-governance. Synchronic norms of plan rationality track conditions of a planning agent's synchronic self-governance. (The argument for this goes by way of a Frankfurt-inspired approach to synchronic self-governance, one that highlights the role of one's relevantly coherent standpoint in guiding one's thought and action. See Bratman 2018g.) And the diachronic norm of rational plan stability tracks conditions of a planning agent's self-governance over time. (As I discuss in the following, the argument for this goes by way of the model of a planning agent's self-governance over time that is defended in the present essay.) This tracking thesis articulates a basic commonality across these norms, a commonality that helps make sense of these norms. Second, on the assumption that we have a pro tanto normative reason to govern our own lives and that we have the capacity for such self-governance,[56] we infer, given the tracking thesis, that we have a pro tanto normative reason in favor of conformity to these norms in the particular case.

The idea in (B) is not that the role of these rationality norms in a planning agent's practical thinking in a particular case reduces to adding the cited normative reason to the scales in a process of weighing reasons. The role of these rationality norms is in structuring the temporally extended plan-shaped practical thinking within which such weighing of reasons is located. This structuring of one's weighing of reasons is grounded in one's framework of prior, partial plans, a framework that poses problems and filters options: we need to avoid the myth of the unstructured weighing of reasons. The normative reason of self-governance cited in (B) provides a source of reflective support for the rationality norms at work in this framework-providing role of our prior, partial plans; it does not supplant that framework-providing role.

The present essay concerns the diachronic self-governance central to (B). The view, roughly, is that a planning agent's self-governance over time normally involves (1) planned temporally extended activity, (2) synchronic self-governance during relevant times along the way and within a time frame induced by the underlying plans, (3) plan-infused cross-temporal interconnections that are analogous to the interpersonal interconnections characteristic of shared intentional agency,[57] and (4) an end in favor of one's self-governance over time.[58] The end in (4) helps support

Appendix: Acting Together With Oneself Over Time

coordination between self-governance at times along the way, as in (2), and the cross-temporal interconnections in (3).

These conditions of diachronic self-governance include, but go beyond, the condition that the same person is acting over time. They go beyond mere psychic tidiness over time. And they fit with the metaphor that in diachronic self-governance, one is acting together with oneself over time.

What is the status of this end of one's self-governance over time? Well, on the one hand, there is no assumption that this end is necessary for all intentional agency. On the other hand, however, my proposal is that this end is not simply one contingent human end among many. Instead, my proposal is that it is for us an entrenched end that plays fundamental roles in our human lives. This is so even though this end is not strictly essential for mind or agency. My proposal is that this end plays a role that is to some extent analogous to that of our concern with quality of will in P.F. Strawson's theory (Strawson 2003) of the role of the reactive attitudes in our lives.[59]

A central claim is that this end in favor of one's diachronic self-governance helps support norms of plan rationality. How? I assume that self-governance, synchronic and diachronic, is a pro tanto human good; and I assume that when we add to this the end in favor of one's diachronic self-governance we get a pro tanto normative reason in its favor. And self-governance over time involves self-governance at times along the way. So, given the end of one's diachronic self-governance and the capacity for such self-governance, we arrive at a pro tanto normative reason to conform in the particular case to conditions of self-governance, synchronic and/or diachronic. So, we arrive at a pro tanto normative reason to conform in the particular case to both synchronic and diachronic norms of plan rationality, given that these norms track conditions of relevant self-governance.

It does not follow that in every particular case, there is undefeated normative reason to conform to the rationality norm. Nevertheless, the presence of a pro tanto normative reason for conformity in an extremely wide range of particular cases, taken together with two-tier pragmatic support for the general role of these rationality norms in our human, plan-infused practical thinking, helps support the reflective stability of a human planning agent's acceptance of these norms. Both this two-tier pragmatic support in (A) and the grounding role of an end of diachronic self-governance in (B) depend on contingent but fundamental features of our human minds. So, the theory involves, as Elijah Millgram (2019) has emphasized, a psychologism about plan rationality.

We can summarize some of these ideas about our end of diachronic self-governance as follows:

(a) This end is entrenched in our human lives in a way that parallels the status of a concern with quality of will in Strawson's theory of holding responsible.

(b) Given the pro tanto value of our self-governance, this entrenched end supports a pro tanto normative reason in favor of specific cases of a planning agent's self-governance over time.
(c) Norms of plan rationality, both synchronic and diachronic, track conditions of corresponding forms of self-governance.
(d) Given (c), the normative reason in (b) helps support the reflective stability of those basic norms of plan rationality.

This takes me, as anticipated, to an important concern: will the normative reason in (b) be present sufficiently generally to play its role in (d)? Sarah Paul (2014) provides a statement of this worry:[60]

> It seems to me that most of us do not care about perfect self-governance, even as an ideal. We also care about things like existential spontaneity, losing control, rolling the dice and letting the world decide, and other more Romantic ideals. For an agent with these multifaceted values, a life that is perfectly self-governed would not in fact be successful relative to her varied concerns. That is, if she actually took the opportunity to be self-governing whenever it was available, she would be flouting her own values.
> . . .
> If this is the correct way to understand the extent of the ordinary concern for self-governance, then it seems false to say that most of us have a reason for the necessary constitutive elements of self-governance in every instance in which it is possible over a series of instances.
>
> (p. 345)

There are two ideas here. There is, first, the idea that if we did value self-governance in each particular case, we would be committed to valuing a life in which we are in each and every case self-governing. But second, we do not value such "perfect self-governance". And my initial reply here is that valuing – or, as I have been saying, having as an end – self-governance in each case need not be rationally agglomerative.

Consider that, on certain views about belief, I can rationally believe of each ticket in a lottery that it will lose and still not believe all tickets will lose. Or I can rationally believe of each proposition in my book that it is true but not believe all the propositions in my book are true. Again, I can rationally intend each action in a lengthy temporally extended series of actions without, strictly speaking, intending the entire series.[61] Analogously, I might coherently be such that in each instance of potential diachronic self-governance, I value that self-governance in that instance but yet do not value universal, "perfect" self-governance. The end of

Appendix: Acting Together With Oneself Over Time 99

diachronic self-governance that we need for our theory of plan rationality is not rationally agglomerative.

But why think we do value diachronic self-governance in (pretty much) *each* case, even if this valuing is non-agglomerative? Suppose in a particular case, I value "existential spontaneity". Why think I also value diachronic self-governance in that case? Here we can again learn from Strawson.

Strawson saw appeal to our concern with quality of will as part of the best explanation of our patterns of reactive attitudes and our practices of holding responsible. But he also noted that we do on occasion bracket our concern with quality of will, sometimes as "relief from the strains of involvement" (Strawson 2003, p. 82). Nevertheless, as I understand Strawson's view, this bracketed concern remains in the background and continues to be available to provide reflective support for our practices of holding responsible.

And my proposal is that an analogous point holds for one's end of diachronic self-governance in a specific case. Appeal to this end is part of the best explanation of our human, plan-shaped practical thinking. Granted, in a particular case, I might bracket this end – perhaps as "relief from the strains of" acting together with myself over time – and be guided instead by a concern with "existential spontaneity". Nevertheless, my end of diachronic self-governance remains in the background. And that background standing is enough for this end to help support a normative reason for self-governance in that particular case. While I do not explicitly treat this end as reason-providing in my present case, it continues to help support a normative reason that would be available, on reflection, as support for basic norms of plan rationality. So, by appealing to this non-agglomerative and bracketable end of one's self-governance over time, we can agree with Paul that "most of us do not care about perfect self-governance" but still defend (d).[62]

I have been speaking of a rationality norm of diachronic plan stability, but I have not yet spelled out the details of that norm. Here there is a methodological dis-analogy with our reflections on the synchronic rationality norms. In the synchronic case, we start with a prior grasp of the main ideas of plan consistency and coherence at a time; we then go on to note how such plan consistency and coherence are central to self-governance at a time. (As noted, this is where we draw on Frankfurtian ideas about such self-governance.) In the diachronic case, it is less clear, pre-theoretically, what the precise rationality norms are. Here we seek a kind of reflective equilibrium between our formulation of this rationality norm, our model of self-governance over time, and the proposed connection between plan rationality and a normative reason of self-governance. And this has led me to the following norm of default rational stability of prior intention (Bratman 2018f, p. 217):

> *Diachronic Plan Rationality* (DPR): If S is a planning agent who is capable of diachronic self-governance then the following is, defeasibly, pro tanto irrational of S:
>
> (a) S is engaged in a planned temporally extended activity that has so far cohered with both synchronic and diachronic self-governance.
> (b) Given her present standpoint, a choice to continue with her planned activity would cohere with that standpoint and so cohere with her continued synchronic self-governance and, in part for that reason, with her diachronic self-governance. And yet
> (c) S makes a choice that blocks her continued diachronic self-governance.

Avoiding a violation of this norm is a condition of a planning agent's self-governance over time, as that is understood within our model of that self-governance. So, given a normative reason for and the capacity for such diachronic self-governance, one has a normative reason to avoid such a violation. This rationality norm itself draws on the very idea of diachronic self-governance; but there is no objectionable circularity, since our model of diachronic self-governance, as in the present essay, is articulated without depending on this rationality norm. Nevertheless, the fit between this model and this norm contributes to the reflective theoretical equilibrium we seek.

Condition (b) in this norm requires that a choice to continue with one's planned activity coheres with one's diachronic self-governance. As discussed in Section 8 of the present essay, one way such a choice can fail to cohere with one's diachronic self-governance is by failing to fit into a cross-temporal structure of attitudes that includes not only one's past but also one's future attitudes. This is why going ahead as planned and drinking the toxin, in Kavka's famous case, would normally not cohere with one's relevant diachronic self-governance. So, it is not an implication of DPR that refusing to drink the toxin in that case would be pro tanto irrational.

In the background are Sartre's young man and Holton's puzzle about rational willpower. Applied to Sartre's young man, our model of diachronic self-governance entails that if he shuffles away from his prior intention to stay with his mother, to a new intention to fight with the Free French, he in this respect falls short of diachronic self-governance. To draw on our metaphor: he is not fully acting together with himself over time even though at each time he is acting for sufficient reason. DPR then

Appendix: Acting Together With Oneself Over Time 101

says that this failure is, defeasibly, a pro tanto rational failure. In this way, DPR articulates a modest conservatism.

A key here is that the young man really did earlier decide/form the intention to stay with his mother. While this decision/intention was underdetermined by his reasons then, it is nevertheless now in place.[63] And once it is in place, it engages pressures of self-governance-tracking diachronic plan rationality in favor of its retention (absent a change of assessment of the underlying reasons, as when he newly comes instead to see his political loyalties as overriding).[64]

In contrast, the application of our model of a planning agent's diachronic self-governance to cases of potential willpower is more complex. Suppose one follows through with one's prior resolution in the face of anticipated temptation even though one's standpoint comes initially to favor the temptation. For this to be a case of diachronic self-governance, it needs to be a case of synchronic self-governance. (Recall condition (2) of diachronic self-governance.) So, one's end of diachronic self-governance needs to re-shift one's standpoint at the time of the temptation so that one's standpoint returns to favoring willpower. So, in this case, the end of diachronic self-governance needs to play a role that goes beyond its roles in Sartre's case. In this willpower case, this end not only (i) is itself a normal background condition of being a diachronically self-governed planning agent and (ii) helps, as an entrenched end, to provide a normative reason in support of the rationality norm DPR; it needs further (iii) to support the cited re-shifting of standpoint in the particular case. That is, this end needs to support this re-shifting if follow through with the prior resolution is to satisfy the synchronic self-governance condition that is built into diachronic self-governance. And in some cases, this end of diachronic self-governance will not do this. But even if it does not do this in a particular case (and so we are without an explanation, by appeal to DPR, of the rationality of willpower in that case), this end continues to play roles (i) and (ii) in the overall theory.

So, we have what we wanted: a model of a planning agent's diachronic self-governance that coheres with and helps support plausible underlying views about plan rationality and associated ends and normative reasons.[65]

Notes

* Thanks to Sarah Paul for helpful comments on an earlier draft of this Appendix.
1 This essay, but not the further Appendix included in this volume, originally appeared in Bratman (2018a, pp. 224–249, using a different style for references). This essay develops ideas about a planning agent's diachronic self-governance that are sketched in Bratman (2018f). I offer a brief overview of the ideas in both of these essays in Bratman (2021). Many of these ideas are drawn from my Pufendorf Lectures, delivered at Lund University in June 2016. I presented earlier versions of the present essay at the II Workshop of the European Network Practical Reason

on "Time in Action" at Oslo University in August 2016; as part of my Franz Brentano Lectures on Practical Philosophy at the University of Vienna in April 2017; and at the Copenhagen workshop on Shared and Temporally Extended Agency in April 2017. Many thanks to the audiences on these occasions and to Philip Pettit, Sergio Tenenbaum, Johanna Thoma, and Gideon Yaffe.

2 Frankfurt (1988, p. 166). See also Watson (1975, p. 216).
3 In saying this, I am supposing that synchronic self-governance can involve self-governance during a relevant, small temporal interval. (This is in the spirit of Sergio Tenenbaum's thought that "a 'synchronic' norm is not necessarily a time-slice norm." See Tenenbaum 2018, p. 456.) Can we say more about such intervals? My tentative proposal is that we look for intervals within which relevant basic concerns and plans are constant, there is not reconsideration of relevant plans, and there are not relevant action plans that specify different stages to be carried out at different times within that interval. Given that we are normally involved in planned temporally extended activities within which our plans specify different stages over time, we can expect these intervals normally to be small. And in any case, once there is reconsideration of a relevant plan, we can no longer continue to understand the process as simply one of synchronic self-governance. Nevertheless, it remains possible that one fails to act in accord with one's standpoint during a relevant interval even if we cannot specify a specific moment in that interval at which this failure occurred. (These comments were aided by correspondence with Sergio Tenenbaum, though they are in the service of an approach to diachronic self-governance that I do not think he would endorse. And see Tenenbaum 2018, pp. 463–464.)
4 This paragraph responds to a query from Gideon Yaffe.
5 Agnes Callard (in conversation) and Jennifer Morton (in correspondence) have pointed to cases in which a breakdown in synchronic self-governance at t results in downstream changes that then support later, associated diachronic self-governance. As I understand it, such later diachronic self-governance begins at a time later than t. But I agree that we might—as it were, by courtesy—speak of the earlier breakdown in synchronic self-governance at t as the time at which, in an extended sense, the diachronic self-governance begins.
6 See Bratman (2018d, p. 143).
7 Granted, even for a planning agent, there may be cases of intentional agency that are not embedded within such planned temporally extended activity: spontaneously scratching an itch, perhaps. But in such cases of spontaneous activity, the question of whether the agent is diachronically self-governing does not arise in a clear way.
8 For this last idea, see Bratman (2007b, pp. 28–33). And see Yaffe (2000, Chapter 3). This paragraph draws from Bratman (2018f).
9 See Bratman (2007d) and Bratman (2018f).
10 See Bratman (2007d, p. 239), where I call these "self-governing policies". For an overview of my approach to a planning agent's self-governance at a time, see Bratman (2017).
11 Sartre (1975). The problem I note in this paragraph owes to Broome (2001, esp. pp. 114–119).
12 I owe the terminology of "shuffling" to Richard Kraut (in conversation). In Bratman (2018d) I call this brute shuffling.
13 Bratman (2018d).
14 Shoemaker (1984, p. 95).
15 See Ferrero (2012, p. 160).
16 An argument that goes beyond my earlier discussion of a planning agent's self-governance over time in Bratman (2018d).
17 McClennen (1990), McClennen (1998), Ainslie (1992).

Appendix: Acting Together With Oneself Over Time   103

18 McClennen (1998, p. 25).
19 I make a related point in response to a similar idea from George Ainslie in Bratman (1999b, p. 48). As I note there, Frank Döring makes a related point in response to McClennen.
20 Carol Rovane explores a related parallel between "long-term activities" and "*joint* activities" in Rovane (1998, pp. 144 ff).
21 Bratman (2014).
22 Since these intentions, as it were, interlock with themselves, they involve a kind of reflexivity.
23 As I indicate in *Shared Agency* (Bratman 2014, pp. 76–77), such a belief condition is, strictly speaking, too strong if what we are seeking are necessary conditions for shared intention. But since what we are seeking is, rather, sufficient conditions for robust forms of shared intention, it is reasonable to appeal here to such a belief condition. (And see note 30.) More generally, in *Shared Agency*, I do not claim that the conditions highlighted there (and cited here) are strictly necessary for shared intention or shared intentional action. I leave open the possibility of other, perhaps weaker, forms of shared agency. However, my conjecture here is that these strong conditions of shared agency help give us an apt model of a planning agent's diachronic self-governance.
24 In my *Shared Agency*, I discuss—and note important complexities concerning—the mirror image of this idea, namely, the idea that shared agency involves "quasi-Lockean" interconnections between relevant participants. See Bratman (2014, pp. 97–97 and 128).
25 A further, interesting question that I will not try to pursue here is whether, and to what extent, this shared agency model can help us understand the legal doctrine of *stare decisis*.
26 Bratman (1987, p. 5).
27 While my intention persists from t_1 to t_2, it will also normally be filled in with further sub-plans. The persistence of intention that is characteristic of planned temporally extended agency is compatible with filling in the partial, hierarchical structure that is normally involved in prior intention. (I am responding here to an inquiry from Thomas Smith.)
28 The idea that relevant contents of intentions can be tacit or implicit is also an aspect of the background view of shared intention. See *Shared Agency*, Bratman (2014, pp. 104–105). I also note there the possibility that "certain less demanding social psychological phenomena might in certain cases to some extent functionally substitute for these more demanding attitudes of each" (Bratman 2014, p. 105). And we can allow for an analogous possibility in the intrapersonal case. So, in the shared case and in the intrapersonal case, there are analogous possibilities of non-explicit but implicit content and less demanding functional substitutes.
29 See my remarks in section 6 about the snowball effect.
30 Here I am mirroring the belief conditions cited in the above model of shared intention, where that model aimed at sufficient conditions for robust shared intention. As mentioned in note 23, we could weaken those belief conditions somewhat, and then those weaker belief conditions would be reflected in our account of relevant shared agency analogues. But to keep our discussion manageable, I put this complexity aside here.
31 The example owes to Seamus Miller. I discuss it in Bratman (2014, p. 100).
32 See Holton (2009). And see Bratman (1999c, 2018e, f). In this paragraph, I draw from that last essay.
33 See Bratman (1987, p. 82), and Bratman (2018c, pp. 114–115). In a standard case of a snowball effect, the new reason to stick with one's prior intention is induced by an initial stage in the execution of that intention (e.g., buying a

nonrefundable airplane ticket), a stage whose aim is not that of inducing such a reason. Here I extend the idea of a snowball effect to include cases in which the new reason is induced by activity (e.g., making a side bet) whose aim is to induce that reason.
34 This is a general theme in Bratman (1987).
35 Here I am disagreeing with Holton's approach in Holton (2009).
36 Paul (2011).
37 There is a parallel here with Bas van Fraasen's "Reflection" principle in van Fraasen (1984). Related ideas are in Paul (2015) and Arthur Lau (unpublished manuscript). I discuss these ideas further in Bratman (2018e), Section IV.
38 This parallels concerns that have been raised about certain apparently basic norms of practical rationality. See note 44.
39 A related idea is in Bratman (2007c).
40 A related idea is in Bratman (2018e).
41 I made some efforts in this direction in Bratman (2007c), at pp. 271–274 and 278, but I now think that these efforts will not apply in a sufficiently general way to cases of potential willpower.
42 Sobel (1994, p. 249).
43 In exploring the idea of preferences that are "influenced by the previously chosen plan of action", Rabinowicz notes the parallel with Sobel's paper. Such preferences are at the heart of Rabinowicz's model of "wise choice". But, as I go on to note in the text, we can ask whether giving such significance to continuity with the past is an undefended concern with mere cross-temporal mental tidiness. To answer we need to embed such cross-temporal continuity within a larger framework. And that is what the appeal to diachronic self-governance – an appeal to which I turn in the following – tries to do.

That said, both Sobel and Rabinowicz highlight an idea that is also part of the model I will be discussing, namely: that, however, we understand this concern for cross-temporal continuity, it is one concern among others and can be overridden in a particular case. Thus, Rabinowicz: "The influence of the previously accepted plan on my preferences at node n may, but need not, be decisive." Rabinowicz (1995, p. 606).
44 An analogous worry is at the heart of a challenge that has been posed by Joseph Raz and Niko Kolodny to norms of plan rationality. I agree with these philosophers that if these norms were simply responsive to mere psychic tidiness, then it would be unclear why they should have normative significance. But in Bratman (2018f) and Bratman (2018b), I argue that these norms are not simply responsive to mere psychic tidiness: they are responsive to conditions of self-governance. In turning later in this discussion to an end of diachronic self-governance, I am pursuing a related strategy with respect to present issues about diachronic self-governance. See Raz (2005) and Kolodny (2008). Talk of "psychic tidiness" is from Niko Kolodny (2007, p. 241).
45 Kelly (2004, esp. pp. 73–75).
46 One consideration in favor of appeal to this specific end is that this appeal fits well with a plausible theory of plan rationality. I explain this in Bratman (2018f) and (Bratman 2018b). This connection with issues about plan rationality is also relevant to my assessment of an alternative, intellectualistic strategy developed by J. David Velleman. In his "Centered Self", Velleman says: "my intellectual drives . . . favor fulfilling my past intentions". (Velleman 2006, p. 272). But, as I note in Bratman (2018f), this will lead to a cognitivist treatment of basic norms of plan rationality, and there are good reasons to be wary of such a cognitivism.
47 Paul (2014), Tenenbaum and Raffman (2012, esp. section III); Andreou (2014), Andreou and White (2010).

48 This is the parallel with views of Sobel and Rabinowicz anticipated in note 43. It is also a feature of Velleman's view cited in note 46.
49 Raz (1986, pp. 325–356).
50 Kavka (1983).
51 This is a basic idea in Bratman (1999c) and Bratman (2018e).
52 Bratman (1999c), Section IX.
53 Sartre (1984, p. 612).
54 See esp. Bratman (2018b) and Bratman (2019a).
55 Chapter 4 of this volume.
56 I discuss the significance of this second qualification in Bratman (2018g).
57 See esp. sections 4 and 5.
58 See esp. section 6 and 7.
59 See esp. Bratman (2018b) in which I argue that this end of diachronic self-governance plays a keystone role in a human planning agent's reflectively stable package of ends and norms.
60 For similar objections, see Millgram (2019) and Rudy-Hiller (2020).
61 (Bratman 2018g, note 7). And see Shpall (2016) for extended discussion.
62 These last two paragraphs expand on brief remarks in my 2018b, pp. 15–16. The parallel with Strawson's version of bracketing owes to Carlos Núñez.
63 Nefsky and Tenenbaum may understate the significance of this point in their (Chapter 8 of this volume, note 38).
64 Concerning this last qualification, see my 2018d, pp. 147–148.
65 For a challenge, see Tenenbaum (2019). My replies are in Bratman (2019b).

References

Ainslie, George. 1992. *Picoeconomics: The Strategic Interaction of Successive Motivational States within the Person* (Cambridge: Cambridge University Press).

Andreou, Chrisoula. 2014. "Temptation, Resolutions, and Regret," *Inquiry* 57 (2014): 275–292.

Andreou, Chrisoula & Mark D. White, eds. 2010. *The Thief of Time: Philosophical Essays on Procrastination* (Oxford: Oxford University Press).

Bratman, Michael E. 1987. *Intention, Plans, and Practical Reason* (Cambridge, MA: Harvard University Press. Reprint 1999 Stanford: CSLI Publications).

Bratman, Michael E. 1999a. *Faces of Intention* (Cambridge: Cambridge University Press).

Bratman, Michael E. 1999b. "Planning and Temptation," as reprinted in Bratman 1999a, 35–57.

Bratman, Michael E. 1999c. "Toxin, Temptation, and the Stability of Intention," as reprinted in Bratman 1999a, 58–90.

Bratman, Michael E. 2007a. *Structures of Agency* (New York: Oxford University Press).

Bratman, Michael E. 2007b. "Reflection, Planning and Temporally Extended Agency," as reprinted in Bratman 2007a, 21–46.

Bratman, Michael E. 2007c. "Temptation Revisited," as reprinted in Bratman 2007a, 264–274.

Bratman, Michael E. 2007d. "Three Theories of Self-Governance" as reprinted in Bratman 2007a, 222–253.

Bratman, Michael E. 2014. *Shared Agency: A Planning Theory of Acting Together* (New York: Oxford University Press).

Bratman, Michael E. 2017. "A Planning Theory of Self-Governance: Reply to Franklin," *Philosophical Explorations* 20: 15–20.
Bratman, Michael E. 2018a. *Planning, Time, and Self-Governance: Essays in Practical Rationality* (New York: Oxford University Press).
Bratman, Michael E. 2018b. "Introduction: The Planning Framework," in Bratman 2018a, 1–17.
Bratman, Michael E. 2018c. "Agency, Time, and Sociality," as reprinted in Bratman 2018a, 110–131.
Bratman, Michael E. 2018d. "Time, Rationality, and Self-Governance," as reprinted in Bratman 2018a, 132–148.
Bratman, Michael E. 2018e. "Temptation and the Agent's Standpoint," as reprinted in Bratman 2018a, 149–167.
Bratman, Michael E. 2018f. "Rational Planning Agency," as reprinted in Bratman 2018a, 202–223.
Bratman, Michael E. 2018g. "Intention, Practical Rationality, and Self-Governance," as reprinted in Bratman 2018a, 76–109.
Bratman, Michael E. 2019a. "Précis of Planning, Time, and Self-Governance," *Inquiry*. https://doi.org/10.1080/0020174X.2019.1663000
Bratman, Michael E. 2019b. "Planning, Time, and Self-Governance: Replies to Andreou, Tenenbaum, and Velleman," *Inquiry*. https://doi.org/10.1080/0020174X.2019.1663003
Bratman, Michael E. 2021. "Plan Rationality," in Ruth Chang and Kurt Sylvan, eds., *The Routledge Handbook of Practical Reason* (New York: Routledge), 514–525.
Broome, John. 2001. "Are Intentions Reasons? And How Should We Cope with Incommensurable Values?" in Christopher W. Morris and Arthur Ripstein, eds., *Practical Rationality and Preference: Essays for David Gauthier* (Cambridge: Cambridge University Press), 98–120.
Ferrero, Luca. 2012. "Diachronic Constraints of Practical Rationality," *Philosophical Issues* 22 (2012): 144–164.
Frankfurt, Harry. 1988. "Identification and Wholeheartedness," as reprinted in Harry Frankfurt, *The Importance of What We Care About* (Cambridge: Cambridge University Press), 159–176.
Holton, Richard. 2009. *Willing, Wanting, Waiting* (Oxford: Clarendon).
Kavka, Gregory S. 1983. "The Toxin Puzzle," *Analysis* 43 (1983): 33–36.
Kelly, Thomas. 2004. "Sunk Costs, Rationality, and Acting for the Sake of the Past," *NOUS* 38 (2004): 60–85.
Kolodny, Nico. 2007. "How Does Coherence Matter?" *Proceedings of the Aristotelian Society* 107 (2007): 229–263.
Kolodny, Nico. 2008. "The Myth of Practical Consistency," *European Journal of Philosophy* 16 (2008): 366–402.
Lau, Arthur. 2013. "Temptation, Resolution, and Epistemic Self-Trust," unpublished manuscript, Stanford University.
McClennen, Edward. 1990. *Rationality and Dynamic Choice: Foundational Explorations* (Cambridge: Cambridge University Press).
McClennen, Edward. 1998. "Rationality and Rules," in Peter A. Danielson, ed., *Modeling Rationality, Morality, and Evolution* (Oxford: Oxford University Press), 13–40.

Millgram, Elijah. 2019. "Review of Planning, Time, and Self-Governance," *Notre Dame Philosophical Reviews* 2019.05.15.
Nefsky, Julia & Tenenbaum, Sergio. 2022. This volume, essay 8. "Extended Agency and the Problem of Diachronic Autonomy."
Paul, Sarah. 2011. "Review of Richard Holton's *Willing, Wanting, Waiting*," *Mind* 120 (2011): 889–892.
Paul, Sarah. 2014. "Diachronic Incontinence is a Problem in Moral Philosophy," *Inquiry* 57 (2014): 337–355.
Paul, Sarah. 2015. "Doxastic Self-Control," *American Philosophical Quarterly* 52 (2015): 145–158.
Rabinowicz, Wlodek. 1995. "To Have One's Cake and Eat It Too: Sequential Choice and Expected-Utility Violations," *Journal of Philosophy* 92 (1995): 586–620.
Raz, Joseph. 1986. *The Morality of Freedom* (Oxford: Clarendon).
Raz, Joseph. 2005. "The Myth of Instrumental Rationality," *Journal of Ethics and Social Philosophy* 1, no. 1 (2005).
Rovane, Carol 1998. *The Bounds of Agency: An Essay in Revisionary Metaphysics* (Princeton, NJ: Princeton University Press).
Rudy-Hiller, Fernando. 2020. "In Defense of a Strong Persistence Requirement on Intention." *Synthese*. https://doi.org/10.1007/s11229-020-02719-8
Sartre, Jean-Paul. 1975. "Existentialism Is a Humanism," in Walter Kaufmann, ed., *Existentialism from Dostoevsky to Sartre*, rev. and expanded (New York: Meridian/Penguin), 345–369.
Sartre, Jean-Paul. 1984. *Being and Nothingness* (Hazel Barnes translation) (New York: Washington Square Press).
Shoemaker, Sydney. 1984. "Personal Identity," in Sydney Shoemaker and Richard Swinburne, eds., *Personal Identity* (Oxford: Basil Blackwell).
Shpall, Sam. 2016. "The Calendar Paradox," *Philosophical Studies* 173: 801–825.
Sobel, Jordon Howard. 1994. "Useful Intentions," in his *Taking Chances: Essays on Rational Choice* (Cambridge: Cambridge University Press), 237–254.
Strawson, Peter. 2003. "Freedom and Resentment," in Gary Watson, ed., *Free Will* (Oxford: Oxford University Press), 2nd ed., 72–93.
Tenenbaum, Sergio. 2018. "Reconsidering Intentions," *Noûs* 52, no. 2 (2018): 443–472.
Tenenbaum, Sergio. 2019. "On self-governance over time," *Inquiry*. https://doi.org/10.1080/0020174X.2019.1663014
Tenenbaum, Sergio & Raffman, Diana. 2012. "Vague Projects and the Puzzle of the Self-Torturer," *Ethics* 123 (2012): 86–112.
van Fraasen, Bas. 1984. "Belief and the Will," *Journal of Philosophy* 81 (1984): 235–256.
Velleman, David J. 2006. "Centered Self," in his *Self to Self* (Cambridge: Cambridge University Press), 253–283.
Watson, Gary. 1975. "Free Agency," *Journal of Philosophy* 72 (1975): 205–220.
Yaffe, Gideon. 2000. *Liberty Worth the Name: Locke on Free Agency* (Princeton, NJ: Princeton University Press).

5 The Structures of Temporally Extended Agents

Luca Ferrero

1. Introduction

We are temporally extended agents: we persist over time and much of what we do takes time – sometimes a very long time. It is easy to characterize our temporal nature negatively: we are not purely instantaneous agents, who only live and act for an instant. But a positive characterization is not straightforward. For there are many ways in which agency and agents might extend over time.

In this chapter, I offer an overview of the main ways in which agents might extend over time, and I sketch what I take to be the characteristic structure of extended human agency. I first introduce pure momentary agents, which only exist at (and care for) the present moment. They exemplify a degenerate form of extended agency. I then show how agency can be extended in two distinct but combinable modes: the ontological, which gives rise to simple continuous agents, and the conceptual, which gives rise to agents who conceive of and care about distal times and have minimal planning abilities. Our extended form of agency combines both ontological and conceptual extension. Even so, we are still limited by the temporal locality in the operation of our psychological and executive powers. To account for this locality, I introduce the notion of "temporal selves", as the loci of immediacy in the agent's determination of their psychology, conduct, and practical standpoint. I argue that the passage of time generates, by itself, the threat of temporal alienation from distant temporal selves. A genuinely extended agency requires temporal identification, that is, the sharing, by separate temporal selves, of a temporally extended and integrated practical standpoint. This temporal identification cannot be produced simply by temporal identity as continuity. What is required is rather temporal identity in what I call "the mode of unity and integration". This identity, I argue, does not precede temporal identification; it is rather co-constituted with it. I then offer a preliminary account of the complex structure of the units of integration for agents who aspire to persist in the mode of unity and integration. I close by sounding a cautionary note: the complex structure of integration, although familiar

DOI: 10.4324/9780429259845-8

to us in the everyday handling of our extended agency, is often missed by standard philosophical accounts, which tend to focus on too simple models of our extended agency.

2. Temporally Extended Agents

2.1. Pure Momentary Agents

Consider *pure momentary agents*. These agents only exist for a moment, they only act at that moment, and they only care about what is going on at that moment.[1] By "moment", I refer to the minimal temporal interval over which these agents can perform what, for them, is an executively basic action. Hence, these agents are not instantaneous; they exist and act *over* time, but their duration is, *modulo* their agential powers, minimal.

Pure momentary agents are not causally isolated. Their actions are partly shaped and constrained by what happened prior to the agents' existence. In turn, their actions can partly shape and constrain what happens after these agents disappear. However, in our universe (at least at the macroscopic level) there is no such thing as action-at-a-temporal-distance, hence, any distal effects of these momentary actions can only be mediated and indirect. Finally, these agents do not care about the indirect effects of their momentary actions: by their nature, these agents genuinely and fully live only "in the present moment".

Pure momentary agents illustrate the degenerate form of temporally extended agency. What does it take for agency to be genuinely extended over time? There are two basic modes of extension. The first is ontological: the agents themselves persist longer than a single moment. The second is conceptual: even if the agents exist only momentarily, they have the capacity to conceive, execute, and care about their momentary actions on account of at least some of their distal outcomes. The two modes can be combined, as it happens for agents like us. But I will first consider them separately to isolate their respective contributions to extended agency.

All temporal agents, regardless of their mode or modes of extension, suffer from the same limitation in executive powers as pure momentary agents: executive powers are always *temporally local*. That is, these powers are always exercised *at a particular moment,* and their *direct* effects are necessarily proximal. The distal effects of any specific and momentary exercise of executive powers, i.e., of any "momentary action", are always indirect, even for non-momentary agents. This entails that many temporally extended pursuits need to be supported, at least from time to time, by exercises of local executive powers at separate times. That is, much of what extended agents can accomplish over time requires *sequences* of momentary steps – momentary exercises of contemporaneous local executive powers. No matter how extensive these powers might otherwise be, their distal effects are always necessarily indirect. This is a fundamental constraint on temporal execution that applies to all kinds of diachronic agents.

2.2. *Ontological Extension*

To understand the contribution of the ontological mode of temporal extension, let's consider "simple continuous agents". These agents persist over an extended period by being temporally *continuous* over that period (for present purposes, it does not matter whether this continuity is that of organisms, bodies, brains, psychologies, etc.). Although these agents persist past a single moment, their executive powers and cares are, like those of pure momentary agents, only focused on the present moment.

What difference does the extended existence of these agents make to their temporal agency? Unlike the actions of pure momentary agents, some of the momentary actions of simple continuous agents might affect their future circumstances and actions (in turn, some of their present actions might have been affected by their past circumstances and actions). Even if simple continuous agents have no conception of the effects of their momentary actions on their future circumstances, sequences of momentary actions might have interesting cumulative long-term effects, and an external observer might be inclined to describe as being extended activities. Consider a pigeon pecking seeds. This foraging behavior is present-directed; the pigeon is only concerned about eating seeds in its immediate vicinity. But as long as seeds continue to be available in its vicinity, the pigeon might continue foraging, at least for a while. Throughout this interval, the pigeon could be correctly described as engaged in the extended activity of "pecking seeds" even if the pigeon has no sense of this activity as temporally extended.[2]

Even if the agent is unaware of these extended activities as extended, their extension does not exist simply in the eyes of the beholder. Some of these activities might make an actual difference to their agents. The activities' cumulative effects might affect the agents *as* extended entities. For example, although the pigeon's foraging is temporally local in both execution and conception, this conduct can have cumulative beneficial effects for the pigeon as an extended organism. The pigeon does not immediately metabolize all the food it gathers; hence, the extended foraging benefits the pigeon past the interval of the actual foraging.

In the pigeon example, the cumulative effects result from the mere repetition of the same kind of simple action. More complex cumulative effects can be produced by stringing together momentary actions of different kinds. When so, the extended activity might be more structured, provided that each momentary step can build upon the effects of the previous ones and, in turn, prepare the stage for the following ones. In our world, these favorable conditions for this temporal extension apply to many simple continuous agents. For instance, biological organisms, even of the simplest kinds, do not sustain themselves by starting literally from scratch at each and every moment, nor are they normally caught up in the mere repetition of the very same simple action.

Thanks to the sequencing of the effects of past momentary actions on the present and future configuration of the agents' circumstances, bodies, and minds (including, in case, the effects of psychological retention and learning), even simple continuous agents can engage in sequences of momentary actions that give rise to complex extended activities. These sequences can stretch over long intervals, even if the agent has no relevant conception of or care for these sequences under the extended description. These sequences can be remarkably beneficial to the agents as extended agents, even if these agents are clueless about this temporal extension. A plausible conjecture is that most, if not all, non-human organisms are simple continuous agents of this sort.

Under the right circumstances, this kind of extended agency can produce remarkable outcomes, even in the absence of any understanding of its extended structure by its own agents. Nonetheless, because of the lack of the corresponding conceptual capacities to appreciate and care for this extension as such, there is something adventitious about this temporal extension. The existence of this structure need not be accidental – often, it has been selected for on account of its functional benefits. But its operation appears to lack the kind of structural unity of full-fledged extended agency, where the unfolding of the activity is supported not simply by the agent's persistence in the mode of continuity but also by a conception of the very structure of the extended activity as extended.

2.3. *Conceptual Extension*

A second way to extend agency is by conceptual means. Even if agents do not persist long enough, they might care for the distal effects of their actions and engage in them in light of their conception of these distal effects. Consider pure momentary agents again. Imagine that, while they still exist only momentarily, they are now able to engage in momentary actions out of the combined capacities to understand, predict, and care for the distal effects of their momentary actions.

The new conceptual abilities allow such agents to choose their momentary actions on the basis of the calculations of the distal effects of these actions. But notice that these effects are, by the very nature of momentary agents, only *ballistic*; these agents can initiate a causal chain but cannot directly guide or control its distal future unfolding.[3] The ballistic effects might include the operation of various devices and the contributions of other future momentary agents (who, in turn, might be expected to choose their momentary actions out of their own calculations). The calculations can thus go well beyond the mere anticipation of simple chains of brute efficient causation. In principle, sophisticated momentary agents might extend the reach of their agency quite far into the future, especially when they can rely on the future collaboration of other momentary agents.

Crucial for this sophisticated calculative power is the ability to form a *synoptic* view of the unfolding of the effects of momentary actions. This view requires more than the capacity to track the unfolding of chains of efficient causality. It also requires an understanding of overall patterns and structures in the causal chains. These patterns span across temporal intervals and often go beyond the simple sequential ordering of momentary steps (which might include, as noted earlier, the momentary actions of other agents).

Equivalent, if not identical, outcomes might sometimes be brought about by different sets of intermediate steps (these sets can be different both in their composition and in the temporal ordering and location, both relative and absolute, of their components). When this is so, it is usually because these outcomes depend on the structural integrity or unity of the overall pattern of steps, which can be partially independent of specific sequences of intermediate steps.

The combination of the capacities for sophisticated calculations and synoptic views gives rise to a *minimal planning* ability: the ability to devise *plans* for the future unfolding of momentary actions and to choose how to act according to these plans.[4]

It might seem a stretch to speak of "plans" in this context given that the products of these calculations cannot, by the very nature of momentary agents, guide and control their future conduct. But we ordinarily speak of plans in this way even when talking about ballistic actions (a failure to land a Mars rover, say, might be described as not "going according to plans" even if we have no direct control of the landing). What is unusual in the case of momentary agents is just that their plans are entirely ballistic. As such, these plans guide the agent who originates them only once – i.e., only when the agent initiates the sequence. But the content of these plans might be accessible to other momentary agents at later times and guide them accordingly. The plan might be rediscovered by future momentary agents on their own, "passed along" the chain of implementation, or made publicly available for future reference.

For present purposes, we might imagine that these momentary agents are akin to Bratman's (1999: 28) "frictionless deliberators", who perform complex deliberative calculations and make a choice among the possible courses of action at a single moment and at no cost to them. This is, of course, an idealization. But this idealization helps highlight what is in principle achievable by the mere ballistic agency of agents who only exist momentarily but have sophisticated future-directed conceptual and calculative abilities. Looking at these agents helps us factor out, even if only notionally, the differential contributions of the two distinct modes (the conceptual and the ontological) of extending agency over time.

As we saw in 2.2, mere ontological extension raises the worry that the extension of agency is adventitious. Is there a similar worry with an extension by conceptual means only? Yes and no. Given the presence of a plan, the relation between the various steps is no longer accidental, provided that the plan continues to guide the unfolding of the steps (and that everything goes non-deviantly according to the plan). However, momentary agents have no guarantee that their plans are going to guide the future unfolding of the sequence, given that these agents must necessarily rely on the collaboration of future momentary agents, over which they have no direct control. There is always the risk that future agents might not collaborate or only do so accidentally (i.e., the future agents might end up contributing to the sequence for reasons that were neither endorsed nor expected by the earlier contributors).

To remove the residual accidentally, it seems that we need a conceptually sophisticated agent who persists for longer than a moment. This agent could directly guide the unfolding of one's plans. Genuine, non-accidental, extended agency seems to require the combination of ontological *and* conceptual extension. This might not seem surprising. However, the mere combination of the two modes of extension might not be sufficient to give us a genuinely extended agency. This is because of the pervasive constraints of temporal locality, which affect not just our executive powers but also, as I am about to argue, the operations of both our psychology and practical standpoints.

3. Temporal Locality

3.1. Temporal Selves

At the root of the temporality of agency is the locality in the exercise of executive powers: all temporal agents can *directly* exercise their agency only at their present moment. From the point of view of any momentary execution, the future extension of agency is necessarily indirect; it is mediated either by brute causality or by other momentary exercises of agency at later times. Temporal locality, however, affects more than the mere exercise of executive powers.

The immediacy constraint on executive powers is just one aspect of the temporal locality that shapes our temporality. The operations of our psychology exhibit a similar immediacy. First, there is immediacy in receptivity, as manifested in the distinctive phenomenology of present experience. Second, there is immediacy in our spontaneity – as manifested, for instance, in the acquisition, rejection, or revision of judgment-sensitive attitudes (such as beliefs and intentions), which always take place at the present time. In other words, there is no such thing as psychological action at a temporal distance. We can *directly* acquire, reject, revise, or operate with any mental attitude only at the present time and via the contemporaneous exercise of our present rational and mental powers.

Sure, a mind can reach into the past and the future. But it can do so only either by retention and anticipation (which still take place at the present time) or by the contents of present attitudes (which can make immediate transtemporal reference at a distance, both prospectively and retrospectively). These are powerful means that allow agents to reach outside of their present time. Yet they still work only through the present operation of our psychology on contemporaneous attitudes. The direct operation of our psychology is always *temporally local*, and we relate to it with a distinctive *immediacy*.

Let me introduce the notion of "temporal self" as the locus of the necessarily *immediate* and *temporally local* exercise of psychological and executive powers. This is how I will understand this notion, which is often used but hardly ever articulated in moral psychology and in the literature on practical rationality.

It is important to resist the temptation to assimilate these "moral psychological" temporal selves to the instantaneous time-slices of persons, as these slices are used in the literature on the metaphysics of transtemporal identity. In that literature, the notion of a time-slice is not specific to persons or agency. It is rather used to address general questions about temporal identity and temporal ontology (including such matters as the difference between endurantism and perdurantism, the nature of the temporal continuum and its parts, etc.).

The temporal selves that matter in moral psychology are different from time-slices both in duration and dynamic. First, a locus of psychological and executive immediacy stretches both in the past and in the future. The length of this stretch is comparable to what James (1890) calls the *specious present*.[5] Second, the locus moves seamlessly with the passage of time. Unlike time-slices, which are just discrete frozen snapshots or slices of infinitesimal duration, temporal selves are dynamic.

Because of the limited time horizon of immediacy, as time passes, the locus of immediacy inexorably loses direct access and control over what was previously within its range of immediacy. Once this happens, a new temporal self, centered on what is now the new present time, replaces the previous one, which becomes a *distinct* temporal self – a past self. A similar dynamic plays out for future selves. They, in turn, can become present and then past selves, just with the passage of time. Over the agent's lifetimes, there will be a continuous succession of distinct temporal selves, each one as a distinct center of psychological and executive immediacy over the limited timespan of the temporal self's existence.

A couple of clarifications are in order. First, temporal selves are not what I called *pure* momentary agents at 2.1: temporal selves are part of an extended agent, and their psychology, motivation, and cares are not necessarily present-directed. Their locality is a matter of the immediacy of the *operations* of psychological and executive functions, not of the objects of such operations. Temporal selves rather resemble momentary agents with sophisticated conceptual capacities (including the capacity of minimal planning, see 2.3).

Second, because of the moving interval of immediacy, the succession of temporal selves is not, strictly speaking, a procession of utterly separate temporal selves. It is rather a succession of *partially overlapping* selves. (For instance, some portions that are in the proximal past of a given self – of its window of retention – are going to be part of the proximal future of an overlapping earlier self – of the latter self's window of pretension, so to say.) Because of the short duration of the specious present, however, this overlap does not last for long, and it can thus be ignored when dealing with standard questions about diachronic moral psychology.

3.2. The Locality of Practical Standpoints

In addition to the temporal locality of the exercises of executive and psychological powers, all temporal agents need to contend with the locality of the practical standpoint. I am using "practical standpoint" in the broadest possible way to refer to what is variously referred to in the moral psychological literature as what determines the agent's true or deep self; what "speaks for the agent" in what the agent does, thinks, and feels; what the agent fully "identifies" with; what lies at the core of the agent's self-governance; etc.[6]

For the purposes of this chapter, I do not need to subscribe to any specific account of the nature of the practical standpoint. All that I need is the claim that agents like us have practical standpoints that determine where each of them *stands* in two related senses: first, the standpoint gives sufficient unity and integrity to the agent, thereby delimiting what counts, in the agent's acting, thinking, and feeling, as genuinely one's own; second, the standpoint orients and guides the agent's conduct in a way that makes this conduct genuinely imputable to the agent (rather than to *external* determinants, including those portions of the agent's psychology from which the agent is alienated).

The practical standpoint is usually understood as the standpoint of an extended agent: it articulates the agent's stance, as an extended subject, on her exercises of psychological and executive powers over time. Even so, any practical standpoint is always realized, so to say, at specific times, and it can directly guide only the agent's thought and conduct that are contemporaneous with the present realization of the extended standpoint. This is because the guidance of a practical standpoint always takes place via the operations of psychological and executive powers. Hence, a standpoint, even if extended in content and conception, always operates *locally* first, as realized in the present standpoint of the agent's present temporal self.

By the very nature of a practical standpoint, a sufficiently integrated agent cannot be genuinely alienated from one's contemporaneous practical standpoint (although such an agent might harbor some ambivalence and unclarity about that standpoint). But at the present time, it is always possible to be alienated from an extended practical standpoint that it is supposed to be presently realized only because it has been endorsed by the agent at some *other* time. Ultimately, it is always in the hands of the contemporaneous temporal self to determine what the agent's practical standpoint is going to be at that time (for the same reasons why the exercise of executive and psychological powers is always in the same hands). The agent at the present time is the ultimate arbiter of whether to continue to support an extended practical standpoint that comes from the past: there is no immediate identification at a temporal distance.[7]

It is the mere passage of time that gives rise to the possibility of a *temporal alienation* from a practical standpoint that comes from the agent's past. No temporal agent is immune from the threat of temporal alienation. Fortunately, there is a silver lining. The threat of this alienation is the counterpart of the possibility of temporal *identification*, which is, as I will argue later, the key to a non-adventitious extension of agency over time. Before doing so, however, I need to discuss an important distinction between two notions of temporal identity.

4. Two Kinds of Temporal Identity

4.1. Appealing to Temporal Identity

Genuine, non-adventitious, extended agency requires a combination of both conceptual and ontological extension. Simply put, the agent must both persist over time and act out of an adequate conception of their extended existence. This combination, even if necessary for genuine extended agency, is not yet sufficient because of the temporal locality in the operations of both minds and practical standpoints. Even if the agent persists over time, their temporal selves are still the loci of the immediate exercises of executive and psychological powers.

In principle, the temporal selves might engage in extended activities in a ballistic form. Once a temporal self has made their momentary contribution to a given extended activity, the success of the activity lies in the hands of the momentary contributions of future selves. But these contributions are not guaranteed, because there is no assurance that the future selves will continue to endorse the same extended practical standpoint that supported the activity in the first place.[8]

The agent is not powerless against this threat. If she has adequate resources, the agent might try to force or cajole future collaboration – by setting up pre-commitments, for instance.[9] But these would be measures of last resort: genuinely extended agency cannot rely on the systematic (even if benign) manipulation of one's future selves.[10] The question facing us, thus, concerns how an agent could make sure to engage in genuine, non-adventitious, and *non-manipulated* extended agency in spite of the locality of both execution, psychology, and practical standpoint.

It seems that the agent could easily secure genuinely extended agency by appealing to one's identity via the notion of a shared practical standpoint. An agent who is, at present, reluctant to continue to embrace a shared practical standpoint might reason as follows: "Despite my present initial reluctance, I am going to embrace the shared standpoint because it comes from *my* past and it stands for *who I am* as an extended agent. I embrace this standpoint because *it is me*!"

This suggestion sounds very plausible, but we must tread carefully here. According to this suggestion, what is supposed to make a difference is that the practical standpoint is coming from *my own past*. However, there are two different notions of temporal identity that might be at play here: temporal identity *as continuity* and temporal identity *in the mode of temporal unity or integration*. These two kinds of identities work differently and neither of them, unfortunately, can offer the kind of support for the shared practical standpoint that we are looking for. Or so I am about to argue.

4.2. *Identity in the Mode of Unity or Integration*

Let's start with temporal identity as continuity (identity-c, hereafter). It is undeniable that temporal selves are part of the same *continuous* agent. However, by its nature, continuity is compatible with massive transformations in the agent's psychology and practical standpoint, especially over the longer term. Hence, a temporal self's acknowledgment that she is identical-c with a self at an earlier time still leaves open whether she *should* take up the practical standpoint she had at the earlier time. This is not to deny that continuity might induce some stability by way of psychological inertia or the causal effects of earlier steps, which might make it easier to continue activities already underway (what Bratman 2010: 10 calls the "snowball effect"). But what is needed to respond to the threat of temporal alienation is not just a stable tendency in favor of identification but a robust rational support for it.

Consider now *temporal identity in the mode of unity or integration* (identity-i, hereafter). When an agent sees herself as temporally unified or integrated, she is not just continuous over time. She rather tries to keep the different portions of her existence together, according to some standards of diachronic coherence or unity. For present purposes, we do not need to consider (nor endorse) any specific characterization of these standards. What matters here is only that there are some standards of this kind that guide the agent in securing her unity and integration over time.

Actual success at meeting these standards is not required to be identical-i. What is required is only that, throughout a given period, the agent acts out of a certain self-conception: a self-conception as an extended agent who is committed to trying to live up to the standards of diachronic unity. Whereas identity-c requires actual continuity, identity-i does not require actual integration but only a stable commitment to it – which is why I called this "identity in the mode of integration".

Unfortunately, the appeal to identity-i cannot help thwarting the threat of temporal alienation. The problem is that identity-i presupposes the very stability of the practical standpoint that it is supposed to ground. In order to have the stable self-conception required by identity-i, this self-conception needs to be locally supported, that is, to be central to the practical standpoint of each temporal self. And the shared practical standpoint must be deemed, by each temporal self, as non-accidentally stable across time. Each temporal self needs to see itself as contributing to the carrying out of the commitment to temporal integration by non-manipulated collaboration with the other temporal selves out of a shared practical standpoint.

Hence, a direct appeal to identity-i cannot help us respond to the threat of temporal alienation. The appeal to identity-i cannot overcome the resistance of any temporal selves who refuse to endorse the shared practical standpoint. A reluctant temporal self is not going to be rationally compelled to endorse the practical standpoint on account of the claim that they are *already* identical-i with an earlier self. Claiming this pre-existing identity begs the question. The correct order of justification runs in the opposite direction: endorsement of the practical standpoint is necessary to establish identity-i rather than the other way around (compare Korsgaard 1989: 113). This is not to deny that the existence of a prior convergence on the shared standpoint might be a consideration in favor of continuing to sustain that standpoint. This convergence might help overcome the temptation of temporal alienation. But the possible contribution of a pre-existing identity-i in *further extending* this identity *to the present time* is not to be confused with the claim that the threat of temporal alienation can be defeated by the mere appeal to a pre-existing identity-i that *already holds at the present time*.

4.3. *Inter-Self Cooperation*

I have argued that that appeal to temporal identity, either as identity-c or identity-i, does not offer an adequate response to the threat of temporal alienation. Is this worrisome? At this point, someone might suggest that we should just accept the existence of a deep and insurmountable barrier between temporal selves. This barrier makes impossible any genuine, non-accidental, and non-manipulated temporal extension of agency as a *single, extended, and integrated* agent.

This might not be a reason to despair because we can still get temporal integration on the model of collective or shared agency, where the participants are not distinct extended agents but separate temporal selves. In other words, by analogy with inter-personal cooperation, we can get individual temporal integration by way of what might be called "inter-self" cooperation. Or so the proposal goes.

Like ordinary inter-personal shared activities, the joint enterprises of separate temporal selves would respect the distinction between their separate practical standpoints. The cooperation requires the convergence of the distinct standpoints in supporting the joint enterprise. The convergence, even if based on an extensive overlap in the content of the distinct standpoints, never amounts to a *merging* of these standpoints into a single, albeit shared, standpoint. In other words, the distinct temporal selves might come together as a "we" but not as a single "I".

Is this a plausible account of our diachronic agency? The analogy between diachronic agency and inter-personal bargaining or cooperation is a common trope in the literature on diachronic rationality and moral psychology.[11] Usually, the analogy is not meant as a full-blown account of diachronic agency or rationality in terms of temporal selves as ontologically prior to extended agents. But there are some authors who are more open to the possibility of the ontological priority of temporal selves (e.g., McClennen 1997; Ainslie 2001). And there is at least one case of full support for the primacy of temporal selves: Strawson (2004). In addition, Strawson argues that a stronger kind of temporal integration (especially one organized around a single narrative) might do more harm than good. In his view, we would be better off leading an "episodic" life: a life as a succession of distinct temporal selves which, despite their continuity, do not identify with each other as the self-same (integrated) agent.

In my view, an extended agency that results from an inter-self cooperation among distinct temporal selves is an open possibility. Hence, I agree with Strawson that we have a choice between different possible kinds of temporal integration, including the refusal of any such integration. This choice is not imposed by any pre-existing identity-i. But unlike Strawson, I do not think that stronger kinds of integration are necessarily prone to do more harm than good. However, I will not be defending this claim here.[12] My present goal is only to spell out the nature of this integration, given the constraints of temporal locality and the threat of temporal alienation.

5. Temporal Identification

5.1. A Locus of Extended Agency

In the case of inter-self agency, the transtemporal collaboration arises from distinct practical standpoints, which converge on a shared goal but only out of distinct practical standpoints. The collaboration is not generated by any structural pressure *internal* to a *single* practical standpoint.

By contrast, "temporal identification" (t-identification, henceforth) imposes such pressure. By t-identifying with other selves, a temporal self shares a single practical standpoint that is no longer centered at any specific moment. This is the standpoint of an *extended* agent, a standpoint that spans the entire interval of the t-integration (which might be shorter than the agent's lifespan, see 5.5).[13]

Continuous temporal selves are subject to the diachronic constraints of minimal planning that guides their momentary contributions to the implementation of extended activities. These constraints are imposed by the instrumental demands of the extended pursuits. The shared standpoint introduces new rational pressures and constraints that are *internal* to the standpoint of an extended and integrated agent. Examples of these new pressures are the demands for diachronic consistency in the pursuit of multiple activities and for the stability of future-directed intentions (which is why the shared standpoint requires a much richer form of planning capacities, see Bratman 2022). The extended agent also becomes a suitable unit for the enjoyment (and correlated calculation) of cumulative and synoptic burdens and benefits (including those of various temporal goods)[14] and for compensatory adjustments and trade-offs that, by default, cannot be imposed across separate agents without special justification (e.g., accepting earlier costs in return for larger future benefits).

These pressures help bind the temporal selves together and harness their momentary contributions to serve the larger unit of integration. These constraints and pressures work by leveraging the capacity to have a synoptic view of temporal structures and patterns,[15] a capacity that is now turned onto the unity of integration itself rather than simply on distinct pieces of extended conduct.

Once in place, the constraints work top-down. They frame and bind the temporal selves' exercises of their psychological and executive powers, which are now subordinated to the larger unit of integration. This is how the separation between the selves is supposed to be overcome. Psychological and executive powers are still exercised at separate moments, but the locality of momentary practical standpoints is partially overcome by their merging into a single extended standpoint. I say "partially" because the shared standpoint is unitary in structure and content, but it still needs to be realized locally, i.e., it still needs to be endorsed by each temporal self.

The integration via t-identification gives rise to an extended locus of imputability: the overall conduct, including its momentary stages, is now primarily and directly imputed to the integrated and extended agent.[16] This is different from the imputability of merely continuous activities, which are *of* the extended agent only indirectly, i.e., parasitic on the primary attribution to the temporal selves who are held together only by continuity. The integration via t-identification is also different from the

Structures of Temporally Extended Agents 121

imputability of inter-self cooperation, where the selves come together as agents with numerically distinct standpoints. It is only with t-identification that the relationship between the temporal selves becomes genuinely *intra*-personal.

5.2. Dual Perspective

Although t-identification overcomes one dimension of separation, the responses to the conceptual constraints and rational pressures of integration still occur at specific moments via the immediate operations of the temporal selves located at those times. Hence, the top-down direction (i.e., from temporally synoptic to temporally local) in conception, imputability, and normativity goes together with the bottom-up direction in actual operation and execution.

The co-existence of these two directions explains the dual perspective that the extended integrated agent can take over oneself at any given time. The integrated agent can see oneself from both (a) the synoptic perspective – as an integrated unit that extends over a stretch of time and (b) the local perspective – as a very short-lived center of the immediate exercise of psychological and executive powers (exercises which take place in sequential concert with the local exercises by the other centers of immediacy within the same unit of integration).[17]

The duality of perspectives is also reflected in the *dynamic* structure of the shared practical standpoint. The temporal selves do not necessarily share a fully fixed standpoint; they rather share a standpoint that mixes stability and robustness, on the one hand, with open-endedness and plasticity, on the other. This mix reflects the need to secure extended integration, *while* the standpoint unfolds *over* time via the sequence of local momentary realizations.

5.3. T-Identification and Identity-i

T-identification is required to secure identity-i. Whereas identity-c can be taken for granted as the necessary precondition for t-identification, identity-i neither precedes nor grounds the existence of a shared practical standpoint; it is rather co-constituted with it. This is why one cannot appeal to a pre-existing identity-i to fend off the threat of temporal alienation. At any given time, one avoids alienation by t-identifying *at that time* with one's past and future selves, *thereby* securing – right at that time – one's identity-i as an extended integrated agent.

When settling on an extended activity in the mode of integration, the agent at the present time is offering to one's future selves an *invitation* to take up the pursuit at the later time in the same mode of integration, that is, to take it up by t-identifying at that time with the shared standpoint. What is offered to the future selves is a package to contribute to the continuation of the pursuit in question in the mode of an integrated and extended agent – something that a future self can do only by accepting to share the extended and integrated practical standpoint, *thereby* securing one's identity-i with the past and, in turn, issuing a similar invitation to one's future selves.[18]

This invitation is different, both in source and in object, from the invitation made to a future self when one is seeking only inter-self cooperation rather than intra-personal integration. In the inter-self case, the invitation both comes from and is directed at temporal selves conceived as *distinct* loci of agency. In the intra-personal case, the invitation, even if it comes at a particular time, comes from the integrated unit, the extended agent, and its object is the continuation of that same unit.

Notice that the latter invitation is issued by a temporal self but only in its role as the momentary realization of the extended agent. It is somewhat trickier, however, to characterize the addressee of the invitation. The invitation is addressed to the locus of immediacy at a later time; in this sense, it is addressed at a future temporal self. Yet, the invitation is for this future self to integrate: in receiving and accepting it, the future self *thereby* gets incorporated into the larger unit.

This is not a two-step process, as if an already existing temporal self, existing as separate from the unit of integration, were *first* to receive the invitation and *only then* merge with the larger unit. Rather, the locus of immediacy at the later time determines *right there and then* whether it is going to be a realization of the integrated unit, which is thereby extended to embrace this moment,[19] or stand out as a distinct temporal self, as a separate locus of agency and imputability.[20]

5.4. *The Phenomenology of Ordinary T-Integration*

The articulation of t-integration in terms of an "invitation" to a future temporal self might appear to be hyper-intellectualized. One might reasonably protest that it does not resemble at all our ordinary experience of extended agency. If anything, when we try explicitly to articulate how our agency can extend over time, it seems more natural to make a naïve appeal to our identity-i as the *pre-existing* condition that is sufficient by itself to remove the worry of temporal alienation (see 3.2). There is something to this concern, but I think it only speaks to the ordinary operation and phenomenology of temporal identification, not to its more general and basic structure.

Normally, t-identification occurs by default. From moment to moment, an adult human being usually acquiesces – seamlessly, tacitly, and unreflectively – to t-identify with (and thereby sustain) an extended practical standpoint and the associated self-conception as an extended locus of agency in the mode of integration.[21] The deliberative questions that are usually at the forefront of our attention concern specific exercises of our agency against the background of an inarticulate appreciation of our transtemporal identity as identity-i. That is, we usually frame these deliberative questions against the background of an extended practical standpoint, which we take for granted. This is why it is tempting to see our extended identity-i as a *given* rather than as an achievement of temporal identification. Ordinary experiences of seamless t-integration obscure that we are constantly, albeit usually tacitly and effortlessly, sustaining our identity-i as the background framework for the more specific practical questions that occupy our attention.

The role we play in shaping and sustaining the shared practical standpoint and the associated extended locus of agency can become apparent to us when we face major challenges to the stability of our standpoint – for instance, when we undergo a "transformative experience" (see Paul 2014) or engage in some radical re-assessment of our standpoint. Situations of this kind put explicitly in question our t-identification and, with it, the status of our temporal identity. Hence, it is no exaggeration when we describe these situations as "identity crisis", given that in those cases the persistence of our identity-i is indeed at stake.

Similarly, one might occasionally face questions concerning how to deal with very distant future portions of one's life under the expectation that one will undergo radical changes in one's practical standpoint (whether because of mere drift or a sudden transformative experience). In these cases, appeal to an allegedly pre-existing identity-i is of no help: what is at stake in contemplating these scenarios is exactly whether one should now commit to an integrated standpoint, that is, whether to t-identify with these distal portions of one's continuous life. Cases of this sort make talk of distinct "selves" apt even outside of philosophical theorizing.

The special situations I have just described are a better guide to the basic structure of extended agency (i.e., to the idea of identity-i as something to be achieved via t-identification) than the phenomenology of ordinary t-identification. These special situations highlight how extended agency is to be shaped and sustained in the face of urgent and significant threats of dissolution or radical reconfiguration. But the need to secure identity-i is also present under ordinary circumstances, even if in those circumstances the need can be more easily met. We normally secure identity-i in a straightforward and implicit manner *just by* and *in* engaging with our ordinary practical reasoning and acting.

Hence, we should not hyper-intellectualize t-identification. For beings like us, much of t-identification takes place by default and unreflectively, especially over shorter time intervals. In the very short term, just outside of the range of the specious present, we should expect a default, implicit, and inertial continuity of temporal identification. This default continuity is produced by the standard operation of our psychological retentive capacities (which secure the basic persistence of individual psychologies) in combination with the relative stability of our local surroundings. Ordinarily, from moment to moment, we should expect a *default proximal temporal identification* and, as a result, an inertially and implicitly stable practical standpoint. This t-identification is what goes together with the ordinary phenomenology of our continuous psychological life.[22]

The range of default proximal t-identification can extend beyond the very short term, especially if the agent lives under circumstances that are stable and, for the most part, engages only in activities that unfold within the temporal horizon of the stable circumstances. Under these conditions, the threat of temporal alienation only appears as a remote metaphysical possibility since the agent is under little pressure to question one's default t-identification.

Imagine day-to-day agents who live in a fairly stable and predictable environment and only engage in repetitive daily activities with no long-term preoccupations. The unit of integration of these agents could just extend for 24 hours, with no pressure to question their default t-identification within that time horizon and no pressure to extend the identification past that time horizon. Outside of the daily horizon of ordinary t-identification, day-to-day agents might be like the simple continuous agents I introduced in 2.2. They are carried into the distal future by mere continuity, by the iteration of their daily integrated activities, which never extend past the daily horizon. Their practical standpoint might slowly change over time by drift. But given the time horizon of their concerns, they are unlikely to be bothered by any such changes.

What happens if day-to-day agents are explicitly confronted with a drastic change in standpoint? Consider a day-to-day agent who is suddenly prompted to think about financial planning for their retirement decades in the future. Should this agent necessarily and immediately t-identify with her future self who would be affected by their current financial choices? I do not think so. This agent might decide to handle the matter in the interself mode. It is ultimately up to her, given her nature and circumstances, to determine the extent of her horizon of t-identification, especially past the range of the default proximal identification.

What is the standard extension of default identification? This is hard to tell. Many factors contribute to it, including the reliability of retention mechanisms, the temporal extension of the projects normally undertaken by the agent, and the stability and predictability of the agent's circumstances relative to the standard extension of her projects. Besides, cultural, societal, and institutional pressures play a role in setting expectations and providing scaffolding for the standards units of integration, which might range over quite different temporal spans.[23] One possible temporal horizon is, obviously, the agent's entire life. But the structures of t-identification and identity-i, by themselves, do not entail that the maximum horizon is necessarily the best, let alone the only possible one.

5.5. Temporal Glue

The difference between identity-i and identity-c is apparent when we consider what keeps the agent together over time – the temporal glue, so to say. For identity-c, the glue is *causal*. That is why the direct connections between the temporal selves can only be local. The causal glue also gives rise to the distinctive topology of identity-c: the topology of lines of continuity. For identity-i, instead, the glue is *normative*. The unity of the standpoint and the locus of imputability are the products of a combination of conceptual constraints, rational pressures, norms of imputability, and the self-conceptions built around them.[24]

Although the normative connections of identity-i ride on top of the causal ones, they give rise to a much more complex topology. Integration depends in part on the properties of the agent as a whole (such as diachronic coherence, narrative structures, etc.). These properties often arise via non-local yet direct relations across several elements of the agent's psychology and conduct (such as cross-temporal referential links among attitudes, see Bratman 2010: 10).

There are three dimensions of the unit of integration that complicate its topology: its shape, length, and dynamic.[25]

Shape – Although there are different possible accounts of what makes an agent continuous (say, the body, the psychology, etc.), temporal continuity comes only in one shape, that of the line. And the question of whether a temporal agent is continuous with another self is not a matter of degree. Strictly speaking, a temporal self cannot be continuous with only a portion of another distal stage. If there is an uninterrupted chain of momentary connections between two temporal selves, these selves are as continuous as they can possibly be, despite any changes that might have occurred in the meantime.[26] Integration, instead, comes in many different forms and degrees. Two temporal selves that are part of the same unit of integration might still have features that are not completely or fully unified across them. And what gets to be included within a unit of integration might change over time. There is no simple shape of integration that corresponds to the line in the case of continuity, unless we take the entire life of an agent with all of its elements to be the only possible unit of integration. But this choice does not seem to be necessitated by the notion of temporal integration as such.

Length – Whereas identity-c lasts for the agent's entire life (death is the permanent loss of continuity), identity-i need not extend that far. As we have seen earlier, we can conceive of day-to-day agents, whose unit of integration goes no further than a day. An agent's entire lifetime might just be a succession of shorter units of integration along the line of continuity (these units might either be utterly separated from each other or partially overlapping). It is possible to argue that identity-i should extend across an entire life, but this is not something forced by the mere nature of temporal integration. And even so, there are different kinds of lifetime integration. For instance, one might integrate into the "maximizing" form, taking the unit of integration as the proper locus of accumulation of mere additive goods (such as the duration of life, or utility, which are indifferent to their temporal location within a life). Alternatively, one might integrate in a "narrative" form, where the life is the span of one or more narrative arches and the goods that one might accrue, via closure or resolution, depend on their relative or absolute location within a life.

Dynamic – Identity-c has a simple dynamic: the center of immediacy moves along the continuous line, whence the succession of temporal selves. For identity-i, instead, there are many moving parts, both inside and outside of the unit of integration. The three main parts are: first, the center of immediacy which moves with time. This is also true of identity-c, but in identity-i the movement is internal to the unit of integration. Even if everything else stays fixed, this movement might create some trouble for integration. For instance, if the agent discounts past or future costs and benefits in a non-linear way, the mere passage of time might induce diachronic inconsistencies (see Andreou 2017). Second, the unit of integration itself might move. If the unit does not cover an entire life, the agent might take herself to be moving over time as a unit (on top of the movement of the center of immediacy). For instance, as time goes by, some portions of the remote past might be dropped from the unit of integration (say, because they are either forgotten or no longer deemed worth caring about). Conversely, future portions that were initially deemed inaccessible or not worth caring about might now get included. Third, the unit that moves might also change its shape and length, possibly going through gradual but eventually radical metamorphosis in both structure and content.

Let me illustrate some of these dynamics by using Parfit (1984: 327)'s famous example of the Russian Nobleman. The Nobleman embraces socialism at his young age but anticipates a radical change in political ideals by the time he gets old. Using my terminology, the young Nobleman and the old Nobleman are identical-c. Some practices, such as the legal ones, might be sensitive only to this identity (for instance, the old Nobleman might be held legally liable for debts incurred by the young Nobleman). But identity-c need not determine the unit(s) of temporal integration. Indeed, in Parfit's original presentation, both the young Nobleman and the old Nobleman consider their distant selves as distinct units of integration. If so, if there is any project to which they might contribute directly, they are supposed to do so only in the inter-self (or better, the "inter-unit") mode. This is a relatively simple scenario that aptly describes situations in which there are clearly separate units of integration. The easiest way to create this separation is through either a sudden and drastic conversion, or what Paul (2014) calls a "transformative experience".

Consider now a variation of this case, in which the change in political ideals takes place by a slow drift over several years. This complicates the dynamic of the units of integration. Imagine the middle-aged Nobleman, who is now more politically moderate but not entirely detached from the political views of his youth. He might still endorse portions of his earlier practical standpoint. He might actually consider his current standpoint as a rational development of the earlier one. To that extent, there is a partial overlap between the units of integration (the unit centered on the young man and the one centered on the middle-aged one). There might be projects initiated in his youth to which he is willing to contribute to this day, out of the shared practical standpoint centered on his present self. But he is not embracing all of the past projects, even if, in the past, he deemed them inseparable from the ones he continues to endorse now. In this way, although his young self would not take himself to be integrated with the middle-aged one, the latter one takes his unit of integration to reach into portions of his youth. In a similar fashion, the middle-aged Nobleman partially identifies with his future old-age self since he anticipates that only a portion of his current standpoint will be retained by then. In turn, it is possible that the old Nobleman might still find some grounds for a partial integration with his middle-age standpoint, but none with his young one.

In the latter scenario, the direct relationship between the old and the young Nobleman resembles that of the simpler scenario and can still be modeled as an inter-self interaction, since the two units of integration are separated. But how are these two units supposed to relate to the middle-aged Nobleman? And how is the middle-aged Nobleman supposed to relate to the two units, given that he might be supporting projects that cover all three stages of his life? Extending the unit of integration to the entire life is an option but not a straightforward one, since there are portions of the distal stages that he does not endorse. Unlike non-branching identity-c, identity-i is not transitive. However, can distal selves simply ignore the fact that, along the line of continuity, there are going to be partial overlaps in units of integration? That is, can a temporal self who at least partially integrates with a later one simply ignore that this later self, in turn, is going partially to integrate with an even later one?

The dynamic of partial overlap is something that temporal agents might have to reckon with. A simple inter-unit model does not work here because there is no complete partition into utterly separate and static units of integration. Here I am not trying to offer answers to these questions. I only want to point out that the dynamics of temporal units and practical standpoints raise thorny issues that have received limited attention in the literature, even if they seem to offer a more accurate picture of the unfolding of our diachronic agency and identity.[27]

There are also complexities internal to each unit of integration. For instance, in cases of temptation and temporary preference reversal, the present self might be in conflict with a larger unit of integration that encompasses the present self. In these cases, should we model the situation in terms of inter-self interaction? The model seems appropriate because the transitions in practical standpoint are very sudden (temptation often works by inducing sudden preference or judgment reversals at the present time). However, the reversal is only temporary, unlike what happens in standard inter-self interactions. This is a well-known set of issues (see, for instance, Bratman 2007: Chapter 12; 2018: Chapter 7), but we still need a comprehensive account that covers all kinds of changes of practical standpoint, both internal and external to the units, both static and dynamic (including such phenomena as temptation, drift, transformative experience, and what Callard (2018) calls "aspiration" – the "distinctive form of agency directed at the acquisition of values").

6. Conclusion

6.1. Some Methodological Remarks

I will conclude my preliminary investigation in the structures of diachronic agents with a couple of methodological remarks. Because of the complexity of the topology of integration, we need to pay attention to the second-order dynamic of the units of integration. The extended agent, considered at a particular moment in time, is already under first-order dynamic pressures. For she is supposed to figure out what to do now to contribute to extended projects over potentially changing circumstances while integrating with past and future stages of that same unit of integration. At a first pass, the agent relies on the expectation of a shared practical standpoint to tie together the momentary contributions of her various temporal selves. The availability of the shared standpoint, however, is threatened if the unit of integration changes in shape, size, and substance with the passage of time. This second-order dynamic needs to be accommodated by any sufficiently adequate account of diachronic agency and identity.

Unfortunately, there does not seem to be a straightforward answer to the problems raised by the second-order dynamic. One strategy is to move to a more generic and possibly higher-order unit of integration, which could re-absorb many of the changes as, in a sense, some sort of internal noise. But this strategy might end up emptying the unit of integration of much of its substantive content. The risk is that of being left with nothing more than the purely formal unity of a maximally extensible but otherwise empty self.[28] As tempting as this solution might be, we should be cautious about losing the ability to account for the concrete diversity and complexity of our extended agency.

Other strategies might make a similarly problematic tradeoff between simplicity and descriptive adequacy. We should be mindful of this danger if we are tempted to settle for structurally simpler accounts. The temptation is to model diachronic agency and identity on one of the two more philosophically manageable extremes. On the one hand, one might give prominence to the constraints of locality and the special place of the present moment, thereby adopting a picture that denies genuine integration in favor of inter-self interactions. On the other hand, one might give pride of place to temporal integration by a unitary agent but take the integration necessarily to extend over the entire lifetime (for instance, in the form of a stable standpoint and self-conception organized around a single master narrative).

The trouble with these extreme models is that they miss at least two dimensions of complexity and their associated dynamics. First, within a single life, we can find a mix of various modes of extension (i.e., mere continuity, inter-self and inter-unit interactions, and stronger integration). Second, even within a single unit of integration, there can be tensions between different perspectives, since the very same unit can be experienced and observed from different temporal vantage points (at the present time, retrospectively, or prospectively) and at different time-scales, not to mention the effects of possible changes in the size, scope, and substantive content of the units of integration.

We are temporally integrated agents. Or better, we aspire to be temporally integrated, and we often succeed at it. But integration is an ongoing achievement that can take many different and dynamic forms. Temporally integrated agents might come in various shapes and sizes, on top of lines of mere continuity. To the extent that integration is valuable, there is a legitimate pressure to secure some structural stability and reduce some of the dynamic complexity in the lives of integrated agents. But in trying to develop an adequate theory of diachronic agency and identity, we should be wary of the temptation to assume that the most viable and valuable units of integration necessarily match the simpler philosophical models currently on offer.

Notes

1 I use "care" as an umbrella term to refer to the components of an agent's practical standpoint, such as desires, preferences, intentions, policies, saliencies, priorities, sensibilities, cares, attachments, and values.
2 Notice that this example does not rest on each pecking action having some clearly defined boundaries (say, the action terminates when the pigeon's neck reaches back by a certain angle). The same would be true of momentary actions that are part of a continuous flow but in which the agent has, at any given moment, only a present-directed orientation, even if an orientation that continues to move ahead as the time passes.
3 On ballistic actions, see Stout (2018).
4 Full bloodied planning agency introduces additional demands (see 5.1).
5 Prosser (2017: 146) describes the specious present as a temporal interval of several seconds, a kind of "psychological present" associated with short-term

130 Luca Ferrero

  memory, to be contrasted with the even shorter interval of present conscious perceptual experiences. See also Paul's (2017: 266) characterization of the specious present as the basic "subjective temporal unit of *agential* experience of the self", my emphasis.
6 For an overview, see Jaworska (2022).
7 At issue here is only the locality of the operation of the standpoint, not its content. A practical standpoint can have non-local content. It might even be possible to argue that it would be hard, if not impossible, to have a standpoint that is entirely characterized as "momentary" in content—see, for instance, Korsgaard (1989: 113–114) and Bratman's (2018) discussion of diachronic self-governance.
8 [See Bagnoli, Chapter 9, this volume.]
9 [See Arruda, Chapter 7, this volume.]
10 See the discussion of "diachronic autonomy" in Ferrero (2010).
11 For two examples from very different debates, see Dorsey (2018) and Bratman (2018: 9).
12 The best case for preferring stronger kinds of integration would show that there are some kinds of goods or values that can only be made available to or pursued by temporally integrated agents. For a preview of such an argument, see Ferrero (2009).
13 Two important precursors of the role of t-identification via shared practical standpoint are Korsgaard (1989) and Schechtman (2007; 2008).
14 For a taxonomy of temporal goods, see Ferrero (2022).
15 Compare Schechtman's (2014: 100–103)'s discussion of the "diachronic holism" of narratives.
16 I use "imputability" as a generic term that is neutral on the possible distinction between answerability, accountability, and attributability, on which see Smith (2012).
17 The duality of perspective has been forcefully argued by Schechtman (2020). Unlike her, however, I do not take the extended perspective to necessarily cover the agent's entire life. Notice also that when she contrasts a unified existence with a disjointed and discontinuous one, she is concerned, like me, about the separation of temporal selves, which is compatible with continuity as identity-c.
18 My account of the structure and content of the "invitation" appears to parallel that of Schechtman (2008: 417), which I discovered only when I was putting the finishing touches to this paper.
19 The structure here is reminiscent of the "paradox of self-constitution" in Korsgaard (2009: 19; see also 41ff.): "there is no *you* prior to your choices and actions, because your identity is in a quite literal way *constituted* by your choices and actions", whence the difficulty of adequately characterizing not only who receives the invitation but also who issues it.
20 This is not to deny that there are cases when a two-step description seems apt. This might happen when the agent is explicitly contemplating whether fully to integrate with a distant portion of their life over some temporal gap, rather than with the continuation of an ongoing integrated unit as described earlier. In this situation, however, at issue is not whether a temporal self is to integrate with an integrated unit, but whether two already extended units of integration should merge into an even larger one.
21 The extent and mode of the default t-identification that I describe here are similar to the extension of the agential perspective of the "subjectively enduring self" described by Paul (2017). See also Schechtman (2007: 162) for a defense of the "largely implicit and automatic" operation of self-conceptions of integration.

22 In the very short term, the agent might suddenly change the course of action because of unexpected occurrences such as serious emergencies, but this is not to be confused with a radical and sudden discontinuity in practical standpoint, which is a much rarer occurrence.
23 For a defense of the social and cultural determinants of personal temporal identity, see Lindemann (2014), Doris (2015: Chapter 8), and Schechtman (2020: 102).
24 For the normative character of diachronic unity, see Korsgaard (1989).
25 The topology that I describe here is quite different from the complex topology illustrated by Dainton (2008: 405), who is only concerned with the effects of multiple *branching* of lines of identity-c via fissions and fusions, not with identity-i. In my view, the issue of branching continuity has played an over-sized role in debates about personal identity, but I am not going to argue for this here. For present purposes, the distinction between continuity and integrity stands regardless of questions about branching. To accommodate branching scenarios, I think that one could just rephrase everything I say here in terms of quasi-identities: q-identity-c and q-identity-i.
26 Sometimes we speak of being "more or less" continuous, but this is an inaccurate way of talking; what we usually mean by degrees of continuity is either degrees of *connectedness* between adjacent stages, which are the building blocks of continuity, or the extent of similarities between non-adjacent stages which are nonetheless genuinely continuous.
27 To the best of my knowledge, the philosophical work most sensitive to the multi-dimensional and multi-perspectival character of agents' temporal identity is that of Schechtman (2007, 2008, 2014, 2020).
28 For a discussion of this threat, see Millgram (2015).

References

Ainslie, G. (2001). *Breakdown of Will*. Cambridge University Press.
Andreou, C. (2017). Dynamic Choice. In E.N. Zalta (ed.), *The Stanford Encyclopedia of Philosophy* (Spring 2017 Edition), https://plato.stanford.edu/archives/spr2017/entries/dynamicchoice/
Bratman, M. E. (1999). *Faces of Intention*. Cambridge University Press.
Bratman, M. E. (2007). *Structures of Agency*. Oxford University Press, USA.
Bratman, M. E. (2010). Agency, Time, and Sociality. *Proceedings of the American Philosophical Association*, 84(2), 7–26.
Bratman, M. E. (2018). *Planning, Time, and Self-Governance: Essays in Practical Rationality*. Oxford University Press.
Bratman, M. E. (2022). Planning Agency. In L. Ferrero (ed.), *The Routledge Handbook of the Philosophy of Agency*. Routledge.
Callard, A. (2018). *Aspiration: The Agency of Becoming*. Oxford University Press.
Dainton, B. (2008). *The Phenomenal Self*. Oxford University Press.
Doris, J. M. (2015). *Talking to Our Selves: Reflection, Ignorance, and Agency*. Oxford University Press.
Dorsey, D. (2018). Prudence and Past Selves. *Philosophical Studies*, 175(8), 1901–1925.
Ferrero, L. (2009). What Good is a Diachronic Will? *Philosophical Studies*, 144(3), 403–430.

Ferrero, L. (2010). Decisions, Diachronic Autonomy, and the Division of Deliberative Labor. *Philosophers' Imprint*, 10(2), 1–23.

Ferrero, L. (2022). Diachronic Agency. In L. Ferrero (ed.), *The Routledge Handbook of the Philosophy of Agency*. Routledge.

James, W. (1890). *The Principles of Psychology*. H. Holton and Company.

Jaworska, A. (2022). Agency and Identification. In L. Ferrero (ed.), *The Routledge Handbook of the Philosophy of Agency*. Routledge.

Korsgaard, C. M. (1989). Personal Identity and the Unity of Agency: A Kantian Response to Parfit. *Philosophy and Public Affairs*, 18(2), 101–132.

Korsgaard, C. M. (2009). *Self-Constitution: Agency, Identity, and Integrity*. Oxford University Press.

Lindemann, H. (2014). *Holding and Letting Go: The Social Practice of Personal Identities*. Oxford University Press.

McClennen, E. F. (1997). Pragmatic Rationality and Rules. *Philosophy and Public Affairs*, 26(3), 210–258.

Millgram, E. (2015). *The Great Endarkenment: Philosophy for an Age of Hyperspecialization*. Oxford University Press.

Parfit, D. (1984). *Reasons and Persons*. Oxford University Press.

Paul, L. A. (2014). *Transformative Experience*. Oxford: Oxford University Press.

Paul, L. A. (2017). The Subjectively Enduring Self. In I. Phillips (Ed.), *The Routledge Handbook of Philosophy of Temporal Experience: Routledge Handbooks in Philosophy*. Routledge.

Prosser, S. J. (2017). Rethinking the Specious Present. In I. Phillips (Ed.), *The Routledge Handbook of Philosophy of Temporal Experience: Routledge Handbooks in Philosophy*. Routledge.

Schechtman, M. (2007). Stories, Lives, and Basic Survival: A Refinement and Defense of the Narrative View. *Royal Institute of Philosophy Supplement*, 60, 155–178.

Schechtman, M. (2008). Diversity in Unity: Practical Unity and Personal Boundaries. *Synthese*, 162(3), 405–423.

Schechtman, M. (2014). *Staying Alive: Personal Identity, Practical Concerns, and the Unity of a Life*. Oxford University Press.

Schechtman, M. (2020). Glad it Happened: Personal Identity and Ethical Depth. *Journal of Consciousness Studies*, 27(7–8), 95–114.

Smith, A. M. (2012). Attributability, Answerability, and Accountability: In Defense of a Unified Account. *Ethics*, 122(3), 575–589.

Stout, R. (2018). *Ballistic Action: In Process, Action, and Experience*. Oxford University Press.

Strawson, G. (2004). Against Narrativity. *Ratio*, 17(4), 428–452.

6 Agency and Time

Abraham Sesshu Roth

What sense can be made of the idea that practical matters are *settled* by decisions and intentions? If we take this idea seriously, it might seem that we are led to an implausible picture of the agent somehow reaching outside the temporal order to determine in direct fashion some future state of affairs. I think we can avoid this consequence and yet maintain a robust conception of settling. But this will require articulating how one can act directly on a prior intention and appreciating the distinctive role of intention in preserving reasons for action.

1. An Ambiguity about Settling, and a Dilemma about Decision

Is there something special about one's attitude toward a prospective action when deciding or intending to do it? Philosophers often appeal to the idea of *settling* to distinguish decision or intention from other possible attitudes toward some prospective φ-ing, such as merely entertaining the possibility, or expecting it, or finding it attractive or worth doing. But the verb *to settle* has become a term of art invoked in importantly divergent ways. We get to the first use of the term by thinking about how a decision affects *the agent*. Once a decision has been made and an intention formed, the agent *is settled* on a course of action to pursue. She stops considering alternatives and attends to bringing about the goal decided upon. Decision and the resulting intention thus play a distinctive role in the agent, manifest in patterns of thought and behavior that lead toward the agent acting in the way she decided to. The picture that emerges is one of getting the ball rolling, so to speak. No longer is the agent merely entertaining the possibility of φ-ing, or deliberating about whether to do it; she's now committing to it and moving toward it, both in her thinking (ruling out alternatives or incompatible projects) and in taking the preparatory steps and willing the necessary means (Bratman 1987). Call this *intransitive* settling.

In contrast, the *transitive* use of the term involves the thought that when, for example, you decide and intend to attend a lecture tomorrow, what you're settling is the matter of *your being at the lecture*. This seems to be more than just getting the ball rolling to attend the lecture. A decision understood merely as getting the ball rolling needn't say anything more than that the agent is constituted in a distinctive way so as to be settled on this goal. But deciding to be, to think, and to behave in certain ways *now*, and thus get the ball rolling on attending the lecture is not quite deciding the matter of lecture attendance. It is compatible with a number of things that fall short of a decision that settles the matter in the transitive sense, such as pursuing a course of action to leave open the possibility of attending, perhaps to see whether attending is really something that you want or are able to do. Being intransitively settled on attending the lecture is likely to be a *part* of what goes on when one decides to attend. But deciding understood as transitively settling the matter seems to involve something more as well.

What more? For now, I want to emphasize that it is the matter of attending the lecture, rather than merely your current condition, that is settled. It was an open question whether you would attend the lecture, and you resolve it by deciding: yes, I'll be there.[1] To say that what I've resolved is to be in a state now that tends to lead to attending the lecture doesn't quite seem to cut it. Part of the thought here is that it's my choice whether or not to be at the lecture. In the normal course of things, the domain over which one can exercise choice over what to do ranges beyond one's immediate psychological and physical conditions. Normally, I choose to attend the lecture; I am not so unfree, so constrained or put upon, that my choice is limited to making some effort to get to the lecture in the hope that things will work out. This point is reinforced by the thought that one must reasonably think that successful φ-ing is under one's control if one is to be in a position to decide and intend to φ (let alone avow it). It's not clear how to make sense of this stricture on decision and intention unless it involves a transitive conception of settling.

This is to say that the decision and the corresponding intention to φ are committal about the φ-ing. The intransitive notion of settling falls short of this, whereas the transitive settling does not. At this point, it might be objected that intransitive settling *does* have an element of commitment. We introduced *being settled* in the intransitive sense as what distinguishes intention from merely desiring to φ. In intending the end, one pursues the means and rules out conflicting goals. Was this not committal, at least compared to merely desiring the end? Yes, but it is nevertheless something less than full-out commitment to the φ-ing. For example, if all that I'm doing is setting myself to attend the lecture and getting the ball rolling on doing so, then *being at the lecture* is not necessarily a "fixed point" in practical reasoning concerning matters *subsequent* to the φ-ing. My being intransitively settled on φ-ing is a fact about me, and it is a sad truth that what I aspire to is not the same as what I accomplish. My decisions nevertheless appear to involve commitments that outstrip those psychological facts, and this is significant for individual planning as well as for what others count on me to do.[2] All of which points to a role for transitive settling in our understanding of decision and intention.

So we have settling$_i$ understood as the agent *being settled* on a goal and getting the ball rolling toward it. And we have a transitive notion of settling$_T$ understood as the agent *settling some (prospective) matter*. The planning considerations highlighted by Bratman are often deployed to articulate the distinctive settling role of intentions. Although some of the planning considerations distinguish intentions from desire in terms of characteristic of settling$_i$, it appears that other planning considerations invoke the stronger settling$_T$, such as when we make use of the decision to φ to resolve further practical issues downstream from the φ-ing.[3]

But now we have a dilemma. Deciding and thereby intending to φ later appear to be more than being (intransitively) settled$_i$ on φ-ing; it is a transitive settling$_T$ that one will φ. On the other hand, undertaking to φ very often can involve a very drawn out and episodic process, only the temporally proximate end of which is available to the agent at the outset. Whatever I decide or do now cannot have a *direct* impact on what I do at some temporal remove. Thus, it seems that I cannot do anything more than get this process going. This suggests that being settled$_i$ is all that is available to me. I can at best take steps now that I hope or expect will have an influence on subsequent follow through on my part. And if that is all that I can do, then how could a decision ahead of time involve my settling some practical matter in the stronger transitive sense? It appears that either we give up on any robust notion of deciding and intending matters beforehand or else we are committed to the implausible thought that one can in magical or transcendent fashion reach out of the temporal process in which one is embedded to settle in some direct way a future state. Call this the Dilemma about Decision.[4]

2. Alternatives to Transitive Settling?

Can transitive settling be metaphysically tamed by operationalizing it in terms of the measurable steps of in transitive settling? Or might we make do without transitive settling altogether while retaining a viable conception of decision and intention? In this section, I will consider some purported alternatives and argue that in one way or another they are committed to transitive settling. The discussion will allow us to introduce two further issues in connection with transitive settling: normativity and transparency.

Start with **aiming**. I suggested that transitive settling is important for intentions and decisions establishing fixed points that can be taken for granted in reasoning about subsequent matters. If my intention to φ doesn't settle whether I φ, then the planning concerning those matters would have to be conditional: if I actually get around to φ-ing, then I can go on to do such and such; but if not, then I'll end up doing something else. Why can't we be satisfied with this? How realistic could it be to hope for more? There's only so much that one can settle, and what lies beyond can at best be managed with conditional planning. More importantly, even if the intention to ϕ won't serve as a fixed point for planning matters *subsequent* to ϕ-ing, it might serve as a fixed point *for matters leading up to* the prospective ϕ-ing. Unlike a mere desire to ϕ, *aiming* at it has me taking steps now so as to bring about or secure as best as I can the hoped-for ϕ-ing. Aiming, therefore, might be a realistic alternative to transitive settling that can nevertheless capture some of the planning elements that we want in our understanding of decision and intention.

One concern with the aiming proposal is that it fits most naturally with situations where what is targeted is not something that involves in any intimate or intrinsic way the agent herself. Thus, when I take a basketball shot, my aiming and releasing the ball is the extent of what I do. If I do it well, then causally and temporally downstream from my involvement the ball goes in the basket. This is what we might be tempted to think in light of the Dilemma about Decision: all that is available to me is what I can do now, so I had better aim well right now. Still, a disanalogy between, on the one hand, my aiming at something and, on the other, my making a decision to ϕ down the road is that in the latter *I will be on the scene then to perform the ϕ-ing*. That is not typical of the case of aiming, and I think it leads to problems.

To see why the aiming metaphor is problematic for our purposes, we need to bring out a normative element to decision and settling that we haven't yet addressed. Suppose I take my basketball shot and it does not go in. Assuming that a defender didn't block it, the problem lies with my aim – what I did when releasing the ball. In contrast, suppose I reach a very reasonable decision to ϕ later but then for no good reason fail to act on it. It seems that the proposal in terms of aiming is relegated to saying that I in effect did not aim well in the initial stage of decision-making, and there was no real problem with my subsequent agency when the ϕ-ing was supposed to be executed. We could of course say that the subsequent inaction amounts to a failure to conform with the prior intention. But on the current proposal, that was a problem with the prior aiming in failing to bring about what was targeted, which involves, among other things, getting myself later to act to ϕ. Aiming is not well suited for an account of decision and intention in the contexts in which they are commonly deployed – temporally extended and episodic processes in which the agent plays a recurring role; the agent on the scene at the time of action is in some sense under some rational pressure to act in accord with the prior decision and intention. That is missing from the proposal in terms of aiming.

The worry with the proposal in terms of aiming points to a normative and committal element to decision reflected in the *transitive* notion of settling. If deciding and intending are merely setting oneself in a way that gets the ball rolling, then it's not clear that one would be at fault later if for no good reason the intention "doesn't take hold" and one does not act on the decision. If all I'm doing is getting the ball rolling and depending on an unfolding temporal process, what happens later is as it were out of my hands. It seems quite possible that later I could take up the matter with my mind changed as to what to do. This sort of thing happens all the time. But from the perspective of decision and intention, *I'm not supposed to change my mind* unless there is some good reason to. The notion of aiming neglects the downstream normative situation, when the agent is to act on the prior intention.[5]

Let me turn to another alternative to transitively settling one's ϕ-ing, namely, that of *leaving open the possibility* of ϕ-ing. The proposal is to leave space for one's later self, as the agent on the scene, to do his or her thing. All one can do now is to ensure as best as one can that the ϕ-ing is available to one at a later time. We should recognize that this is a departure from settling as it is often understood and thus is a revisionary proposal. However, it is motivated by the recognition that the agent is on the scene at a later time and is presumably accountable for performing it; it's not just a matter of poor aim at the time of decision. Moreover, there is the hope that at least some of the patterns of reasoning constitutive of intention-based commitment might be retained – in particular those that lead up to the ϕ-ing. Consider, for example, means-end coherence. Suppose I intend to ϕ, which on the current proposal is understood not as something settled but as something that I am leaving open as a live possibility. Now, suppose that ψ-ing is necessary for ϕ-ing. So, it seems that I should intend ψ. After all, if I don't ψ, I won't leave open the possibility of my ϕ-ing. Thus, we seem to make sense of the requirement to intend the necessary means.

Or do we? Presumably, the ψ-ing, which is meant to leave open the possibility of ϕ-ing, is itself not transitively settled. It, too, is left as an option when the time comes. But if ψ-ing is merely left open and is not transitively settled, then it's not clear that I've left open the possibility of ϕ-ing. I intend to make quiche tonight and need eggs to do this. The store closes shortly, and there are no other places to get eggs. If making quiche is to be a real option for me tonight, then I *have* to get the eggs. I can't just be leaving open the possibility of getting eggs. The latter might be enough for there being the epistemic possibility that I'll make eggs tonight; for all I know, I might be able to make quiche tonight because I might have eggs. But the notion of possibility for intention must be stronger: if I intend to make quiche tonight, then I'm to ensure that eggs are available for cracking tonight. And if I am merely leaving open the possibility of getting eggs, then for all I know, making quiche might not be available to me tonight. For the moment, making quiche is a possibility, but as the night progresses, it very well may not be if I don't get those eggs. Thus, the proposal in terms of leaving open the possibility, if it is to capture means-end coherence, will require intending the means in a sense stronger than merely leaving open the possibility.

Suppose this is right, and that a proposed alternative to transitive settling will in one way or another inevitably be committed to some form of transitive settling in some instances. In light of the concerns raised by the Dilemma about Decision, it would appear that the only thing we could transitively settle would be of something that is not at a temporal remove – something right at this or the very next moment. This would be an unfortunate result. The problem is that for many decisions ahead of time, there simply isn't anything for me to do the very next moment. It seems that we're forced to hypothesize some special *volitional act*, a special settling of a matter – namely, the matter of being in the psychological state of intending or being decided. That is, one's decision to ϕ is not a settling of the matter of one's ϕ-ing but rather a settling of some fact about one's immediate psychology. But, first, we saw that this is – if anything – just to get the ball rolling and is not fully committal, at least with respect to the ϕ-ing. And, second, this seems to get things backward. I am not in a position simply to decide or settle what psychological state I'm in: I don't usually decide or intend to be in the state of being so decided. Rather, familiar cases of decision have to do with things like writing a paper, getting some exercise, or going to the store. In so deciding and transitively settling these matters, I am as a result settled$_i$ on going to the store, exercising, or writing. My being settled$_i$ on ϕ-ing thus exhibits something reminiscent of the transparency of the mental discussed in some of the literature on self-knowledge (e.g. Moran 2001). I am able to transitively settle (decide on) being in a psychological state of being settled$_i$ on going to the store by *deciding to go to the store*. But the settling involved in deciding to go to the store was what we were trying to get a handle on in the first place.[6]

So far, to avoid the Dilemma about Decision, we've considered a couple of proposed alternatives to transitive settling. But the normative element of settling, along with transparency, makes it challenging to avoid a seemingly problematic transitive settling.

3. Just a Matter of Normative Power?

Another reaction to the Dilemma about Decision is to seek some more plausible way in which one may directly affect one's prospective ϕ-ing. One approach makes use of the quite plausible thought that decision and intention involve commitment in some normative sense. Thus, we might draw inspiration from some recent literature on promising for the idea that in deciding to ϕ, I exercise a normative power to make it the case that I would be at fault if I were not to follow through.[7] Or, to use terms more familiar from the philosophy of action, my decision or intention has a distinctive world-to-mind direction of fit, so that I am able, simply by deciding and forming an intention to ϕ, to make it so that my future ϕ-ing is in some sense *fitting*. Although there may be skepticism in some quarters about the possibility of exercising normative power at will along these lines,[8] it would appear to be less objectionable than the thought that I could have a transcendent power to affect the future directly in a more concrete, non-normative sense. Nevertheless, I think that this reaction to the Dilemma about Decision is also problematic. The exclusive focus on appropriateness of the action – whether it is fitting – neglects what's fundamental to agency. My decision to ϕ is not just a matter of manipulating the normative facts, for example, to make it so that I'm at fault for not ϕ-ing. This concern with accountability may be a part of it, but it neglects what's crucial: securing the ϕ-ing. We've left out the more immediate influence we aspire to have over the future ϕ-ing. That being said, there does seem to be something about the idea of the manipulation of the normative facts that is suggestive. Perhaps the normativity in question needs somehow to be closer to agency than what we have in something like promising as it is standardly understood.

4. On the Way to a Non-Transcendent Conception of Transitive Settling: Governance

The first step toward avoiding the problematically magical understanding of transitive settling – one that is committed to some form of psychological action at a (temporal) distance – is to avoid assimilating transitive settling with some sort of immediate or direct causation. The only plausible way to exercise influence over one's future action is through a non-transcendent, temporally bound process. Transitive settling must involve some such process and cannot invoke immediate causal influence. So, how should this process be understood?

No doubt some process associated with being settled$_i$ on ϕ-ing figures causally in subsequent ϕ-ing. As was indicated earlier, when one settles$_T$ the matter, one will be settled$_i$. And there is no reason to deny that being settled$_i$ will have a causal role in bringing about the ϕ-ing. What more do we need to add to intransitive ϕ-ing to get a satisfactory understanding of transitive settling that avoids the magical action at a temporal distance?

One thing missing from the picture of getting the ball rolling (settling$_i$) is that the agent, when it comes time to act, is *governed* by the intention. Suppose, for example, that in the morning, I decide and intend to go to the lecture tomorrow, and to go by bike. As a result of the decision, my various activities become regulated and fit into a rational order. For example, later in the afternoon, I set about replacing the slowly leaking inner tube on the bike. My intention is not merely to fix the tire; I'm doing so in order to go to the lecture. The intention to go to the lecture tomorrow (by bicycle) regulates the present activity of fixing the tire. It explains why, for example, I'm fixing the tire now rather than on the weekend several days hence.

This example brings out how the intention doesn't merely trigger behavior but governs a stretch of it. Having formed the prior intention, I am, as the agent at the time of action, *subject to a rule* that entails in this case that I'm supposed to be fixing my tire this afternoon. In contrast to the proposal in terms of aiming, this notion of governance essentially involves the idea of there being an agent at the time of action: there has to be an agent to be governed, after all. The suggestion is that we explore the possibility of modeling transitive settling in terms of governance.

The rules that govern what I do are put in place by my prior decision and intention to attend the lecture. I would want to resist characterizing this "putting in place" as something like the act of issuing a decree. Most people don't think of their decisions explicitly in those terms. Nevertheless, the suggestion is that something like the regulation of action is what underlies transitive settling. That is, the transitive settling underlying decision is to be understood in terms of the governance of subsequent action by rules that apply in virtue of that decision.

How should we understand the relevant notion of governance so that it might serve as a model for transitive settling? The first and perhaps most important thing to notice is that when acting on a prior intention, I'm acting for the reasons that went into the decision. To return to our example, there's a point to my fixing the tire; it's not merely so that I can ride. The reason I'm fixing it is whatever consideration that went into my prior decision to attend the lecture and to go by bike.[9] Suppose that I decide to ϕ, but that when I go on to ϕ, I do so for reasons that have nothing to do with the considerations that went into the decision. Then it seems that I wasn't acting on the prior decision and that it didn't settle or govern subsequent behavior. So it seems that acting for reasons that went into the prior decision is necessary for the sort of governance we have in mind.[10]

But subsequently acting for the same reasons that went into the deciding so to act is not by itself sufficient for governance.[11] Explaining why points to what more is needed. If my decision is to settle beforehand the matter of my ϕ-ing, then it's important that when it comes time to act and no potentially defeating considerations have emerged, I must not arrive *anew* at the intention or decision to ϕ. After all, if it takes a renewed intention or decision to ϕ, then the matter was not (transitively) settled ahead of time by the decision. In light of this, consider how someone who has decided to ϕ but when it comes time to act, re-opens deliberation about whether to do so. After thinking the matter through, our fickle agent as it turns out decides again on ϕ-ing and decides to do so for the *same* reasons that went into his prior decision. Though the agent ϕ-s and does so for the same reasons that went into the prior decision, that prior decision was undermined in that it failed to settle and govern what the agent subsequently does. Thus, it seems that acting for the same reasons that went into the prior decision is not sufficient for diachronic intention-based governance.[12]

5. Intention Serves to Preserve and Transmit Reasons

If the agent is governed by the decision to φ, she must be intending to φ but not in a way that would be to intend it anew. At the time of action, there must be an *immediate uptake* of the intention deriving from the prior episode of decision-making. There is, in this uptake, a sensitivity to the content of the intention – it has to be understood – and also a sensitivity to the sorts of considerations that would call for revising it. But, absent defeaters, this uptake does not require the agent at the time of action to rehearse the reasons underlying the prior decision/intention and re-decide the matter. Rehearsing the reasons would be to take the matter of what to do as open when precisely the opposite is supposed to be the case (Roth 2004).

So, governance requires *immediate* uptake. I would argue that the immediate uptake of the intention – this *acting directly* on it so to speak – requires in turn the transmission of and entitlement to those reasons that went into the prior decision. Why think this? Well, it's unlikely that when one is acting directly on an intention, one is not at all acting for reasons. And I'm not sure how else reasons would enter into the picture of immediate uptake. Let's consider some possible alternatives for comparison. We've already noted that acting directly on the intention precludes the agent rethinking the matter, even if she arrives at the same reasons. And we've set aside cases where the agent slavishly adopts the prior intention with no regard to the underlying reasons for that prior intention, for that is a tyrannical form of governance that doesn't seem to be relevant for our purposes (see note 11). How else might we understand acting directly?

One proposal, in some ways attractive, is that one regards the prior intention and decision as a reasonable course of action to follow given that one thinks of oneself generally being reasonable, trustworthy, or reliable. One might think this because we have empirical evidence to that effect. Or there may be some a priori consideration that supports a default presumption of self-trust and hence warrants a reliance on one's own prior decisions.[13] I don't think that this can be the full story. First of all, it doesn't get right what we take intuitively to be the reason for which one is acting. The current suggestion is that my reason for φ-ing when acting on a prior intention to φ is that to act on my prior intention is to rely on a conclusion reached by a trustworthy resource – oneself in this case. But this reason of course cannot be a reason that would figure in my forming the decision in the first place. The reasons that do go into deciding, for example, to attend the lecture have to do with learning something, being entertained, supporting a friend, fulfilling duties to the department, etc. And wouldn't those be the reasons that answer why one is so acting?[14]

Second, the proposal distorts the normative force of the prior decision. The decision is supposed to settle what one is to do. But the current proposal would assign the prior decision the normative force of another consideration or reason, something to figure in one's current practical problem of whether to act on the prior decision to ϕ. In effect, one would treat one's prior self as an advisor or expert, and not as the agent that settled the matter. Whereas, in principle and absent defeaters, one does not even face the practical problem of whether, given the level of trustworthiness one attributes to one's past self, one should act on one's prior decision. One should just act in the way that has already been decided upon.[15]

We've considered several problematic accounts of how, when acting directly on an intention, one is related to reasons for which one is acting. When one is acting directly on an intention, one is acting for a reason. But the intention to ϕ does not itself count as a reason. One is, rather, acting for the reasons that went into deciding and intending so to act in the first place. And yet, one's connection with the reasons at the time of subsequent action (so that one counts as acting for those reasons) is *not* a matter of accessing the reasons by rethinking or redeciding the matter. For that would undermine my having settled the matter beforehand. My favored alternative, then, is that intentions serve to *preserve* reasons that went into decision. This thesis is distinct from the idea that the reason for acting on the intention is that we have empirical or even a priori justification to think that it is advisable to rely on one's prior self. The crucial role of intentions for our purposes is that they transmit the reasons that went into one's decision.[16]

Why speak of *intention* as preserving reasons? Why not just appeal to the idea that one *remembers* the intention and the underlying reasons? I think that invoking memory is fine, so long as we keep in mind that we are not merely retaining the belief that one intended or decided to ϕ and the belief that we so intended for such and such reasons. Rather, memory must be understood as retaining the intention itself, with all of its normative force (and thus the reasons underlying the intention).[17] The normative force of a *belief* that one has at some point decided or intended to ϕ is quite different from the normative force of the intention itself; the belief that one has intended lacks the relevant decisive or committal element characteristic of intention and is compatible with thinking that one was confused or mistaken in so intending. Only if memory is understood as preserving the intention itself with all of its normative force will we be able to make sense of having decided and settled some matter beforehand.

The entitlement to the reasons that went into the prior decision and the corresponding ability to act directly on the prior intention account for how one's prior intention governs subsequent action. This strikes me as the most promising way to make sense of the idea that one can transitively settle the matter by deciding ahead of time. Reasons transmission, by way of acting directly, is crucial for governance and transitive settling.[18]

Governance depends upon the willingness of the governed in taking up the relevant intentions. We're seeing now that it matters how the intentions are taken up if governance is going to serve as a model for transitive settling. One must act *directly* on the intention issued by the prior decision, and this requires the preservation of and entitlement to the reasons that went into the decision.

The proper response to the Dilemma about Decision accepts that our influence over some future state of affairs is non-transcendent. The temporal and causal process through which we exercise this influence must involve acting directly on a prior intention, with the intention understood as preserving the reasons that went into the prior decision/intention formation. I think that something like this is what's needed to do justice to the transitive settling implicit in decision without falling back to the picture of just getting the ball rolling.[19] Governance of later actions is secured through a process that involves the agent's immediate uptake of the intention and rational entitlement to the underlying reasons.

6. Diachronic Constraints on the Reasons for Which One Acts

I want to close with a remark on possible challenges to the view sketched here. The proposed solution to the Dilemma about Decision is committed to the idea that the reason for which one acts can sometimes depend, crucially, on what goes on at times outside the circumstances of the action. In particular, when acting on a prior intention, the reasons for which one is acting are those that figure in why it is that one so decided in the first place. The picture is one where fundamentally diachronic elements figure in the preservation and transmission of the reasons for which one acts.

If the prior decision has implications for the nature of the reasons for which one acts, it would presumably also have implications for cases where one fails to act. This might be used to criticize the reasons transmission thesis central to our solution to the Dilemma. Suppose I have conclusive reasons to ϕ, and then go on to decide and intend to ϕ. Suppose further that no defeaters emerge and it's time for me to ϕ. We've seen that if I do ϕ, then there's a rational credit to which I'm entitled. My ϕ-ing is for the reasons that went into my prior decision, and my ϕ-ing is done for those reasons even if I don't rehearse those reasons again. But, by the same token, it seems that if I were to fail to ϕ, then there is a *rational* failing – an automatic rational debit as it were. The prior decision and intention have secured the relevance of certain reasons and considerations for the rational assessment of my subsequent behavior, and my inaction – my failure to ϕ – has rational consequences. But suppose, in addition, that my failure to ϕ was simply due to my forgetting the prior decision. This may be unfortunate, but it doesn't seem right to count it as a rational failing. It appears, nevertheless, that on the view being defended here, I am forced to say that the failure to φ in the case of forgetting is a rational failing. So, this is a reason to reject the reasons transmission picture of intention.[20]

What to say? Suppose that I've decided to go to the store but forget to go. If this means that I simply am unable to recall the fact that I made this decision, then it does seem that this is a form of forgetfulness that doesn't count, in itself, as a sort of rational failing. It would be akin to the case where I forget that it was the beech tree and not the elm that has the smooth bark. Imagine, for example, that one cannot recall having an intention one had long ago, but one with no practical relevance now: at some point, I intended to learn some piece for the piano that came from a soundtrack of a movie I liked. Then I went on to learn it. Some years later, I quit playing altogether. It might be unfortunate to be unable to recall this interesting fact about what I had intended, but it is hardly a rational failing. However, as we noted earlier, memory isn't merely a matter of recalling facts or propositions. It is also for the preservation of "live" attitudes such as intention with its distinctive normative force, attitudes that figure in ongoing rational processes. If the forgetting in question is a failure to retain such an attitude with its normative force, then it does seem that such a forgetting amounts to a genuine rational failing. The intention as reason preservation thesis gets this right.[21]

In conclusion, we can take seriously the idea that practical matters can be settled ahead of time, without taking on board an implausible action at a diachronic distance. Intentions preserve and transmit the reasons for action that went into one's decision to act. Our entitlement to those very reasons when we act directly on the intention is the crucial missing element of the transitive settling fundamental to diachronic agency.[22]

Notes

1 I leave for another occasion the implications the distinction between transitive and intransitive settling might have for debate over cognitivism about intention—the view that to intend to φ entails belief that one will φ. See Grice (1971), Harman (1986), Velleman (1989), Bratman (1987), Setiya (2008), and Paul (2009a, b).
2 As with the case with Moore's Paradox, what one is rationally committed to when one judges or decides (or when one has corresponding attitudes like belief or intention) extends beyond and is distinct from facts about one's psychology. Thus, even though there are very many true propositions that I don't believe, I am never in a position rationally to believe "P and I don't believe P". And although many of my beliefs are false, I am not in a position to say "not-P, and yet I believe P". Likewise, the suggestion is that one is never in a position rationally to think, for example, of some specific φ-ing one has decided upon that one won't do it. And this is the case even though it is quite possible, and indeed often the case that one does not live up to one's decisions.
3 Might we account for the planning subsequent to the φ-ing as a matter of intransitive settling conjoined with a cognitivism about intention? That is, with intransitive settling and a belief that one will φ, we might think that we can make plans downstream from the φ-ing. Cognitivists will have to tell

some story about the belief in φ-ing, and my worry is that any plausible story along these lines will presuppose transitive settling: for central cases, the belief that one will φ is grounded on φ-ing being transitively settled (or at least the transitive settling of some more immediate ψ-ing by means of which one φ-s).

4 See Bratman (1987, 5) for the imagery of intention's ghostly hand reaching to the future to control at a distance what one does then. He conjures the image precisely to convey its implausibility.

5 A number of views might fall under the generic proposal of aiming sketched here. These would include views that see transitive settling as merely initiating a causal process. It also includes views that invoke strategies of precommitment, where deciding or intending is compared to a situation where one has a strong incentive to follow through on the intention. To give an extreme example, you hire a thug to beat you up if you don't act in accord with your own decision. On the precommitment versions of the aiming view, the agent is recognized as on the scene at the time of action. But the agent, in virtue of having made some prior decision, faces certain costs in failing to act on that decision. These costs serve as reason to act in accord with the prior decision. Suppose the agent nevertheless acts against the prior decision. Then the fault, again, would lie with the agent when she intended in the first place; after all, she didn't set up the incentives properly. Even if the agent at the time of action was confused about the incentives and should have followed through, this confusion seems to be a different kind of normative or rational failure from that of not acknowledging the force of the prior intention. And, again, the relevant normative failure, on this sort of aiming approach, lies with the agent qua intender who failed to foresee how the agent at the time of action would be confused about the incentives associated with following through. For a critical survey of a number of proposals that arguably fall under the heading of aiming, see Ferrero (2006). Ferrero finds a number of things objectionable about these approaches, but a recurring concern is that of manipulation that compromises the rational governance of the agent by reasons at the time of action (e.g., at 103), whereas my concern is that these proposals don't capture the normative force of the prior intention for the agent at the time of action.

6 I think that in transitively settling something, you come into a distinctive mental state. But this doesn't entail that entering into such a state is itself an action.

7 Shiffrin (2008), Owens (2006).

8 Hume (1740/1978, 524) (3.2.5.14).

9 This is an important point about how reasons for action are involved with acting on prior intentions, which is not to say that it is not in need of some theoretical discussion, elaboration, and qualification (see Roth 2017). The observation can be reinforced by considering some familiar problems agents run into. For example, sometimes in doing something I forget my reason for doing it. Nevertheless, I am doing it for the reasons that went into my having decided and intended to do it. Think of when you go down the hall to the main departmental office but suffer a senior moment and forget why you were going. The reason is the one that went into why you earlier decided to go – to fetch a printout. That you are acting on the intention to go to the office is enough to ensure that you are acting for the reason that went into forming the intention – even if that reason has slipped your mind.

10 What about cases where one slavishly acts to conform to one's prior decision irrespective of the reasons? I suppose that this might be a form of governance, albeit of a tyrannical sort. Acting for reasons that went into the prior decision would seem to be necessary for a non-tyrannical form of self-governance.

11 Might there be supplemental reasons, new reasons that support acting in accord with prior intentions? Maybe. And I don't rule out that reasons that support acting on one's prior intentions more generally. But the main issue is the decision, and (as we shall see) how it and the resulting intention transmit reasons. Governance requires that we not be acting on new reasons in a way that potentially challenges the authority of the prior decision; the new reasons might reinforce the authority of the prior decision. Of course, sometimes there are considerations – one-off defeaters or more systemic reasons – for not being governed by one's prior intentions.
12 This would seem to be an objection to Ferrero, who doesn't think that diachronic agency requires that intentions and decisions need settle what one does in the future (2006, 111, 112). Rather, the agent is settled on φ-ing insofar as there are conclusive reasons in favor of φ-ing and she has a continued sense of the force and authority of those reasons (113). Ferrero goes on to suggest that this assessment of the reasons and sense of their stability then warrants a prediction that one will φ. One concern here is how to understand the idea of a "sense of stability" of the reasons. It seems that if the reasons are indeed recognized as stable, then in a sense, one would (absent defeaters) take them for granted. But it seems that what Ferrero says amounts to the suggestion that one retains with respect to stable reasons the sort of attention, indeed vigilance, more appropriate for reasons that are in flux and hard to assess. (Ferrero denies that one must continually renew an explicit judgment about reasons (117); rather, there is a direct acknowledgment of the reasons in one's conduct. I might agree with this if I had a better sense of what he means by this.) In any case, decisions often are made in cases where the reasons aren't so dispositive – Buridan cases, competing perhaps incommensurable values, etc. Ferrero's account would seem not to capture any form of settledness of decisions in such cases.
13 Burge (1993), see also Luthra (2017).
14 Roth (2017), Heeney (2019, 5).
15 A further worry raised by Bratman (1987) is that thinking of the prior intention as a reason leads to a problematic bootstrapping.
16 For discussion and defense, see Roth (2017) and Heeney (2019). For views like this in the theoretical case, see Schmitt (2006), Weatherson (2016), and on some interpretations, Burge (1993). Schmitt (2006, 221) also cites Roth (2003) as defending a version of the view in the practical case.
17 This is a way of interpreting Burge's views on preservative role. See Burge (1993).
18 In acting on a prior intention, one is entitled to the reasons that went into the decision. I've argued elsewhere that this entitlement justifies the *authority* one has in deciding and settling matters ahead of time. The current argument is somewhat different. The entitlement and the ability to act directly on a prior intention are what account not only for the authority or legitimacy of the prior self in deciding and settling the matter but also for the very ability of the prior self to do so.
19 Though this is not to deny a role the norms and regularities associated with being intransitively settled.
20 See Moss (2015, 3) citing Williamson (2000).
21 Moss says that it is not irrational for having imperfect powers of evidence retention. That of course is true; it's implausible to require perfect powers of retention as a condition of rationality. But that doesn't mean that having some powers of retention is not a condition of rationality. (The argument against preservation thus trades on a confusion between forgetting that is merely an inability to recall a fact, and a forgetting that genuinely undermines some ongoing rational process. If anything, it seems that we need the preservation

thesis to get this case of forgetting right. If we were to hold a synchronic picture, it seems that as soon as one forgets and loses the attitude in question along with its corresponding normative force, then there is no special rational significance in my failure to act. That doesn't seem right.)

22 A version of this paper was presented at the *Time in Action* workshop at the Center for the Study of Mind in Nature at Oslo, organized by Carla Bagnoli. Thanks to everyone there, including Sarah Paul, Christophe Salvat, Luca Ferrero, Michael Bratman, Franco Trivigno, and especially Carla Bagnoli.

References

Bratman, Michael. 1987. *Intentions, Plans, and Practical Reason*. Cambridge, MA: Harvard University Press.

Burge, Tyler. 1993. "Content Preservation". *Philosophical Review* 102, 457–488.

Ferrero, Luca. 2006. "Three Ways of Spilling Ink Tomorrow". In E. Baccarini and S. Prijic-Samarzija, eds. *Rationality in Belief and Action*. Rijeka: Faculty of Philosophy, University of Rijeka, 95–127.

Grice, H. P. 1971. "Intention and Uncertainty". *Proceedings of the British Academy* 57, 263–279.

Harman, Gilbert. 1986. *Change in View*. Cambridge, MA: MIT Press.

Heeney, Matthew. 2020. "Diachronic Agency and Practical Entitlement". *European Journal of Philosophy* 28:1, 177–198. Doi:10.1111/ejop.12479

Hume, David. 1740/1978. *A Treatise of Human Nature*. 2nd ed. Edited by L. A. Selby Bigge and P. H. Nidditch. Oxford: Oxford University Press.

Luthra, Yannig. 2017. "Self-Trust and Knowledge in Action". *Journal of Philosophy* 114:9, 471–491.

Moran, Richard. 2001. *Authority and Estrangement: An Essay on Self-Knowledge*. Princeton: Princeton University Press.

Moss, Sarah. 2015. "Time Slice Epistemology & Action Under Uncertainty". In Tamar Szabó Gendler and John Hawthorne, eds. *Oxford Studies in Epistemology*. Oxford: Oxford University Press, 172–194.

Owens, David. 2006. "A Simple Theory of Promising". *Philosophical Review* 115, 51–77.

Paul, Sarah. 2009a. "Intention, Belief, and Wishful Thinking: Setiya on Practical Knowledge". *Ethics* 119:3, 546–557.

Paul, Sarah. 2009b. "How We Know What We're Doing". *Philosopher's Imprint* 9:11.

Roth, Abraham Sesshu. 2003. "Practical Intersubjectivity". In F. Schmitt, ed. *Socializing Metaphysics: The Nature of Social Reality*. Lanham, MD: Rowman & Littlefield, 65–91.

Roth, Abraham Sesshu. 2004. "Shared Agency and Contralateral Commitments". *Philosophical Review* 113, 359–410.

Roth, Abraham Sesshu. 2017. "Entitlement to Reasons for Action". In D. Shoemaker, ed. *Oxford Studies in Agency and Responsibility*, Vol. 4, Oxford: Oxford University Press, 75–92.

Schmitt, Frederick. 2006. "Testimonial Justification and Transindividual Reasons". In J. Lackey and E. Sosa, eds. *The Epistemology of Testimony*. Oxford: Oxford University Press, 193–224.

Setiya, Kieran. 2008. "Practical Knowledge". *Ethics* 118:3, 388–409.
Shiffrin, Seana. 2008 "Promising, Intimate Relationships, and Conventionalism". *Philosophical Review* 117:4, 481–524.
Velleman, J. David. 1989. *Practical Reflection*. Princeton: Princeton University Press.
Weatherson, Brian. 2016. "Memory, Belief, and Time". *Canadian Journal of Philosophy* 45, 692–715.
Williamson, Timothy. 2000. *Knowledge and Its Limits*. Oxford: Oxford University Press.

7 Sticking to It and Settling
Commitments, Normativity, and the Future[1]

Caroline T. Arruda

One important feature of our lives as agents is our capacity to settle on courses of action and to stick to plans that we make, things that we take to matter, and ways of living our lives. These things can be mundane, such as settling on exercising regularly, or more meaningful, such as sticking to our moral judgments about consuming non-human animals.

This is arguably a central feature of our capacity for agency in that it underscores the diachronic nature of agency itself as well as the diachronic "frame", for lack of a better phrase, that we place on our long-term plans. There are many ways that we might secure what I will dub *agential stability*, or our capacity to stick to the (largely, but not exclusively, long-term) plans that we make, the future-directed intentions that we form, the wholehearted decisions that we make, the policies we adopt, and the aspirations that we have, among others. Here, the suggestion seems to be that intentions alone are not sufficient for the kind of agential stability that we think characterizes robust agency over time.[2] Or, perhaps, we might think that certain kinds of projects or plans are particularly difficult and thus require extra effort on our parts to realize.

Numerous aspects of agency have received significant attention in the literature as sources of what I am calling agential stability, including plans (Bratman 1987, 1999a, 1999b, 2007a, 2007b, 2007c, 2014, 2015), resolutions (Holton 2009), endorsements (Frankfurt 1998a/1971), and being wholehearted (Frankfurt 1998b/1987), among others (e.g., Chartier 2018; Singh forthcoming). In this chapter, I would like to focus on an intuitive aspect of how we might directly achieve agential stability that has received comparatively less attention (with the notable exception of Marušić 2015). Namely, our capacity to make commitments and to be guided by them in our future actions.

At first glance, commitments seem well suited to help us to stick to it, although they are surely not the only way of doing so. People often think that commitments are designed to secure various aspects of the way we exercise our agency over and through time. These include resisting temptation (Holton 2009; Marušić 2015); blocking re-deliberation (Bratman 2004, 2014, 2018; Hinchman 2014; Holton 2009); helping us

DOI: 10.4324/9780429259845-10

to do what we correctly think that we are unlikely to do (Marušić 2015); and ensuring (or providing one route by which to ensure) the diachronic stability of our intentions or decisions (Morton 2013; Morton and Paul 2019; Paul 2021). Commitments seem well suited for these tasks because we think that commitments have at least some characteristics that seem to directly contribute to agential stability. *Prima facie*, they[3]: are forward-looking, are akin to self-directed promises, have potential (although defeasible) forward-looking normative force, and may serve as a way of securing and representing our perseverance (or helping us to strengthen our will) (e.g., Holton 2009; and, to a lesser degree, Morton and Paul [2019] on "grit").

To see how these putative characteristics might enable commitments to contribute to agential stability in the ways described earlier, consider the following two examples:

Example 1: I commit myself to going running each morning at 5:00.
Example 2: I commit myself to being a good friend.

Notwithstanding the fact that (1) and (2) are very different kinds of commitments[4], they shed light on why, on face value, commitments seem well suited for securing agential stability and, upon closer examination, why the situation is more complex than it may initially appear. If we focus on (1), then we see perhaps why commitments may serve some of the functions proposed (although, as I will show, we would be wrong to think that they do so). Intuitively, if I have made the commitment to go running each morning at 5:00, I, at the very least, feel the force of that commitment when I am tempted to ignore my alarm when it goes off at 4:30. At most, I find the commitment to be a source of *reasons* to continue to exercise in that I take the commitment to represent my considered judgments about what is best for me and which I endorse. At least, it is a kind of self-directed promise that I might be loath to break, or perhaps it is a type of conative tool to ensure my perseverance. If any of these glosses is correct, it suggests that commitments themselves carry some (normative, psychological or motivational) force according to which we ought to stick to them. If so, this intuitive picture of commitments suggests that they are, at least, *indirect sources* of agential stability, where stability is understood in terms of our capacity for stick-to-it-ness.

Unfortunately, the situation is more complicated than it may initially have seemed. To see why, consider Example (2), as (1) is not the only type of commitment that we can make. Example (2) is arguably as common, if not more common, than Example (1). Why? More frequently, we commit ourselves to doing things about which we already feel strongly.[5] What's more, we do so to *reflect* this attitude, not necessarily to rebut temptation or to settle our deliberations, among other possibilities.

Example (2) highlights this combination of attitudes that often ground the formation of a commitment, while (1) is, at least typically, the kind of commitment we make precisely because we think we are unlikely to be motivated to do something we plan to do.[6] If this is correct, then we should doubt that commitments are the *source* of the relevant kind of stability in the way often supposed; rather, as I will argue, they are the *vehicles for* it. For the moment, however, these two examples highlight the need for us to investigate more closely our intuition that commitments provide agential stability in the relevant sense *just by virtue of making them*.

To do so, it is necessary to do the following: (1) to determine the specific kind(s) of stability that agential stability comprises; (2) to return to the question of what a commitment is to determine whether it could provide this kind of stability; and (3) to determine whether this (these) kind(s) of stability is (are) connected in any substantive way to normativity, and if so, how so.

In what follows, I make both a negative and (the beginnings of) a positive argument. With these aims in mind, I begin with the negative argument (Sections 1 and 2). I first identify four types of stability that commitments could plausibly provide, using the two guiding examples mentioned earlier to illustrate each type (Section 1). I then show that, by returning to the question of what a commitment is, no plausible picture of commitments can show how they directly confer any of these four types of stability (Section 2).

This result may seem counterintuitive, given the compelling intuitive picture of commitments with which I began this chapter. I argue, contrary to this, that commitments *do* play a role in securing agential stability, but not in the intuitively familiar way (Sections 2.4–3). If commitments provide any sort of agential stability, it is in virtue of their relationship to what we care about, what has import for us or what we value. In this regard, commitments are vehicles for, but not the sources of, what I call normative agential stability. But they are these kinds of vehicles for unfamiliar reasons. Commitments are not themselves normative; rather, it is the reasons that we have to form the commitment in the first place that are the sources of normativity (and, perhaps, stability).

1. Agential Stability

In this section, I begin by outlining an ecumenical picture of what, if anything, might constitute agential stability in the sense of agents helping themselves to "stick to it". I will then identify four types of agential stability that commitments seem to provide. This sets the stage for evaluating whether commitments indeed provide any of these types of agential stability, to which I turn in Section 2.

1.1. Agential Stability: An Ecumenical View

To determine whether commitments can secure agential stability, it is necessary to narrow the focus of the question at hand. There are many ways that *general* agential stability, understood as diachronic stability, can be achieved. Most notably, we might appeal to the rational requirements on intentions (Bratman 2018; Broome 2007), the role of plans in unifying our intentions (Bratman 1987, 2007a, b, c, 2018: esp. Introduction), and the role of intending to intend, among other options. But my interest here is in how agents do this *explicitly and in a fashion that distinguishes what agents achieve from the mere diachronic stability of intentions*. Agential stability concerns how an agent relates to her capacity for agency in ways that explicitly ensure that she sticks to what she intends to do. By contrast, diachronic stability concerns the structures of agency that enable agents to be stable over time when they exercise their agency regardless of whether stability is their direct aim.

Arguably, commitments seem like a natural way for agents to exercise this capacity in an explicit fashion such that they aim at their own agential stability. So what we need to know is whether, indeed, commitments rightfully play this role.

To do so, we need a set of sufficient conditions for agents to count as exercising this capacity, with the caveat that there might be many ways to do so. It is sufficient for agents to exercise their capacity to "stick to it", where sticking to it is a form of agential stability, when they meet the following conditions[7]:

1. At time t, an agent intends to ϕ for reason r, which can be motivating or justifying, at time $t+n$.
2. Φ-ing is sufficiently important or significant (in instrumental, moral, rational, or broadly normative terms) *for the agent* in question such that she *also* explicitly adopts the goal at time t of exercising her agency such that she ensures she intends to ϕ at $t+n$.[8]
3. Adopting the goal in (2) is, as the agent understands it, a way of capturing her interest in sticking to what she intends to do, but it may not be sufficient for her to be successful in doing so.

For the purposes of evaluating the claim about the putative relationship between commitments and agential stability, I shall focus on how agents go about adopting the goal described in (2). Although there are likely many ways that agents might do so, commitments are *prima facie* one way of doing so, given the aforementioned characteristics that they are often thought to have. To determine whether this is true, however, we need a clearer picture of the candidate types of agential stability that commitments might be able to provide.

1.2. Types of Agential Stability[9]

There are numerous ways that agential stability can be achieved. The question that I seek to answer here, however, concerns the types of agential stability commitments might plausibly provide *when agents explicitly make them*.

Stability and "sticking to it" are temporal notions, so the assumption is that making and retaining a commitment does something for us, both over and through time. The question is what might commitments do and why might they be uniquely suited for accomplishing these things (as opposed to merely psychologically functional in these ways but easily replaced by other kinds of attitudes or practices).

With this narrow focus in mind, let's consider the candidate types of agential stability[10]:

Type 1: The stability of intentions over time[11]
Type 2: Blocking or constraining re-deliberation
Type 3: Perseverance or strength of will (broadly understood as types of psychological stability)
Type 4: Normative stability

Given the ecumenical picture of agential stability outlined in the previous section, it is important to note that while we assume that agential stability is primarily a *normative notion*, it need not be understood as such. Rather, if agential stability is understood as an explicit goal that agents can adopt and purse, then there may very well be multiple types of stability that agents can achieve. This includes indirect sources of stability, such as that described in (1) and (2), as well as the psychological or motivational stability of (3) and the stability that comes from the pressure to adhere to what we ought (rationally, instrumentally, morally, etc.) to do. In this regard, we can tease apart the question of whether commitments are the *source* of agential stability from the question of whether they bear normative force and, thereby, provide stability. My focus, at least for the moment, is the former; however, any account of commitments' ability to provide agential stability should be consistent with an account of what, if any, normative force they properly have.

Each of types (1)–(4) represents different kinds of agential stability, but they are all kinds of stability that agents can explicitly adopt such that they are using their capacity to "stick to" what they intend, plan or aspire to do. At the most general level, we have (1), which suggests that commitments enrich or make garden-variety intentions more robust. Since the focus here is on agents making *explicit commitments* with an eye toward explaining how agent secure (at least some of the conditions for) sticking to it, it is important to distinguish (1) from the more wide-spread view in philosophy of action that forming intentions brings on stream commitments, grounded in rational requirements, to follow through on those intentions.[12]

Although not unrelated to (1), (2) captures the kind of stability that we achieve when we block re-deliberation about what we have already decided to do. Blocking re-deliberation contributes to the diachronic stability of our intentions, but it is not directly concerned with it. Rather, it secures the stability of an agent's previous decisions about what to do, and, to a lesser degree, their evaluation of the reasons in favor of that decision. Of course, blocking re-deliberation does not directly ensure that we will indeed follow through on the conclusions of those deliberations, as this is a question of the rational requirements on intention formation and the normative force of our previous decisions. Other things being equal, however, if commitments can serve to block re-deliberation, then perhaps they can secure the kind of agential stability that it represents.

In contrast to (1) and (2), which target the kind of agential stability that accompanies the diachronic stability of our intentions and the non-revisability of the conclusions of our practical deliberation, types (3) and (4) describe rather different kinds of agential stability. Type (3) concerns psychological stability in the face of both *external* challenges (such as conditions that we know might tempt us to act in ways other than planned) and internal challenges (e.g., *accidie*) to an agent's ability to stick to it.[13] As an aside, one might think that "perseverance" and "strength of will" are not equivalent.[14] They are not, at least insofar as perseverance captures our ability to *continue to aim at our ends even when it is difficult to do so,* whereas strength of will captures our ability to *withstand potential underminers to our pursuit of a given end.*[15] I group them here only insofar as, vis à vis the question of agential stability, both represent types of what we might classify as "psychological stability" for agents. Finally, (4) captures the stability that we typically think comes from an agent's appropriate uptake of those things that have normative force for her.

2. Can Commitments Provide Any of These Types of Agential Stability?

With these types of agential stability in view, I shall now consider whether commitments can secure any of them. First, however, a few preparatory remarks are in order. The question to answer here is not simply "Do commitments secure agential stability?", for answering this question has to be guided by some clear criteria. Instead, the following questions will guide my inquiry:

> Q1. Can agents, in making commitments, actually secure the type of agential stability in question at least some of the time, and if so, how so?

Q2. Is this picture of the relationship between commitments and agential stability consistent with a coherent conception of what commitments plausibly are?

Notice that, unlike the ecumenical view of agential stability outlined in Section 1, the idea here is that we need to know whether agents can use commitments when exercising their capacity for explicitly securing their agential stability *such that they have a chance at* actually being successful in doing so, hence (Q1). The motivation for including (Q2) is, however, different. It is worth noting that commitments have received little *direct* philosophical attention. There are exceptions to this generalization (e.g., Arruda ms; Bratman 2004, 2014; Brewer 2003; Chang 2009, 2013; Chartier 2018; Dorsey 2016; Elster 1985, 2000; Gilbert 2013, 2014, 2018; Heim 2015; Hieronymi 2006, 2009; Hinchman 2010; Holton 2009; Killmister 2017; Liberman and Schroeder 2016; Marušić 2015; Michael and Pacherie 2015; Ross 2012; Roth 2004; Schroeder 2013; Sen 1977, 2005; Shpall 2014; Townsend 2015), but very few works engage directly with the question of what a commitment is (cf. Arruda ms; Chartier 2018; Shpall 2014). Since this is not my direct concern in this chapter, I will consider whether different types of (often implicit) pictures of what commitments are fit with the picture of how they might provide any of these four types of agential stability.

Second, a caveat. Some views, such as Bratman's (2004, 2014), posit commitments as part of our general arsenal of stability-ensuring features of agency. On these views, commitments accompany other kinds of attitudes we form (e.g., intentions) even when we do not explicitly make them. This is not the kind of case on which I focus in what follows, and nothing about what I argue here bears on these claims. Instead, I am interested in cases where we make explicit commitments as a way to self-consciously ensure our agential stability by exercising our capacity to stick to it. In this regard, the guiding examples will be used to illustrate each of the aforementioned types of stability: (Example 1) "I commit myself to going running each morning at 5:00"; (Example 2) "I commit myself to being a good friend".

With these examples in mind, let's consider each type of stability outlined earlier.

2.1. *The Stability of Intentions Over Time*

How might commitments (at least partially) secure the stability of intentions over time (for both present and future actions)? A variety of answers have been given, but here is one way of glossing them: commitments, in being future-oriented, provide a link between the intentions we form and the time at which we execute them such that agents might self-consciously aim at securing their own agential stability in making them.

To evaluate this claim, we first need a clearer picture of what a commitment is. In this context, there are two options:

a. Commitments are attitudinal states toward other, first-order attitudes, including (but not limited to) intentions, desires, evaluative beliefs, etc. (Arruda *ms*; Chang 2009, 2013),[16,17,18]
b. Commitments establish a normative relation between a mental state or action and its object (another mental state or action). (Ross 2012; Shpall 2014)[19]

Although each of these claims could be the subject of extensive discussion, the purpose here is to identify two broad classes of views of commitments in order to evaluate the claim about the relationship between commitments and agential stability. The most obvious question that arises is what it means to call commitments 'attitudinal states'. Although I cannot fully answer this question here, we simply need a *prima facie* plausible view. One plausible view is to think of commitments as attitudes toward our other, first-order attitudes. We do not make commitments unless we already hold first-order attitudes about the value of a thing, some goal that we have, etc. If this is right, then they are attitudinal states that agents understand as strengthening the first-order attitude toward which they are directed.

It is worth noting here that (a) and (b) are not mutually exclusive in that one might take commitments to be psychological states *and* to establish the normative relation in question. I take this point, and, in one sense, answering the question of whether commitments can do so is one upshot of argument in this chapter. For the purposes of determining first, however, *whether* they indeed can establish any kind of agential stability (and whether that stability has normative import), it is necessary to treat (a) and (b) as analytically distinct. This is because part of determining whether they can do so depends on what commitments are.

With these two views of what commitments are in view, let's now turn to considering whether they can provide the following kind of agential stability:

Type 1: The stability of intentions over time[20]

If commitments are attitudinal states of the kind described in (a) above, then can they provide this kind of agential stability? There are, I contend, three reasons why they cannot do so, and thus this picture of the relationship between commitments and agential stability does not provide a satisfactory answer to (Q1). First, it is unclear that they can ensure that intentions are stable over time even if they provide agents with a way of being motivated to stick to their intentions. Although motivational strength is one necessary condition for intentions' stability, it is not sufficient. What's more, it is unclear whether they even reliably provide it, for they surely do not provide it by conceptual necessity. Second, even if commitments alone could provide this kind of motivational strength, they would not play a pivotal role in securing the stability of intentions over time; they would rather play a role in explaining how agents take their previously formed intentions seriously or feel some sort of conative pressure to follow through on them. But this does not concern the stability of intentions; it secures the stability of agents' relationship to their intentions and how they regard them relative to other intentions they are considering forming in their stead. Third, it is unclear what commitments would add to the arsenal of tools we already have to guarantee the underlying stability of intentions, including the roles of future-directed decisions (Ferrero 2010), self-governing policies (e.g., Bratman 2018), and the role of rational requirements on intentions (Broome 2007), among others. Each of these aspects of agency seems well suited to ensure the stability of intentions in various forms, particularly the role of self-governing policies (whether understood in the robust sense that Bratman intends 'plans' or more weakly understood as loose, outer-constraints on our future decisions). Commitments, under any reading, do not seem to *add* to the stability of intentions in ways that these well-established features of our agency already help to secure.

But even if we were willing to grant that motivational strength of this kind is somewhat conceptually close to the agential stability that successfully exercising one's capacity for stick-to-it-ness involves, there is an additional problem for this view. It concerns the putative answer it would provide to (Q2). To see why, recall Examples (1) and (2) raised earlier. Other things being equal, these two examples represent different kinds of commitments. Example (1) is primarily self-directed, whereas (2) is primarily other-directed.

If indeed commitments were able to provide the stability of intentions over time described earlier, this would produce an overly narrow picture of what commitments are. Namely, it would render all of them, whether superficially other- or self-directed, as fundamentally self-directed. This is because the commitment's true, underlying content would concern the agent's intention, in (2), to be a good friend and securing the stability of that intention. But this commitment is not, *ex hypothesi*, primarily or fundamentally self-directed; its content is arguably other-directed *even if* we are willing to grant that it *also involves* self-directed concern regarding following through on our intentions. While it may be true that this conception of commitments is, in the end, the correct picture,[21] it is not *prima facie* obviously true. So the combination of treating commitments as psychological states – option (a) – with the claim that commitments can secure the stability of our intentions over time ends up providing an incoherent answer to (Q2).

But there is another option. Perhaps instead of treating commitments as attitudinal states – option (a) – we would get more traction by treating them as normative relations between an attitude an agent has and a state of affairs or an object. This is option (b), which Shpall (2014) articulates in detail. While Shpall does not limit his account to intentions, we can easily apply it to the question at hand. If commitments are understood in this way, can they provide a way for agents to secure the stability of their intentions over time, where this is understood as a form of agential stability?

Recall that the question of stability or "sticking to it" is a question both about future-directed intentions and their persistence and about the non-revisability of present intentions that have a substantive diachronic expression. With this in mind, there are two problems that arise when understanding commitments as establishing normative relations between an agent's attitudinal states and an object or state of affairs.

Let's begin with (Q1). On this picture of the relationship between commitments and agential stability, we encounter two distinct problems in answer to this first guiding question. Let's assume that commitments can be coherently understood as establishing a normative relationship between an agent's attitudinal states (e.g., an intention) and a state of affairs (e.g., the realization of the intention or the revision of the intention).[22] The relevant question here is whether, in providing this specification of what a commitment is, we can identify a path to explaining how it secures, at least some of the time, the stability of those intentions.

I think that this account of commitments does not successfully show how commitments secure intentions' stability over time. It is not clear what commitments so understood would add to a theory of the *stability* of intentions, at least on the assumption that some rational requirements plausibly apply to them. Regardless of whether these requirements are wide or narrow in scope, the point is that the rational requirements on intentions provide for their stability in the sense under consideration here. Following Broome (2005: 324), I define 'requirement' simply as a standard that governs relations among attitudes, including but not limited to beliefs and intentions. Brunero (2008) further develops this definition in terms that do not privilege either the wide- or the narrow-scope view: "[T]he requirements of rationality specify *conflicts among attitude-states* which we should resolve or avoid if we are to be rational. An attitude-state could consist in either the presence or absence of an attitude" (1). In this regard, what it is to conform to rational requirements is to lack conflicts among one's attitudes, whether this requires that one acquires an attitude that one previously did not have or that one rejects an attitude that one currently holds. In this context, if they are narrow in scope, then agents must follow through on the intention to ϕ. If they are wide in scope, agents must either follow through on the intention to ϕ or revise their decision to ϕ. As long as there are some rational requirements on intentions, it is unclear what, if anything, commitments would *add* to their stability over time above and beyond the force of these requirements. In this regard, this combination of claims – viz., that commitments are normative relations and that commitments secure (at least some of the time) the stability of intentions over time – provides an unsatisfying answer to (Q1).

Now, perhaps what they do add is motivational in nature. Nothing about the picture I have thus far laid out rules this out. But this would not be consistent with the picture of what a commitment is that is under consideration. If commitments establish normative relations between an agent's attitudes and some state of affairs logically or conceptually related to that attitude (e.g., by realizing the intention in question), then this relationship is not primarily motivational in nature. It is not logically dependent on an agent's conative states even if its realization for a particular agent at a particular time is. This suggests that this combination of claims produces an equally unsatisfactory answer to (Q2).

Perhaps instead they explain how we understand or represent these rational requirements when we form intentions. If this were correct, then it would require that we explain the sense in which commitments are psychologically efficacious for specific individuals, given their motivational psychology, *in relation to* their understanding of how the rational requirements on intentions apply to them. But this would require us to understand commitments in psychological, not normative, terms. This is inconsistent with the proposal under consideration, and thus it is not a promising solution for this problem.

By way of conclusion, it appears that there is no promising way to show that commitments, understood either as normative relations or as psychological states, can at least sometimes directly secure the stability of intentions over time. Additionally, we can draw the following lesson from testing various views of what commitments *are* in conjunction with this claim about their role in securing agential stability. A view akin to Shpall's distances commitments too much from the lives of agents and what has conative force for them. By contrast, the idea that commitments are psychological states places commitments too close to agents' psychological lives such that their putative force is undermined.

2.2. Blocking or Constraining Re-Deliberation

The previous view of how commitments might secure agential stability proved unfruitful. But there are other types of agential stability that they may very well play a role in securing. In this section, I will consider the claim that commitments secure the following type of agential stability:

Type 2: Blocking or constraining re-deliberation

Here, the suggestion is that when agents make commitments, they secure agential stability (again, at least some of the time) by blocking or constraining how and when they re-deliberate or reconsider decisions they have already made.

In broad brushstrokes, consider how this view might explain the relationship between commitments and agential stability. Let's do so with reference to Example 1. In that case, I made a commitment to go running at 5:00 each morning. On the view under consideration, the suggestion is that commitments serve to block my potential re-deliberation about whether to go running when the alarm goes off and I am tempted to go back to sleep. In this regard, commitments might serve to mitigate the effects of weakness of will, but they would also strengthen those things upon which I have already deliberated *and* about which I am (evaluatively) settled. Similarly, commitments might further serve to specify defeasibility conditions on re-deliberation. In Example 1, we might think that the commitment to go running at 5:00 each morning contains at least an implicit set of conditions regarding when it would be permissible to override the commitment (e.g., illness, injury, etc.).

Broadly speaking, both Holton's (2009) account of resolutions and Bratman's (2004, 2014, 2018) view of self-governing policies are examples of this view.[23] As in the previous section, let's consider how well each of these views of what commitments are meshes with the claim that they secure (at least some of the time) agential stability by blocking re-deliberation.

Let's begin with the claim that commitments are a type of resolution. Resolutions surely provide a clear route for blocking re-deliberation (Holton 2009) and, in this regard, they do secure a form of agential stability.[24] The same is true of policies for self-government. So the real question is whether commitments are coherently understood in either of these two ways. This may seem like a less significant question than whether commitments, so understood, provide agential stability by blocking re-deliberation. Recall, however, that one of the guiding questions is the following:

Q2. Is this picture of the relationship between commitments and agential stability consistent with a coherent conception of what commitments plausibly are?

I contend the real problem with this view is that it presents an incoherent picture of what commitments are, thereby failing to meet the bar set out in (Q2).

Consider first the claim that commitments, in virtue of being a type of resolution, block re-deliberation. The problem here is that if commitments are understood as a species of resolution, we end up being unable to distinguish conceptually or functionally between the two. Why should this matter? There are two reasons why. First, resolutions are designed to help us do things that we judge we will have trouble doing, while commitments need not serve this function. Consider the aforementioned

Example 2. While it is true that commitments *may* be the kind of thing we form when we are having trouble, say, being a good friend, it is not necessarily the case that this is the only context in which we would make such a commitment. We might do so under any number of circumstances that are unrelated to blocking re-deliberation, even if this is one side effect of making a commitment such as this one. One such case might be that of trying to *underscore* the evaluative import we put on certain actions we are already undertaking. By contrast, resolutions are, *ex hypothesi*, uniquely designed to help us to do things we judge ourselves as having difficulty doing.

Second, commitments can be used in cases where we do not directly aim to block re-deliberation. By contrast, resolutions are (or at least should be) made in cases where we judge that we may have a hard time (due to weakness of will, *accidie*, lack of strength of will or temptation, among other options) doing something that we antecedently judge we should or we want to do. It might also be the case that resolutions are used to ensure strength of will even in cases where we have no antecedent reason to suspect that we will fall prey to weakness of will, but that are cases where, to borrow a phrase from Frankfurt (1998/1987), we are wholehearted about a particular course of action. Commitments need not be used in either of these fashions.

So it does not appear that commitments can be coherently understood as resolutions, notwithstanding the fact that resolutions might provide the form of agential stability under consideration. Perhaps instead commitments should be understood, à la Bratman, as policies for self-government, and, in this guise, they block re-deliberation. What is the problem here? Like resolutions, it is clear that policies for self-government serve, *inter alia*, to block or constrain re-deliberation. But the pressing question is whether commitments are best understood as a species of these kinds of policies. I contend that commitments are not coherently understood as policies for self-government. I say this for three reasons. First, it is not the case that commitments are necessarily sufficiently substantive or enduring such that they qualify as *policies* for self-government. There are few constraints on the content of commitments, and, in this regard, the extent to which they necessarily constitute explicit policies for how we want to govern ourselves and exercise our agency is doubtful. They surely represent aspirations for such a thing, but it is not clear that they become policies just in virtue of having made them, which is what this view would require us to say.

Imagine, however, that we could come up with a coherent way of understanding commitments as policies for self-government.[25] One option would be to understand them as standing evaluative guidelines for decision-making that come on stream in cases where they apply to the deliberative situation at hand. This is a type of policy for self-government, and it does seem to capture much of what is conceptually distinctive about commitments themselves. The problem, however, is that while policies for self-government get some of their normative force from what they are, it is unclear whether and where commitments' normative force is located. Simply stipulating that they are policies for self-government might seem to solve this problem, but this solution is merely apparent. It is an open question whether they are indeed necessarily such policies in part because while these policies carry at least some of their own normative force, it is not clear that commitments alone can do so. This is so for two reasons: first, commitments do not have the *de facto* agential authority that policies for self-government have insofar as the latter are directly connected to autonomy while the former are not[26]; second, the policies, in virtue of being *policies*, are designed to be self-binding, while it is not clear that commitments are necessarily self-binding. Consider the two guiding examples with which I began this chapter. While these commitments arguably *represent* things that have evaluative significance for the agents who make them, they are not *directly* self-binding. Arguably, they are binding in virtue of the reasons *why* we made them in the first place.[27] This matters because it suggests that *if indeed* commitments play a role in blocking re-deliberation, they do so only *indirectly*, in part by virtue of their relationship to our evaluative attitudes and judgments. The proposal under consideration takes them to do so *directly*, as though the very making of a commitment brings on stream constraints to deliberation that did not pre-exist its formation.

2.3. *Perseverance or Strength of Will*

Perseverance or strength of will is the third type of agential stability that commitments might provide. These are different, but not unrelated, types of psychological stability insofar as they represent an agent's orientation toward her own actions. Of course, there are many ways that we are oriented toward our own actions. Here, the idea is that commitments are psychologically effective in securing, not simply representing, the way in which we want to persevere as we pursue a given end, and, in this regard, represent a distinctive, explicit kind of orientation we might take toward the ends we have adopted. They may be used to block temptation, to strengthen the sense in which we dedicate ourselves to realizing a particular end, among other possibilities.[28] Consider how this works in Example 1, where I commit myself to going running at 5:00. In this case, the commitment would *help me* to persevere in my realizing my goal insofar as I could appeal to it as a source of motivational strength when the alarm goes off the next morning. It might also help me to remain steadfast in the pursuit of that goal, regardless of whether there are any challenges to my pursuit of it. This would capture commitments' ability to help us to strengthen our wills in cases where we aim to remain steadfast in their pursuit.[29,30]

So, as in the previous sections, we can consider this proposal in light of (Q1) and (Q2). Let's begin with the latter. Commitments are clearly a source of motivational strength, although they need not necessarily be so. Insofar as perseverance and strength of will each requires motivational strength, then it might make sense to explain commitments' motivational force as contributing to providing this strength (although they are surely not the only way to do). In this regard, there is nothing particularly problematic about the answer that this picture of commitments and agential stability gives to (Q2) in that we want any view of what commitments are to explain their motivational role for the typical agent.

By contrast, the problems arise when we consider (Q1). Whether commitments help us to persevere is highly defeasible and depends almost entirely on the psychological make-up of the individual who makes them rather than on the force of the commitment itself. If so, then commitments are not, themselves, the kinds of things that *secure* perseverance, although they may be the kinds of things that certain agents do in order *to motivate* themselves to persevere. To see why, consider Example 1. When my alarm goes off at 4:30, I do not persevere in the face of my sleepiness *in virtue* of the commitment. The commitment arguably *reminds me* to act in ways *such that* I do persevere. Simply consider the counterfactual. I could easily persevere *without the commitment* by appealing to my judgment that running is good for my health or simply forcing myself to ignore my fatigue. This suggests that, first, commitments are neither necessary nor sufficient for *directly* securing perseverance, and, second, that even when they *contribute to it*, they do so in a largely indirect, highly defeasible manner.

Something similar is true for strength of will. Commitments may *encourage* agents to act in ways consistent with strength of will by underscoring the need for such strength or pointing to those things toward which we are antecedently disposed to be strong willed, but they do not *secure* this strength. To see why, consider Example 2. When I consider my commitment to be a good friend to Juan when he is grieving the loss of a loved one, this *points toward* the strength of will I may need to help him cope with his grief under trying circumstances. It does not *secure*, at least not directly, this strength. I have to do that on my own. And, as with perseverance, when they do contribute to it, it is in an indirect, highly defeasible way.

If this is what the proponent of the claim that commitments secure agential stability means, then I have no disagreement with this point. But I very much doubt that this is a substantial or sufficiently regular form of agential stability. In this regard, this picture of the relationship between commitments and agential stability fails to provide a coherent answer to (Q1).

2.4. Normative Stability

The last of the four candidate types of agential stability that commitments may provide is, in one way, the most familiar one. This is the idea that commitments provide normative stability. What specific type of normative stability is this and how is it distinct from the view described in Section 2.1? Here the idea is that commitments *themselves* carry normative force with regard to our decision-making, the ends we pursue, and what we think we have reason to do. They are, at heart, normative notions. This is distinct from Shpall's view discussed in Section 2.1 insofar as his view suggests that commitments *establish* normative relations between an attitudinal state (e.g., an evaluative belief about what one ought to do) and a state of affairs (e.g., acting in light of that evaluative belief), although he does note that commitments exert normative pressure on agents to ensure that they stand in the right kinds of relationships with the objects or state of affairs that follow from their attitudes (2014: 148, 149).[31] On the conception of commitments and agential stability under consideration here, however, the idea is that the *commitment itself carries normative weight* and the normative weight in question is designed to play a direct role in future decision-making (cf. Shpall 2014: 146).

Among the four types of agential stability, the idea of normative stability is the most promising. First, it can account for the two examples, and their respective differences, with which we began. Both are instances of things that we take to have significance, and commitments serve as vehicles for conveying this significance in our deliberations, in the formation of our intentions, and in how we cope with deliberatively difficult matters (e.g., cases where matters are, to borrow a phrase from Ruth Chang (2001), on a par). Second, it explains, in principle, what commitments add to our decision-making, at least in instances where we have explicitly made them. Given that many things have normative import for us, they play an underscoring role in making those things clear to us. Depending on the ground of this import (e.g., does the balance of reasons support it?), they can play a substantive role in adding to the stability of the outcome of that decision-making. This is true even in cases where we revise our judgments. Third, it points to how, in taking things to have import, this import bears on our relationships with our actions (both present and future).

But there are two (mutually exclusive) ways that commitments might provide normative stability:

1. They have inherent normative force by virtue of being akin to self-directed promises and thus being the source of backward-looking reasons.[32]

Or

2. They are vehicles for, or they reflect, the normative force of other things that matter to us, such as reasons and evaluative judgments, among others.

Option (1) is implausible for two reasons. First, it makes commitments' normativity mysterious, and, on at least one reading of bootstrapping,[33] they would fall prey to an unacceptable form of bootstrapping.[34] Second, it is not clear what a self-directed promise is, at least with regard to its genuine normative force. This is because we can always release ourselves from them. This would mean that they cannot be a very dependable source of agential stability. In this regard, (1) produces incoherent answers to both (Q1), in failing to explain how commitments actually secure normative stability, and (Q2), in reducing commitments to the questionable notion of a self-directed promise.

Option (2) is a better candidate for understanding how commitments might provide agential stability in virtue of being vehicles for normative stability. First, it locates commitments' normative force in the reasons we have to undertake the action and to form the commitment toward the action. Second, it provides space for explaining the sense in which commitments represent what Morton (2013: 84) describes as our "normative perspective" – in this case, it is our normative perspective on how we exercise our agency (both at a time and over time). This means it locates commitments' normative force in a diverse array of other normative notions, including reasons we have to undertake an action, evaluative judgments, and rational requirements, among others. In this regard, it has a natural advantage because it preserves the normative force of commitments while underscoring the various ways in which commitments connect up with our other evaluative attitudes. Finally, it is consistent with what Ferrero (2006) describes as the "temporal stability of reasons" that is distinctive of diachronic agency. In this regard, it provides a coherent picture of how commitments contribute to agential stability (Q1), while also maintaining a picture of what commitments are that preserves their distinctive characteristics (Q2).

Notice, however, that this takes the wind out of the sails of the claim that commitments' fundamental role is in helping us to "stick to it". Rather, whatever our capacity for agential stability is and how we exercise it, commitments' role is in providing the relevant background conditions for us to exercise this capacity *in light of that which has normative force*. What remains to be seen is how they do so and what types of normative force they can underscore for us. This raises questions for future consideration about the kinds of normativity for which they can be vehicles (e.g., reasons, evaluative judgments, moral concerns, etc.) and whether they are related solely to agent-relative concerns or both agent-relative and -neutral concerns.

3. Conclusion: Remarks on Commitments and Normative Stability

Given space constraints, I cannot provide a full account of the ways in which commitments provide normative stability. However, I take this conclusion as an opportunity to provide a sketch of the sense(s) in which commitments are one salient type of vehicle for it.

Broadly speaking, commitments are vehicles for representing what we care about, what we judge ourselves to have reason to do, etc. There are (at least) two ways that commitments are vehicles for normative stability in cases where we explicitly make them: (1) they reflect the normative force of the reasons we take ourselves to have for undertaking the action toward which the commitment is directed; (2) there are reasons to adopt the commitment itself, thereby exercising what Hieronymi (2006) calls "evaluative control", and thus they are indirect sources of normative stability when we want to make ourselves into certain kinds of agents.

If what I have suggested is correct, then this means that commitments are not uniquely or specifically future-oriented (again, except in some literal sense) nor are they *directly* action-oriented. Rather, they are what we might call import-oriented in ways that agents take to bear on how they exercise their agency. In this regard, they do not necessarily secure any of the kinds of agential stability discussed earlier. Still, they have broader relevance for future decision-making than any of the views under consideration suppose *precisely because* they are vehicles for that which we take to have normative significance. Moreover, they provide a highly defeasible source of normative stability in being vehicles for what matters to us and what we judge ourselves to have reason to do. In this regard, they are clearly an indispensable part of our capacity to stick to it, but not in the ways that we might typically or even intuitively suppose.

Notes

1. I presented earlier versions of this paper at CSMN-Oslo and GRIN Montreal. I am grateful to my audiences, especially Carla Bagnoli, Luca Ferrero, and Mauro Rossi, for their questions, which surely improved the argument I provide here. I owe the notion of "stick-to-it-ness" to Mark Schroeder, who raised a question about commitments and this feature in response to a paper I presented at the Annual NYU Abu Dhabi Workshop on Normativity and Reasoning. This chapter is an attempt to answer his question. I am grateful to Carla Bagnoli for extensive comments on an earlier draft of this chapter.
2. This is one way of reading the significance of Bratman's notion of plans.
3. For a more detailed discussion of some of these features, see Arruda (2020: Section 13.1.1).
4. Including the fact that (1) is self-directed, non-moral, and arguably grounded in agent-relative reasons, while (2) is other-directed, moral, and arguably grounded in agent-neutral reasons.

5 Chang (2009) takes them to be ways of *creating* reasons to do things that matter, such as reasons to take care of one's partner in light of one's love for him, her or them.
 6 For a lengthy treatment of this idea, see Marušić (2015).
 7 Notice that the conditions for *exercising the capacity* to stick to it and the conditions for *successfully sticking to it* are analytically distinct, although, ideally, the former will provide *at least* necessary conditions for the latter. The list mentioned earlier specifies conditions for the former, as this paper is concerned with the question of how agents secure their own agential stability.
 8 Compare this with Holton's (2009: 11) picture of resolutions as involving first-order intentions to ϕ, where ϕ-ing is something that the agent takes to be difficult for her to achieve, and a second-order intention not to "let that [first-order] intention be deflected".
 9 We can distinguish between the question of what a commitment is and what making a commitment does or accomplishes. One way of reading the argument in this paper is that it forces us to consider the question of what a commitment is (and whether, indeed, it accomplishes the things that we think that it does).
10 This is not a mutually exclusive list, as commitments might provide more than one of these types of stability if indeed they provide any of them. For the purpose of evaluating the claims about the relationship between commitments and stability, however, it is necessary to distinguish analytically among different types of stability that commitments might provide.
11 The includes both the stability of decisions about how we will act at a future time and the everyday case of the gap between intention formation and action.
12 For an example of this view, see Bratman (2004: 336–337).
13 I use the idea of "external" and "internal" challenges rather loosely here, as it is clearly possible that some challenges (e.g., addictive behaviors) that are literally internal may be experienced by the agent as external insofar as they are outside of her direct (or even indirect) control. Also, it is not clear that, say, *accidie* is always or only an internal challenge, particularly depending on its causal etiology. I thank Carla Bagnoli for pushing me to consider *accidie* in this way.

The idea here is only to highlight that if commitments do secure agential stability by virtue of helping to secure our capacities for perseverance or strength of will, then they would be doing so *in the face of* etiologically and experientially different kinds of challenges to the stability of an agent's will.
14 I am grateful to Carla Bagnoli for encouraging me to discuss this point.
15 I owe this way of thinking of strength of will to Carla Bagnoli.
16 As an example of this view, consider Ruth Chang's (2013) proposal that commitments have a broadly volitional component.
17 Commitments can be classified broadly as "attitudinal states" or propositional attitudes. For my purposes here, not much hangs on this distinction, as the same problems plague any of these more specific proposals (although see Arruda *ms* for a discussion of why this difference might matter for answering the question of what a commitment actually is). To draw the relevant contrast with (b), I will group all of these views together.
18 There is a third option, which is not relevant for the proposal under consideration but bears mention here. Sen (1977, 2005) denies that commitments are attitudes and instead takes actions to be committed when they are undertaken for the pursuit of others' goals (rather than for the sake of our own welfare). We do not, on Sen's view, make commitments; rather, we engage in committed actions.

19 Shpall describes his view as follows:

> There are two features of rational commitments that I want to draw attention to as a point of departure. First, to be rationally committed to A is to stand in a normative relation to A. Such commitments cannot be analyzed purely in terms of the actual attitudes one has; Adam might not believe that the world was created in six days even though he is committed to believing it. An agent's actual attitudes constitute the ground of his rational commitments—that is, what makes it the case that he has the commitments that he does—but not the commitments themselves. The commitments themselves are normative, in the sense that they put genuine pressure on the committed agent to form the attitude to which he's committed; and this pressure obtains independently of how he thinks about it. Thus rational commitment is, on the face of it, a normative relation: it cannot be reduced to the attitudes one takes towards the object of one's commitments, and to stand in the commitment relation is to be under the grip of some distinctive form of normative pressure.
>
> (149)

By contrast, Ross (2012) takes mental states to bring on stream commitments to follow through on those mental states (most obviously, intentions), which forecloses deliberation about them. In this regard, I treat views like Ross's, which are not directly views of commitments, in Section 2.2.

20 Holton (2009) puts it thus:

> Once formed, intentions have a tendency to persist. They have what Bratman calls stability. Stability is not, of course, absolute. Sometimes we revise our intentions, and it is quite rational that we do so . . . Stability can best be understood as a shift in the threshold of relevance of information: some information that would have been relevant in forming an intention will not be sufficient to provoke rational reconsideration once an intention has been formed.
>
> (2–3)

The obvious question, to which Holton then turns, is what constitutes the relevant information such that we can rationally revise our intentions. More simply, and more directly germane for my concerns in this chapter, we might wonder what makes intentions stable *in cases where we aim at their stability*. The view under consideration in this section claims that commitments might be a vehicle for achieving this more specific kind of stability. For Holton, intentions are "intrinsically stable" such that they "engender a mindset that treats them as stable" (6–7). If he is right, then this already limits the purchase of the view under consideration about the role of commitments in, to use his phrase, engendering this mindset.

21 I make such an argument in Arruda (ms).
22 I say this because there are independent questions concerning the nature and force of this normativity, but the answer to this question does not affect the argument here.
23 Compare with Ross (2012), who takes commitments to *settle* future deliberation in that mental states, such as intentions, "commi[t] one to acting in some way".
24 Holton (2009) describes resolutions as follows:

> Clearly, if it is to work, a resolution has to be something that holds firm against temptation. At one extreme we could think of them simply as intentions with an especially high degree of stability. But that doesn't seem to get it right. It is no part of the nature of a resolution that it will

be effective; the point is rather that it is meant to be. At the most intellectual level, resolutions can be seen as involving both an intention to engage in a certain action, and a further intention not to let that intention be deflected. Understood in this way they involve a conjunction of two simpler intentions, one first-order and one second-order (i.e., an intention about an intention). So, when I resolve to give up smoking, I form an intention to give up, and along with it I form a second-order intention not to let that intention be deflected.

(11)

It is worth noting that Holton takes resolutions to be a special combination of first- and second-order intentions. In the treatment mentioned earlier, I take only the idea that resolutions, however they are understood, to function to block redeliberation about our intentions, and thus commitments might be a species of them if they can serve this function. Whether they are to then be understood as a species of intention, à la Holton's proposal, is not relevant for the argument under consideration here.

25 To see how this might work, consider Bratman's (2004: 336–337) account of individual commitment. On his view, individual commitments involve higher-order (e.g., second-order) forms of endorsement of first-order, volitionally significant attitudes (e.g., desires). At the very least, these endorsements are responsive to what we take to be reasons in favor of acting on our volitionally significant attitudes. On a more demanding picture – and one that informs the view under consideration earlier – they are responsive to agents' overall policies for self-government.

As should be clear, I am not analyzing or evaluating Bratman's specific view, as it does not exactly fit the picture of agential stability and commitments that I am evaluating. Still, it is the broad inspiration for this proposal, and it serves as a helpful touchstone when considering the arguments mentioned earlier.

26 This is true even if we grant that we can form genuinely unjustified policies for self-government in that they have some *de facto* authority, however defeasible.

27 I return to this idea that commitments are vehicles for that which has normative significance in Section 3.

28 The closest approximation to this view is Marušić (2015: esp. 122, 175), who argues that commitments are aspirations or resolutions to do what we have very little evidence we are likely to do.

29 The closest approximation of this view, taken very broadly, is Morton and Paul's (2019) account of grit. They write,

> Sincerely committing to a difficult end should be consistent with subsequently making the rational decision to quit and invest one's resources in a more viable alter- native, and this decision should be governed in part by the evidence bearing on the chances of success. On the other hand, we agree with the Sartrean insight that the way an agent should think about the evidence bearing on activities she herself is committed to is potentially different from the way an impartial observer would reason about the same body of evidence.
>
> (189)

On their picture, commitments play a role in the service of grit, but policies in favor of being gritty are defeasible (unlike some pictures, such as Holton's, of perseverance or strength of will):

> [W]e have pro tanto reason to have evidential policies that are grit friendly. A grit-friendly evidential policy will result in some degree of inertia in

> the agent's belief about whether she will ultimately succeed, relative to the way in which an impartial observer would tend to update on new evidence. As a consequence of committing to a goal, the agent's threshold should go up for how compelling new evidence must be before she revises her belief about the likelihood of succeeding if she continues to try.
>
> (Morton and Paul 2019: 194)

30 Cf. Holton (2009: 113), who takes strength of will to be precisely that which we use to block temptation. Interestingly, he takes willpower to be an independent agential ability that is not reducible to some combination of a special set of intentions, beliefs, and desires. In this regard, if he is correct, it would go some way in bolstering the view under consideration in this section – viz., that commitments help us to exercise this ability.

31 Shpall (2014) writes,

> Rational commitments, like the commitment to believe what you know to follow from one of your beliefs, and moral commitments, like the commitment you take on by making a promise, share several important underlying features. I'll suggest that they are indeed two instances of one normative relation, the relation of being committed. And this relation is distinct from those—especially the relation of having a reason, and the relation of being required—that philosophers have recognized and invoked in constructing their theories.
>
> (146)

32 For a discussion of this option and what goes wrong with this picture, see Arruda (2020).

33 I address the question of different kinds of bootstrapping, and whether or not there might be an acceptable form of bootstrapping, in Arruda (provisionally forthcoming). For specific issues associated with commitments and bootstrapping, see Bratman (1987), Chang (2013), Ferrero (2006: 103, 2010), Holton (2009), and Marušić (2015).

34 Compare with Chartier (2018: 4):

> *Ex ante*, commitments and the subsidiary choices that implement or support them can contribute directly or indirectly to shaping preferences and dispositions that influence our subsequent choices. *Ex post*, commitments can constitute or generate reasons for action that it would be inappropriate for us to ignore.

References

Arruda, C. (2020) "Commitments and Collective Responsibility," in D. Tollefsen and S. Bazargan-Forward (eds.), *The Routledge Handbook of Collective Responsibility*, New York: Routledge.

Arruda, C. (ms) *Enriching Practical Reason*.

Bratman, M. (1987) *Intention, Plans, and Practical Reason*. Center for the Study of Language and Information.

Bratman, M. (1999a) "Shared Intention," reprinted in *Faces of Intention: Selected Essays on Intention and Agency*, New York: Cambridge University Press, 109–129.

Bratman, M. (1999b) "I Intend that We J," reprinted in *Faces of Intention: Selected Essays on Intention and Agency*, New York: Cambridge University Press, 142–161.

Bratman, M. (2004) "Three Forms of Agential Commitment: Reply to Cullity and Gerrans," *Proceedings of the Aristotelian Society* 104: 329–337.
Bratman, M. (2007a) "Introduction," in *Structures of Agency: Essays*, Oxford: Oxford University Press.
Bratman, M. (2007b) "Planning Agency, Autonomous Agency," in *Structures of Agency*, Oxford: Oxford University Press, 197–232.
Bratman, M. (2007c) *Structures of Agency*, Oxford: Oxford University Press.
Bratman, M. (2014) *Shared Agency: A Planning Theory of Acting Together*, Oxford: Oxford University Press.
Bratman, M. (2015) "Shared Agency: Replies to Ludwig, Pacherie, Petersson, Roth, and Smith," *Journal of Social Ontology* 1(1): 59–76.
Bratman, M. (2018) *Planning, Time, and Self-Governance: Essays in Practical Rationality*, Oxford: Oxford University Press.
Brewer, T. (2003) "Two Kinds of Commitments (and Two Kinds of Social Groups)," *Philosophy and Phenomenological Research* 66(3): 554–583.
Broome, J. (2005) "Does Rationality Give Us Reasons?" *Philosophical Issues* 15: 321–337.
Broome, J. (2007) "Wide or Narrow Scope?" *Mind* 116(462): 359–370.
Brunero, J. (2008) "The Scope of Rational Requirements," *The Philosophical Quarterly*: 1–22.
Chang, R. (2001) *Making Comparisons Count*, New York: Routledge.
Chang, R. (2009) "Voluntarist Reasons and the Sources of Normativity," in D. Sobel and S. Wall (eds.), *Reasons for Action*, New York: Cambridge University Press.
Chang, R. (2013) "Commitments, Reasons, and the Will," in R. Shafer-Landau (ed.), *Oxford Studies in Metaethics*, Vol. 8, Oxford: Oxford University Press.
Chartier, G. (2018) *The Logic of Commitment*, New York: Routledge.
Dorsey, D. (2016) *The Limits of Moral Authority*, Oxford: Oxford University Press.
Elster, J. (1985 [1979]) *Ulysses and the Sirens: Studies in Rationality and Irrationality* (revised ed.), Cambridge: Cambridge University Press.
Elster, J. (2000) *Ulysses Unbound: Studies in Rationality, Precommitment, and Constraints*, Cambridge and New York: Cambridge University Press.
Ferrero, L. (2006) "Three Ways of Spilling Ink Tomorrow," in E. Baccarini and S. Prijic- Samarzija (eds.), *Rationality in Belief and Action*, Rijeka, 95–127.
Ferrero, L. (2010) "Decisions, Diachronic Autonomy, and the Division of Deliberative Labor," *Philosophers' Imprint* 10(2): 1–23.
Frankfurt, H. (1998a [1971]) "Freedom of the Will and the Concept of the Person," in *The Importance of What We Care About*, Cambridge: Cambridge University Press, 11–25.
Frankfurt, H. (1998b [1987]) "Identification and Wholeheartedness," in *The Importance of What We Care About*, Cambridge: Cambridge University Press, 11–25, 159–176.
Gilbert, M. (2013) "Commitment," in H. LaFollette (ed.), *The International Encyclopedia of Ethics*, New York: Blackwell Publishing, 899–905.
Gilbert, M. (2014) *Joint Commitment: How We Make the Social World*, Oxford: Oxford University Press.
Gilbert, M. (2018) *Rights and Demands: A Foundational Inquiry*, New York: Oxford University Press.

Heim, J. (2015) "Commitments in Groups and Commitments of Groups," *Phenomenology and Mind* 9: 74–82.
Hieronymi, P. (2006) "Controlling Attitudes," *Pacific Philosophical Quarterly* 87(1): 45–74.
Hieronymi, P. (2009) "Two Kinds of Agency," in L. O'Brien and M. Soterieu (eds.), *Mental Action*, Oxford: Oxford University Press, 138–162.
Hinchman, E. (2010) "Conspiracy, Commitment, and the Self," *Ethics* 180: 526–556.
Hinchman, E. (2014) "Narrative and the Stability of Intention," *European Journal of Philosophy* 23(1): 111–140.
Holton, R. (2009) *Willing, Wanting, Waiting*, Oxford: Oxford University Press.
Killmister, S. (2017) *Taking the Measure of Autonomy: Self- Definition, Self-Realisation, and Self-Unification*, New York: Routledge.
Liberman, A., and Schroeder, M. (2016) "Commitment: Worth the Weight," in E. Lord and B. Macguire (eds.), *Weighing Reasons*, New York: Oxford University Press.
Marušić, B. (2015) *Evidence and Agency: Norms of Belief for Promising and Resolving*, New York: Oxford University Press.
Michael, J., and Pacherie, E. (2015) "On Commitments and Other Uncertainty Reduction Tools in Joint Action," *Journal of Social Ontology* 1(1): 89–120.
Morton, J. (2013) "Deliberating for Our Far Future Selves," *Ethical Theory and Moral Practice* 16(4): 809–828.
Morton, J., and Paul, S. (2019) "Grit," *Ethics* 129(2): 175–203.
Paul, S. (2021) "Plan B," *Australasian Journal of Philosophy*. doi:10.1080/00048402.2021.1912126
Ross, J. (2012) "Rationality, Normativity, and Commitment," in R. Shafer-Landau (ed.), *Oxford Studies in Metaethics*, Oxford: Oxford University Press.
Roth, A. S. (2004) "Shared Agency and Contralateral Commitments," *The Philosophical Review* 113(3): 359–410.
Schroeder, M. (2013) "Scope for Rational Autonomy," *Philosophical Issues* 23: 297–310.
Sen, A. K. (1977) "Rational Fools: A Critique of the Behavioral Foundations of Economic Theory," *Philosophy & Public Affairs* 6(4): 317–344.
Sen, A. K. (2005) "Why Exactly Is Commitment Important for Rationality?," *Economics and Philosophy* 21(1): 5–14.
Shpall, S. (2014) "Moral and Rational Commitment," *Philosophy and Phenomenological Research* 88(1): 146–172.
Singh, K. (Forthcoming) "What is an Aim," in Russ Shafer Landau (ed.), *Oxford Studies in Metaethics*, Oxford: Oxford University Press.
Townsend, L. (2015) "Joint Commitment and Collective Belief," *Phenomenology and Mind* 9(9): 46–53.

8 Extended Agency and the Problem of Diachronic Autonomy*

Julia Nefsky and Sergio Tenenbaum

1. Introduction

It seems to be a humdrum fact of human agency that we often act on intentions or decisions that we have made at an earlier time.[1] At breakfast, you look at the Taco Hut menu online and decide that later today you'll have one of their avocado burritos for lunch. You're at your desk and you hear the church bells ring the noon hour. You get up, walk to Taco Hut, and order the burrito as planned.

As mundane as this sort of scenario might seem to be, philosophers have raised a problem in understanding it. If you are simply abiding by this morning's decision, how are you acting autonomously? Your earlier self seems to be calling the shots; if you are just acting accordingly, without thinking through it or in some other way trying to ensure that the past decision conforms to your present standpoint, it is not clear how this amounts to an exercise of your present autonomous agency. It seems, rather, that your earlier self has succeeded in slaving you to her own purposes. She was the one who wanted (intended, judged it to be good, etc.) to have an avocado burrito; in simply following through, your current self seems to be just an automaton performing the commands left behind by your former self.

Of course, you might not allow yourself to be shackled by your earlier self. You might refuse to follow anything but your own present judgments: you will only go to Taco Hut if this is what you judge you should do right now, and once at Taco Hut will only eat the avocado burrito if that is what you want to eat once there. But if this is the way you generally operate, this seems to block your ability to make effective future-directed decisions. If you will always open up the question of what to do when the time comes, acting only on your present judgments, then you cannot successfully decide in advance what to do later. But, as we have said, this is an ability that we do seem to have and employ frequently.

The puzzle, then, is one of explaining how the future self can do the bidding of her past self without losing her autonomy. Or, as Luca

DOI: 10.4324/9780429259845-11

Ferrero puts it, how can our future-directed decisions be "effective without being manipulative"[2]? Let's call this "the Problem of Diachronic Autonomy".

Philosophers raising the Problem of Diachronic Autonomy take it to show that there must be reasons or rational requirements to follow through with our past decisions. They claim that unless our decisions put rational pressure on us to follow through, we cannot solve the problem.

We argue that there is no Problem of Diachronic Autonomy. There is, in other words, no puzzling situation that needs explaining. Consequently, there is no need coming from this purported puzzle to think that our future-directed decisions generate reasons or rational requirements to follow through. The "future self" can do the bidding of the "past self" without giving up its autonomy because, very simply, the past self is the *same agent* as the future self. In following through with my decision, I am acting on my own freely-formed intention; this is straightforwardly autonomous. There is nothing puzzling or difficult here.[3] Indeed, we argue that the Problem of Diachronic Autonomy, as specified, is ultimately incoherent: it implicitly relies on two inconsistent conceptions of human agency. We then consider other possibilities for what people might have in mind in thinking that there is a special problem of diachronic autonomy and argue that none of them work either. There is no relevant difference between the diachronic case, in which I make a future-directed decision and later act on it, and the synchronic case, in which I act immediately on a decision about what to do in the present.

2. Attempts to Solve the Alleged Problem

In this section, before turning to our own view in the next, we will discuss other philosophers' proposed solutions to the problem and give some initial reasons to be unsatisfied with these views.

David Velleman argues that we can only solve the Problem of Diachronic Autonomy if in making a future-directed decision one gives one's future self reason to follow through with it:

> The only way to control our future behavior without losing future control, I believe, is by making decisions that our future selves will be determined to execute of their own volition; and the only way to determine our future selves to do something of their own volition is by giving them reason to do it. Hence future-directed intentions or commitments must be capable of providing reasons to our future selves. Unless we can commit ourselves today in a way that will generate reasons for us to act tomorrow, we shall have to regard our day-older selves either as beyond the control of today's decisions or as passive instruments of them.[4]

Velleman recognizes that some people's normative intuitions oppose the idea that our decisions generate reason to follow through with them: they "think that abiding by a commitment for its own sake is foolish".[5] But, he says, whatever your normative intuitions are on the matter, the question of whether there are such reasons is settled by the need to solve the Problem of Diachronic Autonomy. A fact about human agency is that we have the ability to decide for our future selves without undermining our future autonomy, and – Velleman claims – we can only make sense of this fact *if* our decisions generate reasons to follow through.

How does making a future-directed decision generate reason to follow through with it? Velleman does not give a full answer, but he does sketch an idea of at least one way this could work: namely, if we accept his view that autonomy is the constitutive aim of action. He writes:

> [I]f autonomy is the constitutive goal of action, and hence the internal criterion of success for action, then reasons for acting will be considerations relevant to autonomy . . . And we can at least hope that reasons of this kind will be generated by future-directed decisions.[6]

Like Velleman, Sarah Paul claims that for a future-directed intention to serve its function of settling a deliberative question, "the agent must view the fact that she has formed that very intention as carrying a distinctive weight that is independent of the weight of the reasons favoring the intended action".[7] Paul's story of how this works is different from Velleman's. Paul focuses on cases in which one's options are on par or incommensurable.[8] So, take a case in which you decide to go to Taco Hut for lunch, but in which lunch at Taco Hut is, in your assessment, completely on par with lunch at Fajita Palace. In such a case, there is no direct cost to breaking with your decision when lunchtime comes and going to Fajita Palace instead. But, Paul claims, there is "an indirect cost" to not following through with your decision: it gives you evidence that your decisions do not determine what you will do, and this evidence erodes your ability to treat your decisions as authoritative when there are benefits to be gained from doing so – for instance, in cases in which you are using future-directed decisions to try to avoid temptations or to try to cooperate with others.[9] So, in Paul's view, our decisions generate reasons to follow through because following through with them helps maintain our capacity to treat our decisions as authoritative, and this is a useful capacity to have.

While the details of their proposals differ, Paul and Velleman agree that our future-directed decisions must give us reason to act accordingly because without this we cannot make sense of how future-directed decisions can decide deliberative questions effectively without being manipulative. So, on both of their views, I have reason to go to Taco Hut and order the avocado burrito coming from the fact that I decided in the morning to do so. Let r be the reason in question.[10] The problem with both proposals is that now when I go to Taco Hut and order the burrito, the reason I do so is (in part) r. But r is, by definition, not the reason why I formed the intention to order the burrito in the first place. I formed the intention to order the burrito because it would be a delicious lunch. So, a view like Paul's or Velleman's only vindicates my autonomous acting on a past decision at the cost that I do not act on the same reasons for which I made the decision. I now eat my burrito to preserve my autonomy or to preserve my capacity to make effective future-directed decisions, rather than (or, rather than just) because it would be a delicious lunch. A picture on which I conform with my decision but for different reasons from those for which I made the decision does not seem to be an accurate or acceptable picture of how our future-directed decisions guide our actions.[11]

Furthermore, such a picture seems at risk of actually undermining, rather than providing an explanation of, diachronic autonomy. On this picture, it is by giving you this new reason that your decision exerts control over your future actions, and because it exerts control via this reason, this is supposed to make the control non-coercive.[12] But does this make it non-coercive? On this view, my past self is doing something (deciding) that gives my present self a reason that it would not otherwise have had to act according to my past self's will. Controlling someone's behavior in this way can be a way of coercing or manipulating them. As Ferrero writes, controlling your future behavior by "introducing features extraneous to the original merits of the case" is precisely what happens in "manipulative forms of distal self-control like pre-commitments".[13]

Velleman's and Paul's idea seems to be that the control my past decision exerts is not coercive because it goes *through* my rational deliberative capacities, appearing in the reasons that I entertain in deciding for myself now whether to go through with the decision, rather than bypassing my deliberation with brute causal force. But this argument does not work. My decision to give my wallet to the person who threatens "your money or your life" also goes through my rational deliberations: their threat gives me a reason to give up my wallet, a reason that outweighs my reasons to keep it. But that surely does not make this threat a non-coercive way of exerting control, nor does it make giving up my wallet a case of purely autonomous agency.

Perhaps, though, the specific sort of reason that one's past self gives one's future self on Velleman or Paul's account helps explain why the situation is non-coercive. After all, not all cases of giving someone a reason to act as you wish are cases of coercing them.[14] But looking at the content of the reason does not seem to help here. The content is, in very rough and general terms, something like: "*I* decided to ϕ and if you don't do as I – your past self – decided, then your agential capacities will be compromised in such-and-such a way".[15] Giving someone this sort of reason to ϕ certainly seems coercive.

There are two ways philosophers have avoided having the future self acting for different reasons from those that came into the decision, while preserving the idea that the decision controls future behavior non-coercively by changing the rational deliberative scene for the future self. The first one, proposed by Bratman, is to argue for wide-scope rational requirements governing the relation between future-directed intentions and their later execution. If the rational pressure that past decisions exert on our current selves is determined by wide-scope requirements, we need not say that these decisions generate new reasons to act. A second possibility, proposed by Ferrero, is that decisions give us new exclusionary reasons – that is, second-order reasons to exclude certain kinds of reasons from our deliberations. This would also avoid the conclusion that the past decision creates a new reason for action. We will consider each of these views in turn.

Let's start with the proposal that we are diachronically autonomous when following through with a past intention insofar as and because doing so is in conformity with a wide scope rational requirement. Bratman's proposal for the wide scope rational requirement is:

(D) You ought (If you intended at t_1 to X at t_2 and throughout $t_1 - t_2$ confidently took your relevant grounds adequately to support this very intention, to X at t_2.)[16]

Now, to be clear, Bratman himself does not present D as a direct response to the Problem of Diachronic Autonomy. Rather, Bratman argues in a different way that diachronic autonomy requires D. That is, he argues that in order to have diachronic autonomy (or, in his terminology "self-governance over-time"[17]), we need D, but he does not argue for this by appeal to the puzzle about how our past decisions can control our behavior without undercutting our autonomy.[18] In this section, we will look at D as a response to the Problem of Diachronic Autonomy (even though Bratman himself does not present it that way). But as we will explain later, at the end of Section 3, our main point carries over to Bratman's actual argument as well.

If we put rational requirement D as a response to the Problem of Diachronic Autonomy, the idea would be as follows: since your past self made the decision to ϕ, this limits what it is rational for your current self to do: either your current self must change (if she hasn't already) her assessment of the relevant grounds *or* she must follow through. Following through, then, is an exercise of your autonomous agency, just an exercise that is – rightly – responsive to the rational constraints that the past decision puts in place.

While invoking a rational requirement in this way might avoid positing new first-order reasons, it is not clear that this view does any better at capturing following through on one's past decisions as autonomous.

Whether one appeals to new reasons created by past decisions or to rational requirements whose antecedent is partly made true by a past decision, the past decision controls my future conduct by way of rational pressure on me to follow through. Putting rational pressure on someone to act as you wish can be a way of manipulating or coercing them; it does not make a difference whether the pressure is coming from a first-order reason or from a rational requirement. Suppose I want you to do my laundry. My clothes are very dirty from gardening, and I feel lazy after all the hard work. I ask you if you would mind taking on the task. You refuse. You explain that you have more important things to do today than my laundry: you have big plans to thoroughly clean your house. In light of this information, I run into your house, scatter my dirty laundry on the floor, and blockade the doors and windows so that you cannot get rid of it. I know how meticulous you are when you clean: so meticulous that you wouldn't consider the task complete if there was a single article of dirty clothing on the premises. Since there is a rational requirement for means-end coherence, I have made it such that you are now rationally required to either abandon your cleaning project or to do my laundry. In this way, I have put rational pressure on you to do my laundry. This is, quite obviously, a case of coercing or manipulating someone. By manipulating the rational requirements that apply to you, I am interfering with your autonomy.

Ferrero's response to the Problem of Diachronic Autonomy seems to avoid this problem. According to Ferrero, rather than a new first-order reason or a rational requirement, my future-directed decision gives rise, under certain circumstances, to a second-order exclusionary reason to follow through with it. On his view, we make future-directed decisions because our finite capacities require that we have a "division of deliberative labour"; if I expect that I am in a better position to deliberate now than I will be at the time of the action, I should decide now what I will later do. But if this is true, and I decide now to ϕ later, it would be wasteful and "risky" to reopen deliberations when it comes time to ϕ. The fact that I deliberated in good conditions thus creates an exclusionary reason not to reconsider first-order considerations in favor or against ϕ-ing, and to instead simply act on the basis of my knowledge of my previous decision. This exclusionary reason is – Ferrero says – "maximally protected", meaning that it cannot be defeated by first-order considerations. Such exclusionary, maximally protected reasons are generated by an agent's past decision as long as (a) "the agent's deliberative conditions at [the time of the action] have not improved over the conditions at [the time of the decision]"; and (b) "there is a reasonable expectation that she would reach the same conclusion if she were to deliberate in conditions as good as those she enjoyed [when she made the decision]".[19]

So, Ferrero's solution to the Problem of Diachronic Autonomy is that, insofar as you are following through with your past decision when conditions (a) and (b) hold, you are exercising your autonomous agency in doing so, because in doing so you are responding to the exclusionary reason that your decision gives you – a reason that says to "ϕ without any further ado".[20] Now, like the other views, Ferrero's account tries to vindicate one's diachronic autonomy by saying that one's past decision puts a certain sort of rational pressure on you to follow through. But, unlike the other views, this sort of rational pressure does not seem at risk of being coercive. The "pressure" to follow through comes entirely from my current self's recognition that my past self deliberated better than (or at least, as well as) I could expect to deliberate now based on our shared practical perspective.

The first thing to notice is that in Ferrero's view acting on my past intention is exactly like acting on expert advice. I act on my past intention because I recognize that it would be better, or at least expectedly better, to act on a "borrowed opinion"; it's just that the borrowed opinion comes from my past self. But is this plausible? It seems to us that there is an important difference between following through with my past decision and deferring to the advice of an expert.[21]

A related objection is that if conditions (a) and (b) must be satisfied in order for acting on your past decision to count as autonomous, then the scope of cases of diachronic autonomy would be very limited. Take our original example of acting on one's earlier decision to have lunch at Taco Hut. It seems unlikely that either (a) or (b) is satisfied in that case. I'm probably in a much better position at lunchtime to deliberate on what kind of meal I would enjoy for lunch. And it might also be true that there is no reasonable expectation that I would reach the same conclusion if I were to deliberate again when lunchtime comes (under equally good conditions to my original deliberations). After all, I know that I often change my mind when I reconsider my lunch options. But despite the fact that (a) and (b) are probably not satisfied, I still seem perfectly autonomous if I do not reconsider and simply act on my earlier intention and go to Taco Hut.[22]

Perhaps – one might suggest – this means that Ferrero should drop or modify conditions (a) and (b), so that the maximally protected, exclusionary reason applies *even if* I am in a better position now to deliberate about the matter, and even if I would reach a different conclusion were I to deliberate now under equally good conditions. This way he could still capture the Taco Hut case (and others like it) as a case of diachronic autonomy. But the problem with Ferrero's account is not just that (a) and (b) are likely not satisfied; it's also that it is simply not plausible that there is a maximally protected, exclusionary reason not to re-check first-order considerations in the Taco Hut case. There surely would be nothing wrong if, while walking to Taco Hut, I reconsidered my decision and chose to go to Rawesome instead on the basis of the fact that Rawesome has healthier options than Taco Hut. Ferrero might try to argue that there is something wrong with reconsidering: it would be a waste of my deliberative resources. But why think that? As I walk to Taco Hut, deliberating about lunch might be no worse of a use of my faculties than humming "The Wheels on the Bus" in my mind. So, Ferrero's appeal to maximally protected, exclusionary reasons does not seem to work to explain why I am autonomous when I act on my decision to go to Taco Hut. Since there is nothing unusual about the Taco Hut example, the point will carry over to many more cases of acting on my past decisions.

3. It Was Me All Along

Despite the variations in their views, all four philosophers agree on the same general point: that our past decisions must give us reasons or rational requirements to abide by them, because without this we cannot make sense of our diachronic autonomy. We now will argue that this general idea is a mistake.

The Problem of Diachronic Autonomy asks: when I follow through with my decision to have an avocado burrito for lunch, how is it that I am acting autonomously? How is it that I am not being coerced or manipulated by my earlier self, if it was my earlier self who settled the question for me of what I will have for lunch? Our view is that there is nothing puzzling or difficult to explain here. The answer is simple: I am acting autonomously when I go to get the avocado burrito because *I* was the one who decided to get the burrito – not someone else. I am not being coerced or manipulated by someone else (my earlier self) into executing their will, instead of my own. Rather, I am a temporally extended agent, and so it is the same self (me!) who intends and performs the action. This is the commonsense response to the Problem of Diachronic Autonomy. And this commonsense, simple answer turns out to be the correct one.

This answer relies on accepting that our agency is temporally extended.[23] It requires, in other words, denying a time-slice conception of our agency: a conception on which myself-at-t_n is a different agent from myself-at-t_m. But the philosophers who raise the Problem of Diachronic Autonomy recognize that we are temporally extended agents. They do not want to subscribe to a time-slice conception. Rather, they present the problem specifically as a problem in understanding the diachronic nature of our agency. The fact that we are temporally extended agents means that we can decide now and execute later, and they think that, in cases in which we do this, the temporal distance between the decision and the execution creates a puzzle. They think, in other words, that *given* that (A) we are temporally extended agents, there is a problem in understanding how (G) our future-directed decisions can guide our actions without being manipulative. Our claim is that once we accept A, there is, in fact, no problem at all in explaining how it is that G.

Extended Agency and Diachronic Autonomy 181

In fact, more than that, it seems that in order to be able to formulate the supposed problem to begin with, one must implicitly rely on both of these two mutually inconsistent conceptions of human agency – a time-slice conception and a temporally extended conception. First, to set up the problem, we need a temporally extended conception of our agency. On a time-slice conception, your relation to your past selves is of the *same type* as your relation to other people. So, your past self can only decide – or, settle a practical question – for you in the sense that someone else can settle a practical question for you. Someone else can settle a practical question for you by making a convincing argument, or by offering you an incentive that you cannot resist, or by forcing your hand, or by some other causal shenanigans. But none of these are the same as forming an intention for yourself to act on at a later time. On a temporally extended conception of our agency, on the other hand, you – as a single agent – persist through time, and so you can form an intention now about what you will do later, and then, later, act on it. Since the Problem of Diachronic Autonomy is a problem about cases in which we form intentions for ourselves to act on at a later time, it thus requires a temporally extended rather than time-slice conception.[24] But second, in setting up the puzzle, we must implicitly assume a time-slice conception of our agency. It is only on a picture under which my earlier self is a *different agent* from my later self that simply acting on my earlier freely-formed decision could even look like a case of being coerced or manipulated.

It is worth noting that the time-slice conception of agency is often relied upon in the language the previously mentioned philosophers use in discussing the problem. While they are explicitly recognizing and studying the cross-temporal features of our agency, the time-slice conception seems to creep in. Paul, for instance, asks, "Finding myself with an intention formed last week to go to the dentist today, why should I allow these instructions from the past to guide *my* action – permit myself to be manipulated by the 'dead hand of the past', so to speak?"[25] Velleman writes that the only way of making sense of our diachronic autonomy is if we "make decisions that our future selves will be determined to execute of *their own* volition",[26] and he talks about what it takes for a person's intention from the past to become a "volition of his current self" – for the "volition to become *his own*".[27] Ferrero, in discussing an agent who follows through with her decisions without sensitivity to the conditions required for the exclusionary reason to apply, writes:

> [The agent's] uncritical acceptance of a past decision . . . [does not] respect her autonomy at a later time, since . . . she is uncritically submitting to the dictates of the prior self, with no guarantee the they might make her do what *she* would autonomously choose if *she* were to decide *for herself* at t_{act}.[28]

All of these ways of talking treat the self who formed the intention as a different agent from the one who might act on it.[29]

Once we consistently recognize the temporally extended nature of our agency, we see that the relation between future-directed intention and future doing is no different than the relation between current intention and current doing. That is, at least as far as autonomy is concerned, there is no difference between the diachronic and the synchronic case. In either case, if (a) you intended, (b) you acted, and (c) you acted because you intended, then you acted autonomously.[30] The passing of time between the initial formation of the intention and the execution does not change this. Of course, the passing of time does give you more of an opportunity to rethink the decision and change your mind. But often we don't rethink our decisions; often we are simply moved to act by the intentions we formed earlier. I might decide now to call my Grandma Doris when I finish writing this paragraph. Having formed that intention, when I get to the end of the paragraph, I might simply close my computer, pick up the phone, and dial. That is, the future-directed intention that I formed might simply persist and directly cause my intentional activity of calling my grandmother, without any new exercising of my rational deliberative capacities. The philosophers in question think that if this is the way things go, then "our later selves would lack autonomy of their own, since they would find their limbs being moved by the decisions of earlier selves".[31] But things are quite the opposite. If I formed the intention of my own accord, and this intention moves me to act, that is *paradigmatically* autonomous. To think that being moved to act directly by the intention I formed earlier would be a case of lacking autonomy is, again, to mistakenly treat my future self and past self as two different agents.

On our view, future-directed decisions are effective at settling deliberative questions in virtue of the fact that, in the absence of interference, we will act on them, exactly like in the synchronic case. They do not gain their ability to control our future behavior via some pressure they put on our future deliberations. Rather, they can control our future behavior because we act on them.[32]

In sum, the answer to the question of how I am acting autonomously when I follow through with my future-directed decision to ϕ is simple and commonsense. I am acting autonomously when I ϕ because *I* decided to do it: I am following through with my own decision. There is no need to invoke special reasons or rational requirements in order to explain this.[33] And for this very reason, this commonsense account of diachronic autonomy does better than the others in terms of how autonomous we turn out to be. That is, it does better than the others at capturing following through on one's past decision as autonomous (and this despite the fact that those other accounts put more effort into the task). On all other accounts, my current self would not have been autonomous *but for* the fact that it is responding to rational pressure imposed on it by my earlier

Extended Agency and Diachronic Autonomy 183

self. To the extent that this counts as a way of being autonomous at all, this is a rather distorted, minimal kind of autonomy.[34] On our account, on the other hand, I am autonomous when I follow through with my future-directed decision in the most basic and full sense: I am autonomous because I am acting on my own, non-coercively formed decision.[35]

Before moving on, we want to come back to Bratman's argument. As we said earlier, Bratman does not himself argue for D, his rational requirement for intention stability over time, by appeal specifically to the Problem of Diachronic Autonomy. He argues for D, instead, by appeal to his account of what diachronic autonomy, or – in his terminology, "self-governance over time" – consists in. We now want to argue that our main point applies to Bratman's argument for D as well.

In arguing for (D), Bratman is particularly concerned with "Buridan's Ass" and incommensurability cases, in which our reasons support multiple incompatible courses of action. In such cases, in the absence of a rational requirement to stick with one's decisions, a rational agent could engage in "brute shuffling"; she could abandon a previously formed intention to ϕ in favor of an intention to ψ while having no reason to prefer ψ-ing over ϕ-ing (as long they are equally good or incommensurable). Bratman claims that brute shuffling in this way undermines your self-governance over time. On Bratman's conception, "self-governance essentially involves . . . guidance and control by attitudes that help constitute a sufficiently unified point of view, a point of view that constitutes the agent's . . . practical standpoint".[36] And, Bratman thinks, brutely shuffling from one equal value or incommensurable option to another means that one does not have a unified point of view over time. Thus, conforming to the rational requirement to either change your assessment or follow through with your decision is required for being self-governing over time.

If this argument succeeds then, at least on Bratman's conception of diachronic autonomy, it would be true that diachronic autonomy requires conformity to a rational requirement to follow through with one's past decisions. So, autonomy in the diachronic case would not be – as we have claimed – the same as autonomy in the synchronic case.

But the argument does not seem to us to succeed – at least, not if we accept that our agency is temporally extended. As Bratman himself agrees, a unified point of view over time must admit of change; a practical standpoint evolves over time and, at least as long as such changes are rational, not manipulated, and not in some other way undermining of the agent's self-governance, they do not threaten the agent's self-governance over time. But "shuffling" in incommensurability and equal value cases seems to clearly count as an unproblematic change in the agent's attitudes over time. If – while I shuffle – each time I form a new intention, I do so on the basis of an enduring "practical perspective" that provides sufficient grounds for it, then all my decisions and actions over this time frame are being guided by the same fundamental point of view. So, this is a clear instance of being guided by a "unified point of view". Thus, even if we adopt Bratman's conception of autonomy, violations of (D) do *not* seem to threaten our autonomy over time.[37]

Now, if we assume a time-slice conception of agency, such that the self who decided to ϕ and the self who decided to ψ were different agents, then it might indeed be hard to think that there is a unified point of view. But this lack of unification would be a result of the fact that they were two different selves. Two different selves reaching different conclusions from the same "information" (namely, that the options are on par or incommensurable) might not seem to have a unified point of view. If we reject the time-slice conception, there is no difficulty in seeing the point of view from which the agent shuffles from her decision to ϕ to her decision to ψ as a unified one.[38]

To further illustrate the point, think of a (quasi)-synchronic shuffling case: a case in which there are no time gaps between the shuffles. Suppose you are deciding between two shirts, a red and a blue one, and you reach the conclusion that the two choices are completely on par. You tell the salesperson: "I'll take the red". As he is about to pick up the red shirt, you say: "No, the blue!", then "Actually the red", and finally "No, definitely the blue". You are certainly exhibiting indecisiveness, but you do not lack a unified point of view that is guiding and controlling your actions. Your point of view is that the two are on par, and that it is, thus, a toss-up of which one to go with. There is nothing substantially new introduced if we add time gaps between the shuffles (e.g., if I decide to go with the red shirt, put it on hold and go for lunch, and then switch to the blue shirt when I come back to make the purchase).

4. Isn't the Diachronic Case Special?

Our claim is that there is no special problem in understanding our autonomy in acting on past decisions: it is just like acting autonomously on decisions we make at the moment. But it is important to be clear that this is a broader and stronger claim than just that the Problem of Diachronic Autonomy, as specified in Section 1, is not really a problem. Even if you grant that the Problem of Diachronic Autonomy, as specified, does not itself amount to a real problem, you might propose that there is another important difference between the diachronic and the synchronic case that explains why there is indeed a special problem in understanding how we can be autonomous in the diachronic case. In this section, we discuss three such arguments.

The first such argument appeals to the fact that in the diachronic case, there is the opportunity to change one's mind. One can change one's mind over time, but one cannot (or at least should not) be of two minds *at a time*. Doesn't this show that there is a special problem in explaining why we are autonomous when we act on past decisions?

But why would it? First notice that if an agent changes her mind about her evaluations or overall preferences but acts – despite this – on her earlier views, she is *not* acting autonomously. Such a case would be, at best, a case of *akrasia*. Few philosophers argue that an agent in such a situation would be manifesting diachronic autonomy. So, the case in which an agent changes her mind but nonetheless acts on her past decision cannot be said to pose a special problem for explaining diachronic autonomy, since that just wouldn't be a case of diachronic autonomy.[39]

Perhaps, though, the claim is not that actual cases of changing one's mind pose a problem for understanding diachronic autonomy, but rather that the *possibility* of changing one's mind in the diachronic case poses the problem. That is, even if you do not in fact change your mind, and you do act on your past decision, there is no guarantee that you would have stuck with that decision *had* you deliberated further in the time that elapsed between making the decision and acting. The fact that you could have changed your mind might be thought to pose a problem for understanding how you are autonomous when you simply follow through.

But once we move to merely possible changes of mind, there doesn't seem to be any interesting difference between the diachronic and synchronic cases. In the synchronic case, it is also often true that *had* you deliberated further you might have come to a different decision. Suppose I deliberate and decide to bake a cake "right away". It is true that further deliberation might have changed my mind and even revealed to me that I ignored some important preferences that I have or that I was too quick to conclude that I prefer my homemade cakes to the store-bought ones. But deliberation must come to an end at some point, and the fact that I *could have* continued deliberating, and even the thought that were I to continue to deliberate I would probably end up deciding something else, does not threaten my (synchronic) autonomy when I proceed to bake the cake.

The diachronic case is just an instance of this same general phenomenon. Sometimes deliberation ends because we are convinced that no further deliberation would change our mind. But sometimes deliberation ends because we ran out of time, were too tired, didn't think it was worth the effort, etc.[40] Of course, when making decisions in such circumstances, I might have second thoughts or change my mind as I start acting on the decision. However, if I do not have second thoughts and do not change my mind, this is no threat to my autonomy. Acting on the outcome of such deliberations is perfectly autonomous. There is no difference introduced by the diachronic case other than the time lag between the decision and the action. Of course, if we think that the time lag makes it the case that the person who decides and the person who acts are not, in the relevant sense, the same person, then the introduction of the time lag would be significant. But, as we said earlier, all of those concerned with diachronic autonomy are committed to (and indeed must be committed to) the identity of the agent through time.

So, the first argument fails: the possibility of changing my mind does not pose any special problem for understanding our diachronic autonomy. In neither the diachronic case nor the synchronic case, does the fact that further deliberations might have resulted in a different decision threaten the autonomy of acting on the decisions that we do make.

Perhaps, though, the distinctive problem of diachronic autonomy comes from a particular sort of risk that one will change one's mind, namely, the risk of temptation. This is the second argument. Suppose I know that tomorrow evening my cousin will call and ask if I want to go to a karaoke bar. However, I promised my aunt that I would have her quilt ready by the day after tomorrow, and if I don't spend all of tomorrow evening sewing, the quilt will not be ready on time. I think that I really should finish the quilt on time, but I suspect that tomorrow I might end up finding a way to rationalize joining my cousin. I thus make a resolution, or at least form an intention, today that I will stay home sewing the quilt tomorrow evening. When the time comes to act on my intention, I recognize that I might be tempted to reconsider my decision and go to the karaoke bar instead. I thus make a special effort not to reopen the question about my evening plans; I keep chanting to myself "quilt for auntie!" so that I'll not deliberate on this issue. I avoid deliberating exactly because I suspect that my current evaluative standpoint would lead me to make a different decision.

There seems to be a real challenge to our understanding of my autonomy here that finds no parallel in the synchronic case; it seems that we need to understand how acting on an intention that I formed exactly so as not to act on my current evaluative standpoint could be an expression of my autonomy. After all, at least on some conceptions of autonomy, in order to act autonomously, my actions must somehow express my evaluative standpoint or a motive that I (truly) endorse.

But is there really no "synchronic parallel" to such a case? In the karaoke case, I avoid reopening the deliberative question because I am aware that the proximity of a certain kind of enjoyment could warp my practical standpoint. Specifically, I am aware that, were I to deliberate now, my reasoning would be corrupted by the nefarious influence of the propinquity of the satisfaction afforded by karaoke singing. But similar impediments to my deliberative capacities can be present in synchronic temptation cases. Suppose my wedding ring falls into the bottom of a cold and deep pool. I immediately jump into the pool to try to recover it. As I dive into the cold water, I realize that I might be tempted to give up pursuing the ring in order to avoid the pain and discomfort I'm enduring. Fearing this possibility, I avoid thinking about the pros and cons of continuing in my search for the ring, and instead just keep chanting to myself "must get the ring" until I snatch it from the bottom of the pool. This is not a case of deciding in advance to do something that I suspect I will be tempted not to do when the time comes. I never formed a prior intention to save my ring in such a situation. But here, as in the diachronic temptation case,

I avoid deliberating, and so avoid acting according to deliberation from my current practical standpoint, because I fear that doing so would lead me astray.

We can see what the two cases have in common: in certain contexts, I realize that my best judgment is not the one that would be formed by careful deliberation at the time of action, because I realize that some part of my evaluative standpoint has been corrupted. I thus rely on judgments or motives that I form (or have formed) in other ways. In the diachronic case, I rely on a judgment that was made in the past. In the synchronic case, I simply act on my desire to save the ring without allowing myself to consider the merits of the other options. In both cases, I refuse to open deliberation due to my realization that it might lead me astray. In the diachronic case, my action relies on prior deliberation, but given the assumption that we are temporally extended agents, why should this make any difference to the question of whether or how my action is autonomous? Whether the best judgment or motive happens to lie in the present or in the past, in both cases, I act on an intention that expresses *my* best judgment or motive.[41]

Let's turn to the third argument. The third argument says that there is a crucial difference between the diachronic and synchronic cases that we have overlooked, namely, that it is possible to manipulate your future self. Even though the past self is the same agent as the future self, you can manipulate your future self, and – the claim goes – this shows that there is a special problem in understanding our autonomy when we act on past decisions.

It is true that it is possible to manipulate my future self. There are two ways in which I can do this. First, I can create "coercive" incentives for my future self, with the aim – for instance – of avoiding temptation.[42] For example, I can make sure that I do not have ice cream for dessert by making it the case that when the time comes for dessert the "cost" of getting ice cream will be artificially high: I can give away all the ice cream that I have in my freezer so that the only way for me to have ice-cream for dessert would be to make a special trip to the grocery store across town. Second, I can try to bind my future self in a way that blocks my future self from having any choice on the matter when the time comes. For instance, I might hypnotize myself now, so that when I later hear the theme song of "Days of Our Lives", I will walk to my office (because otherwise I would watch the show and get no work done).

But while I can indeed manipulate my future self in these ways, this does not give rise to any special problem in understanding diachronic autonomy. This is because there is nothing distinctive about the possibility of manipulating oneself in the diachronic case: both varieties of diachronic self-manipulation have synchronic counterparts.

Starting with the second kind of case, we can imagine a synchronic version of the hypnosis example. Imagine that *while* the theme song of

"Days of Our Lives" is playing, I hypnotize myself to walk to my office when I hear the theme song of "Days of Our Lives". I thereby immediately (before the song is over) walk to my office and get to work. There is no temporal distance here between the hypnosis and walking to my office. But I am, nonetheless, clearly manipulating myself into walking to my office.

The first variety of self-manipulation (giving myself coercive incentives) is also possible in the synchronic case. Suppose I am eating the leftovers off my dinner guests' plates as I clean the dishes. The leftover morsels of food are so tempting, but I also think to myself that I should not be eating little pieces of partially consumed food off other people's plates. So, as I am driving the fork to my mouth with my right hand, I pour detergent onto the food with my left hand to make it significantly less desirable. Since I know I will not like the taste of detergent, I stop eating the leftovers.

As these examples of synchronic self-manipulation reveal, there is nothing distinctive about the possibility of manipulating yourself in the diachronic case. Technological obstacles make synchronic cases of self-manipulation less common than diachronic cases, but they are not impossible and do sometimes happen. Thus, it is a mistake to think that the possibility of self-manipulation poses a special challenge in understanding cases in which we do act autonomously on our past decisions.

Indeed, on the contrary, reflection on diachronic self-manipulation cases helps illustrate why acting directly on my past decision is a straightforward, paradigm case of acting autonomously. In the self-manipulative ice cream example, when I eat fruit for dessert instead of ice cream, the relationship between my past decision to have fruit for dessert and my current eating of fruit for dessert is deviant. Rather than the past decision directly causing me to eat fruit for dessert when the time comes, the past decision spurred me to set up incentives so that I would, when the time comes, abide by my decision. Indeed, when I eat the fruit for dessert, I am not *acting on* my past intention to eat fruit for dessert at all. Rather, I am acting on a new intention to eat fruit based on my current evaluation of the options. The case involves self-manipulation[43] because I interfered with the factors that I knew would come into my evaluation of the options.

Suppose instead now that I decide this afternoon to have fruit for dessert this evening; I go about my other business for the rest of the day, and after dinner, I simply *act on* my earlier decision. I get out a bowl of strawberries from the fridge and eat it. In this case, the relationship between my past decision and the action that executes it is not deviant. I eat strawberries simply and directly because I decided to, and that's all there is to it. Nothing could be more straightforwardly autonomous than that.

5. Time-Slice Agency and Diachronic Autonomy

Our account of autonomy in acting on past decisions appeals to the fact that our agency is temporally extended; we claim that once we recognize this fact, there is no distinctive problem in understanding our diachronic autonomy. As we mentioned, some people dispute that we are temporally extended agents and subscribe, instead, to a time-slice conception of human agency. We think that the time-slice conception is mistaken, but more relevantly for our purposes in this chapter, so do the philosophers concerned with the Problem of Diachronic Autonomy. Not only do they happen to subscribe to a temporally extended picture of our agency, but they also need to if they are interested in giving an account of future-directed decisions. In this section, though, we want to briefly consider the time-slice conception of agency, and look at a version of the Problem of Diachronic Autonomy that might be thought to arise on such a conception.

Here is the time-slice conception's version of the problem: while there is no such thing as one's past self literally deciding for one's future self, there is something like it that happens all the time. Our past selves very often, somehow or other, seem to control our future selves. Our past selves make what *look like* decisions for our future self (even though they cannot really be doing anything different in kind from advising or commanding). And our future selves often seem to simply follow those dictates, without question. It sounds then that the life of the average person involves constantly being manipulated by other people (i.e., her past selves) – a terrifying prospect! But at least, in standard cases of my present time-slice following the dictates of my past time-slice, it doesn't *feel as though* I'm being manipulated; rather, I regard myself as acting autonomously. How can this be? We can call this the "Time-Slice Problem of Diachronic Autonomy". It isn't a problem that concerns our diachronic agency, since our agency is not diachronic, on such a conception. But it is a problem that concerns how one time-slice can maintain its autonomy in these diachronic situations.

How to understand a time-slice view in this context is a complicated issue. What we will do here is just briefly explain why we think that the Time-Slice Problem of Diachronic Autonomy is not a distinctive problem for those with a time-slice conception. That is, we will argue that there is no special problem for the time-slice conception in explaining our autonomy in diachronic situations, and rather – much like we argued in the case of the cross-temporal conception – as far as autonomy is concerned, there is *no interesting difference* between the diachronic and synchronic cases.

The difference between acting autonomously and not is not a difference in whether you are acting *in accordance with* your preferences, or judgments, etc. First, one can act in accordance with one's current preferences without being autonomous at all; one can end up with one's most preferred outcome due to deviant causes or fortuitous circumstances. Second, I can be fully autonomous, even though I have made a mistake of calculation, overlooked an important aspect of my situation, etc., such that I am not acting in accordance with my current preferences. The difference between acting autonomously and not is a difference in whether you are being *guided by* your own judgments, or evaluations, or some such thing. Autonomy requires that my action is properly guided by my judgments, evaluations, or preferences, or that my action is the outcome of my (possibly implicit) deliberations. But deliberation, or any process or event that will count as "being properly guided", takes time. So, even in the "synchronic" case, in which I act immediately on a decision that I have just made (with no time gap), autonomy seems to require at least a causal relation between items that exist at different times or extend through time. It is, thus, not clear how a time-slice agent can be autonomous at all unless autonomy is a relation that the time-slice agent bears to its past selves. The process of deliberation or of being guided by one's judgments, preferences, or evaluations spans more than a moment and thus must operate through more than just the present time-slice agent. If this is right, then even on the time-slice conception, there is no special problem in understanding our autonomy in the diachronic case. Autonomy, even under that conception, must be by its very nature diachronic.

6. A Concluding Thought

If we reflect on the nature of action, it is not surprising that there is no special problem of diachronic autonomy. Any action takes time to execute; there is no such thing as action that occurs in a mere moment. So, there is no truly "synchronic" case. Because actions always take time, intentions must always operate over time. The intention that I have at the beginning of action must sustain my action throughout its duration. When I walk to the library, my intention needs to persist until I reach the library. While I could reconsider what I am doing partway through, most often I do not. Most commonly, as I make my way through the city blocks to my destination, I do not redeliberate, reconsider my reasons, or even rely on exclusionary reasons not to reopen the question; I simply continue to act on the same intention. The difference between this case and the "diachronic case" that was supposed to pose a special puzzle is only a matter of the length of the time that elapses between forming the intention and (completely) executing it.

Though it certainly does lend some support, noticing that all action is diachronic is not enough to establish that there is no special problem of diachronic autonomy concerning future-directed decisions. Even if all actions take time, it could be that once we are talking about decisions concerning the not-merely-immediate future, the puzzle arises. It could, in other words, be that once the time that elapses crosses some rough threshold, something additional is needed than in the more "synchronic-like" cases to make sense of how we are autonomous in following through with the original intention. Our argument shows that this is not so: it shows that a difference in degree does not make for a difference in kind in this case.

Notes

* For very helpful comments on earlier drafts of the paper, we would like to thank Michael Bratman, Luca Ferrero, Kim Frost, Amelia Hicks, Dana Howard, Hanti Lin, Berislav Marusic, Sarah Paul, Regina Rini, Tina Rulli, John Schwenkler, Itai Sher, Matthew Silverstein, Walter Sinnott-Armstrong, Karen Stohr, Larry Temkin, Mike Teitelbaum, and Stephen White. We would also like to thank audiences at Duke University, the 2015 Workshop in Ethics at Dartmouth University, the 2015 St. Louis Annual Conference on Reasons and Rationality, the Belief Rationality and Action Over Time Workshop in Madison, the 2017 Meeting of the Israeli Philosophical Association, and the Varieties of Agency Workshop at Stanford University and departmental colloquia at Universidade de Campinas, Universidade Federal do Rio de Janeiro, and Université Paris I (Panthéon-Sorbonne). We greatly profited from the discussions in all these venues.
1 In this paper, we use "future-directed intention" and "future-directed decision" interchangeably. More precisely, our view is that a future-directed decision is a kind of future-directed intention, namely, one that is formed by deliberation. There are other future-directed intentions that are not formed by deliberation, but this doesn't matter for our purposes here. So we can, for simplicity, use the two terms interchangeably.
2 Ferrero 2010, p. 1.
3 There is, of course, a lot of disagreement about what it takes for an action to be autonomous. This does not matter for our purposes. As long as you accept that for my act to be autonomous, I must at least act on my own intention (or reasons, or desires) than we have what we need for the arguments we want to make. While there will be other conditions for an act to count as autonomous beyond that basic one, it is that basic one that is at play in the Problem of Diachronic Autonomy: the concern is that if I act directly on my past decision, then I am not acting on my *current self*'s intentions (or desires or reasons) and am instead being manipulated by my past self.
4 Velleman 1997, p. 46.
5 Velleman 1997, p. 49.
6 Velleman 1997, p. 49. Velleman explains that on a *maximize utility* conception of the aim of action, there is no room for a future-directed decision to ϕ to generate reason to ϕ. On such a conception, one only has reason to ϕ *if* doing so maximizes utility. So, if Velleman is right that our future-directed decisions must generate reason to follow through, then the maximizing-utility conception cannot be correct. He explains: "If an action were the sort of thing whose success or failure could be judged solely by utility-maximizing considerations, then it wouldn't be the sort of thing that we could decide on today in a way that would necessarily give us reason to perform it tomorrow . . . But action *is* that sort of thing—it *is* behaviour over which rational agents have diachronic autonomy" (Velleman 1997, p. 49).
7 Paul 2014, pp. 349–350.

8 Such cases are useful in thinking about whether a decision to φ generates reasons to φ, since they rule out that other reasons to φ (e.g., that it's easier to φ than to take the other options) are what are really doing the work.
9 Paul 2014, p. 351.
10 For Paul, *r* is, roughly, that every time one follows through with a decision this helps maintain (or, at least, avoids eroding) one's ability to understand one's own decisions as authoritative, and this is an ability that we have an interest in maintaining. For Velleman, *r* is something like: following through will preserve my autonomy (or, some other reason connected to the constitutive aim of action, autonomy.)
11 Velleman might reply to this objection as follows: while the future-directed decision generates reason to follow through with it, one would only act *for* this new reason if one reconsidered before following through. If one does not reconsider, then one might simply follow through with the original decision, acting for the original reasons. If this is Velleman's view, this avoids the objection that on his account, I must be eating the avocado burrito at least partly in order to preserve my autonomy. But even if Velleman can avoid that first objection in this way, this does not help with the issues we will raise in what follows. This is because even if I need not act *for* the new reason, it is still true – on his account – that the existence of this new reason is doing the work of explaining why my following through is autonomous. That is, whether or not I explicitly entertain it or act for it, his solution to the Problem of Diachronic Autonomy is that I have this new reason and that this new reason is (part of) what justifies my following through with the decision. The new reason is something I should take into account if I do reopen the question, and if I do not reopen it, the reason is still doing "behind-the-scenes" work in justifying my action and explaining it as autonomous. This is enough for the next objection we make, and it is enough for our general critique in Section 3.
12 In this essay, we use the terms "manipulation" and "coercion" fairly loosely to capture the ways of interfering with someone's agency that are of concern in the Problem of Diachronic Autonomy. Interpersonal coercion often involves threats, but, of course, intrapersonal coercion could not be threats-based. But in the interpersonal case too, coercion need not involve threats: it can occur through acts that constrain the agent's choice situation. If I set up an automated electric shock system so that every Tuesday, if you do not come visit me, you will receive a very painful shock, I am coercing you into visiting me on Tuesdays, even though I have not issued any threat.
13 Ferrero 2010, p. 1.
14 In particular, we often can give others positive incentives to act as we wish without coercing them. (For example, "if you help me move, I'll buy you a nice dinner".) Interestingly, it is hard come up with a clean case of giving *yourself* a "positive" incentive. If I promise myself ice cream as an incentive to finish unpacking, it might seem as though I'm giving myself a positive incentive. But ice cream, in this example, must be something that I have access to unless I withhold it from myself. So, it seems more accurate (or, at least, equally accurate) to characterize this as a case of negative incentives: the incentive is that unless I finish the unpacking, I will withhold ice cream from myself.
15 This should not be read as a threat. It is, on the accounts in question, what you *make true* by deciding for your future self, rather than something you threaten to do to your future self. It looks, thus, more like the case of coercing by setting up an electric shock system (see footnote 12), rather than coercing via threats.
16 Bratman 2012, p. 79; we have rephrased it into "You ought (If p, to q)" form.
17 Bratman notes that "self-governance over time" for him is the same idea as "diachronic autonomy" for Velleman. See Bratman 2012, p. 87, n. 26.

Extended Agency and Diachronic Autonomy 193

18 It's worth noting that Bratman does raise the Problem of Diachronic Autonomy elsewhere. For instance, in "Toxin, Temptation and the Stability of Intention", Bratman writes that a theory of instrumentally rational planning agency "needs to be responsive to a fundamental tension": "On the one hand, a planning agent settles in advance what to do later. On the other hand, she is an agent who, whatever her prior plans, normally retains rational control over what she does when the time comes. Following through with one's plan is not, after all, like following through with one's tennis swing. We need to do justice to both these aspects of planning agency" (Bratman 1999, p. 60).
19 Ferrero 2010, p. 10. Ferrero imposes further conditions, but they do not affect our argument. We cannot do justice here to all the aspects of Ferrero's interesting discussion of the division of deliberative labor.
20 Fererro 2010, p. 13.
21 What this difference is will become clear in the next section. Note that we don't deny that there might be special cases in which following through on your past decisions is like following expert advice. Our point is that this is not the normal case of acting on a past decision. See footnote 33 for more on this.
22 You might propose that this is because where I am going to have lunch is a rather unimportant decision. Maybe the conditions for autonomy are not as strict in fairly trivial cases like this. But most of our actions on the basis of future-directed intentions are, in the grand scheme of things, rather minor. And it's not that trivial that pursuits are immune to failures of autonomy. It would be very different, for instance, if my action was the result of the subliminal but infallible effect that Taco Hut commercials have on my mind. My following through with a decision I made this morning, even if the decision was made under less than ideal circumstances, seems to bear no resemblance to this kind of manipulation.
23 We are not assuming any particular solution to the problem of personal identity over time, nor are we assuming that there is no such problem. We do assume, as we will presently explain, that human agents, or persons, persist through time such that – for instance – myself from this morning is (in the normal case) the same person as myself from this afternoon. But we do not assume or require any particular account of how this works. Whatever the correct account is of what makes it the case that myself from this morning is the same person as myself from this afternoon, this should be fine for our purposes here, and thus we can remain neutral on this difficult question.
24 Now, the time-slice conception might have its own version of the Problem of Diachronic Autonomy. We will discuss this briefly in Section 5.
25 Paul 2014, p. 339.
26 Velleman 1997, p. 46, our emphasis.
27 Velleman 1997, p. 47, our emphasis.
28 Ferrero 2010, p. 15, our emphasis.
29 In "A Planning Agent's Self-Governance Over Time" (Bratman 2018, reprinted in this volume), Bratman is explicit that, at least for him, these ways of talking are metaphorical. He doesn't think there are literally multiple agents at play; it is just one agent acting at different times. The metaphor, though, he thinks is helpful (pp. 230–232). But the worry is that, without the metaphorical talk of more than one agent, the problem simply disappears. See footnote 38 for more details.
30 There will likely be other conditions that must be satisfied for the act to count as autonomous (e.g., that there are no deviant causal chains), but this does not make a difference to our point.
31 Velleman 1997, pp. 45–46.
32 It should be clear that we do not claim to have shown that future-directed decisions never generate reasons or rational requirements to follow through with them. What we are arguing is that there is no argument for such reasons

or rational requirements *from* the Problem of Diachronic Autonomy: we do not need them in order to explain how it is that our future-directed decisions effectively control our behavior or how it is that we are autonomous when we act on them. This does not rule out that there may be some totally other sort of argument for them.

33 To clarify: this is our understanding of normal, typical cases of acting on past decisions. We don't want to deny that there could be unusual cases in which acting according to one's past decision is like following the advice of an expert. Suppose that I am walking in the park and see a group of people practicing Tai Chi. Tai Chi has never appealed to me before, but this time, it suddenly does. I decide that I will sign up for Tai Chi classes. Immediately, after making the decision, a stray baseball hits me on the head and I am knocked unconscious. When I wake up, I have no persisting intention to sign up for Tai Chi and indeed no memory of having made the decision. If I later remember having made the decision and, on the basis of this memory alone (without having any idea whatsoever what reasons I might have had to sign up for Tai Chi), sign up for classes, this would seem to be a case of treating my past self's decision as something like expert advice. But this is far from the normal case of acting on a future-directed decision. In the normal case, the decision either is or gives rise to an intention that persists over time, and which I act on (so long as there is no interference, like a change of mind).

34 Ferrero might be excepted from this charge. But still the kind of autonomous agency at work in his account – namely, the kind that we exercise when we defer to the advice of another – is hardly paradigmatic autonomy and arguably is less than ideal.

35 Assuming, of course, there is nothing else going on to take away from the significance of this fact.

36 Bratman, "Time, Rationality, and Self-Governance", p. 77.

37 For a similar critique, see Ferrero 2012, p. 160.

38 In his "A Planning Agent's Self-Governance Over Time", Bratman tries to further back-up his argument that diachronic self-governance requires (D) by arguing that temporally extended planning agency is largely analogous to interpersonal shared agency. When one forms a future-directed intention for one's future self, this is *analogous* to (even though not the same as) trying to act jointly with another person. To be self-governing over time, then – Bratman argues – one must coordinate with and be responsive to one's past intentions in the same sorts of ways that agents acting together must coordinate and be responsive to each other's intentions. It is not clear to us, though, that the analogy really works in the way that Bratman says it does, if we truly accept that your future self who acts is not a different agent from your present self who decides. (For instance, rather than – as Bratman's analogy seems to require – following through on a future-directed intention to A involving having a new intention to A that interlocks with one's past intention to A, it can simply involve retaining one's intention to A over time and acting on it. If that's right, then the analogy does not hold.) But more importantly: even if the analogy does largely hold, it does not seem to us to support a rational requirement against shuffling, provided that we really are – as Bratman intends to – accepting that it is only an analogy, and there is really only one agent. If there is one agent with a single practical perspective that equally supports both φ-ing and ψ-ing all along, then while one would, of course, not be following through with one's intention to φ if one shuffled to intending to ψ instead, there is no reason to think that this amounts to a breakdown of self-governance of any kind.

39 Even those who think that agents ought to act on their past resolutions when facing potential judgment or preference shifts, do not think that agents should act contrary to their current judgments. Holton, for instance, argues that an agent should not reconsider her resolution, exactly because she knows that were she to reconsider she would abandon her resolution and, in that case, it would not be rational to act according to the resolution. See Holton 2004. Bratman considers a view on which rationally resisting temptation involves acting contrary to one's current judgment in "Toxin, Temptation, and the Stability of Intention". But in a later paper, he rejects that understanding of rationally resisting temptation (see Bratman 2014).
40 And, of course, sometimes we do not even deliberate.
41 Our reply to this argument does not depend on this particular description of what makes these actions autonomous; it does not even commit us to accepting that these actions are indeed autonomous. All that we need for our purposes is the claim that the synchronic and diachronic cases are perfectly parallel in the relevant respects.
42 See the classic discussion of such cases in Ainslie 2001.
43 If it does. Some might want to deny that this case and the analogous synchronic case involve self-manipulation at all, since in both cases, the agent is following her best judgment. This is fully compatible with our view; our claim here is that even if we grant that these cases involve self-manipulation, they do not show a disanalogy between the synchronic and diachronic cases.

References

Ainslie, George. 2001. *Breakdown of Will*. Cambridge: Cambridge University Press.

Bratman, Michael. 1999. "Toxin, Temptation, and the Stability of Intention", in Michael Bratman, ed. *Faces of Intention*. Cambridge: Cambridge University Press.

Bratman, Michael. 2012. "Time, Rationality, and Self-Governance", *Philosophical Issues* 22:1, 73–88.

Bratman, Michael. 2014. "Temptation and the Agent's Standpoint", *Inquiry*, special issue on Choice Over Time, Sergio Tenenbaum, ed. 57:3, 293–310.

Bratman, Michael. 2018. "A Planning Agent's Self-Governance Over Time", in Bratman, M, eds., *Planning, Time, and Self-Governance: Essays in Practical Rationality*. Oxford University Press, 224–249.

Ferrero, Luca. 2010. "Decisions, Diachronic Autonomy, and the Division of Deliberative Labor", *Philosopher's Imprint* 10:2, 1–23.

Ferrero, Luca. 2012. "Diachronic Constraints of Practical Rationality", *Philosophical Issues* 22, 144–164.

Holton, Richard. 2004. "Rational Resolve", *Philosophical Review* 113:4, 507–535.

Paul, Sarah. 2014. "Diachronic Incontinence is a Problem in Moral Philosophy", *Inquiry*, special issue on Choice Over Time, Sergio Tenenbaum, ed. 57:3, 337–355.

Velleman, David. 1997. "Deciding How to Decide", in G. Cullity and B. Gaut, eds. *Ethics and Practical Reason*. Oxford: Oxford University Press, 29–52.

9 Hard Times:
Self-Governance, Freedom to Change, and Normative Adjustment[1]

Carla Bagnoli

In deliberating about action, we consider whether and how our present choice respects our past and envision a future that we would welcome as a result of what we do. Current debates in action theory take this concern to be distinctive of temporally extended agents. However, it is possible to conceive of temporally extended agents who are not concerned with organizing and harmonizing themselves over time because they do not experience any significant changes. Human agents, conversely, often face hard choices because their present concerns conflict with their past plans. Humans strive for coherence: they design future actions while feeling the burden of duties contracted in the remote past or pressed by commitments they regret making. Despite the heavyweight of their past deliberations and decisions, these agents conceive of themselves as free to revise their plans, reassess the claims of the past, and question whether commitments arising from lapsed relations still provide compelling reasons for action. This freedom is an agential power, as well as an ethical and political priority: it is related to the right to develop one's own conception of a flourishing life.[2]

My argument will be that to fully understand the freedom to change and develop, we have to characterize the predicaments of temporal rational agency in ways that have largely escaped current debates. Such debates construe the challenge faced by temporal agents in terms of tradeoffs between the value of temporally distributed options.[3] The present is understood to exert a distinctive pull; part of the philosophical problem is to establish whether this pull is normative as well as motivational. From this perspective, the main concern for theories of diachronic agency is to explain the transmission of agential authority over time despite the corrosive effect of time passing. Correspondingly, their task is to provide normative devices that stabilize the agent's practical standpoint by counteracting the threats to diachronic coherence (e.g., in the guise of principles, plans, future-directed intentions, pre-commitments, self-nudging, self-commands, etc.). The virtues of willpower, grit, and resoluteness are consequently identified as the core modes of exercising rational self-governance under temporal constraints.

DOI: 10.4324/9780429259845-12

In contrast to the perspective mentioned earlier, this chapter calls attention to cases of cross-temporal dissonance. Such cases arise because temporal agents thrive on their freedom to change views and in time develop new categorical concerns; their deliberative powers are directly invested in this endeavor. This characterization imposes a shift in perspective: the problem becomes how to account for normative adjustment. Correspondingly, the task is to ensure that rational self-governance can be effectively exercised despite the modifying motivational structure of the will. The distinctive mode of temporal agents' rational self-governance is dynamic, in the sense that it draws on a plastic network of normative, affective, cognitive, and meta-cognitive competences. Such higher-order capacities secure self-governance over time in more complex ways than those envisioned by current theories of diachronic agency.[4] The resulting conception of dynamic self-governance is marked by ambivalences and dissonances, but it is robust enough to tolerate normative change without leaving us with a multitude of scattered selves.

I shall argue that freedom to change is vital to the developmental dynamics of self-governance; it is therefore a requirement of dynamic practical rationality to protect it by fostering suitable normative adjustments. In Section 1, I present the standard view of the predicaments of temporally extended agency. The standard view centers on the alleged privilege of the present stance. In Section 2, I provide two arguments for non-reconsideration of past intentions and plans, both of which are designed for the case of temptation. In Section 3, I show that these arguments cannot be extended to cases of diachronic conflicts of ideals or normative indeterminacy. In Section 4, I address some examples of dissonance that I take to be paradigmatic of temporal agency. I do so in order to show that rational self-governance does not require diachronic coherence in the form of intentional stability or volitional integrity. In Section 5, I account for the meta-cognitive and affective resources available to temporal, interdependent, and mutually vulnerable agents to foster dynamic self-governance. In Section 6, I reassess the predicament posited by the anchorage of practical deliberation in the present. To this purpose, I distinguish the subjective and the objective dimensions of the normative authority of reasons for action. In Section 7, I argue that various forms of alienation are part of the processes of normative adjustment that underpin the dynamics of self-governance distinctive of temporal agents.

1. The Predicaments of Diachronic Agency: The Standard View

The fact that human agents are temporal living subjects raises difficult philosophical questions about the sort of rational self-governance that they can achieve. Current debates primarily focus on the predicaments that human agents encounter insofar as they are temporally situated, temporally extended, and temporally constrained. In the face of these problems, the job of rational deliberation is to correctly assess the intertemporal trade-off between temporally distributed options from the agential perspective. Temporal agents are represented as a sequence of selves that succeed one another in time. The main difficulty in implementing deliberative tasks is that past, present, and future are asymmetrical (Hare 2015). Generally, the present stance is said to be privileged because (i) it is causally active, whereas the future and the past are not; (ii) it is epistemically accessible in a way that the past and the future are not; and (iii) it exercises a special kind of pull that tends to be overriding in deliberation.

All these claims are contestable. However, I am concerned here with the third claim, which motivates the view that deliberation is constitutively biased to the present because it is anchored to it.[5] Indeed, one needs to place oneself in time in order to deliberate; this placement requires awareness of one's temporality and the temporal constraints that apply to the context of choice. Timing action is a key problem for temporally situated agents; this problem is not separate from the problem of describing the action to be brought about.[6]

The anchorage of deliberation in the present has different implications for the requisites of practical rationality depending on how its special pull is construed. On the *motivational* construal, the present stance is privileged because it is motivationally effective. Temporally situated agents therefore tend to act on the present ranking of options. Although this characterization does not tell us anything about the rational justification of the present ranking, it is expected to play a role in the explanation of rational action, since it indicates that rational action naturally flows from the agent's motives. The contrary case, in which motives and reasons for action diverge and rational action does not spring from the agent's motivational set, is harder to explain. It also raises issues regarding whether and how reasons unsupported by motives can effectively guide action. Any plausible account of rational action should thus explain how motives and reasons are related. On the *normative* construal, the present is the stance representative of the agent and hence the *locus* of agential authority: it is "where *the agent* stands".[7] For this reason, most theorists agree that the present ranking normally exerts a special normative pressure in deliberation. This special normative pressure is legitimate, unlike the tempting force of present desires.

These construals are not mutually exclusive but interestingly intertwined.[8] They both frame the problems of diachronic agency in distinctive ways. First, there is a general question about the very possibility of diachronic agency. If diachronic agents naturally tend to privilege their present ranking of options, how can temporally extended intentional actions be carried out, if at all? Second, there are specific issues about the requisites of practical rationality. Empirical studies point out that humans have an inbuilt bias toward the present that leads to future and past discounting. The philosophical question is under what conditions these attitudes are rationally justifiable or else undermine rational self-governance. Under conditions of uncertainty, it might be prudent to discount the future in favor of the present ranking, even with the prospect of a smaller reward. However, not all cases of future discounting are justifiable responses to uncertainty; some appear to be akin to irrational impatience.[9] Likewise, past discounting – as in Parfit's famous example of pain preferred to be in the past (Parfit 1984, pp. 156–166) – makes sense for temporally extended agents projected into and invested in the future. However, it is debatable whether this attitude is rationally justifiable or else a form of arbitrary partiality.

Temporality is generally regarded as the source of agential fragility, a radical tendency to self-disorganization (e.g., on the construal of temporal bias toward the present, which leads to discounting the future or the past and thereby undermines rational self-governance over time). I shall argue that this characterization of the challenges posed by temporality is too narrow and oversimplified. It encourages the view that the paradigmatic predicament of temporality is temptation, i.e., the case in which an agent is committed to a normative principle (plan or intention) but is tempted to violate it because of the present urgency of a desire. The characterization is also misleading in that it underestimates the importance of normative change and the constructive and structuring roles of affective temporal attitudes.

In discussing this general view, I shall refer to "the dominant model", because prominent theories of action share salient elements. The dominant model does not affirm that temporally extended agents lack the capacity to pull themselves together over time. On the contrary, the whole normative enterprise is put in place to contrast with the entropic tendency due to temporality. The philosophical question is whether, why, and how the norms of practical rationality regulate our vulnerability to time passing (e.g., by ruling out temporal bias as irrational).[10]

2. Two Arguments for Diachronic Coherence

Temporal agents who are aware of their temporality deliberate by taking into account the possibility of change, although not all changes are predictable or determinable in all their normative ramifications.[11] Temporally extended agents therefore face the problem of deliberating so as to fulfill their present commitments while keeping open the prospects of undetermined change.[12]

The prevailing approach in decision theory calculates the costs of reconsidering and abandoning a plan according to two main deliberative procedures: straightforward maximization and constrained maximization. The latter limits the spectrum of options to those compatible with prior plans and commitments. These calculations are possible insofar as the relevant normative changes are expressed in the uniformed language of preferences. This language facilitates commensuration but is inapt for capturing the subtlety and nuances of our deep emotional engagement with the practices of valuing. In moral philosophy and action theory, two major arguments support the claim that the norms of practical rationality prohibit temporal bias for the sake of rational self-governance over time. Both arguments assume that rational agents have reasons to foster rational self-governance over time, insofar as they are temporally extended.

First, the impartialist argument is that all forms of temporal bias are irrational. They are a form of arbitrary partiality akin to self-interestedness, which undermines rational agency. For Thomas Nagel, the rational stance of practical deliberation is timeless; any time-sensitive exception to practical principles is analogous to a plea in favor of oneself.[13] The view that practical judgments are rooted in time makes them hostage to temporal bias and dissociated from the conception of agency as temporally extended. If practical judgments had different contents across time, "then practical reasoning would be an area divorced from the conception of oneself as being equally real over time".[14] Notably, this position departs from the purely instrumental view of practical rationality, which is compatible with partialities of all sorts. In some of its formulations, the impartialist argument rests on the philosophical assumption that all rational agents are alike in the relevant respects.[15]

A second argument, proposed by Michael E. Bratman, derives the normativity of the requirement of diachronic stability and coherence from the normativity of self-governance. The requirement of diachronic stability is said to protect an intrinsic interest of temporally extended agents, on the assumption that incoherence undermines the structure of their will.[16] Broadly speaking, the will is conceived of as a faculty that maintains intact resolutions and blocks the reconsideration of previous intentions.[17] The principle of non-reconsideration of previous intentions seems designed to fit the case of temptation. In this case, it is rational to resist the force of the present ranking of options in order to protect diachronic rational self-governance. To this purpose, Bratman formulates a modest and fairly plausible principle of practical rationality. The principle requires that the revision of previous general policies be blocked on the condition that retention and non-reconsideration promote the agent's own end.[18] Bratman's argument for the stability of prior intentions is based on instrumental rationality and exploits the countervailing force of counterfactual regret: stability over time is "grounded in the central concerns of the planning agent with its own future, concerns that lend special significance to future regret".[19] If the planning agent anticipates that she will experience regret if she violates her general policy, such regret blocks the evaluative judgment in support of revision. The anticipation of regret amounts to the anticipation of a breakdown of agency over time, because and insofar as past intentions, principles, and policies are taken to be representative of the agent's stance. To ignore the pressure of present desires and goals has its own costs, but it protects the agent from alienation. The condition of alienation is generally taken to signal a failure of agential authority.[20] Similar arguments may be invoked to support resoluteness and similar virtues of grit, self-mastery, and willpower, which all facilitate self-governance.[21]

My argument in the next sections does not plainly contradict Bratman's principle of modest conservativism, insofar as this principle is formulated in terms of *pro tanto* reasons to favor conformity to prior plans. However, my argument presses the case that temporally structured agents may more often than not appeal to defeating reasons in the activity of exercising self-governance over time; their concern for the future takes the form of a careful reexamination and adjustment of prior plans. This is not to deny that plans (principles and intentions) play a crucial background framing role, as Bratman holds.[22] My suggestion is that they effectively do so in virtue of their being indeterminate and hence adaptable and revisable.[23] Self-governance seems better served by openness to autonomous normative change than by *pro tanto* diachronic stability.

3. Diachronic Conflicts of Ideals and Values

Temptation is not the only case in which the stability and rational authority of temporal agents are threatened. A more problematic case is that of global value changes, which require a global reassessment of responsibilities, obligations, and commitments. This case challenges the view that the present stance has normative priority.[24] As Thomas Nagel puts it:

> It may happen that a person believes a one time that he will at some future time accept general evaluative principles – principles about what constitute reasons for action – which he now finds pernicious. Moreover, he may believe that in the future he will find his present values pernicious. What does prudence require of him in that case? Prudence requires that he takes measures which promote the realization of that for which there *will* be reason. Do his beliefs at the earlier time give him any grounds for judging what he will have reason to do at the later time? It is not clear to me that they do, and if not, then the requirement of prudence or timeless reasons may not be applicable.[25]

Nagel distinguishes between changes in mere preferences and radical changes of values. Changes in preferences pose no problem for compensation over time. However, radical changes of value do, because they are disruptive of identity (on the assumption that identity rests on psychological continuity and some forms of motivational stability). For this reason, the latter are akin to conflicts among different persons. Whereas comparison and compensation are regarded as almost automatic in the case of intrapersonal conflicts of preferences, they are problematic in interpersonal conflicts of value and, by analogy, in the case of diachronic intrapersonal value conflicts. Similarly, building on the analogy between interpersonal and intrapersonal conflicts of ideals, Derek Parfit holds that agents cannot act on convictions and concerns that they do not have at the time of acting, any more than they can act on someone else's plans. If this is correct, then there are temporal constraints on the reasons that can be acted upon, even though the present stance has no normative priority. Importantly, these constraints are not (only) psychological but seem to pertain to the logic of rational thinking.[26]

Both Nagel and Parfit focus on cases in which agents can anticipate the direction of change. Nagel therefore suggests that they "*may* have a clear view of the matter" and be able to formulate a practical judgment in terms of timeless reasons. If an agent presently anticipates that his future ideal is worthless, then there are no prudential reasons to sacrifice the present for the future. Otherwise, there is a demand to have "a certain prudence about keeping open the paths to eventual respectability". This demand is advertised as a requirement of practical rationality. However, the scenario depends on values and beliefs that the agent holds at a present time, so it is not obvious that this anticipatory strategy respects the sort of timeless view that Nagel defends. Ultimately, Nagel recommends that we give priority to reasons and values that present agents expect to be stable across time. He hence takes stability to underwrite agential authority.

The considerations that block compensation across time count against the extension of Bratman's instrumentalist argument for non-reconsideration to the case of diachronic intrapersonal conflicts of value. The argument is still based on the premise that "the functional roles of prior intentions and plans include settling relevant practical matters in a way that supports the cross-temporal intention-interconnections that are characteristic of planned temporally extended activity".[27] According to Bratman, this principle also holds in the face of persistent normative underdetermination. Take, for instance, the case of Sartre's student debating whether to join the resistance or assist his ailing mother. In the absence of relevant changes to the description of options or the background context of choice, vacillation is irrational. It amounts to "brute shuffling": that is, shifting preference over a course of action on no rational ground.[28] Even when shuffling is not self-defeating, it undermines rational self-governance and thus agential unity. However, the success of the argument that discounts the present by anticipating a future regret crucially depends on the hypothesis that "the agent stays the same" throughout.

Furthermore, the extension of the regret-based argument from the case of temptation to that of shuffling oversimplifies the general problem of diachronic self-integration. It assumes that motivational stability and formal coherence are necessary requirements of self-governance over time. This equivalence can also be rejected from an impartialist perspective. For instance, Nagel (1986) admits that adopting a timeless view of one's life may be "objectively unwise", because such a view requires systematic control of one's first-order motives.[29] On a timeless view of rational agency, all diachronic conflicts are understood on the model of temptation; diachronic stability is ensured by imposing systematic control on first-order motives. Nagel identifies the costs of the timeless view in terms of the willpower model. However, the costs may be higher and of a different kind, as I shall argue shortly.

The acknowledgment of the drawbacks of the timeless view leaves us with a substantial problem concerning how we should conceive of rational self-governance for temporally structured rational agents for whom shifts in value and normative changes do not occur only in exceptional and catastrophic circumstances. Shifts and transitions are instead inherent to the agents' nature; they are ordinary, to be expected, and protected as allowing for growth and development. We may gain insights by refocusing on the deliberative efforts of agents who are at pains to adjust to normative changes they have sought and responsibly undertaken.

4. The Dynamics of Normative Adjustment

Values are key modes of cross-temporal organization and play a large role in practical deliberation, but they may be conflictual. It is not obvious that the most perceptive way of dealing with conflicts of values, whether in synchronic or diachronic rational deliberation, is to treat them as akin to incoherence.[30] It is also questionable whether temporal rational agents should preserve rational self-governance by resisting normative change, even though they are recognizably striving for volitional harmony. In fact, agents engage in rational self-governance precisely to achieve such harmony. In this section, I discuss some examples of normative adjustment to diachronic changes in values. In these examples, the awareness of the temporality of one's agency takes center stage. The cases are presented from within the subjective perspective of the agent who is transitioning from one cluster of values to another, rather than comparing rankings of options that pop up at subsequent times. On these occasions, agents learn how to govern themselves by enduring ambivalences and engaging in shuffling, even though their attitudes do not track any qualitative change in the options' features. The emphasis on the difficulty of normative adjustment has two objectives: first, to provide an alternative framework for the study of global normative changes, and second, to uncover a large array of underappreciated practical resources available to temporal agents.

CASE 1: PROJECTION. A teenage girl, Mary, decides not to terminate her pregnancy, even though she recognizes that her decision lacks adequate rational grounding.[31] Mary positively anticipates that she will love her child, so that her future life will be shaped by maternal love. This hopeful anticipation is not a prediction, nor is it an exercise in prospection understood as a speculative activity about how the future will unfold.

Rather, *hope* allows Mary to project herself into a future in which she will have acquired categorical reasons that will make her present choice non-regrettable, although unwise on some descriptions. Whether this future prospect will indeed materialize partly depends on concurring factors that are not under Mary's volitional control, because they involve another person's will (namely, the child's).[32] However, Mary's projection can be justified by a reasoning of the sort "I will be glad to have had a child".[33] Importantly, this reasoning is transformative and generative, in that it has an agency-enhancing and a self-fulfilling effect. It raises the chances that Mary's projected prospect will be realized by setting in motion a complex set of co-reactive attitudes that elicit – and in some cases demand – specific emotional responses from the child (e.g., loving Mary back, resenting her absence, engaging lovingly with her, attending to her, etc.). Categorical concerns such as love for one's child arise and grow in time, and hence contingently, but they do not do so independently of the exercise of the agent's rational and deliberative capacities. Mary's reasoning, hopeful attitude toward the future, and loving attitude toward her future child all contribute to shaping how the future unfolds.

On the standard account, Mary exhibits diachronic incoherence: she accepts normative reasons not to have a child but adopts contrary normative reasons whose existence is dependent on having had the child. However, this diagnosis mischaracterizes the complexity of Mary's situation. In fact, her full acceptance of life as it is shows that the categorical concerns generated by her hopeful attitude have been successfully integrated. What blocks regret or other self-disapproving attitudes – which would be coherent with the early assessment about the imprudence of continuing with the pregnancy – is the categorical concern rooted in the decision not to terminate the pregnancy. This concern is nourished through a personal relation and sustained by self-enhancing attitudes such as love and gratitude. The generative aspect of reasoning and hopeful projection can be appreciated and assessed only in retrospect. Looking back, a mature Mary still thinks that it was *unwise* having a child as a teen, but this judgment is not contradicted by the heartfelt gratitude for how things came about after her decision. A reasonable sense of self-contented reward for her successful efforts prevails over the judgment of ineptitude and immaturity concerning her younger self. The point is that a major normative transition has been successfully completed: Mary is rationally self-governing while mindful of a meaningful past.

CASE 2: *INTEGRATION*. Nadja is an athlete. She was born and raised in a traditional Islamic country from which she emigrated as a teenager. Nadja has slowly and painfully developed a conception of the good life that incorporates values at odds with her cultural heritage. The adoption of new values has backward- and forward-looking normative effects: it enables Nadja to interpret and describe her past in different terms and provides her with new action-guiding reasons. As a result, she retains only some of her traditional behavior and justifies it on newfound normative grounds. She wears the veil when and because she likes it; she is selective about food but not because she observes *haram*. Although Nadja's global evaluative arrangement has changed, she still experiences ambivalences; she often feels divided between habits and novel reasons for action. For instance, she feels uneasy – almost guilty – for not fasting during Ramadan. Do these feelings show that Nadja is "in the grip" of the traditional norms that governed her childhood? Are such norms a remnant of a past that makes legitimate claims on her? Do these claims run deeper than she likes to admit, representing the vital roots of her identity, or are they unwarranted demands to be overruled and set aside as irrational? These questions have tormented Nadja for a long time. Facing conflicts between habits and current reasons for action, she has agonized about what to do. As time goes by, she finds herself measuring her behavior according to traditional norms. However, she is no longer prepared to consider her refusal to abide by these norms as a moral failure or violation, nor does she take her need for self-assessment as proof that the old habits are sources of valid normative reasons. Even so, the traditional norms are not just obstacles standing in her way or external threats to her agential authority.

There is a clear sense in which Nadja is synchronically and diachronically incoherent. As she harbors deontic attitudes associated with the violation of norms that she no longer endorses, she is also in a state of normative dissonance. However, this does not constitute evidence that she is not properly self-governing. On the contrary, Nadja's ambivalence results from a sustained exercise of autonomy. She is capable of reflecting upon her ambivalent attitudes, scrutinizing her reasons, and disciplining herself accordingly. When she eats meals during Ramadan, she knows that she is not committing a crime; she reflectively monitors her guilty feelings, judging them as rationally ungrounded and yet meaningful. Nadja is forcefully and constantly working on adjusting to changes and draws on a powerful reservoir of rational and affective capacities to undertake this task. Importantly, such affective and rational capacities are activated in response to others. For instance, she may often deliberate under normative pressure to conform to her new peers. She may thus feel the urge to rationally account for her dissonant attitudes to herself in the course of an ongoing self-investigation *and* in the context of social negotiation with members of her relevant community. These are important social and self-reflective dimensions of normative adjustment. They press toward normative self-integration but tolerate emotional dissonances that mark her vivid awareness of the value of her past allegiances and loyalties within a newly formed conception of the good life and her identity.

CASE 3: *RETROSPECTION*. As a young woman, Louisa agreed to marry an older man she did not love. She was persuaded by her father's presentation of statistical facts about marriage.[34] As a mature woman, she realizes that her marriage was based on a profound misunderstanding of what makes for a good life. She recognizes her bad judgment and misplaced trust. Her retrospective assessment of her marriage is based on a new set of values that delineate a novel practical vantage point. This vantage point is tinged with anger and regret. We can imagine a pensive Louisa next to the window, gazing sadly at foreclosed opportunities. Although the realization that she misjudged the prospects of marriage closes off some avenues, it also puts things in an entirely new perspective. The realization thus poses a deliberative question: what *now*? The burden to respond to the question rests heavily on Louisa's shoulders, but she is not completely free from her past in envisioning her future. Some of her past commitments claim and deserve a place in her deliberation, although they undergo a thorough reassessment that drains a significant amount of her deliberative resources. Adjusting to her novel condition requires Louisa to determine that some of the obligations rooted in shared plans have not survived, while others remain alive and intact, or changed in nature (e.g., enforced by law, rather than imposed by marital love). These are three different ways in which the legacy of the past is carried on through unsettling changes. Each requires pervasive normative adjustments and calls for distinctive forms of normative integration.

5. The Dynamic Structures of Rational Agency

These examples illustrate the complexities of the modes of self-governance by normative adjustment to emergent values and constraints that arise out of personal development or in the context of social negotiation with others. For temporal agents such as humans, normative change is no accident. It is a constitutive aspect of their nature as living beings with a conception of their selves and of the good life – a conception that is susceptible to refinement and development. For such beings, motivational unity or volitional integrity is not a given; when it occurs, it might be at the expense of autonomous growth. Normative change should not be regarded solely as a dangerous source of diachronic coherence that undermines self-governance. It is in fact vital to the proper exercise of practical rationality. Second, these examples show that the temporality of agency does not entail any restriction on the form of practical reasoning available to temporal agents. They are not limited to instrumental reasoning or strategic interactions. On the contrary, their predicament is that they acquire categorical concerns over time. To adequately account for temporally structured agency, we therefore need a different and more varied characterization of the constraining effect of temporality – a characterization that does not exclude the appeal to non-instrumental practical reasoning in the face of contingencies.[35]

To cope with these contingencies, temporal agents count on various capacities that enable them to keep a broad temporal focus in deliberating about what to do. These are meta-cognitive capacities such as prospection, meta-representation, and meta-cognition, and a large network of inter-related emotional attitudes.[36] Prospection involves the representation and evaluation of possible futures; it comprises a broad range of skills. Meta-cognition enables the evaluation and control of prospection and plays a crucial function in activating alternative scenarios (e.g., in envisioning what others think) and in counterfactual reasoning about how things might have been. Meta-representation allows for monitoring and managing one's cognitive capacities over time (e.g., by relying on memory or compensating for memory lapses). These meta-cognitive capacities work together with temporally structured emotional attitudes. For instance, anticipation is associated with distinctive emotional attitudes; it affects evaluative dynamics by shaping the ways in which alternatives are imagined or by altering their salience. Cross-temporal comparison and compensation can be blocked or facilitated dynamically depending on how well these meta-capacities are activated. However, the possibility of comparison and compensation in diachronic conflicts does not rest solely on meta-cognitive capacities. It also depends on the freedom to acquire, integrate, and adjust to new categorical concerns in social contexts: that is, by negotiating one's place in the relevant normative community.

Appealing to the organizing role of emotional capacities allows for a richer understanding of the subjective experience of value transitioning by showing patterns of emotional transmutation (e.g., Mary's transmutation of regret into gratitude, Nadja's transmutation from guilt into pride, and Louisa's transmutation of hope into disappointment). Philosophical descriptions of conflicts often adopt a dichotomous language for capturing the role of subjective normative attitude in deliberation (e.g., preference/indifference or regret/affirmation).[37] This simplification underdescribes the varieties of subjective responses to normative reasons and leads to an underestimation of the deliberative resources, normative powers, and practical capacities of temporally structured agency. Emotional attitudes work as normative cross-temporal structures that govern temporal agents over time. They fulfill an organizing function because they are themselves dynamic structures.[38] The organizing function of emotional attitudes differs in kind from the one exercised by normative structures such as norms, plans, and policies.[39] The latter structures foster diachronic stability by providing guardrails against disruptive forces: they are not themselves safe against the corrosive force of time. Their significance and authority alter in time so that they do not constitute a definitive barrier against fragility. Emotional attitudes, conversely, maintain and conserve a memory of past values and commitments, and of their role in one's life, even when such values and commitments have lost any normative authority and no longer represent a source of compelling reasons for action. Together with meta-cognitive capacities, these affective capacities shape descriptive and normative expectations about one's own deliberative performance, trace changes in the salience of alternatives over time, and help select the objects of rational choice. Emotional attitudes make a normative change visible and salient in reflection, but they also offer deliberative guidance throughout one's normative adjustment because they convey the authority of reasons. Attention to how various emotional attitudes emerge, wane, or transform into one another gives us a better understanding of how temporal agents relate to the reasons for action that they have embraced over time. Perplexed agents like the protagonists of Section 4 engage in intense rationalization of their ambivalent emotional attitudes.[40] This activity is conducive to self-organization over time, in that it contributes to regulating and integrating emotional and normative reactions. It thereby attenuates the dysfunctional effects of ambivalence and ameliorates the efficacy of practical reasoning. Building on these complexities, we can reconsider the issue of the present anchorage of deliberation as illustrated in Section 1.

6. Changes in Subjective Authority

The claim that deliberation is anchored in the present has the advantage of directly relating reasons to motives in its explanation of rational action. The connection with motives seems particularly important *if* self-governance is understood in terms of volitional integrity or wholeheartedness, as in Harry Frankfurt's theory.[41] On this view, ambivalences and alienation are cases of fragmentation of the mind; they induce a practical irrationality analogous to self-contradiction in the realm of thought. The dynamics of temporal agency illustrated in Section 4 gives us reason to doubt that there is a strict equivalence between rational self-governance and wholeheartedness. From this new perspective, the core philosophical issue is how normative reasons transition while temporal agents maintain rational authority across time. To address the latter question, I propose that we distinguish between the subjective and the objective dimensions of the normative authority of reasons.

Subjective authority captures the subjective experience of the authority of reasons, thus capturing the stance of temporally structured rational agency. It stands in contrast to objective authority, which fits rational agents "as such": that is, independent of temporal constraints on rational agency.[42] A reason for action has subjective authority over an agent if the agent experiences normative pressure to constrain deliberation about alternative ends incompatible with the action that the reason recommends, engage in relevant means-end deliberation, and act on such a reason unless this is rationally defeated. There is no one unique way for agents to experience the normative pressure of reasons. This is why it is so important to attend to the way agents feel and to consider the richness of one's affective network as an asset in the exercise of practical rationality. The examples provided in Section 4 urge us to conceive of rational guidance as dynamic, such that its normative pull is exercised through a complex array of temporally oriented emotional attitudes. This is not only a matter of phenomenological accuracy. It is also a theoretical point: we can reconceive emotional dissonance in terms of the discrepancy between different dimensions of the authority of reasons, which can be expressed and finely articulated through varieties of concurrent emotional attitudes. By calling the dimension of subjective authority into play, and its connection to the network of affective capacities, we can better explain the special relation that temporal rational agents bear to their own normative history. We are also in a better position to explain how their normative history shapes agents' practical agency and sense of identity.

The objective authority of reasons for action may not be subjectively felt as such. This discrepancy is not due solely to the fact that temporal agents are prone to temporal bias, temptation, and other kinds of practical irrationality. It may also be that objective reasons, which should be compelling for rational agents "as such", give little guidance unless the context of action is specified. In the scenarios from Section 4, temporal agents have normative reasons, grounded on independent sources, to which they relate differently across their lives. The distinction between subjective and normative rational authority allows us to acknowledge that reasons for action are sensitive to time, without conceding that the present anchorage of practical deliberation makes it inevitably biased toward the present. Normative reasons for action may lose subjective authority over time and become external constraints on the self. However, acknowledging this does not commit us to the view that temporal location matters directly and independently in the formation of reasons for action.[43]

7. Dynamic Self-Governance and Alienated Reasons

The norms of dynamic practical rationality do not necessarily foster integrity and autonomy in a manner that demands wholeheartedness. Temporal agents normally tolerate a certain amount of alienation and ambivalence, as transitions are temporal achievements.[44] Indeed, this is part of these agents' rational capacity to adjust to circumstances and respond rationally to contingencies: it is one significant asset of instrumental rationality (understood as rationality that is strategic to achieve long-term plans), which can be locally inconsistent with present goals. For instance, on the basis of overt instrumental reasoning, rational agents may decide to detour from their general plan and adopt a goal that is blatantly in contrast to it. They do so because they know that this is a winning strategy in the long run to support their general plan. One might say that in this case, the present goal is not *really* incoherent with the large plan. However, this description hides an important peculiarity of temporal agency. Present goals may contribute in many ways to the realization of a general long-term plan and do not always do so directly. They can be locally incoherent and yet indirectly useful. Ambivalences and local inconsistencies can and should be tolerated for the sake of global rational self-governance.[45]

Second, rational self-governance is not a solitary affair. The legitimate claims of others importantly shape and constrain rational deliberation over time. Although such claims may become obligations from which the agent feels alienated, they nonetheless provide reasons for action. This is because the agent's practical stance is permeable by others. It is permeable not only insofar as some of the agent's normative reasons are the result of joint and communal deliberation or rational bargaining with others, but also because the claims of others represent objective constraints whose authority does not alter across time, depending on the deliberative anchoring of the agent. To this extent, temporally structured agents are mutually vulnerable and interdependent. Furthermore, personal relations modify the normative contents of the agential stance not merely by supplying an additional set of external reasons but also by shaping it internally. The example of Mary illustrates how the mother–child relation dynamically shapes the perspectives of the two agents involved. There is a time over which the relation develops; during that time, the agents involved reciprocally affect one another. Although the relation is mutual, how it unfolds and how the agents normatively adjust to one another remain largely unpredictable issues. To this extent, the normative changes effected by personal relations are open-ended, non-predictable, and assessable only in retrospect.

In sum, temporal agents are entitled and rationally committed to protecting their freedom to change and develop. While they put to work their remarkable capacities for adjusting through relevant transitions, they often, and as a consequence, find themselves conforming to reasons that are both alien and objectively binding. The dynamic view thus confronts us with a new question: namely, how much alienation is tolerable. My tentative answer is that the limit is set by the self-defeating impact of alienated reasons on one's global normative arrangement. When alienated reasons predominate, undercutting goals and plans vital to rational agency, rational agents face the threat of disintegration. I take this phenomenon to be rare but not impossible.

Conclusion

I have argued that the main challenge of temporal agency is not to counteract the entropic effect of time passing, but to protect the freedom of growth and change while respecting past commitments and responding appropriately to the legitimate claims of others. It is a requirement of practical rationality to protect freedom and foster normative adjustment. This entails that formal consistency across time is not necessary for rational self-governance over time. In fact, formal consistency might be an impediment to autonomy – in particular in its relational and social dimensions.

Hard Times 211

The thrust of my argument is that temporal agents have the capacities and the right to develop their own conception of a good life; in the process of doing so, they acquire novel categorical concerns. This acquisition requires thorough normative adjustments, during which some reasons may be defeated and drop out, while others may lose subjective authority and become external constraints. These normative dynamics are importantly related to the agent's history and identity. Their normative significance can be traced by attending to the specific emotional transitions that the agent undertakes. The argument establishes that the model of diachronic self-governance marked by volitional integrity and exercised by subsequent acts of willpower does not capture the challenges of temporality. Temporal agents do strive for volitional harmony, but they avail themselves of more complex modes of self-governance and self-integration over time. These complex modes may require agents to negotiate their place and their membership in the relevant normative community by engaging in ambivalent emotional attitudes. The appreciation of the normative role of such ambivalences and local inconsistencies furthers our understanding of temporally structured rational agency. Ultimately, the focus on normative adjustment suggests that dilemmas that seem untreatable may dissolve over time, apparently groundless shuffling may generate new rational grounds for action, and abrupt radical conversions may be integrated in retrospect.

Notes

1 This chapter was completed during my first term as a Visiting Fellow at All Souls College at the University of Oxford, Michaelmas 2021, and discussed at the KJuris Seminar at Kings College, London, on Dec. 8th, 2021. Previous drafts were presented at the Moral Philosophy Seminar at the University of Cambridge, the workshop on Temporal Agency at the University of Oslo, the University of Pennsylvania, and Humboldt University in Berlin, in 2017. I am grateful to these audiences for their comments, and especially to Cristina Bicchieri, Tim Crane, Christel Fricke, Rainer Forst, Stephan Gosepath, Edward Harcourt, Jean Heal, Jennifer Hornsby, Laurent Jaffro, Onora O'Neill, Joseph Raz, Massimo Renzo, Abe Roth, and Caj Strandberg. Elijah Millgram read several drafts of this paper, and every time with constructive advices and insightful comments; this work is dedicated to him, with friendship and admiration.
2 Rawls writes that "free persons conceive of themselves as beings who can revise and alter their final ends and who give first priority to preserving their liberty in these matters" (Rawls 1974, p. 641). The capacity to form, revise, and rationally pursue conceptions of the good is a moral power; the capacity to exercise this moral power is the "highest-order interest" of citizens, see Rawls (1999, pp. 475–476) and related to liberty of conscience and freedom of association, Rawls (2005, pp. 332–335). Although this chapter is confined to the problem of dynamic rational self-governance, the argument builds upon examples that highlight the ethical and political relevance of freedom to change. I hope to address this topic on another occasion.
3 See Bagnoli, "Introduction" to this volume, footnotes 1 and 4.
4 I do not use the terms "dynamic" and "diachronic" synonymously. I use "diachronic" only in reference to the approach to rational choice and action. This

212 Carla Bagnoli

approach takes agents as situated in time; it focuses on intertemporal choices involving trade-offs between outcomes that are diachronically distributed or reiterative choices preference. The task of diachronic theories of agency is to devise strategies that enforce normative reasons through time in ways that overcome local incoherence, see, e.g., Andreou (2020, 2012, p. 30); Bratman 2007; Tenenbaum and Raffman 2012). By contrast, the "dynamic" approach that I defend takes agents to be temporally structured; it refocuses the discussion on the ordinary activities of normative adjustments to global changes in value.

5 Williams (1981, p. 13). "If so, temporal neutrality runs afoul of a kind of temporal bias built into the very idea of intentional action" (Brink 2003, p. 228, and p. 243 n22); see also Brink (2011).
6 As Brink remarks, "this kind of unavoidable temporal bias reflects a fact about ownership and timing of judgment, where that involves not just whose judgments they are but when they are held" (2003, p. 234). Arguably, this is a feature of practical deliberation that sets it apart from epistemic deliberation. This asymmetry can be explained in reference to the alleged motivational effects of a practical judgment about what to do, which partly concerns the temporal focus of action.
7 Frankfurt (1988, 2004); Bratman (2007, p. 98); Korsgaard (1996, p. 372).
8 How to understand the relation between the normative and motivational interpretation is also a matter of debate, one which intersects with the dispute about internal and external reasons. See Williams (1981, pp. 101–113).
9 I leave aside the differences between exponential or hyperbolic discounting, see Andreou (2020).
10 In the tradition influenced by Augustine, finitude is tied to embodiment and consequently to the fragility of the will, in the guise of concupiscence. Interestingly, temptation is not easily distinguished from ambivalence: both are diseases of the will caused by original sin. This view survives in contemporary action theory: for instance, in the guise of the claim that "the desire uses its unchallenged incumbency to silence representatives of the future self" (Korsgaard 2014, p. 193). The capacity for willpower or continence is often understood as the capacity to resist the action-controlling influence of appetite, desire, and emotion, see Sripada (2010); Carver (2015); Morton and Paul (2019).
11 This indeterminacy is due to various forms of uncertainty, both factual and normative. In Section 4, I point out that one source of indeterminacy depends on the fact that the categorical concerns temporal agents develop are relational. They depend on the unpredictable responses and activities of other agents with a mind of their own – as in Mary's example.
12 This indeterminacy opens up different scenarios than those exemplified by Parfit's example of the Russian nobleman. The nobleman's dilemma arises because he anticipates the direction of his future normative change and thus deliberates while knowing the relevant features of his future ranking of options. On the dominant view, the Russian nobleman is beyond the reach of his prior intentions, as if he were another person, cf. Ferrero (2012, p. 155).
13 All reasons are tenseless or timeless, so "the only acceptable reasons are objective ones" (Nagel 1971, p. 96). The distinction between objective and subjective reasons is analogous to the time-neutral/time-relative distinction. A reason for action is subjective if "the defining predicate R contains a free occurrence of the variable p". In Section 6, I provide an alternative account of the predicament.
14 Nagel (1971, p. 71).
15 Nagel (1970, p. 88).

16 The principle of resistance to reconsideration is "grounded in the central concerns of the planning agent with its own future, concerns that lend special significance to future regret" (Bratman 2006, p. 57); see also Bratman (2006, pp. 265, 277). Cf. Frankfurt (1988, p. 166).
17 Bratman (2007, pp. 264–274). Holton identifies weakness of the will as the failure to maintain a pre-existing resolution, in contrast to *akrasia*, in which one acts against one's own concurrent judgment, see Holton (1999, 2004).
18 Bratman changed his views regarding temptation. Bratman holds that in the case of temptation, one should act against current rankings (1999, p. 64). Bratman (2014), on the other hand, argues that in the case of temptation, rational agents are under rational pressure to revise their current ranking. However, they can re-endorse their initial ranking by anticipating future regret if they do not, Bratman (2006, p. 275); see also Bratman (1987, pp. 52–56). In a similar vein, Richard Holton holds that rationality requires a refusal to reconsider past commitments and intentions if tempted, even if the costs of reconsideration are minimal (2009, p. 154). Ferrero defends a qualified form of practical conservativism induced by pragmatic considerations of efficiency and efficacy, rather than stemming from irreducible diachronic constraints (2012, p. 161).
19 Bratman (2007, p. 57).
20 In the literature inspired by Frankfurt (1988), alienation is contrasted with autonomy and integrity. In the final section of this chapter, I will argue that alienated reasons (in Frankfurt's sense) may be the product of an autonomous change in values that required normative adjustment.
21 See Sripada (2010); Morton and Paul (2019).
22 See Bratman 2018, Chapter 4 of this volume and Appendix.
23 Bagnoli (2018b); Millgram (2014).
24 One category of conflicts of value can be found in Parfit's example of the Russian nobleman, Parfit (1984, pp. 327–328). As mentioned in footnote 11, I refocus the discussion on changes whose outcomes are not predictable.
25 Nagel (1970, p. 74).
26 "It would be giving the same weight to what he now believes to be justified and what he now believes to be worthless or contemptible. This is clearly irrational. It may even be logically impossible" (Parfit 1984, p. 155). See also Brink (2003, pp. 225, 228, 2011).
27 Bratman (2016a, p. 5).
28 Bratman (2012, pp. 345–369). Bratman tracks the problem to Broome (2001, pp. 114–119). Although Bratman relates changes over time to temptation and various forms of temporal incoherence, he recognizes that the tension between present preferences and policy gives the agent a reason to reconsider whether she wants a given desire to play a key role in her agency (2007, p. 57).
29 Nagel conceives of prudence as a "first stage in the development of an objective will, whose effect is selecting motives and preferences" (Nagel 1986, p. 133), cf. Nagel (1986, Chapter 8). Brink remarks that to reduce rational self-governance to an exercise of willpower is adequate for the psychology of children (2003, p. 243 n. 17). Cf. Bratman (2007, pp. 278–279).
30 For a classical argument against equating conflicts of values to incoherence, see Williams (1981, pp. 71–82).
31 The example draws from Parfit (1984, pp. 358–359).
32 The absence of regret in the case of a rationally imprudent decision is widely discussed see, e.g., McMahan (2005); Harman (2009); Wallace (2013), pp. 136–137); cf. Bagnoli (2016); Na'aman (2021). Harman and Wallace hold that regret is

blocked by the woman's new attachments, whereas Setyia holds that there is an objective reason to prefer the existence of anybody, independently of subjective relations and attachments. I hold that these cases are better understood in terms of emotions as processes rather than states, see Bagnoli (2017, 2018a) and Na'aman (2021). This view coheres with my defense of a constructivist account of practical reasoning as transformative and empowering and hence governed by activity-oriented norms (Bagnoli 2018b).
33 See Harman (2009) and Buckner, R., and Carroll, D. (2007).
34 The example is modeled on Gradgrind's daughter Louisa in *Hard Times* (Dickens 1854).
35 It is generally assumed that humans have only short-lived motives and are limited to strategic rationality because of their finitude. However, finitude (i.e., limited temporal extendedness) does not entail any limitation on strategic reasoning, although there is no way to establish that finite rational agents have access to all the sorts of reasoning that infinite or disembodied rational agents may have. Furthermore, there is a debate regarding whether the normativity of instrumental reasons rests on non-instrumental reason (see Korsgaard 1999).
36 See Railton (2016); Seligman, Railton, Baumeister, and Sripada (2013); and Carver (2015). On monitoring, see Carver (2005). For an insightful empirical study on the role of higher-order capacities in practical deliberation in the face of temptation, see Bulley and Schachter (2020). The affective network plays a cognitive role insofar as it may be an important source of information in the explanatory account of one's agency. It also plays a role in predictive reasoning, see Thornton and Tamir (2017).
37 See, e.g., Frankfurt (1988); Wallace (2013).
38 There is a growing literature on the dynamic structure of emotions, especially in recent enactivist accounts, see Bagnoli (2022). This line of research stands in contrast to an important trend within another research program that privileges decision-making according to rules, intuitions, and habits; they also commonly deliberate over their options, Gigerenzer, Todds and The ABC Research Group (1999); Gilovich, Griffin and Kahnemann (2002). The role of reasoning in the latter studies is marginal. The appeal to intuitions and emotions becomes predominant (especially when deliberators are pressed by time), on the assumption that one can manage contingencies only by "quick and dirty" heuristics. On my view, conversely, emotional attitudes (e.g., reactive attitudes) are complex modes of valuing, capable of sustaining long-term agential structures; they often provide the necessary interconnections for successful integration over time, see also Railton (2009, 2016, 2020); and Seligman, Railton, Baumeister, and Sripada (2013).
39 Bratman (2007, pp. 267–699). Bratman thinks that agential authority can be defended because of certain attitudes whose "primary role is the constitution and support of Lockean continuities and connections" (Bratman 2007, p. 59). The stance of agency is provided by the recognition that a certain item serves in deliberation as a justifying end of action, Bratman (2007, p. 61).
40 Wilson and Gilbert (2003).
41 Frankfurt (2004, pp. 96, 138–139).
42 In a Kantian fashion, normative authority is understood in terms of rational agency "as such": "The normativity of reasons requires the perspective of a rational agent as such as the standpoint from which all reasons, including those grounded on what motivates an agent from his own point of view, are ultimately assessed" (Darwall 1983, p. 113).
43 In contrast to Nagel (1970), and cf. Brink (2003, p. 220).
44 One may be alienated from one's own values, Velleman (2000, p. 134), Bratman (2003).

45 As Wallace remarks, "an attitude of deep ambivalence would better correspond to the complexities of the history that he looks back on" (Wallace 2013, pp. 185, 181). Some authors have recognized that local and short-term strategies may be effective and agency enhancing in connection with long-term goals and decisions, see Muillanathan and Shafir (2013), and Morton (2012). For an argument against Bratman's attempts to derive the normativity of instrumental coherence from self-governance, and the possibility of self-governance through higher-order intentions to retain first-order incoherence, see Levy (2014). Levy observes that there are costs in efficiency but no incompatibility between means-ends incoherence and self-governance.

References

Andreou, Chrisoula. 2012. "Self-Defeating Self-Governance," *Philosophical Issues*, 22: 20–34.
Andreou, Chrisoula. 2020. "Dynamic Choice," in Edward N. Zalta, ed. *The Stanford Encyclopedia of Philosophy*. Winter 2020 ed., https://plato.stanford.edu/archives/win2020/entries/dynamic-choice/.
Bagnoli, Carla. 2016. "Rooted in the Past, Hooked in the Present: Vulnerability to Contingency and Immunity to Regret," *Philosophy and Phenomenological Research*, 92 (3): 763–770.
Bagnoli, Carla. 2017. "Change in View: Sensitivity to Facts in Prospective Rationality," in Giancarlo Marchetti and Sarin Marchetti, eds. *The Contingency of Fact and the Objectivity of Values*. London: Routledge.
Bagnoli, Carla. 2018a. "Emotions and the Dynamics of Reasons," *Journal of Value Inquiry*, 52 (3): 347–363.
Bagnoli, Carla. 2018b. "Defeaters and Practical Knowledge," *Synthese*, 195 (7): 2855–2875.
Bagnoli, Carla. 2022. "Emotions and Agency," in Ferrero, Luca. ed. *The Routledge Handbook of Philosophy of Agency*, New York: Routledge, 317–328.
Bratman, Michael E. 1999. "Toxin, Temptation, and the Stability of Intention," in *Faces of Intention*. Cambridge: Cambridge University Press, 58–90.
Bratman, Michael E. 2003. A Desire of One's Own. *Journal of Philosophy*, 100 (5): 221–42.
Bratman, Michael E. 2007. "Temptation Revisited," as reprinted in Michael E. Bratman, ed. *Structures of Agency*. Oxford: Oxford University Press, 264–274.
Bratman, Michael E. 2012. "Time, Rationality, and Self-Governance," *Philosophical Issues*, 22: 73–88.
Bratman, Michael E. 2014. "Temptation and the Agent's Standpoint," *Inquiry*, 57: 293–310.
Bratman, Michael E. 2018. *Planning, Time, and Self-Governance*. New York: Oxford University Press.
Brink, David O. 2003. "Prudence and Authenticity: Intrapersonal Conflicts of Value," *Philosophical Review*, 112 (2): 215–245.
Brink, David O. 2011. "Prospects for Temporal Neutrality," in Craig Callender, ed. *The Oxford Handbook of Philosophy of Time*. Oxford: Oxford University Press.
Buckner, Randy L., and Carroll, Daniel C. 2007. "Self-projection and the Brain," *Trends in Cognitive Science*, 11: 9–57.
Bulley, Adam, and Daniel, Schacter. 2020. "Deliberating Trade-offs with the Future," *Nature Human Behaviour*, 4 (3): 238–247.

Carver, Charles S. 2015. "Control Processes, Priority Management, and Affective Dynamics," *Emotion Review*, 7: 301–307.
Darwall, Stephen L. 1983. "Unified Agency," in *Impartial Reasons*. Ithaca, NY: Cornell University Press, 101–113.
Dickens, Charles. 1854. *Hard Times*. London: Bradbury and Evans.
Ferrero, Luca. 2012. "Diachronic Constraints of Practical Rationality," *Philosophical Issues* 22: 144–164.
Ferrero, Luca. ed. 2022. *The Routledge Handbook of Philosophy of Agency*. New York: Routledge.
Frankfurt, Harry. 1988. "Identification and Wholeheartedness," as reprinted in Harry Frankfurt, ed. *The Importance of What We Care About*. Princeton, NJ: Princeton University Press, 159–176.
Gigerenzer, Gerd, Todd, Peter M., and The ABC Research Group. 1999. *Simple Heuristics that Make. Us Smart*. New York: Oxford University Press.
Gilovich, Thomas, Griffin, Dale W., and Kahneman, Daniel 2002. *Heuristics and Biases: The Psychology of Intuitive Judgment*. New York: Cambridge University Press.
Hare, Caspar. 2015. "Time: The Emotional Asymmetry," in Bardon, Adrian and Dyke, Heather, eds. *A Companion to the Philosophy of Time*. Hoboken, NJ: Wiley-Blackwell, 2013, 507–520.
Harman, Elizabeth. 2009. "'I'll Be Glad I Did It' Reasoning and the Significance of Future Desires," *Philosophical Perspectives*, 23 (1): 177–199.
Holton, Richard. 1999. "Intention and Weakness of Will," *Journal of Philosophy*, 96: 241–262.
Holton, Richard. 2004. "Rational Resolve," *Philosophical Review*, 113: 507–535.
Korsgaard, Christine M. 1996. *The Sources of Normativity*. Cambridge: Cambridge University Press.
Korsgaard, Christine M. 2014. "The Normative Constitution of Agency," in Manual Vargas and Gideon Yaffe, eds. *Rational and Social Agency: The Philosophy of Michael Bratman*, Oxford: Oxford University Press, 190–214.
Morton, Adam. 2012. *Bounded Thinking: Intellectual Virtues for Limited Agents*. Oxford: Oxford University Press.
Morton, Jennifer M., and Paul, Sarah K. 2019. "Grit," *Ethics*, 129 (2): 175–203.
Mullainathan, Sendhil, and Shafir, Eldar 2013. *Scarcity: Why Having Too Little Means So Much*. New York: Times Books/Henry Holt and Co.
Na'aman, Oded 2021. "The Rationality of Emotional Change: Toward a Process View," *Noûs*, 55 (2): 245–269.
Nagel, Thomas. 1970. *The Possibility of Altruism*. Princeton, NJ: Princeton University Press.
Nagel, Thomas. 1986. *The View from Nowhere*. New York: Oxford University Press.
Parfit, Derek. 1984. *Reasons and Persons*. Oxford: Oxford University Press.
Railton, Peter. 2009. "Practical Competence and Fluent Agency," in D. Sobel and S. Wall, eds. *Reasons for Action*. Cambridge: Cambridge University Press, 81–115.
Railton, Peter. 2016. "At the Core of Our Capacity to Act for a Reason: The Affective System and Evaluative Model-Based Learning and Control," *Emotion Review*, 9 (3): 1–8.
Railton, Peter. 2020. "Rationalization of Emotion is also Rational," *Behavioral and Brain Sciences*, 43: E43.

Rawls, John. 1974. "Reply to Alexander and Musgrave," *Quarterly Journal of Economics*, 88 (4): 633–655.
Rawls, John. 1999. *A Theory of Justice*. Revised ed. Cambridge, MA: Harvard University Press.
Rawls, John. 2005. *Political Liberalism*. Expanded ed. New York: Columbia University Press.
Seligman, Martin E. P., Railton, Peter, Baumeister, R. A., and Sripada, Chandra S. 2013. "Navigating into the Future or Driven by the Past?" *Perspectives on Psychological Science*, 8: 119–141.
Sripada, Chandra S. 2010. "Philosophical Questions about the Nature of Willpower," *Philosophy Compass*, 5 (9): 793–805.
Tenenbaum, Sergio, and Raffman, Diana. 2012. "Vague Projects and the Puzzle of the Self-Torturer," *Ethics*, 123: 86–112.
Thornton, Mark A., and Tamir, Diana I. 2017. "Mental Models Accurately Predict Emotion Transitions," *Proceedings of the National Academy of Sciences USA*, 114: 5982–5987.
Velleman, David J. 2000. "What Happens When Someone Acts?", in his *The Possibility of Practical Reason*. New York: Oxford, pp. 123–43.
Wallace, R. Jay. 2013. *The View from Here: On Affirmation, Attachment, and the Limits of Regret*. Oxford: Oxford University Press.
Williams, Bernard A.O. 1981. *Moral Luck*. Cambridge: Cambridge University Press.
Wilson, Timothy D., and Gilbert, Daniel T. 2003. "Affective Forecasting," *Advances in Experimental Social Psychology*, 35: 345–411.

Part III
Failures of Temporal Agency

10 Weakness and the Memory of Resolutions

Laurent Jaffro

Contemporary moral theory tends to remain silent about the temporal aspect of practical reasoning. More specifically, it overlooks the portion of our struggle for practical rationality which is due to the challenges of diachronic agency – planning a future conduct, acting on an earlier decision, following a judgment that took place in the past, etc. How can my earlier judgments and commitments exercise the right traction on my later choices and conduct, and how is this a matter of practical rationality? How can they fail to do so, and how is this kind of lapse a distinctive kind of "practical irrationality"? In this chapter, I focus on the moral psychology of *solemn resolutions* – an area, if any, where the diachronic dimension of agency is especially salient.

In his argument against judgment internalism, Russ Schafer-Landau gives this counterexample of a soldier expecting to be called to the front:

> As the days pass, he dwells increasingly on the horrors he may face. His fortitude diminishes accordingly. After several days he is struck by what seems to him a complete absence of motivation to fight. He recognizes the convenience of modifying his moral views. If he embraced pacifism, or at least came to morally oppose the present war, then he could with good conscience justify his unwillingness to fight. But he cannot do this. He thinks himself a coward precisely because of his lack of motivation to do his perceived duty.
> (Schafer-Landau 2005, 150)

This is indeed an excellent illustration of the way in which the successive nature of what is sometimes called the "multiplicity of the self" has moral relevance and forms a background to ordinary weakness of will. It is a case of accidie more than of akrasia, an expression of deep existential weariness rather than a practical lapse. However, when Schafer-Landau draws on this kind of example to argue for the externalist thesis that the connection between judgment and motivation is contingent either on the agent's psychological constitution or on the "perceived content of moral demands" (151), the dimension of temporality does not play any role in his account. In contrast, I will claim that the appropriate basis for an argument in favor of motivational externalism lies in the temporal structure of mental life.

My contention is that disconnections between past resolutions and occurrent motivations are not exceptional but rather grounded in the temporal constitution of agency and practical reflection. The truth of externalism is contingent upon our psychological constitution, although the formal requirements of action-guiding value judgments *per se* plead for internalism. Psychological finitude and the diachronic character of our practical conduct have a part to play in accounting for practical irrationality as well as for the capacity for self-control.

The first part of this chapter follows a lead from Leibniz's account of akrasia and compensatory techniques of self-control: both practical irrationality and self-control are concerned with problems of memory. The second part elaborates on a classification of types of memory and applies it to remedies for weakness of will and thus to self-control over time.

My argument aims to answer two questions. The first concerns the nature of weak agents' normative memory of important resolutions. Not all moral decisions are like Hercules' solemn choice at the crossroads, between pleasure right now and the later, more costly rewards of virtue. However, even agents who are far from being moral Hercules experience significant times of commitment and resolve.[1] What kind or degree of memory is required (and accessible) to stick to one's resolutions?

The second question concerns devices of diachronic self-control that may be useful to agents who are aware of their weakness and willing to cope with it. I will pay particular attention to intrapsychic means such as "personal rules" as opposed to external constraints and will ask whether and how these can act as palliatives for defective normative memory.

1. The Psychological Conditions of the Authority of Important Resolutions

1.1. Combining Existential Externalism With Conceptual Internalism

Do moral or prudential judgments about one's own conduct motivate, and, if so, under what conditions? I stand for existential externalism, that is, a view of the relationship between evaluation and motivation that corresponds to a moderate internalist thesis, when applied exclusively to agents either chronically or constitutively so weak that, according to their own evaluative standards, they are doomed to a frequent gap between evaluation and motivation (often termed "practical irrationality"). At first glance, it seems that this amounts to saying that internalism cannot apply. However, the disjunctive form of moderate internalism, as laid out by Michael Smith, leaves some space to defend existential externalism:

if I judge that I have normative reasons to φ over any other option, then either I am motivated to φ or I am practically irrational (Smith 1994). This statement is not falsified by its application to weak agents – that is, agents who think that they should φ over any other option but tend to fail to φ unless they are helped or externally constrained. Lacking the corresponding motivation, they are affected by akrasia or other forms of weakness of will. Far from representing an exception to a natural connection between judgment and motivation, disconnection is their ordinary condition. However, we may wonder what, if any, difference there is between existential externalism and externalism.

There is indeed a difference. According to existential externalism, the correct understanding of the internal link between judgment and motivation plays a major role in guiding weak agents. Though the fact that they judge they should φ does not suffice to motivate them directly, it may motivate them to take measures so that they succeed in φ-ing. These agents are able not only to have a clear awareness of what their judgment requires from them in practice, but this awareness also influences their conduct and may be indirectly efficacious. Thus, existential externalism differs from externalism tout court in so far as the latter denies any kind of internal connection between judgment and motivation, whereas the former is combined with the view that motivational internalism must be true at the very least of the kind of more rational agents that we would like to be.

We may use the term "guidance" to refer to the indirect and fallible influence of moral judgment on our conduct.[2] Conceptual internalism – the view that the concept of moral judgment requires that it be accompanied by a corresponding motivation – fits with existential externalism, because having that concept is a necessary condition of the guidance that the latter calls for. In order to be guided toward φ-ing, it is not sufficient that I judge that I should φ, it is necessary that I conceive that a (comparatively) rational agent would judge that φ-ing is what should be done and thus would be motivated to φ. The idea that if I were more rational I would be motivated, even though it does not actually provide me with the required motivation, is liable to motivate me to take steps toward doing the right thing. These steps consist of remediation techniques, especially the use of pre-commitments and constraints.

I will first focus on the psychological conditions that make existential externalism true for resolutions and will highlight the contingent practicality that it accounts for, as well as the limited kind of "necessity" that its accomplice, conceptual internalism, maintains.

1.2. Temporality Makes Existential Externalism True

One aspect of our psychological constitution is particularly neglected in arguments for or against judgment internalism in moral theory: the time-dependent nature of psychological states and operations – that is, the fact that they are located in time, that they may be successive as well as simultaneous, and that they do not all have the same duration or durability.

I distinguish *formal* considerations from *material* considerations about time dependence. Material considerations relate to the content of certain psychological states and operations, for instance, having a project for next year, or regretting a social attitude one had yesterday, or yearning for immediate reward. Material considerations about time dependence are familiar to economists and psychologists. Formal considerations have to do with the way in which psychological entities, as entities, are located in time, independently of their contents. No doubt there are relationships between the two kinds of temporal considerations. For instance, one necessary condition for the success of one's project for next year may be the fact that the intentions involved have some persistence. In this chapter, I will limit myself to formal considerations.

Here is one such consideration. For my best judgment to have authority in the long run, it is not necessary that this judgment be constantly present, throughout the succession of my preference sets, say, in the form of a persistent belief. Let us consider two subsequent periods that are distant in time. The first period is that of the formation of the agent's judgment about the best thing to do, which is to ϕ; in short, the evaluative background that matters to the agent. During the later period, the agent has opportunities to ϕ, which were not available in the former period. Then, the agent decides to ϕ and thus complies with the former judgment, which proves its long-term authority over the agent's practical deliberation and action. One might be tempted to think that in order to have such an influence during the later period, the judgment must still be present, either as an occurrent operation or as a disposition. If this were the case, then if the decision happened not to be in line with the previous judgment, we would have to construe the gap between the two as a case of compulsion or division of the self.[3] According to a prevalent view, a judgment cannot have any authority over our current preference set without being co-present with it. Thus, if the normative judgment is co-present with a diverging decision, then we have a case of apparent weakness of will, which may be construed as an internal conflict, and if the judgment is not co-present with the decision, and hence did not persist through time, then there is no weakness involved. Divergence can be explained away as a case of oblivion or change of mind.

It is doubtful that judgments or commitments about one's conduct, especially in the guise of solemn resolutions, are always contemporary with the decisions they are liable to guide and over which they exert authority. This is because there is an important difference in status between p and the judgment that p, where the proposition p is about one's being guided by values, norms, or reasons. That difference in status is connected with the fact that judging is a psychological operation, and as such is located in time, whereas p has the status of a proposition or content. In short, we should apply Frege's remark here: "If a judgment is an act, it happens at a certain time and thereafter belongs to the past" (Frege 1960, 126). Of course, this does not prevent evaluative judgments from being contemporary with desires to act, whether in accordance with them or not. However, it does mean that in many cases, evaluative judgments, especially when they require attention, careful weighing, and thus time for reflection, exert their authority without being present as an occurrent operation, or even as a disposition.

1.3. The Temporal Location of Judgments: A Leibnizian Account

Leibniz accords great importance to the time dependence of psychological states. He argues that full and direct willpower is a myth: the influence of the will on mental operations including willing, as well as the revision of beliefs or desires, is essentially diachronic and indirect. Moreover, according to Leibniz, weakness of will is analogous to a calculation error, in so far as both kinds of failure are partly due to the successive, discursive, activity of the mind. We are partly responsible for those failures, for they are due to our not making enough effort to compensate for memory lapses that are induced by the diachronic structure of agency as well as of reasoning. Leibniz's claim is that moral reflection is similar to a mathematical proof in several respects, especially because both kinds of operations of the mind take place in circumstances that require attention, especially when the question at hand is complex. Since circumstances favorable to calm deliberation rarely converge with the circumstances of action, we are de facto caught in a diachronic predicament. Leibniz also explains that in this situation, evaluative judgments and practical deliberation exert a weak, even faint influence on our choices, through memory alone. This understanding of weakness construes the multiplicity of the self as a succession. One difference from a Kantian view like that of Michael Smith (1994) is that agents draw not on their beliefs about what idealized agents would want but on the evaluative beliefs they have in real life, in favorable cognitive situations in which they have some space for reflection about their reasons for acting and also about the ways of implementing their resolutions. Moments of calm allow for tactical planning in the service of a moral or prudential strategy.

Let us consider the possible relationships between an initial moment of practical reflection, $t1$, and a later moment of weakness, $t2$. According to Leibniz, the normative reasons that are the object of judgment at $t1$ are present to the agent at $t2$ only through memory, for our volitions, as well as our beliefs are determined either by present reasons or by present memories of past reasons. As Leibniz puts it in his "Reflections on the general part of Descartes' Principles":

> Whoever judges of anything becomes conscious either of a present sensation or reason, or at least of the presence of the memory of a past sensation or of the perception of a past reason, although we are often deceived in this by untruthful memory or by faulty attention.
> (Leibniz 2001, 36)

One implication is that practical irrationality does not differ from a calculation error, which is difficult to accept. It is only a matter of inaccurate and superficial memory and defective attention. Another consequence is that agents are not free to judge, although they are free to prepare themselves to judge in so far as they can organize favorable conditions for reflection. Let us apply this to the relationship between one's present desires and one's former resolve in a case of diachronic weakness of will: one's present desires at $t2$ are not aligned with one's former resolution at $t1$, although this evaluative commitment seems to be somehow still present at $t2$. In fact, what is present at $t2$ is not the "cognition" that was present at $t1$ but only the imperfect memory of that cognition.

Leibniz makes a decisive move regarding the topic of weakness of will when he observes that the memory of a reason to act or to believe cannot influence action or belief as original reasons do; there is a significant difference between the two, but it is a difference in degree. So, we may combine without inconsistency the claim that there is a strong link between reasons and motivation and the claim that there are real cases of weakness of will.

In his "Reflections on the general part of Descartes's Principles", Leibniz (2001, 54–56) discusses the manner in which we might improve our reasoning and bring it up to the level of perfection of those who are able to philosophize in the midst of noise and busyness and compares this with a kind of soliloquy, or advice to oneself, as if thought could act as an "external adviser" for oneself. He also insists, interestingly, that mental concentration is not voluntary in the sense that we cannot concentrate at will. Thus, he would not accept what Jeanette Kennett says about our "ability to refocus", that is, to "narrow", "expand", or "restore" cognitive focus in order to realign our desires with our values and thus decrease subjective irrationality (Kennett 2003, 136). We should object that if cognitive refocusing were sufficient as a means of self-control, we would not need techniques of diachronic self-control. Changes in cognitive focus cannot be achieved directly, but only through astute techniques and fortunate encounters. In this Leibnizian setting, self-control cannot consist in what Kennett terms "a rational commitment to act in accordance with evaluation" (Kennett 2003, 38), if this is understood as a voluntary resolution aiming at direct control; instead, it involves the more modest versions she also discusses: diachronic self-control and what she terms "aggregative" self-control, that is, recourse to additional incentives (Kennett 2003, 141).

For Leibniz, the origin of calculation errors lies in the temporal structure of reasoning, which cannot be remediated by the use of evidence in the Cartesian sense, since we should not fully trust "*évidence*" until it is put to the test by reasoning. For the same reason – that is, the temporal structure of mental life – a tendency to diachronic weakness of will is inescapable, although there are ways to cope with it. We cannot be as sensitive to past reasons as we are to our present reasons. As Leibniz puts it: "The finest moral precepts and the best prudential rules in the world have weight only in a soul which is as sensitive to them as to what opposes them – if not directly sensitive (which is not always possible), then at least indirectly sensitive" (Leibniz 1996, 186).

Let us now turn to the other possible relationship between the initial moment of reflection, when we have distinct evaluative perceptions, and the subsequent moment of weakness, when they are confused. We cannot will at will any more than we can judge or believe at will. However, we can make efforts to prevent the foreseeable consequences of our cognitive frailty. We may adopt techniques of diachronic self-control, in order to be "indirectly sensitive". The analogy between past evaluative judgments and past proofs or calculations gives a strong cognitivist flavor to the theory of judgment since it suggests that more attention would suffice to diminish weakness of will. Yet the solution is not that simple. The memory of evaluative judgments involves a gradual or even rapid diminution of attention over time, so that supplementary remedies must be found, which draw not on voluntary attention but rather on routines, constraints, programs, etc.

Leibniz hints at the variety of forms and degrees of memory in this remarkable passage about diachronic akrasia:

> We assume and believe – or rather we tell ourselves, merely on the credit of someone else's word or at best of our recollection of having thought it all in the past – that the greater good is on the better side and the greater evil on the other. But when we do not have them actively in the mind, our thoughts and reasoning which oppose our sentiments are a kind of parroting which adds nothing to the mind's present contents; and if we do not take steps to improve them, they will come to nothing.
>
> (Leibniz 1996, 186)

This seems to involve at least three kinds of memory: the more or less attentive "recollection" of former thoughts, active re-enactment as opposed to merely verbal repetition, and prospective memory. The second part will explore the varieties of memory.

To sum up the Leibnizian view, weak agents are not necessarily driven by ignorance or compulsion alone. Weakness of will may be explained by constitutive conditions – mainly the imperfect memory of evaluative judgments, as well as other circumstantial factors. Weak agents are strong enough to set up tactics of control over time in order to compensate for their defective memory. The extensive and frequent use of constraints and incentives on oneself is consistent with the truth of existential externalism.

1.4. *No Purely Synchronic Akrasia*

One benefit of the existential externalist approach is that it may throw light on the controversy over the reality of akrasia. Some have questioned the existence of synchronic cases of akrasia (see, for instance, Elster 2007, 119–122). Close attention to the temporal aspects of the connections between judgment and motivation suggests that we have conceptual reasons to doubt that *purely* synchronic cases of akrasia exist, although a decisive answer to the question of whether synchronic cases exist would obviously depend upon empirical data. Let us distinguish between pure and mixed synchronic cases:

There is a pure synchronic case at $t1$ if and only if all the following conditions are met:

(1) At t1, the agent is convinced that all things considered, rather than to ψ, she ought to (and can) φ.
(2) She chooses to ψ.
(3) She was not convinced at any $t1$-n that all things considered she ought to φ rather than to ψ.

There is a mixed synchronic case at $t1$ if and only if all the following conditions are met:

(1) and (2) as mentioned previously.
¬ (3) She was convinced at some $t1$-n that all things considered she ought to φ rather than to ψ.

The nature of "all-things-considered" judgments seems to necessarily imply that cases of akrasia cannot be purely synchronic, for this kind of judgment involves reflection, and reflection requires time to reflect. The question of whether there are synchronic cases is an empirical one; however, it has a conceptual basis, since there are requirements attached to the use of all-things-considered judgments. If synchronic cases are never pure, if they are always *also diachronic*, then the memory of the evaluative background that matters to the agent must play some role in the phenomenon of akrasia as well as in self-control.

The same argument rules out purely diachronic cases of akrasia. There is such a case at *t* if and only if all the following conditions are met:

(1′) At *t*1 the agent has an almost extinct memory, akin to hearsay information, that all things considered she ought to ϕ rather than to ψ.
(2) and ¬ (3) as mentioned previously.

This seems to be a case of oblivion rather than of akrasia. Diachronic akrasia requires, among other things, that the agent still remembers enough to maintain the conviction that all things considered she ought to ϕ rather than to ψ. Therefore, we need some degree of memory for diachronic or synchronic akrasia to exist. Now the question is what the nature of that memory is.

2. Memories of Important Resolutions: Retrospective and Prospective

2.1. Which Concept of Memory?

There is a significant difference between the memory of past evaluations, especially when they have strong practical authority, and the memory of past purely cognitive operations. For us to act as we act with resolutions, we need more than simply factual memory. For example, in the case of theoretical proofs, I do not need to redo a proof as long as I am confident that I have proved the theorem or understood the proof and double-checked it. My trust in those earlier operations derives from my trust in my memory. Now, in the case of memory of what might be called solemn moral resolutions (for it is indeed not true of all value judgments but only of those that claim special authority over one's future conduct), it cannot merely be a matter of trusting the factual memory that I made a solemn resolution in the past, as if it were only a matter of now accepting my previous evaluation as a premise of my current conduct. The practicality of moral judgment is not conditioned by its later acceptance; it is embedded in the act of judgment, which has a dimension of commitment. My past judgment is forward-looking and demands that I act in accordance with it. The memory of that judgment is neither an object of trust nor the vector of my trust in it. It is the other way around: at the time of judgment, I entrusted my later self with the task of acting in accordance with that judgment. In other words, contrary to what Leibniz suggests, the memory of important evaluations is not simply the decreasing, sometimes almost extinct, consciousness of previous operations – it is also the mark of a resolution that still requires from me now, albeit faintly, certain attitudes and actions. In short, the kind of memory involved here is not factual but normative.

A first question concerns the nature of the memory of background evaluations in a context of weakness. It seems implausible that, to have authority over time, background evaluations would need to be remembered in the form of personal memory. On the contrary, most of them, including moral norms, seem to be objects of mere factual memory. In many cases, we know and remember that we should not behave in such or such a way, exactly as we know and remember facts about the world. The personal dimension of normative memory has to do with moral or prudential norms to which we have committed ourselves by resolutions made in distinctive moments, in times of crisis, through practical reflection, thorough examination and debriefing of our conduct, and also through moral or vital emotions. A second question concerns ways of coping with that defective memory: what techniques of self-control over time can weak agents use?

To answer these two questions, I borrow concepts of memory from psychologists, using them only as descriptive tools, without taking a stand on empirical matters or on the hypothetical structure of the mind. The main ingredient in this bricolage is the classification of types of memory developed by Endel Tulving, especially his distinction, within declarative memory, between episodic memory and factual, semantic memory.[4] What is most interesting in this approach is that it connects episodic memory to one's sense of oneself and one's ability to imagine one's past or future experience.[5]

2.2. Akrasia as Weak Memory

When speaking of the memory of theorems, Leibniz had in mind something stronger than the memory a schoolboy may have of a theorem that he never proved, and to whom the math teacher never explained the proof. This stronger form is the memory of a proof, and it supposes that one once had access to the whys and wherefores of the particular proposition. Is the kind of memory at work in remembering theorems in this sense factual or personal?

It may be personal in the case of a mathematician able to remember having proved the theorem one week ago (or perhaps many years ago, if the experience was especially memorable). If the experience was distinctive enough, the episodic memory of a theorem might include the fine intellectual emotions one had when seeing the proof. However, mere semantic memory of theorems is sufficient for mathematical work. Episodic or personal memory is not required for the mathematician to recognize the persistent validity of the theorem.

Let us now consider the case of moral or prudential reflection in favorable moments. Having attentively considered the current state of my social relationships and my low level of popularity, on a melancholy evening, I make a resolution never again to ϕ, where ϕ-ing consists in reproaching other people with their shortcomings or their annoying habits. There are several forms that this resolution not to ϕ might have. It might be a promise to someone, or an oath before witnesses, or just a personal resolve, the adoption of a rule regarding my future behavior. What kind of memory of that commitment is necessary at a later time for me to recognize that I should comply with that rule? It depends on the form that my commitment took. If it was an oath before witnesses, or a contract in written form, personal memory is not necessary. It may be sufficient for someone (for instance, a witness) to remind me that I took the oath. The knowledge of the fact that I swore is not necessarily conditioned by the memory of my experience of swearing. The case of promises is perhaps more ambiguous, since promises have both personal and institutional, public dimensions. However, remembering that I promised, without remembering the specific circumstances, may be sufficient for me to feel obligated to comply.[6] In the case of a purely internal resolution, the kind of memory that is necessary (although not sufficient) for me to stick to it is mainly personal. This memory does not necessarily include many details about the content of the experience remembered, but it must include some picture of the cognitive context in which the resolution was thought to be a relevant response. This certainly requires that it incorporate relevant information, and thus elements of semantic memory and knowledge of facts.

Now let us go back to Leibniz's point about diachronic akrasia, which may be reconstructed thus:

> At $t1$, in a moment of calm and thorough reflection, having weighed the reasons, I judge that I ought never to ϕ. Later on, at $tn+1$, in the circumstances of action, I am tempted to ϕ. While I still confusedly remember resolving never to ϕ, I am seduced into ϕ-ing and I do it.

If memory were not at work, it would not be a case of akrasia, since the possibility that my choice may be determined by the memory of the best reasons would be ruled out. If the confused memory of antecedent practical reflection were replaced with a clear and distinct reflection about the best reasons one has against ϕ-ing, it would be a case of akrasia but a synchronic one.[7]

There is an element of commitment in my judging that I ought never to ϕ. This means that in the act of judging, I am not simply aware of the wrongness of ϕ-ing, I also decide that henceforth I shall not ϕ and I intend not to ϕ whenever I might be tempted to do so. Thus, the internalist requirement is minimally satisfied, that is, it is satisfied at the moment of judgment, with the formation of the proper intention.

Time passes. A few days later, I still remember resolving not to ϕ. It is more than the factual memory that somebody sometime judged that ϕ-ing is wrong. What I remember is my judging and committing myself not to ϕ. I remember not only that I resolved, but also *why* I resolved not to ϕ.

I may also remember some particular emotions that were attached to my deliberation or decision, say, a feeling of resentment at the thought of people ϕ-ing about me, or of humiliation at the thought of myself ϕ-ing before witnesses. My re-enacting that experience puts me back in my shoes. Perhaps, the day I made that resolution was marked with a white stone, and the episodic memory of that moment is fresh enough to include access to the reasons I had for resolving never to ϕ and may even include the competing reasons that were responsible for my hesitation about that issue. At this second stage, if I were in a context where I would be tempted to ϕ, I would probably resist ϕ-ing, especially because of my sensitivity to reasons for not ϕ-ing, which personal memory has preserved.

Third stage. A few months later, the judgment that ϕ-ing is wrong is still part of my evaluative background. When people around me express their indignation at the thought of ϕ-ing, I nod my assent. However, the personal memory of my resolve never to ϕ has declined and turned into the mere semantic memory that one should not ϕ. The element of commitment has disappeared. I am no longer sensitive to the reasons I had against ϕ-ing, I just think that ϕ-ing is very bad, in a quasi-vicarious way, as if the thought belonged to someone else. It is no surprise that, when tempted in a provocative social context, I now indulge in ϕ-ing with exquisite excitement and a faint but still unpleasant feeling of guilt. The object of that factual memory is a kind of general norm against ϕ-ing, which is not of particular concern to me. I do not include myself among the people concerned by that rule simply because, although I have not forgotten the rule, I have forgotten my commitment to it.[8]

What matters to this argument about the nature of the memory at work in diachronic self-control is a kind of asymmetry, which Leibniz did not recognize, between the memory of theorems and the memory of one's value judgments that claim to have special authority over one's conduct. Bygone proofs of mathematical theorems are authoritative even though we have access to them only through semantic memory, whereas being an object of personal memory seems to be crucial to the authority of one's resolutions, at least those that are not enforced by institutional or external control. Remembering a decision does not simply amount to remembering *what* one decided (to which we may have access through semantic memory); it should also include remembering one's deciding, what it looked like to make that decision. What is thus re-enacted is similar to the cognitive situation to which our decisive evaluation responded, and especially the way in which it was determined by our consideration of reasons.

Now, although personal memory is required by, and accounts for, the authority of purely personal resolve over time, it is often not sufficient to bind one's future conduct. Self-governance over time requires more robust solutions. This does not mean that personal memory does not play a major role in organizing our future. Most interestingly, according to many psychologists, episodic memory also involves the ability to imagine what one might do or experience in the future and it is thus crucial to our planning activity.

Here again, Leibniz gives a hint:

> When a man is in a good frame of mind, he ought to make himself laws and rules for the future, and then carry them out strictly, drawing himself away — abruptly or gradually, depending on the nature of the case — from situations which are capable of corrupting him.
> (Leibniz 1996, 187)

The mind is "directly sensitive" to "moral precepts" and "prudential rules" (p. 186) only in favorable circumstances that rarely square with the urgency of action. So, the mind must manage to become "indirectly sensitive" by various means: distancing itself from circumstances of temptation, shaping a more favorable environment, drawing on the help of other people, adopting personal rules, etc. Leibniz envisaged a variety of techniques to cope with weakness of will; some of them "abrupt" (such as avoiding any occasion for temptation) and others gradual (such as acquiring good habits). Some techniques draw on objective irreversibility (making it so that options are not available anymore) and others on subjective irreversibility (through a voluntary ban on some options). Leibniz mixes intrapsychic with extrapsychic means.

Weakness of will may be accounted for by constitutional conditions, mainly that of imperfect and limited normative memory, which may also be combined with other circumstantial factors. Weak agents are strong enough to set up what Schelling calls "anticipatory self-command" in order to compensate for their defective memory. Proleptic actions draw on the same resources of personal memory that seem to be crucial to one's sense of oneself over time, to the ability to be guided by norms to which one is committed, and also to picture one's future situation. In the next section, I put intrapsychic means of diachronic self-control to the test.

2.3. Two Challenges

One might say that the reason why resolutions or personal rules are not effective by themselves (that is, not effective without further support, for instance, being publicized so that one knows that there are costs associated with their transgression) does not relate to weak memory of them but is simply a consequence of their voluntary nature. If binding myself not to φ is a matter of willing, then it is no wonder that later on I unbind myself by a new will. As Hobbes said: "Nor is it possible for any person to be bound to himself, because he that can bind can release; and therefore, he that is bound to himself only is not bound" (Hobbes 1991, 184). As Hausman notes, "the notion of a constraint on choice that is self-imposed merely by an act of will seems paradoxical" (2012, 61). So, it is not a matter of weak memory, but literally of weak will.

One prima facie reason to doubt this objection is that it does not square with the phenomenology of the use of resolutions in the context of akrasia. The fact is that people do not account for their inability to stick to their previous resolve by invoking changes of will. The objector might try to explain this by their being afraid of being considered unstable and capricious. In any case, what people do say is that they *forgot* their resolution, not that they canceled it. If the initial commitment consisted in a promise, which does not consist in purely intrapersonal resolve, they would probably say that they were not able to keep their word, failing to remember or forgetting not being an excuse in that case. We should take this phenomenology of forgetting resolutions seriously.

Another interesting challenge may be the following: my proposal construes moral and prudential judgments on important matters, which play a major role during practical reflection, as resolutions – that is, as involving an element of commitment toward future conduct. Thus, evaluative judgments are assimilated to resolutions or personal rules. Then why should we need still other personal rules to enforce those judgments? If our mature evaluative judgment is not commanding enough to prevent us from backsliding, how could intrapsychic devices suffice to keep us on the right track? Either personal rules are effective for governing conduct, or they are not. If they are effective, we do not need further support; if they are not, additional resolutions to comply with the former ones would probably not be either. Indeed, the efficacy of resolutions as purely intrapsychic measures is doubtful, particularly under the hypothesis of constitutionally weak agents. The fact is, however, that people very often double their resolutions with further ones, while they must be aware that these probably will not suffice either. It is here that the question of extrapsychic support in the form of constraints or self-nudges comes in. Yet the question remains why people also persist in drawing on apparently less effective intrapsychic measures. The following is a defense of the remedial function of resolutions.

2.4. How to Remember to Remember: Remediation of Akrasia

In Leibniz's construal of akrasia, the major premise of the practical syllogism ("It is bad to φ in such and such circumstances") is present through a memory that is fainter than occurrent motives to φ. Thus, it is not a case of pure ignorance or oblivion of the premise. It is not a case of mere compulsion either: the motives that lead us astray are not irresistible; they are simply more persuasive than the declining memory of the major premise and of the reasons why we endorsed it. So, what is responsible for akrasia is a combination of faint memory, relative oblivion, the relative authority of value judgments, and the relative seduction of divergent motives.

The construal of akrasia I have argued for adds a few details about the kinds of memory that are involved: there is a risk of akrasia when the relative memory of the major premise, which is initially personal, becomes more factual and impersonal. The element of commitment to the major premise is forgotten. We are personally more concerned with responding to other stimulations, which are more present to the mind.

As to the remediation of akrasia, it may involve, among several devices, the use of new resolutions, which at first glance seem redundant and doomed to failure. Since weak agents tend to be aware that they fail to stick to their resolutions, the question is: why do they persist in drawing on resolutions? One answer is: new resolves constitute a way to remobilize personal memory and are part of our planning effort. Although they are the least effective tactics of diachronic self-control, compared with extrapsychic means, they are very easily available and not altogether useless. Now we need to further examine the role of forward-looking memory.

If we tend to forget our best judgment in the context of action, and if we are acquainted enough with our own weakness, which makes life difficult, we are motivated to find ways not to forget – ways to remember to remember. For that, we need what seems to be, at first glance, yet another form of memory: prospective memory.[9] This prospective memory may consist of "reminders", but probably requires more effective mnemonic means, since intrapsychic reminders are not different from resolutions or the memory of resolutions. Among those more effective means, training (whether of conduct or of attention) is certainly a major one and draws on procedural memory: it consists in acquiring good habits. Another way to remember to remember is to draw on social memory, that is, one's memory of witnesses, institutions, contracts, etc.

Should we consider that prospective memory takes over for the defective personal memory of our resolutions? It seems so, since it is a remedy for the latter's failure or disappearance. But, according to some psychologists, we should instead see prospective memory as collaborating with episodic memory. As Schacter and Addis explain, "the constructive nature of episodic memory is highly adaptive for performing a major function of this system: to draw on past experiences in a way that allows us to imagine and simulate episodes that might occur in our personal futures" (Schacter and Addis 2007, 778). The same resources of experiential memory, which are crucial to one's sense of oneself over time, are mobilized to remember what matters to us and also to plan our conduct in the future.

Thanks to personal memory, we are able to imagine what it would feel like to indulge in ϕ-ing. For instance, we are able to anticipate the feeling of guilt that we would have, which may motivate us to take measures to avoid being tempted to ϕ. Here, experiential memory allows us to plan our conduct. This view might get support from the work R. H. Frank devoted to the role of emotions as commitment devices in the context of intertemporal choice as well as interpersonal interaction:

> "Consider, for example, a person who is emotionally predisposed to regard cheating as an unpleasant act *in and of itself*, that is, someone with a conscience. Such a person will be better able than a person who lacks a conscience to resist the temptation to defect in the current round of repeated prisoner's dilemmas"
>
> (Frank 1992, 280).

The anticipatory feeling of guilt constitutes a penalty attached to the desire for defection. The difficulty is how to assess such recourse to intrapsychic means, since the one who suffers from the cost is also able to waive it. Some have been reluctant to admit that such means are of any use. Schelling has described the problem of diachronic self-control thus:

> The problem is to make oneself behave as one has resolved to behave, especially in moments of crisis or whenever the resolve may lapse, and the tactic is to structure incentives so that even if the original motivation for behaving as resolved should fade or be rationalized away, there remains a forbidding consequence of misbehavior to provide the necessary discipline.
>
> (Schelling 1992, 167)

Schelling's description should be somewhat qualified. My concern is that there could be a misunderstanding of the way in which Schelling characterizes the tactics or solutions to the problem he evokes: the prospect of a "forbidding consequence of misbehavior". For there exist incentives that do not draw on the prospect of consequences, as Schelling well knows – for instance, acting upon the environment of choice by making some options objectively unavailable.

In any case, Schelling construes these tactics as identical with techniques of social control, interpersonal influence through sanctions. This might suggest that self-governance just internalizes techniques for governing others. We would learn to treat ourselves the same way we treat other people, in an educational or disciplinary context. This view is one-sided. I do not see why all the tactics of diachronic self-control should be borrowed from techniques of interpersonal control. Schelling accepts that what he nicely terms a "transfer of knowledge" may work both ways: "If we knew a lot about the way to manage our own behavior, we might be able to transfer that knowledge to managing the behavior of others". However, Schelling insists that since we are far more familiar with a variety of techniques to cope with others' conduct, "the main transfer of knowledge is likely to be from the coping with others' behavior to the coping with one's own" (Schelling 1992, 169). This explains why, among various tactics, Schelling does not give much attention or credit to purely psychological means – that is, "self-imposed rules", which "have to deal with exceptions . . . and with violations" (Schelling 1992, 175).[10]

Some psychologists, however, show a clear awareness of the fact that extrapsychic devices, to which Schelling gives primary importance, are but one family of means of pre-commitment alongside the family of intrapsychic means.

> Of the four possible means of doing this [self-control in a context of discounted expected reward] – using extrapsychic devices, controlling one's attention, using the momentum attached to emotions, and making personal rules – the last is the most complex and has the most far-reaching consequences for the process of choice. It makes some choices more important as precedents than as events in their own right, thereby variously generating the experiences of free will and compulsion.
> (Ainslie and Haslam 1992, 177–178)

In Ainslie's and Haslam's view, which draws on a game-theoretical framework of intrapersonal bargaining, personal rules draw on "private side bets", analogous to public side bets, the latter being a form of "extrapsychic commitment device". "A private side bet is a self-enforcing contract that the person makes with his own future motivational states" (Ainslie and Haslam 1992, 189). For instance, we might adopt the personal rule of not indulging in a glass of wine more than twice a week. If we fail, there is a cost that consists in our being not up to our own expectations. One problem is that, if we do not care anymore, there might be no cost at all, just pleasure. People who draw on personal rules tend to consider that minor exceptions could have a negative snowball effect. According to Ainslie and Haslam, "making personal rules is a learnable skill, similar to the skills required of a lawyer or a negotiator" (Ainslie and Haslam 1992, 190). Perhaps we should consider instead that skill has a built-in psychological ability to influence our future preferences by modifying their context (if we admit that elements of context may be intrapsychic), as I will argue.

2.5. The Impact of Important Resolves on Contexts of Choice

Whereas evaluations are indisputably constitutive elements of preferences and thus directly influence choices, the memory of resolutions also intervenes as a component of the context of choice. In cases where preferences are not in line with previous evaluations, normative memory may influence current choice only through modifying its context. It is a kind of pre-commitment or diachronic self-constraint. Pre-commitments are considered voluntary. However, there is only a difference in degree between that voluntary constraint and the involuntary alteration of the context of our future decisions by the memory of our prior resolutions.

We may thus qualify Hausman's criticism of the view that self-imposed, "purely psychological" constraints, by which "an individual rules out certain alternatives", vouch for the possibility of counterpreferential choice. Hausman discusses thinkers who, like Amartya Sen, draw on this kind of case in order to object to mainstream economic methodology: "Jack might not choose x even though he prefers it to y, because he has excluded x from the set of alternatives from which he can choose" (Hausman 2012, 60). We should understand this exclusion as subjective: ruling out an option without making it objectively unavailable. Hausman's point is that construing this kind of commitment as a case of counterpreferential choice is unconvincing, because it fails to show that through self-imposed internal constraints we do not choose what we most prefer (Hausman 2012, 61–62).

However, independent of the controversy over the possibility of counterpreferential choice in general, we should pay attention to the fact that self-imposed constraints are often counterpreferential in a weaker, diachronic, sense: that is, when resolve intends to structure future conduct by anticipating a reversal of preferences. Thus, resolutions, construed as "contrary inclination defeating" devices (Holton 2009, 77), may be counterpreferential with respect to expected future preferences. This is literally what we try to do with psychological self-constraints: we try to counter our expected preferences, which we presently prefer not to have, drawing on the experience of our own lapses and relapses in a repeated game.

3. Concluding Remarks

3.1. Weak Agency and Bounded Rationality

The foregoing analysis leads to defining constitutionally weak agents as agents whose moral or prudential judgments can influence their choices only or mainly by modifying their contexts. A resolution may fail to directly govern conduct yet may nevertheless indirectly contribute to the implementation of the desired behavior.

At least some of the tactics on which we draw to solve Schelling's problem are not created by human contrivance but are given or at least initiated within our psychological make-up. Resolutions, personal rules, and reminders in the service of a strategy are not artificial products of human contrivance. Herbert Simon's analysis of time constraints suggests that they are already there, in the natural flow of mental life. The way each particular choice is affected by prior decisions de facto constitutes a limitation of future options.

> There is nothing which prevents the subject, or the organization, having chosen one strategy on Monday, from selecting a different one on Tuesday. But the Monday decision, in so far as it has been partly acted out before its reconsideration, has already narrowed down the strategies available on Tuesday.
>
> (Simon 1997, 77)

This particular kind of pre-commitment, which is an aspect of what Simon calls "bounded rationality", is often a side effect of what we have already begun or achieved, but it may also consist in making voluntary use of the faculty of diminishing the range of future options, something made possible by the temporal structure of agency.

"Bounded rationality" and "weak agency" are not synonymous. However, they are closely related, since the former corresponds to the psychological or informational fact that we do not compute all possible consequences of our choices but instead focus on options that seem to us interesting as well as accessible, whereas the latter, weak agency, is not a necessary consequence of the former but draws on it in order to adopt practical solutions (on a similar debate in epistemology, see Morton 2012). There is also much to learn from Simon's distinction between substantive planning – that is, a value-centered decision process – and "procedure planning", which deals with the environment of choice and involves "mechanisms that will direct [an agent's] attention, channel information and knowledge, etc., in such a way as to cause the specific day-to-day decisions to conform with the substantive plan" (Simon 1997, 106–107). In a sense, weak agents dealing with diachronic akrasia have to buttress their resolutions by procedure planning.

3.2. Normative Memory and Practical Identity

Identity is obviously at stake in diachronic self-control. Since what I call practical identity depends on agents' desires and especially on their commitment to a later self, and is thus partly voluntary, we should be careful not to conflate *practical* and *personal* identity and cautious about involving normative memory in the preservation of personal identity over time. On the one hand, there is a close relationship between the question of normative memory and that of practical identity or constancy, quite different from the connection John Locke saw between memory and personal identity. On the other hand, were personal identity to depend upon the memory of an important commitment, being the same person would be somehow voluntary, since it would rest upon the follow-up we would give to the previous resolve. Now, *personal* identity is immune to the greatest inconstancies unless they radically affect our consciousness and ability to assume our former experiences and actions. Normative memory is crucial to *practical* identity, for it involves some degree of constancy and may be jeopardized by radical reversals of views, tastes, and evaluations, especially when we are not able to rationalize deep changes or to cope with them.

If I am correct in this account of the normative memory of important moral and prudential judgments – that they draw on the personal memory of commitments and are liable to decrease and transform into a more impersonal and perhaps purely factual form of memory ("purely" because personal memory always incorporates elements of factual memory) – then we should rather say that personal memory may be a resource both for practical identity and for personal identity but works in different ways at those different levels: the memory of important commitments, desires, and decisions, and the ability to re-enact them from their context, seems to be crucial to practical identity, whereas it does not seem to play a particular role in personal identity, which is concerned with more basic conditions of accountability.

Indeed, practical identity or "constancy" is a vague, though very useful, notion. Sometimes it is quite difficult to distinguish between being faithful to one's previous evaluative judgments and being unable to revise one's prejudices. To change one's mind is not necessarily to be unstable; it may be quite reasonable and valuable if one has reasons to change. The normative force that the memory of a previous judgment conveys may be a source of conformism. Thus, morality, prudence, and rationality, even though they require some degree of coherence between successive preference sets, cannot consist in this coherence. They also depend on the value of rationalization, that is, the process by which we consider what reasons we have for our important preferences.

In the case of weak agents whose conduct is guided by moral evaluations, the influence of normative memory upon action is not due to a general bias toward coherence or psychological unity but rather to the particular importance of those background evaluations for the agents concerned. Although we cannot rule out that the need for psychological coherence over time plays a role in the behavior of all agents (however sensitive to morality they may be), the concept of moral guidance demands that the virtue of constancy not be referred to a *de dicto* need for coherence (for the sake of coherence in general) but rather to a *de re* recognition of the authority of particular evaluations. Some important judgments require us to have enduring resolve.[11]

Notes

1 For an analysis of this kind of engagement, see Betzler (2016).
2 One significant difference between guidance and motivation is that the latter, even though it admits of degrees and may consist in a disposition rather than solely in occurrent volitions, includes a triggering element: being motivated to ɸ per se implies an intention to ɸ – which guidance does not involve. On guidance, see W. D. Falk's seminal "Goading and Guiding" (Falk 1953). On "belief-like attitudes underlying normative guidance", see Railton (2006).
3 For objections to theories of the divided self, see Kalis (2011, Chapter 9).
4 Declarative memory is analogous to knowing-that rather than to knowing-how, and is traditionally contrasted with procedural memory as the faculty for remembering how to do something. Declarative memory is either episodic (memory of one's experiences) or semantic (memory of facts and information about the world). However, the concept of episodic memory on which this essay relies does not give the vivid reliving of the past the centrality that

Tulving attributed to it. I thank Loraine Gérardin-Laverge for pointing this out to me.
5 "Episodic memory" is "memory for personally experienced events" or "remembering what happened where and when", whereas semantic memory is "memory for general facts of the world". A somewhat more elaborate definition holds that episodic memory has to do with one's "autonoetic" awareness of one's experiences in the continuity of subjectively apprehended time that extends both backward into the past in the form of "remembering" and forward into the future in the form of "thinking about", imagining, or "planning for" the future (Tulving 2002, 270).
6 As for the obligation to perform, it is constituted by the promise and its institutional environment, regardless of my own feelings. We are bound to keep our promises for external reasons, while we are bound to follow our self-imposed resolutions for internal reasons only. On this use of the distinction between internal and external reasons, see von Wright (1985).
7 The latter situation, in the absence of temptation, would be quite enigmatic within a Leibnizian framework, since it would go against the principle of psychological determinism to which Leibniz adheres.
8 This is a diachronic version of John Calvin's analysis of akrasia. One problem with requirements that claim to be "universal" (that is, to apply to all agents) is that the judge may omit or forget that they apply to him or her as well (Calvin 1846, vol. 1, p. 242). See Saarinen (2011, Chapter 4).
9 Loraine Gérardin-Laverge drew my attention to the fact that what I call normative memory overlaps with the memory of intentions, which most psychologists consider to be episodic in nature.
10 The objection to personal rules as liable to be overridden at will, also made by Hausman, is discussed in Section 2.3.
11 I am very grateful to Carla Bagnoli and Jacopo Domenicucci for their insightful comments and suggestions.

References

Ainslie, George and Nick Haslam 1992. "Self-Control", in George Loewenstein and Jon Elster, eds., *Choice Over Time*. New York: Russell Sage Foundation, 177–209.

Betzler, Monika 2016. "Evaluative Commitments: How They Guide Us over Time and Why", in Roman Altshuler, ed., *Time and the Philosophy of Action*. London: Routledge, 124–140.

Calvin, John 1846. *The Institutes of the Christian Religion*, translated by Henry Beveridge, 2 vols. Edinburgh: Calvin Translation Society.

Elster, Jon 2007. *Explaining Behavior: More Nuts and Bolts for the Social Sciences*. Cambridge: Cambridge University Press.

Falk, Werner D. 1953. "Goading and Guiding", *Mind*, LXII (246), 145–171.

Frank, Robert H. 1992. "The Role of Moral Sentiments in the Theory of Intertemporal Choice", in George Loewenstein and Jon Elster, eds., *Choice Over Time*. New York: Russell Sage Foundation, 265–284.

Frege, Gottleb 1960. "Negation", in Peter Geach and Max Black, eds., *Translations from the Philosophical Writings*, 2nd ed. Oxford: Blackwell, 117–135.

Hausman, Daniel 2012. *Preference, Value, Choice, and Welfare*. Cambridge: Cambridge University Press.

Hobbes, Thomas 1991. *Leviathan*, edited by Richard Tuck. Cambridge: Cambridge University Press.

Holton, Richard 2009. *Willing, Wanting, Waiting*. Oxford: Oxford University Press.
Kalis, Annemarie 2011. *Failures of Agency: Irrational Behavior and Self-Understanding*. Plymouth: Lexington Books.
Kennett, Jeanette 2003. *Agency and Responsibility: A Common-sense Moral Psychology*. Oxford: Clarendon Press.
Leibniz, Gottfried Wilhelm 1996. *New Essays*, translated by Peter Remnant and Jonathan Bennett. Cambridge: Cambridge University Press.
Leibniz, Gottfried Wilhelm 2001. "Animadversiones in Partem Generalem Principiorum Cartesianorum", in Paul Schrecker, ed., *Opuscules Philosophiques Choisis*. Paris: Vrin, 30–158.
Morton, Adam 2012. *Bounded Thinking: Intellectual Virtues for Limited Agents*. Oxford: Oxford University Press.
Railton, Peter 2006. "Normative Guidance", in Russ Schafer-Landau, ed., *Oxford Studies in Metaethics*, vol. 1. Oxford: Oxford University Press, 3–34.
Saarinen, Risto 2011. *Weakness of Will in Renaissance and Reformation Thought*. Oxford: Oxford University Press.
Schacter, Daniel L. and Donna Rose Addis 2007. "The Cognitive Neuroscience of Constructive Memory: Remembering the Past and Imagining the Future," *Phil. Trans. R. Soc. B*, 362, 773–786.
Schafer-Landau, Russ 2005. *Moral Realism*. Oxford: Clarendon Press.
Schelling, Thomas C. 1992. "Self-Command: A New Discipline", in George Loewenstein and Jon Elster, eds., *Choice Over Time*. New York: Russell Sage Foundation, 167–176.
Simon, Herbert A. 1997. *Administrative Behavior: A Study of Decision-Making Processes in Administrative Organization*, 4th ed. London: Free Press.
Smith, Michael A. 1994. *The Moral Problem*. Oxford: Blackwell.
Tulving, Endel 2002. "Episodic Memory and Common Sense: How Far Apart?", in Alan Baddeley, John Aggleton, and Martin Conway, eds., *Episodic Memory: New Directions in Research*. Oxford: Oxford University Press, 269–288.
von Wright, Georg Henrik 1985. "Probleme des Erklärens und Verstehens von Handlungen", *Conceptus*, 19 (47), 3–19.

11 Inverse Akrasia
A Case for Meta-Reasoning About One's Emotions

Monika Betzler

1. The Challenge

The term "inverse akrasia"[1] is used to describe cases in which an agent acts against her better judgment on account of an emotion. Such cases of akrasia are described as "inverse" because being moved to action by an emotion seems, in the end, to be the more reasonable, better, or right thing to do. Yet, because the agent acts against her better judgment while continuing to retain it, the action remains akratic.[2] The following example introduced by Nomy Arpaly illustrates this phenomenon particularly well:

> Emily's best judgment has always told her that she should pursue a Ph.D. in chemistry. But as she proceeds through a graduate program, she starts feeling restless, sad, and ill-motivated to stick to her studies. These feelings are triggered by a variety of factors which, let us suppose, are good reasons for her, given her beliefs and desires, not to be in the program. . . . One day, on an impulse, propelled exclusively by her feelings, she quits the program, calling herself lazy and irrational but also experiencing a (to her) inexplicable sense of relief.[3]

More precisely, an inversely akratic action is one in which an agent:

(i) judges that X is the best course of action to take;
(ii) performs X in accordance with her better judgment;
(iii) harbors, in the course of carrying out X, an emotion that countervails her better judgment;
(iv) retains her better judgment;
(v) discontinues X as a result of her emotion and performs Y instead;
(vi) is puzzled by her action and cannot make sense of it, although she later comes to believe that Y was the better or right course of action to take.

Cases of so-called inverse akrasia are philosophically challenging: how can it be more reasonable or rational[4] for an agent to proceed with something

DOI: 10.4324/9780429259845-15

that goes against her better judgment and that she herself considered to be bad or wrong at the time of action? Or, to put it differently, how can it *not* be reasonable or rational, given that the action she performed on account of her emotion appears, with hindsight, to have been the best or right course of action to have taken?

In this chapter, I take up this challenge. I first clarify which conditions have to be met if the action propelled by a judgment-countervailing emotion is to stand a chance of being considered both akratic and rational. I then show that neither the standard view, according to which akrasia is a paradigm of irrationality, nor recent proposals that attempt to describe cases of inverse akrasia as rational meet these conditions.

Against this backdrop, I therefore argue that the cases of inverse akrasia as presented in the philosophical literature do not qualify as cases of rational akrasia. The rational thing to do in situations in which we experience judgment-countervailing emotions is to reconsider that judgment and then to revise or reaffirm it in the light of our emotions. I explain in detail how the process of meta-reasoning about our conflicting attitudes, including our emotions, can be carried out. This reveals that cases of inverse akrasia are not irrational in the sense that is propagated by the standard view; they are irrational because the agent fails to meta-reason about her judgment-countervailing emotions. Our synchronic conception of enkrasia (that one should intend to do what one judged best to do), which underlies the standard view, therefore needs to be complemented by a diachronic conception of enkrasia (that one should reconsider one's better judgment and form a new one in the light of new and weightier reasons).

2. *Additional Qualifications*

The phenomenon of inverse akrasia as it stands is severely under-described in the literature. I will therefore start by specifying the conditions that must be met if supposed cases of inverse akrasia can really be described as both akratic and (potentially) rational.

First, if a case like Emily's is really to be regarded as akratic, the agent must act *intentionally* against her better judgment. That is to say, it must have been possible for her to have acted in accordance with her better judgment. This *intentionality condition* has important ramifications for the role that emotions may play in such cases. The motivational force of her emotion cannot be such that it simply overpowers the agent and compels her to act against her better judgment. Rather, she needs to have some kind of control over her emotions and their motivational force. Part of that control could be a desire to maintain these emotional states or to refrain from suppressing them. For the action to be intentional in the akratic sense, the agent must, therefore, be considered to take a particular stand regarding her emotions.[5] Second, and not unrelatedly, if inversely akratic actions are to be regarded as *inverse* and thus *rational* in some to be specified sense, we need to clarify in what way an inversely akratic agent can be considered to act *rationally* on her emotions (the *rationality condition*). How could the fact that she acted on her judgment-countervailing emotion be considered the better or right thing to do? Any answer to that question has to ensure that the connection between the inversely akratic agent's emotions and her action that, in the end, appears to be better or right for her is not arbitrary and thus is not just a matter of "rational luck".

This connection can be interpreted both in a perspectivist and in a more objectivist way. According to the perspectivist interpretation, the action of the inversely akratic agent is considered to be better because, at the time of action, the agent had access to her evidence-based reasons via her emotions. According to the objectivist interpretation, her action appears to be better in the light of considerations that were only accessible from the broader perspective of a more informed observer or from the more informed perspective of the agent's later self as she looks back on her life.

Arpaly's own description of the Emily example clearly suggests an objectivist reading:

> Years later, happily working elsewhere, she [Emily] suddenly sees the reasons for her bad feelings of old, cites them as the reasons for her quitting, and regards as irrationality not her quitting, but rather the fact that she held on to her conviction that the program was right for her for as long as she did.[6]

It is Emily's later self, now "happily working elsewhere", whose more informed, later viewpoint conveys to her – in the light of the experiences she had after giving up her chemistry studies – that she had good reason to act as she did, reasons that only became accessible to her after her career change. Arpaly's objectivist reading, however, does not exclude the possibility that abandoning the program can be interpreted as a case of "rational luck": the fact that Emily came to enjoy her new career cannot serve as a rational explanation for her abandoning her PhD in chemistry at an earlier date. There are at least three possibilities that could account for this explanatory gap.

First, her preferences might have changed because of the new and possibly transformative experiences of her new career.[7] The reasons for which Emily supposedly quit her chemistry program are now based on her new preferences; she did not have these reasons when she formed her better judgment. Second, she might have later rationalized her earlier decision to abandon her PhD in order to give unity to her life. Third, it is possible that the positive experiences of her new job committed her to endorse retrospectively the conditions that made her new career possible.[8]

As a result, I believe that an objectivist reading is unable to defend the claim that there is a relevant connection between Emily's emotions and her action, that is, that she can be regarded as having had sufficiently good reasons to leave the program when she did.

Despite Arpaly's own objectivist interpretation, Emily's action can only be regarded as a true example of rational akrasia (and not as a matter of "rational luck") from a perspectivist point of view. Even if the relevant emotions circumvent the agent's conscious assessment of her reasons *as* reasons, experiencing them must somehow have helped the agent to recognize what constitutes a reason for her. For this to be the case, they must serve as *"proxies* or *substitutes"*[9] for reasons and thus lead Emily to regard the new and relevant evidence as a good reason for quitting the program. It is only when an inversely akratic agent like Emily acts on such emotion-based reasons – that is, on reasons based on the evidence which she finds relevant – that the action she took against her better judgment can be considered "rational" at the time of leaving the program.

Third, in order to be able to specify in more detail the conditions under which emotions that conflict with one's better judgment are likely to make akratic actions rational, it would be helpful to highlight how cases of inverse akrasia can be distinguished from cases of so-called recalcitrant emotions. The latter are emotions (or dispositions to have recalcitrant bouts of a particular emotion) that persist, even though the agent knows full well that these particular emotions are not justified.[10] Phobic states are cases in point. In contrast to such recalcitrant emotions, the inversely akratic agent is moved to action by an emotion that arises due to new experiences she is undergoing after carrying out her better judgment. Even though in cases of inverse akrasia, the agent does not relinquish her better judgment, her emotions are likely to lead her to become aware of new reasons – concerning the truth of what the agent has judged to be best – that are grounded in relevant, experience-based evidence.[11] I call this the *new evidence condition*.

These clarifications highlight three, as of yet unacknowledged, conditions that must be met if cases of inverse akrasia can be described, in principle at least, as both *akratic* and potentially *rational*: (i) the agent must in some sense be able to gain control of the emotions that lead her to act (the intentionality condition); (ii) her emotions must help her to recognize the reasons according to which she acts, and these are reasons that she has at the time of action (the rationality condition); and (iii) the relevant emotions must be a result of the new experiences she has since carrying out her better judgment and which are therefore likely to direct her toward new and relevant evidence (the new evidence condition).

Once these conditions have been made explicit, we will be in a much better position to discuss the explanatory power of the standard view – which holds that akrasia must be irrational – as well as the recent and novel attempts to describe inverse akrasia cases as rational. I will start by examining the standard view.

3. Akrasia and "Irrationality"

There are a number of variants of the standard view. I shall restrict my analysis to the three that have played an important role in the literature.

First, akrasia is believed to be irrational because it violates a rational requirement: our propositional attitudes are required to be coherent.[12] If this requirement of coherence is to be satisfied, an agent needs to make the following conditional true: rationality requires [if she judges X to be best, then she should intend to carry out X]. Accordingly, if the agent does not intend to do X and desires Y or feels that Y is the thing to do – and thus holds an attitude that does not cohere with her judgment that X is best – she then violates enkrasia.[13]

Second, another principle of rationality, the so-called "principle of continence",[14] states that the judgment we hold about X, which we made after having conditionally assessed all the available relevant reasons, should lead us to form the unconditional judgment that X is the right course of action to take. We act irrationally when we fail to go from our conditional all-things-considered judgment of what is the best thing to do in the light of the relevant reasons to an unconditional judgment. When the agent is unable to do this, she then violates the principle of continence according to which one should always do what one concludes is best on the basis of all the relevant reasons.[15] Instead of making her conditional all-things-considered judgment "all-out" or unconditionally, the agent makes an unconditional judgment that contradicts her conditional all-things-considered judgment. The principle of continence, as a principle of rationality, thus concerns the close connection between what an agent believes is best for herself, taking into consideration the relevant reasons available to her and the motives that cause her to act accordingly.

A third variant of the standard view suggests that the particular rationality of making better judgments lies in a further fact: in forming a better judgment an agent is not necessarily endorsing the propositional content of her reasons[16] rather, judgments serve a more pragmatic rationale. Making better judgments is a way of dealing with ignorance and fallibility in the light of particular constraints on time, foresight, and transparency while maintaining her rational agency.[17] When an agent does not know what is really best, making a judgment about the seemingly best course of action to take and then acting on it, rather than not doing anything at all can be seen as an effective means of reaching one's goals (even if one is not completely sure that the course of action is really best). In the case of Emily then, she makes a better judgment in the light of the fact that it is impossible to know fully in advance (if at all) how a particular career choice will unfold. Given that she needs to decide on a career and that choosing one is better than not choosing one, Emily's judgment can be considered as instrumentally rational.[18]

The claim that an agent's akratic action can be rational in cases of inverse akrasia challenges all three variants of the standard view: according to the first variant, an inversely akratic agent is irrational because of her *incoherent* attitudes; according to the second variant, an inversely akratic agent makes an unconditional judgment (underlying her emotion) that *contradicts* her all-things-considered judgment; while the third variant interprets the inversely akratic agent as someone who is *instrumentally irrational* and so does not take the necessary measures to accomplish her goals. In all these variants of the standard view, the inversely akratic agent is seen as someone with a "conflicted mind". Because she cannot make sense of what she does, she is unable to guide her actions rationally.

The different conceptions of rationality that are found in these three variants of the standard view are, however, beset with problems of their own. For example, and with regard to the first variant, it has been argued that it is hard to understand why an agent should be coherent at all.[19] Moreover, as a principle of rationality, coherence requires that a conditional be true (either the agent needs to reconsider her better judgment or she needs to hold attitudes that cohere with her better judgment). Enkrasia as we intuitively understand it, by contrast, seems to presuppose that an agent ought to adhere to the better judgment she formed previously.[20] The requirement of coherence in its proposed form is, therefore, unable to satisfy enkrasia.

Concerning the second variant, it has been questioned whether akrasia can best be described as a contradiction of different kinds of judgments and whether the connection between better judgments and motives needs to be as close as the principle of continence requires.[21] Advocates of the third variant are confronted with the "wrong kind of reasons" problem; pragmatic considerations about settling a question (rather than not settling it) seem to be the wrong kind of reasons. The particular authority of a judgment is determined by its reasons, which must be based on the evidence and not on pragmatic considerations.[22]

Much more can, of course, be said about all the variants of the standard view and the criticisms to which these variants give rise. But even if it is the case that Emily, for example, holds incoherent attitudes, violates the principle of continence, and/or is instrumentally irrational, none of the variants of the standard view consider whether she may in some sense be in control of her emotions, whether her emotions may direct her toward reasons that potentially outweigh the reasons favoring her initial better judgment, and whether her emotions may be based on new evidence. In short, none of these variants refer to the aforementioned conditions necessary for cases of inverse akrasia to be regarded as being both akratic and rational. Consequently, they are also unable to demonstrate that inversely akratic cases are irrational in not fulfilling these conditions.

There are two related factors that explain why the variants of the standard view are too limited in scope. First, all the variants manifest synchronic requirements of rationality that concern particular mental attitudes, their combinations, and the actions ensuing from them at a particular point in time: an agent needs to have a coherent set of attitudes at a particular time, or she has to be able to judge unconditionally according to her conditional better judgment and act accordingly at a particular time, or she needs to adhere to the judgment she made at a particular time in the light of the various constraints she faced and then act accordingly. All these variants apply to an agent at a particular point in time. None of them take into consideration that an agent might need to reconsider the better judgments she made previously and revise them in the light of new and weighty reasons. The aforementioned conditions that need to be met if cases of inverse akrasia are to be viewed as being, in part at least, potentially rational, must account for the fact that agents, as well as their reasons and circumstances, change *over time*.

Second, none of the three variants take into account the normative import of emotions. But emotions can direct an agent toward reasons based on new evidence that she has acquired since making her previous better judgment. Even though better judgments are, in part at least, formed precisely so that an agent can bring matters to a close and refrain from re-opening the issues they are meant to settle, it is striking that all the variants of the standard view disregard the fact that there is more to rationality than just synchronic requirements. Since new evidence can call into question an agent's better judgment – evidence that her emotions may have led her to – we need an account of rational agency that will help an agent to assess when to reflect on her emotions and when to reason from them to reconsider the better judgment, so that the agent is able to maintain her rational agency *over time*. The threshold for reconsidering a better judgment must certainly be high, given that the very reason for forming a judgment is to try and avoid the need to reconsider the better judgment at a later date. However, the threshold cannot be meant to rule out reconsidering better judgments under any circumstances.[23]

Even though the standard view can be taken to describe cases of inverse akrasia as synchronically irrational, it cannot show that they are diachronically irrational. This is due to the fact that it takes into account neither the new evidence condition nor the relevant connection between the agent's emotions and her evidence-based reasons (that is, the intentionality and the rationality conditions). If Emily can be shown to fulfill these conditions, she might therefore qualify as an agent who is rational over time.

4. The "Rationality" of Akrasia

Proponents of the view that cases of inverse akrasia are rational, however, justify their claim by pointing out that this is so because the agent affirms the violation of her earlier better judgment retrospectively. She affirms it because, as it turns out, by acting against her better judgment she made the right decision, which reveals, they maintain, that akratic actions can be (or become) rational. As a result, they argue that the standard view needs to be revised.

The first lesson they draw from cases of inverse akrasia is that better judgments should not have any privileged status, since they are the same as beliefs.[24] In addition, emotions, it is argued, may be more effective at directing an agent toward her reasons than her beliefs, even if the agent is not necessarily aware that this is the case.

As a result, they maintain that two equally important conditions typically associated with the standard view should be given up: namely, that (i) the actions the agent judged best must be based on her *conscious* and *deliberated* assessment of her reasons and (ii) the agent's actions must always be guided by her response to reasons *as reasons*. Agents can be regarded as goal-directed entities that monitor, by way of various subsystems, what is best for them, but not assessing, let alone acting *for*, any particular reason.

The emerging picture, however, does not satisfy the aforementioned conditions for inverse akrasia to be described as both intentional and rational. It remains unclear how an agent can control and thus guide her actions if she lets herself be driven by her emotional subsystem. Similarly, it remains obscure how the emotions that arise from an inversely akratic act can be linked to the agent's reasons – a link that any viable account of inverse akrasia would need to explain.[25] Moreover, what speaks against a revisionary account of rationality in which the intentionality and rationality conditions of enkrasia are renounced is that emotions do not necessarily direct us toward our reasons, let alone toward the best reasons we have; emotions can be exaggerated, erroneous, or otherwise inappropriate.[26] If we want to regard inverse akrasia as an intentional and rational phenomenon of some kind, we need to provide an explanation as to how an agent can distinguish between her emotions that point to reasons from those that do not. And we need an explanation as to how an agent can have some kind of control over her emotions so that she can be understood to be *guiding* her "reason-tracking" emotions.

In view of this challenge, a second proposal has been advanced: the agent fulfills the conditions that are necessary for akrasia to be rational if she is regarded as someone who more generally endorses her emotions. The agent is thus understood to be connected to her reasons because she exercises guidance control over her emotions: she only consciously steps in when there is a risk that the emotional subsystem will lead her in the wrong direction.[27] Otherwise, she endorses it as "reason-tracking".

This second proposal, however, does not explain how a rational agent would know when her emotions are, in a particular case, reason-tracking, and how to distinguish her reason-tracking emotions from those that do not reason-track. A third proposal presents such a criterion: it is only those emotions that cohere best with a person's character and/or are consistent with the broad basis of her more deeply held values, ideals, commitments, and beliefs that can thus serve as proxies to reasons. Only by responding to her emotions, which are in harmony with her "whole self"[28] or are part of "the overall thrust of the agent's system of reasons as it bears on the context of action",[29] can an agent be truly directed toward her reasons.

Consider, however, the infamous mafioso, who – after much reflection – arrives at the judgment that it would be in his best interests finally to try and become a decent person. Hardly surprisingly, though, he decides to act against his better judgment when he learns of a forthcoming drug deal in which he is desperate to participate. It seems implausible, however, to claim that it is his desire to take part in the drug deal that leads him to undertake what he considers is a more reasonable action just because this desire stems from his moral character or is rooted in his more deeply held values. Apart from the fact that the action in question is immoral, it cannot be regarded as being more reasonable, because the mafioso formed his better judgment precisely in order to become a better person by overcoming these character-based desires. This character-based account cannot, therefore, provide the sought-after distinction between emotions that lead an agent toward reasons and those that do not.

Hence, none of these revised accounts of rational agency are convincing enough to enable us to describe cases of inverse akrasia as rational.[30] Even though they all try to fulfill the new evidence condition and take the normative import of emotions seriously, they fail to meet the aforementioned intentionality and rationality conditions: they are unable to show how an agent's emotions can help her to identify her reasons for acting and how her emotions can be regarded as rationally guiding her.

To sum up, the standard view asserts that an agent who acts against her better judgment on account of an emotion she cannot make sense of acts irrationally. However, because of its synchronic conception of rational agency, the standard view fails to recognize that we sometimes have weighty reasons to revise our better judgments and so we should thus let ourselves be guided by our emotions that have directed us toward these reasons.

Although these new accounts of rational agency in which cases of inverse akrasia are taken to be rational recognize that we can be confronted with new evidence toward which our emotions have directed us, they are unable to show exactly how an agent can be connected to these evidence-based reasons via her emotions. Only when an account is able to demonstrate this connection will an agent be able to guide herself using the reasons toward which her emotions directed her at the time of action.

In the light of this dialectic, my aim now is to reinstate the agent as reasoner and to show how meta-reasoning about her attitudes can help her to satisfy the conditions necessary for inverse akrasia cases to be viewed, in principle at least, as rational.

5. Meta-Reasoning About One's Emotions

Let us return to the Emily narrative. I will first highlight in what ways she did not satisfy the conditions necessary for her case to be described as both akratic and rational. Against that backdrop, I will then show what it takes for an agent like Emily to act rationally before finally explaining in more detail how an agent can meta-reason about her emotions so as to maintain her rational agency over time.

It remains unclear whether the act of quitting the program, which Emily had originally judged to be her best course of action, can be viewed as intentional, let alone rational in any relevant sense. After all, she retains her better judgment, despite her countervailing emotions, and she herself regards the fact that she abandoned the program because of her emotions as "irrational". This suggests that she is not in control of her emotions, nor is it evident that she would have managed to stay in the program at all (and thus fulfill the intentionality condition). The emotions she experienced propelled her to act in a way that does not make her appear to be someone who guides her actions. Even though the fact that she abandoned her PhD seems, with hindsight, to have been the right decision for Emily's future self; at the time of action she did not give up her program because of the evidence that was available to her and which allowed her to identify it as a reason for doing so. It is not even clear that her emotions provided the right sort of access to her reasons. Therefore, she cannot be described as being rational either.

Arpaly's Emily also differs from standard cases of akrasia, however, since the factors that make Emily abandon her PhD are – even unbeknown to her – *not* those that she had at the time that she formed her judgment. In addition, these considerations are not reasons that are the result of any inclinations that her judgment was meant to overrule. In contrast to the standard view of akratic action: (i) Emily failed to consider that her emotions directed her toward new evidence, which she should have regarded as a sufficient reason to reconsider her judgment and (ii) she reaffirmed her better judgment, despite the evidence provided by her emotions that she should engage in a new pattern of enkratic reasoning. After all, her emotions result from the experiences she has after carrying out her better judgment. In short, although she fulfills the new evidence condition, she cannot process the new evidence and use it as a reason for reconsidering her better judgment. In order to maintain her rational agency over time,

Emily needs to view her judgment-countervailing emotions as potential proxies to reasons. However, to be able to do this, she needs to distinguish between emotions that are proxies from those that are not. I believe that the only way that Emily can do this is for her to reflect on her emotions and thereby find out which of them helped her to identify her evidence-based reasons. In this way, she can be considered to guide her actions by *her* reasons.

This type of reflection constitutes a case of *meta-reasoning*. First-order reasoning concerns the evidence-based reasons that we take ourselves to have and which enables us to form attitudes, such as better judgments, beliefs, or emotions in response to those reasons. Meta-reasoning, by contrast, involves the attitudes that we have already acquired in response to our reasons; in this sense, it is second-order reasoning about those attitudes and their appropriateness with regard to the evidence-based reasons toward which they are directed.

More precisely, by meta-reasoning, an agent can examine the nature of the attitudes she has acquired – such as her beliefs, desires, intentions, and emotions – and the objects at which they are directed, ascertain whether they are, or continue to be, appropriate, and whether they serve their functions well. Meta-reasoning thus individuates an attitude, specifies its content, and assesses its correctness and functionality. The central purpose of meta-reasoning is that an agent can reconsider her attitudes in the light of new evidence-based reasons and thus preserve the appropriateness of her attitudes by either revising or reaffirming them.[31]

I will start by discussing *why* and *when* an agent like Emily should meta-reason, then I will look at the *objects* of meta-reasoning, and finally, I will explain in detail *how* one can meta-reason in practice.

Why, one might then ask, should someone like Emily decide to meta-reason about her emotions and reconsider the judgment that she has already made after having assessed her reasons?

Two points should be made here. First, we are all fallible and, since our reasoning is always incomplete, it is inevitable that we will make mistakes when forming our judgments. Indeed, if we were omniscient, there would be no point in reasoning.[32] Hence, it is constitutive of our reasoning to realize that we might not get it right: reasons can be overlooked or incorrectly evaluated.[33] After all, when deliberating about the best course of action to take, we do not have recourse to "what-it-is-like" information[34] and hence we cannot know for sure what is really best for us.

Second, we are creatures who move through time. New evidence might emerge, earlier evidence-based reasons can lose their importance, while weightier reasons based on new evidence might suggest that we should reconsider the judgments we made earlier. Following Emily's experiences in the graduate program, the deliberative conditions of her case improve.[35]

However, even if we agree that better judgments do not settle matters for good, we should not reconsider our better judgments for just any old reason. So, what kinds of factors can determine *when* it becomes appropriate to reconsider our judgments? In the case of Emily, the continued reoccurrence and strength of her negative emotions would seem to provide sufficient grounds for Emily to start questioning her initial judgment to study chemistry and to meta-reason about her emotions.

To be able to expand on *how* Emily can meta-reason about her emotions, it would be helpful to give a more precise definition of emotions. It is a widely held view among philosophers of emotion that emotions typically: (i) have a particular phenomenology; (ii) are intentional attitudes that are directed at particular objects; (iii) have a "formal" object that specifies standards of appropriateness; (iv) are associated with action tendencies; and (v) serve a particular function, that is, they lead us to respond to particular environmental challenges that affect our well-being.[36]

Emotions thereby contain two sources of intentional content[37]: they (that is, the phenomenal component of our emotions) represent the body's capacity to interact with the environment (i, iv) and they are directed at particular objects. Accordingly, they can be assessed as being appropriate or inappropriate in the light of two different standards: the "formal" object and the particular function of certain emotions (ii, iii, v).

Given the two sources of intentional content and taking into account the types of attitudes that emotions are considered to be, Emily could proceed, in a number of steps, to meta-reason about her emotions:

First, she could focus on what her emotions are telling her about her body by consciously becoming aware of their phenomenology. She could thus find out what information her feelings are revealing about her body's "*potential* or *preparedness* for certain environmental interactions".[38] For example, Emily might physically feel that she is not being drawn to anything and she may also have a strong sense of being trapped. She might discover that her feelings of restlessness stem from a sense of nervousness and uncertainty about how she should respond or deal with her situation, that her sadness is related to a sense of loss and ties in with the sense of isolation and disconnectedness that she feels, and that her lack of motivation reflects a sense of weakness. All these feelings have a negative valence and correspond to her desire to avoid various forms of social interaction[39]; unsurprisingly, she finds herself withdrawing from her environment. By becoming aware of her feelings and what they indicate about her body, however, she would be able to recognize that she is suffering from insecurity, loss, and a sense of exclusion in relation to her situation.

Second, Emily could conceptualize her feelings and find out with which particular emotion types they are associated. Her feelings of restlessness and her sense of insecurity might, in part at least, be correlated with her fear of failure; she might be afraid of doing badly in her studies. Emily could examine her feelings of sadness and her low spirits and discover that they are related to her regret about not being able to develop her natural talents. Her lack of motivation and her sense of exclusion might be related to the shame she feels for not living up to the expectations of both her parents and her supervisors. Emily could come to recognize that her feelings of insecurity, loss, and exclusion are typically aroused by the negative emotions of fear, regret, and shame. Emily could thereby draw on her past experiences to deal with these particular emotions.[40]

Third, once able to conceptualize her feelings in these ways, Emily would be able to analyze the objects of her emotions and ascertain whether the objects or situations of her emotions render these particular kinds of emotions appropriate. She could reconceptualize the emotions she associates with her feelings, once she has identified the respective objects of her emotions. For example, she could analyze whether the regret that correlates with her feelings of sadness is directed at the fact that she misses her friends or that she misses cultivating her other talents. Since her regret might be directed at a number of different objects, she needs to try and ascertain what these possible objects might be. She could consider whether she would continue to feel sad and regretful if she were to devote more time to her friends. If her sadness and regret were to lessen, then she would be able to conclude that she had simply been lonely; her work environment would then not be the cause of her regret. Similarly, she could try and see whether she would acquire a more positive outlook toward her work if she were to remove other potential grounds for her regret and its underlying sadness. Perhaps she feels regret because she lacks acknowledgment, which is something that she could discuss with her supervisor. In all these instances, Emily would come to realize that her negative emotions arose from circumstances that were unrelated to her decision to do a PhD in chemistry. She could then make changes to her life by dealing with these emotions. If these attempts were to fail, she could try vividly engaging with her regret[41]; she might then come to realize that her regret is, in fact, directed at an object or a situation that represents an important loss which is connected to her studies. It might turn out that Emily's sadness is related to the fact that she is deeply concerned about the kind of laboratory work that she is expected to do. She thus regrets not being able to do something that she finds rewarding.

Fourth, and once she has identified the objects of her individual emotions, she could examine whether the situation in which she finds herself makes these emotions appropriate. She could think about the "formal object" of the emotions she has identified. Do her situation, her field of study, and the relationships she has with the people with whom she needs to interact justify her fear of failure? Would she be distressed if she were to lose them, so that regret would be an appropriate response? And to what extent do they rightfully convey that she is not living up to the standards that she expects of herself, so that the feeling of shame would be a rational response? Emily would then be in a position to meta-reason about the particular features of her situation that might justify her emotional reactions. For example, she might find out that her fear of failure is indeed justified, given that, in order to be successful in her studies, she needs to have abilities that she does not, in fact, possess.

Were she to realize, through the process of meta-reasoning, that her emotions and their intentional content are appropriate, Emily would still have to ascertain whether the evidence-based reasons that make her emotions appropriate are sufficient for her to believe she should revise her initial judgment to study chemistry. If Emily's fear, regret, and shame can only be removed by her giving up her studies, then Emily will have a weighty enough reason to reconsider her initial pattern of enkratic reasoning. To be sure, the fact that her emotions can be linked to her weighty reasons needs to be balanced against the reasons that led her to make her better judgment in the first place. But if the reasons disclosed by her emotions prove weightier than the reasons for which she made her initial judgment, Emily would no longer be able to justify her judgment that chemistry was the best option open to her. Accordingly, she would no longer be able to justify her intention to study chemistry. She would, therefore, be forced to conclude that she should revise her previously held judgment; in this way, Emily would be able to preserve the appropriateness of her attitudes. However, if the emotions that led her to revise her better judgment are linked to reasons that are less weighty than the ones that led her to make her judgment, then Emily could reaffirm her judgment and dissociate herself from her emotions.

If Emily were to engage in these ways of meta-reasoning about her emotions, she would come to satisfy a new principle of rationality, namely, *enkrasia over time*. Given the reoccurrence and strength of the emotions countervailing her better judgment and which have come to light because of what she experienced while carrying out her better judgment, she might discover that she has an overwhelming number of reasons for "inverting" her pattern of reasoning from a first-order enkratic pattern to a meta-reasoning pattern in which judgments are reconsidered in the light of the emotions that she regards as warranted. This would help her to avoid the irrationality that arises from not revising her previously made judgments, despite the emergence of new evidence, and it would qualify her as a reasoner, that is, as someone who is able to examine which of her emotions are linked to her evidence-based reasons. She would no longer be in a state of akrasia, but she would have been able to resolve the conflict between her attitudes; thus, because she reconsidered and revised her better judgment using newly acquired evidence by meta-reasoning about her emotions, she would be able to satisfy enkrasia over time.

The aforementioned conditions that are necessary for inverse akrasia to be described as rational can only be met when an agent is able to meta-reason about her emotions in these ways. The interesting and perhaps surprising result, however, is that once these conditions are met and the agent is able to distinguish appropriate emotions from those that are not, she would then be able to continue meta-reasoning using the emotions that she came to consider as appropriate and which would lead her to revise (or otherwise reaffirm) her previously made judgment. Hence, the agent, if she is to be rational, would no longer remain in a state of conflicting attitudes, a state of mind that would cause her to act akratically. Rather, if the agents fulfill the conditions necessary for inverse akrasia cases to be described as rational at all, the agent must re-establish enkrasia over time by relinquishing (or reaffirming) her better judgment and forming a new one.

In cases of inverse akrasia, the agent's action cannot be regarded as a rational act. These cases do, however, show that there are different ways of establishing enkrasia. We do not only form better judgments at a particular point in time in order that we can guide ourselves over time; cases of inverse akrasia suggest that we also need to reconsider our previous better judgments in the light of changing reasons and circumstances. Not engaging in such a process amounts to a specific kind of irrationality, namely, that we wrongly reaffirm the better judgments we made, rather than revise our enkratic reasoning patterns in the light of new evidence. We thus violate the requirement to satisfy enkrasia over time.

6. Objections and Responses

In order to further substantiate the claim that an agent can rationally extract herself from cases of inverse akrasia by meta-reasoning, we need to deal with a number of objections.

First, it can be quite costly in terms of time and effort to revise a judgment that one has already started carrying out. Decisions to change one's career or study programs are cases in point: our lives have already been shaped by our decisions, so abandoning what we have already settled on can be seen to amount to a waste of time as well as have a severe impact on our self-understanding and on the meaning of our lives. As a result, we might worry that the cost of revising a judgment is in itself a strong enough reason *not* to reconsider it. Even though better judgments might generate second-order pragmatic reasons, that is, reasons not to consider other reasons that question our better judgments,[42] it seems plausible to suppose that these second-order pragmatic reasons supervene on the first-order reasons on which our better judgment is based. If these first-order reasons are outweighed by the new reasons registered by the agent's emotions, these second-order pragmatic reasons might still be able to intensify, or add weight to, the first-order reasons. But when the reasons registered by an agent's emotions remain stronger, it is rationally justified to revise the judgment, in spite of the costs. Admittedly, there will be many cases in which we cannot be sure about our balance of reasons. We need to be aware, however, that it can be costly when we both reconsider and revise better judgments, as well as when we fail to reconsider them. While reconsidering and revising a better judgment might threaten our self-understanding and sense of self-control, failing even to reconsider a better judgment could cause an agent to lead an inauthentic and thus less meaningful life. It takes courage, to be sure, to make a wise decision, but the fact that revising our better judgments and incorporating the ensuing changes into our lives will be costly is not, however, an argument against meta-reasoning.

A second concern is that the agent in question might wrongly take her own emotions to be appropriate when they are, in fact, exaggerated or inappropriate. This might occur, for example, if the agent suffers from traumatic experiences that make her likely to consider that many situations wrongly demand such an emotional response. If we are to rule out that emotions that have been erroneously assessed can lead us to become aware of new reasons, it might prove helpful to look in more detail at an aforementioned feature of emotions, namely, that they serve a particular function: they enable us to respond to particular challenges in our environment and so protect or enhance our well-being. In meta-reasoning about her emotions, an agent can examine whether a particular emotion serves its function well. Emily might find out, for example, that she tends to have strong emotional reactions to situations that are new to her. She might find out that her lack of self-esteem can be attributed to traumatic childhood experiences, which in turn explains why she interprets new situations as being threatening (although her response is inappropriate as she has the capacity to deal with such supposed threats). As a result, she may come to realize that her particular emotional reactions do not serve her well-being. Fear of novelty and lack of self-esteem are likely to hold her back, both professionally and personally. By meta-reasoning, we can determine and eventually try and rid ourselves of emotions that have a wayward causal history.

A third objection, however, is that meta-reasoning does not necessarily achieve what it sets out to achieve, namely, to make our emotions more transparent. After all, we have a tendency to confabulate, we are fallible by nature, and we are encouraged by our over-intellectualized picture of emotions to believe that meta-reasoning about our emotions will always lead us to become aware of our reasons. This skepticism also explains why in many cases we are left at a loss as to whether we should work on our emotions in order to rid ourselves of them or whether we should trust them.[43] What makes things worse is the fact that meta-reasoning itself is prone to error. The way we meta-reason might be affected by our strong negative emotions or it might be driven by our strongly held beliefs about ourselves. There is a possibility that an infinite regress might arise, for we would need meta-meta-reasoning to assess whether our meta-reasoning is in fact reasoning about our attitudes and not rationalizing, which is determined by the attitudes we have already acquired.

In response to this objection, I concede that meta-reasoning about our attitudes cannot eliminate human fallibility. It can bring us closer, however, to attaining appropriate attitudes as we are only able to engage in such a process of meta-reasoning if we distance ourselves, to some extent at least, from our attitudes (including our emotions). Therefore, it does not follow that our meta-reasoning is overdetermined by our emotions, even though it might not be completely independent of them. Meta-reasoning is still a process in which an individual agent holding particular attitudes engages. It is independent enough of our attitudes, however, to allow us to improve our reason-responsiveness and coherence. In addition, we have at our disposal a number of options that can help us to reduce our chances of being fallible: we can ask for advice, arrange psychotherapy sessions, and look for peace and quiet. Meta-reasoning about our emotions will not help us to obtain an objective, fully informed, and infallible perspective of our attitudes, but it will at least bring us closer to discovering the reasons for our attitudes, which will lead us to revise our better judgments.

7. Concluding Remarks

I have tried to show why the cases of inverse akrasia that are presented in the literature are philosophically challenging. First, it is a challenging task to explain how an agent who acts against her better judgment on account of an emotion can plausibly be said to act rationally: she does not act against her better judgment for a reason and she affirms her action much later, believing that she had good reasons to act akratically.

Second, I tried to show that cases of inverse akrasia are not rational but rather exhibit a particular kind of irrationality: the agent tries to satisfy synchronic enkrasia by adhering to her better judgment, yet she finds herself acting on her emotion. Instead, she should have established enkrasia over time by meta-reasoning about her emotion and by reconsidering her better judgment, before revising or reaffirming it. As agents, we need to guide ourselves over time. Since we, as well as our reasons and circumstances, change over time, it is important that we reconsider the correctness of our enkratic reasoning pattern. The emotions that countervail our better judgment prompt us to reconsider our better judgments as they can direct us toward new evidence-based reasons. It is only when an agent is able to meta-reason about her judgment-countervailing emotions that she will be able to rationally resolve the cases in which there is a conflict between her better judgment and her emotions.

Meta-reasoning is not an easy process and it is not always clear how we should proceed; it certainly cannot eliminate our human fallibility. I should also point out that this is not an exhaustive account of how we should meta-reason. My aim has been to provide an outline of how meta-reasoning about our emotions can help us to extract ourselves rationally from so-called inversely akratic cases and thereby satisfy enkrasia over time.[44]

Notes

1. The term "inverse akrasia" was introduced by Arpaly and Schroeder (1999), 162, to describe cases in which "*akrasia* results in what, for lack of a better word, might be called rightdoing of one sort or another. That is, the *akratic* course of action is superior to the course of action recommended by the agent's best judgment. Because these cases reverse our usual expectations from akratic actions, we call them cases of inverse *akrasia*". Bennett (1974) was the first to present such cases (although he did not use the term "inverse akrasia") in his discussion of Mark Twain's fictional character Huckleberry Finn.
2. I use the term "akrasia" to denote specific cases of weakness of will: an agent acts akratically if she intentionally acts against her better judgment, even though another course of action was open to her.
3. Arpaly (2000, 504).
4. I use the terms "reasonable" or "rational" in a broad sense here.
5. This presupposes a cognitivist account of emotions. I will come back to this in Section 5.
6. Arpaly (2000, 504).
7. See, e.g., Paul (2014, Chapter 2).
8. See Wallace (2013, 96–108) for such a view.
9. See, e.g., Brady (2013, 129f). See also Bagnoli (2018, 348), and Tappolet (2003, 115).
10. Cf.: D'Arms and Jacobson (2003, 129); Brady (2009, 413); Benbaji (2013, 577).
11. There may be other sources of reasons, but the cases of inverse akrasia discussed in the literature focus on the new experiences that an agent makes after having carried out her better judgment.
12. See Broome (1999, 398–419).
13. The principle of enkrasia typically states that there should be coherence between an agent's better judgments and her intentions, not between her better judgments and emotions. However, if an agent acts in accordance with the emotions against her better judgment, she clearly does not intend to do what she judged best and thus violates the principle. In Broome (2013, 425), the author presents a formulation of the principle of enkrasia with additional qualifications. A discussion of these qualifications is, however, beyond the scope of this paper.
14. According to Davidson (1980), 41, the principle of continence states that we should "perform the action judged best on the basis of all available relevant reasons".
15. Davidson (1980, 41–43).
16. See Owens (2009), 121–137. See also McHugh (2011, 246).
17. Cf. Audi (1990, 280). See also: McIntyre (2006, 293ff.); Wedgwood (2013, 488); and Owens (2009, 135f).
18. Cf. Owens (2009, 126).
19. See Kolodny (2005) and Levy (2015).
20. This is called the "asymmetry problem". See Schroeder (2004) and also Kolodny (2005). This criticism has been taken up by philosophers wishing to amend Broome's conception of rational requirements. See, e.g., McHugh and Way (2018, 153).
21. See, e.g., Watson (1977); Taylor (1980); and Mele (1987).
22. These problems are strikingly similar to those discussed in the debate on pragmatic encroachment. See, e.g., Roeber (2018, 171–195).
23. See Bagnoli (2017, 137ff.).
24. See Arpaly (2000) for such a view.
25. See also Jones (2003, 188f.).

26 Arpaly (2000) admits to this, but nowhere does she clarify how cases of irrational emotions can be distinguished from so-called reason-tracking ones.
27 See Jones (2003, 196f.).
28 See Arpaly and Schroeder (1999, 173). See also McIntyre (2006, 392f.).
29 Audi (1990, 280).
30 See also Brunero (2013, 550f.).
31 I draw from McHugh and Way (2018, 153–174).
32 See Baker (2016) for an interesting argument on why omniscience excludes deliberation.
33 Hrishikesh (2017, 74f.) maintains that cases of inverse akrasia can be described as rational because forming a better judgment is itself "irrational".
34 See Paul (2014, Chapter 2).
35 Cf. Moller (2009, 664), who refers to meta-reasoning in cases in which bias distorts our deliberations. In cases of inverse akrasia, it is not bias but new experiential information that questions our previous deliberations. See also Elga (2005, 115–124).
36 See, e.g., Deonna and Teroni (2012, Chapter 1).
37 See Cochrane (2017, 1454–1475).
38 Cochrane (2017, 1466). See also Deonna and Teroni (2012, 87ff.).
39 Cochrane (2017, 1466) outlines eight dimensions – including positive-negative valence, power-weakness, certainty-uncertainty, and a sense of social connectedness-isolation – that help to characterize an agent's physical reactions to emotions (which he terms "bodily feelings") and clarifies how they convey content about the agent's body in relation to her environment.
40 See Cochrane (2017, 1469ff.).
41 Moller (2009, 663) highlights the importance of engaging vividly with the particular aspects of a situation so as to improve one's deliberative condition.
42 Cf. Scanlon (2004, 251).
43 See Hinchman (2013, 540ff.), who believes that it is a person's self-mistrust that governs how an agent should reason.
44 Earlier drafts of this paper were presented at the Institute of Philosophy, School for Advanced Study, University of London, and at LMU Munich, the University of Göttingen, Johannes Gutenberg University Mainz, the University of Postdam, the University of Lisbon, and Victoria University of Wellington. I benefited considerably from the feedback, for which I am extremely grateful, given to me by members of these audiences. I am particularly indebted to Carla Bagnoli, who, besides giving me the opportunity to contribute to this volume, also provided me with valuable written comments, as did Thomas Buchheim, Hili Razinsky, Fabrice Teroni, and Anna Wehofsits.

References

Arpaly, Nomy. 2000. 'On Acting Rationally against One's Best Judgment', in: *Ethics* 110 (3), 488–513.

Arpaly, Nomy and Timothy Schroeder. 1999. 'Praise, Blame and the Whole Self', in: *Philosophical Studies* 93 (2), 161–188.

Audi, Robert. 1990. 'Weakness of Will and Rational Action', in: *Australasian Journal of Philosophy* 68 (3), 270–281.

Bagnoli, Carla. 2017. 'Change in View: Sensitivity to Facts and Prospective Rationality', in: Giancarlo Marchetti and Sarin Marchetti (eds.): *Facts and Values: The Ethics and Metaphysics of Normativity*. New York and London: Routledge, 137–158.

Bagnoli, Carla. 2018. 'Emotions and the Dynamics of Reasons', in: *The Journal of Value Inquiry* 52 (3), 347–363.
Baker, Derek. 2016. 'Deliberators Must Be Imperfect', in: *Philosophy and Phenomenological Research* XCIII, 321–347.
Benbaji, Hagit. 2013. 'How is Recalcitrant Emotion Possible?', in: *Australasian Journal of Philosophy* 91 (3), 577–599.
Bennett, Jonathan. 1974. 'The Conscience of Huckleberry Finn', in: *Philosophy* 49 (188), 123–134.
Brady, Michael S. 2009. 'The Irrationality of Recalcitrant Emotions', in: *Philosophical Studies* 145 (3), 413–430.
Brady, Michael S. 2013. *Emotional Insight: The Epistemic Role of Emotional Experience*. Oxford: Oxford University Press.
Broome, John. 1999. 'Normative Requirements', in: *Ratio* 12 (4), 398–419.
Broome, John. 2013. 'Enkrasia', in: *Organon F* 20 (4), 425–436.
Brunero, John. 2013. 'Rational Akrasia', in: *Organon F* 20 (4), 546–566.
Cochrane, Tom. 2017. 'The Double Intentionality of Emotional Experience', in: *European Journal of Philosophy* 25, 1454–1475.
D'Arms, Justin and Daniel Jacobson. 2003. 'The Significance of Recalcitrant Emotion (or, Anti-quasijudgmentalism)', in: *Royal Institute of Philosophy Supplements* 52, 127–145.
Davidson, David. 1980. 'How is Weakness of the Will Possible?', in: *Essays on Actions and Events*. Oxford: Clarendon, 21–43.
Deonna, Julien and Fabrice Teroni. 2012. *The Emotions: A Philosophical Introduction*. London: Routledge.
Elga, Adam. 2005. 'On Overrating Oneself... and Knowing It', in: *Philosophical Studies* 123 (1/2), 115–124.
Hinchman, Edward S. 2013. 'Rational Requirements and "Rational" Akrasia', in: *Philosophical Studies* 166 (3), 529–552.
Hrishikesh, Joshi. 2017. 'What's the Matter with Huck Finn?', in: *Philosophical Explorations* 20 (1), 70–87.
Jones, Karen. 2003. 'Emotion, Weakness of Will, and the Normative Conception of Agency', in: Anthony Hatzimoysis (ed.): *Philosophy and the Emotions*. Cambridge: Cambridge University Press, 181–200.
Kolodny, Niko. 2005. 'Why be Rational?', in: *Mind* 114, 509–563.
Levy, Yair. 2015. 'Normativity and Self-Relations', in: *Philosophical Studies* 172, 359–374.
McHugh, Conor. 2011. 'Judging as a Non-Voluntary Action', in: *Philosophical Studies* 152 (2), 245–269.
McHugh, Conor and Jonathan Way. 2018. 'What is Good Reasoning?', in: *Philosophy and Phenomenological Research* XCVI (1), 153–174.
McIntyre, Alison. 2006. 'What is Wrong with Weakness of Will?', in: *The Journal of Philosophy* 103 (6), 284–311.
Mele, Alfred R. 1987. *Irrationality: An Essay on Akrasia, Self-Deception, and Self-Control*. New York: Oxford University Press.
Moller, Dan. 2009. 'Meta-Reasoning and Practical Deliberation', in: *Philosophy and Phenomenological Research* LXXIX (3), 653–670.
Owens, David. 2009. 'Freedom and Practical Judgment', in: Lucy O'Brien and Matthew Soteriou (eds.): *Mental Actions*. Oxford: Oxford University Press, 121–137.

Paul, Laurie A. 2014. *Transformative Experience*. Oxford: Oxford University Press.
Roeber, Blake. 2018. 'The Pragmatic Encroachment Debate', in: *Noûs* 52 (1), 171–195.
Scanlon, Thomas. 2004. 'Reasons: A Puzzling Duality?', in: R. Jay Wallace et al. (eds.): *Reasons and Value: Themes from the Moral Philosophy of Joseph Raz*. Oxford: Oxford University Press, 247–268.
Schroeder, Mark. 2004. 'The Scope of Instrumental Reason', in: *Philosophical Perspectives* 18 (1), 337–364.
Tappolet, Christine. 2003. 'Emotions and the Intelligibility of Akratic Action', in: Sarah Stroud and Christine Tappolet (eds.): *Weakness of Will and Practical Irrationality*. Oxford: Oxford University Press, 97–120.
Taylor, C. C. W. 1980. 'Plato, Hare and Davidson on Akrasia', in: *Mind* LXXXIX (356), 499–518.
Wallace, R. Jay. 2013. *The View from Here: On Affirmation, Attachment, and the Limits of Regret*. Oxford: Oxford University Press.
Watson, Gary. 1977. 'Skepticism about Weakness of Will', in: *Philosophical Review* 86 (3), 316–339.
Wedgwood, Ralph. 2013. '*Akrasia* and Uncertainty', in: *Organon F* 20 (4), 484–506.

12 Individual Time-Bias and Social Discounting

Brian Hedden

1. Introduction

Many of us, as individuals, seem to care more about our nearer futures than our further futures. Consider a choice between getting one chocolate bar now versus getting two chocolate bars in a month's time. If you would prefer getting the one chocolate bar now, that is indicative of your being *time-biased*, and in particular *biased toward the near*, to use Parfit's (1984) helpful phrase. Similarly, consider a choice between a less painful operation tomorrow and a more painful operation a year from now. Again, if you would prefer the latter over the former, that is indicative of your being time-biased.

On a social level, many policy decisions are and should be made using cost–benefit analysis. When the costs and benefits accrue at different times, as is typically the case, we can conceptualize the procedure as first aggregating the costs and benefits *at each time* and then aggregating those net costs or benefits *over time*. There are significant difficulties even with aggregating costs and benefits at a single time (having to do in particular with issues of incommensurable values), but setting this problem aside, how should costs and benefits be aggregated across time? Economists typically employ a *social discount rate*, which gives costs and benefits accruing in the farther future less weight than those accruing in the near future.

In this chapter, I am concerned with so-called *pure time preference* or *pure discounting*, in which it is well-being itself that is discounted. I therefore set aside other reasons why one might seem to give greater weight to the near future than the far future, having to do with uncertainty, decreasing marginal utility for resources and anticipated wealth gains, and what John Broome (1994, 139) calls "the fertility of technology".[1] In what follows, I use "individual time-bias" and "social discounting" to refer only to the discounting of well-being itself with respect to time.

My focus in this essay is on the relation between the normative status of individual time-bias and the normative status of social discounting.

DOI: 10.4324/9780429259845-16

Does what we say about individual time-bias constrain what we should say about social discounting, and *vice versa*? In Section 2, I show that while earlier theorists took them to be closely connected, there has emerged a near-consensus among economists and philosophers that the two issues are largely independent, so that the normative status of the one entails nothing about the normative status of the other. This is puzzling, for as I suggest in Section 3, the strongest arguments for and against the permissibility of individual time-bias carry over to the case of social discounting, and *vice versa*. And if the same arguments apply with equal strength in both the individual and the social case, then there is strong pressure to draw the same conclusion about each and thereby conclude that individual time-bias and social discounting have the same normative status. In Section 4, I consider a possible disanalogy between individual time-bias and social discounting, namely, that one's treatment of one's own future selves falls only within the domain of rationality, whereas our treatment of future generations falls within the domains of morality and justice. Drawing on recent work in ethics, I reject this disanalogy and suggest that one's treatment of one's future selves can in fact be immoral or unjust. I conclude that individual time-bias and social discounting should in fact be treated in parallel and that they have the same normative status.

2. The Consensus

Some theorists have thought that whether people are, or permissibly may be, individually time-biased has implications for what the proper social discount rate is. Sidgwick (1907) endorsed a position on which both individual time-bias and social discounting are impermissible, and for the same reason, namely, that they fall afoul of a principle of aggregation. Here is Rawls (1999 [1971], 259) discussing Sidgwick's view in the context of the debate over optimal societal rates of saving:

> Just as the good of one person is constructed by comparison and integration of the different goods at each moment as they follow one another in time, so the universal good is constructed by the comparison and integration of the good of many different individuals. The relations of the parts to the whole and to each other are analogous in each case, being founded on the aggregative principle of utility. The just savings principle for society must not, then, be affected by pure time preference, since as before the different temporal position of persons and generations does not justify treating them differently.

Other theorists have thought that a non-zero social discount rate is justified, and moreover that it is justified in part because individuals themselves are, or may permissibly be, time-biased with respect to their own well-being. Schelling (2000, 833) expresses the view as follows, though he himself rejects it:

> [T]here is a near consensus among these economists that the appropriate discount rate should be conceptualized as consisting of two components . . . The first is pure time preference and . . . deals with the impatience of consumers and reflects their inborn preferences of immediate over postponed consumption . . . The second component reflects the changing marginal utility of consumption with the passage of time.[2]

Despite these alleged connections between individual time-bias and social discounting, there is now a near-consensus that the normative statuses of the two are independent. Expressing this common sentiment, Cowen and Parfit (1992) write,

> Even if this attitude [time-bias] is not irrational, it cannot justify an intergenerational discount rate. Perhaps individuals may rationally prefer smaller benefits, because they are in the nearer future. But this argument has no next step. Pure time preference within a single life does not imply pure time preference across different lives.

Statements of the same view can be found in Cline (1992) and Greaves (2017). Unfortunately, these authors do not give a further argument to back up the claim that the two issues are independent. Cowen (ms, 5) goes further. He writes that "Time preference within a life, however, cannot be extrapolated directly to time preference across different lives". His argument seems to be that individual time-bias derives from impatience or a distaste for waiting. Within a single life, having a benefit accrue later rather than sooner does involve that individual's having to wait. But across lives, when a benefit accrues to a future person rather than a presently existing one, it is not the case that any waiting is involved. As Cowen (ibid, 6) notes, "The passage of time before our births does not involve waiting".

Along similar lines, Schelling (2000, 834) argues that "Any time preference pertinent to discounting the long-term benefits of greenhouse gas abatement cannot have anything to do with impatience. The alleged inborn preference for earlier rather than later consumption is exclusively concerned with the consumer's impatience with respect to his or her *own* consumption".

As we will see, however, we need not think of individual time-bias as being rooted in impatience or a distaste for waiting, and so the fact that impatience does not extent across lives fails to show that the permissibility of individual time-bias is independent of the permissibility of social discounting.

Rawls (1999 [1971]) also endorses the claim that individual time-bias and social discounting are independent, though he does so for quite different reasons. Rawls maintains that both individual time-bias and social discounting are impermissible, but he thinks (*contra* Sigdwick) that the reasons for the impermissibility are different in the two cases. Unlike Sidgwick, Rawls (1999 [1971], 259) thinks that since "the principles of justice are not extensions of the principles of rational choice for one person, the argument against [social discounting] must be of another kind" from that of Sidgwick. He proceeds to give an argument against social discounting based on his own, non-utilitarian, theory of justice.[3]

3. Parallel Arguments

Is this consensus correct? Is the normative status of individual time-bias really independent of the normative status of social discounting? One way to answer this question is to look at the arguments that have been advanced for or against the permissibility of the one and to see whether each such argument applies with equal force for or against the permissibility of the latter. That is the tack I will pursue in this section. And while I cannot hope to survey every possible argument that has been or might be advanced in this domain, I will suggest that the strongest arguments for and against the permissibility of individual time-bias carry over with equal force to the case of social discounting, and *vice versa*. This yields good, though certainly not decisive, inductive grounds for concluding that they have the same normative status.

In some cases, the arguments that have been advanced in the context of individual time-bias have also been advanced in the context of social discounting. This is the case for arguments against the permissibility of these attitudes. But in other cases, parallelism has not been recognized. In particular, it has not been recognized that prominent arguments in favor of the permissibility of individual time-bias carry over to the case of social discounting. Indeed, these arguments are, to my knowledge, known only in the philosophical literature and have not been discussed by economists interested in either individual time-bias or social discounting. Thus, bringing these powerful arguments in favor of individual time-bias to the attention of theorists interested in social discounting is one of the aims of this essay.

3.1. *Arguments Against Permissibility*

There are two main arguments against the permissibility of both individual time-bias and social discounting. They are simple but powerful. The first appeals to arbitrariness. In the individual case, the thought goes that it is arbitrary to care differently about your different time-slices merely due to their differing locations in time. Well-being is well-being, no matter when it occurs, and so individuals should not discount their own well-being with respect to time.

It is easy to see that the same argument applies in the case of social discounting, and indeed, it has been made by numerous philosophers and economists (see Sidgwick 1907; Ramsey 1928; Pigou 1932; and Cline 1992, among others). The well-being of future people is still well-being and so should not be treated as less important than the well-being of presently existing people merely due to its temporal location.

The second argument appeals to diachronic inconsistency. If you as an individual are time-biased, then your attitudes will be diachronically inconsistent (unless your time-bias takes a specific form). Suppose that at all times, you prefer one chocolate bar right away over two a month from then. But you also prefer two chocolate bars 13 months in the future over one chocolate bar 12 months in the future. Then, your preferences will shift with the passage of time. Initially, you prefer the two chocolate bars 13 months in the future over one in 12 months time, but as the date approaches, you will come to prefer the latter over the former.

This is potentially problematic, since it can lead to self-defeating courses of action. Suppose it is now January 1, 2022. You start off with a ticket entitling you to one chocolate bar on January 1, 2023. I offer you the option of exchanging that ticket for one entitling you to two chocolate bars on February 1, 2023, at the cost of a small fee. You accept, since you prefer the latter ticket to the former. But being time-biased, your preferences switch, and by late December 2022, you prefer the first ticket over the second. I offer you a chance to make the switch, again for a small fee, and you accept. You thereby wind up with the same ticket with which you started, minus the fees. This is a sort of diachronic exploitability familiar from the money pump argument for transitivity of preferences and diachronic Dutch Book arguments in Bayesian epistemology. Of course, the same diachronic exploitation can take place on a social level. We can imagine a society or state that discounts the future in an analogous way that results in vulnerability to self-defeating courses of action.

On both an individual and a societal level, such vulnerability to diachronic exploitation can be avoided by discounting the future *exponentially*. Being an exponential discounter amounts to having a constant discount rate (not discounting the future at all trivially qualifies as a form of exponential discounting). As Parfit (1984, 160) puts it, a person discounts exponentially if she discounts "at a constant rate of n per cent per month. There will always be the *same* proportionate difference in how much this person cares about two future events". That is, the proportionate difference between the weight assigned to two different times depends only on how far apart in time they are and not on how far either is from the present time. For instance, if (individual or societal) well-being today is assigned twice the weight of well-being a year from now, then exponential discounting requires also assigning well-being ten years from now twice the weight of well-being eleven years from now. In an important result, Strotz (1955–6) proves that exponential discounting will not lead to any exploitable shifts in preferences over time.

But while exponential discounting avoids diachronic exploitability, it nonetheless has problematic implications. First, exponential discounting with some positive discount rate involves not only caring more about the near future than the far future but also caring more about the distant past than the recent past. After all, exponential discounting involves having the proportionate difference in the weights assigned to well-being at one time versus another depending only on how far apart those points in time are and not on their location relative to the present. In response, one might propose a modified version of exponential discounting on which one treats all past times the same and applies a constant discount rate to future times only. But this move reintroduces diachronic inconsistency, with preferences switching due to the mere passage of time. It is tempting to think that this particular sort of diachronic inconsistency is innocuous and hence untroubling. Greaves (2017, 406) writes that "the *only* sort of inconsistency that can result from the discounting structure in question is the phenomenon of foreseeable regret" and that it will not lead one to pursue self-defeating courses of action. But as we will see in Section 3.3, this tempting thought is mistaken; in certain circumstances, treating the past differently from the future can yield diachronic exploitability.

Second, exponential discounting leads to extreme differences in the weights assigned to well-being at different times, when those times are far enough apart. As Broome (2013, 150) notes, discounting at a rate of 1% per year entails that the "7,000 casualties of the battle of Marathon in 490 BC work out to be far, far worse than would be the slaughter of every single person alive on Earth today". And of course these extreme implications of exponential discounting apply not only with respect to past times but also with respect to the future.

In any event, individual time-bias or social discounting that takes a non-exponential form is vulnerable to diachronic exploitation, and even exponential discounting may be unattractive on these independent grounds.

3.2. *Arguments for Permissibility: Demandingness*

We now turn to arguments in the other direction. In this subsection, I consider one argument in favor of social discounting and argue that it applies also to the case of individual time-bias. The argument is that a positive (pure) discount rate is needed in order to prevent our obligations from being overly demanding. It can be overly demanding for two reasons.

First, consider optimal savings theory (Ramsey 1928). Assuming a broadly consequentialist aim of maximizing the good, how should each generation's income and wealth be allocated between immediate consumption, on the one hand, and savings and investment, on the other?

Immediate consumption improves the well-being of those doing the consuming, while savings and investment improve the well-being of those in the future. But as Arrow (1997, 1) notes, in standard economic models, "with zero time preference and a long horizon, the [required] savings rates become inordinately high, possibly approaching one as the horizon goes to infinity." The technical details are complex, but the basic point is simple. Suppose that some generation has the option of foregoing some consumption for the sake of investing in the future. With an infinite time horizon, "Each unit [of resources] sacrificed would yield a finite utility loss to the first generation, but to compensate there would be a gain, however small, to each of an infinity of generations" (Arrow 1997, 5). Hence, any sacrifice in consumption for the sake of saving and investing is on balance good, if we assume a zero discount rate. And even without an infinite time horizon, the optimal savings rate may nevertheless come out excessively high. Thus, a positive social discount rate is needed to avoid the implication that current people ought to take on extreme sacrifices for the sake of future generations.

Second, consider existential risks such as risks of the extinction of humanity from asteroids, gamma-ray bursts, global pandemics, the expansion of the sun into a red giant phase, and the like (Bostrom and Ćirković 2008). The premature extinction of the human race at some time yields a massive loss of well-being, and so huge expenditures on existential risk reduction may be justified by even a small reduction in the probability of extinction (at some time). Arguably, this is grounds for thinking that we should be spending far more than we currently are on policies to mitigate these risks (Posner 2005; Bostrom 2013). But even advocates of increased efforts to mitigate existential risk may balk at the thought that we ought to spend, say, a majority of our budgets on such efforts. Posner (2005, 152), himself an advocate of increased mitigation efforts, argues:

> [N]ot to discount future costs at all would be absurd . . . For then the present value of benefits conferred on our remote descendants would approach infinity. Measures taken today to arrest global warming would confer benefits not only in 2100 but in every subsequent year, perhaps for millions of years. The present value of $100 billion received every year for a million years at a discount rate of 0 percent is $100 quadrillion, which is more than even Greenpeace wants spent on limiting emissions of greenhouse gases.

In my view, this demandingness worry is not a good argument for a positive pure social discount rate. Insofar as we are worried about excessively demanding obligations, we would do better to reject the broadly consequentialist theory assumed as background. (It is worth noting in this regard that overdemandingness is a familiar objection to consequentialism, or at least utilitarianism, even setting aside long or infinite time horizons; see Scheffler 1982.) Perhaps some rights-based theory should be adopted in its place.[4]

Nevertheless, what I want to point out is that analogous motivations (even if they are not good ones) could also be used to support individual time-bias. As an analogue of the debate over the optimal social rate of savings, we can consider the optimal rate of savings for individuals. How much should individuals allocate to immediate consumption, and how much to saving and investment? If humans lived long enough, we would get the same sorts of results that worry Arrow in the social case, being required to make intuitively excessive sacrifices for the sake of our later selves. A positive discount rate with respect to one's own well-being would avoid this result. As an analogue of the point about existential risks, we can ask how much humans should spend (or more generally, what sacrifices they should undertake) to extend their lives or otherwise avoid death. Depending on the costs of various life-extending efforts and their probabilities of extending life by certain amounts of time, we may get the same sorts of results that worry Posner in the social case, being required to devote intuitively excessive portions of our incomes to pursuing gene therapies, telomere-protection efforts, and so on (not to mention strict diet and exercise). Again, being time-biased would allow one to avoid these implications.

Of course, it might be suggested that the demandingness argument for individual time-bias doesn't go through, since while society is potentially eternal, individuals' lives are necessarily finite. But in fact, society has a finite duration as well. The sun is projected to expand and turn into a red giant and sterilize the earth's biosphere in around 3.5 billion years. And even if humans manage to colonize other planets, the universe will eventually become too cold to support life (Adams 2008). And if we set aside these astrophysical considerations, it is not clear that there is any in-principle reason why an individual could not exist indefinitely.

As with the social case, I doubt whether these demandingness considerations are good motivations for the permissibility of individual time-bias. But my main point is simply that even for this somewhat dubious motivation for social discounting, there is an analogous motivation for individual time-bias.[5]

3.3. *Arguments for Permissibility: Future Bias*

We turn now to some more compelling arguments. In this and the following two sections, we will look at arguments that have been advanced in support of the permissibility of individual time-bias. But they have not, to my knowledge, been taken note of in the literature on social discounting. This is unfortunate, since once again these arguments carry over to the social case.

We have so far been dealing with time-bias understood as caring more about the near future than about the far future. This is what Parfit (1984) calls "bias toward the near". But there is another form of time-bias, which he calls "bias toward the future". You are biased toward the future if you prefer that your pleasures are in the future and your pains in the past, even if this means a somewhat worse lifetime pleasure to pain ratio. More generally, it involves weighing the well-being of your future selves more heavily than the well-being of your past selves.

There is a strong intuition that it is permissible, and perhaps even required, that one be biased toward the future (though see Dougherty (2011) and Greene and Sullivan (2015) for dissenting views; see also Hare (2015) for a survey).

If bias toward the future is indeed permissible, this puts pressure on the view that bias toward the near is impermissible. As Parfit (1984) emphasizes, many of the same reasons for thinking that bias toward the near is impermissible apply to bias toward the future as well. So there is a strong case for the conditional that if bias toward the near is impermissible, then bias toward the future is also impermissible.

First, bias toward the future, like bias toward the near, can be charged with arbitrariness. Well-being is well-being, no matter when it occurs. So it would be arbitrary to weight the well-being of various temporal selves differently due merely to their differing locations in time.

Second, bias toward the future, like (non-exponential) bias toward the near, yields diachronic inconsistency. Here is a case from Dougherty (2011) to illustrate the point. Suppose you must undergo one of two courses of surgery. The early course involves 4 hours of painful surgery on Tuesday and 1 hour of painful surgery on Thursday. The late course involves no surgery on Tuesday and 3 hours of painful surgery on Thursday. Being biased toward the future, on Monday, you will prefer the late course over the early course, as it involves a lesser amount of future pain relative to Monday. But on Wednesday, you will prefer the early course over the late course, as it involves a lesser amount of future pain relative to Wednesday.

One might think that the diachronic inconsistency resulting from bias toward the future is innocuous since it is practically inert; you cannot affect whether some event occurs in the past versus the future. So this diachronic inconsistency, unlike the diachronic inconsistency associated with bias toward the near, will not leave you vulnerable to diachronic exploitation or performing self-defeating courses of action. But Dougherty (2011) shows that this is not quite right. If you are biased toward the future and also risk averse in a certain way, then there are cases in which you will in fact be led to perform self-defeating courses of action.[6]

Moreover, while it is true that you cannot affect whether some experience of pleasure or pain occurs in the past versus the future, this may not be true of well-being more generally. Many non-hedonic theories of well-being entail that it is possible to affect the well-being of past selves.[7] Consider desire satisfactionism, according to which the satisfaction of your desires adds to your well-being, and their frustration subtracts from your well-being. Crucially, it is not *believing* some desire to be satisfied that adds to well-being, but rather it's in fact being satisfied. Your past selves likely had desires about the future, and hence you may be able to affect whether their desires were in fact satisfied. If your younger self desired that you eventually travel to Africa, you can satisfy that desire by booking a trip.

The preceding suggests that if bias toward the near is impermissible, then bias toward the future is also impermissible. Parfit (1984) himself holds that both are impermissible. But one could instead apply *modus tollens* and hold that bias toward the future is permissible, and so bias toward the near is permissible as well. Thus, the arbitrariness and diachronic inconsistency arguments against bias toward the near must not be sound.

In any event, this argument – from the permissibility of future bias to the permissibility of near bias – applies to the social case as well. There is at least a strong intuition that policy-makers can permissibly assign less weight to the well-being of past people, even if they are in a position to causally affect their well-being by satisfying their future-directed desires. If such societal bias toward the future is permissible, this puts pressure on the widely held view that societal bias toward the near (i.e., pure social discounting) is impermissible. For the same sorts of reasons standardly appealed to in arguing for the impermissibility of societal bias toward the near (namely, arbitrariness and diachronic inconsistency) would condemn societal bias toward the future as well. So if societal bias toward the future is permissible, then societal bias toward the near should be permissible as well, absent some relevant disanalogy between the two. Thus, in both the individual and the social case, the intuition that bias toward the future is permissible supports the claim that bias toward the near is permissible as well.

3.4. Arguments for Permissibility: Bias in One's Favor

It is natural to think that it is permissible to favor one's own interests over others' interests, at least to some degree. But Parfit (1984) argues that this claim is in tension with the claim that individual time-bias is impermissible. After all, if it is permissible to be biased in one's own favor, why should it not also be permissible to be biased in one's own *current and near-term* favor?

Parfit (1984) calls this the *appeal to full relativity*. There are two natural views: that both person neutrality and temporal neutrality are required and that neither is. But the intermediate position, that temporal-neutrality but not person-neutrality is required, is unstable and can be attacked from both sides.

Here it is worth noting that person neutrality can be motivated by the same two considerations that motivate temporal neutrality. First, bias in one's own favor is arguably arbitrary. If well-being is well-being, no matter *when* it accrues, similarly well-being is well-being, no matter *to whom* it accrues. Second, bias in one's own favor yields an analogue of diachronic inconsistency. In particular, it yields cases of interpersonal inconsistency, in which each person prefers performing her member of some set of actions, despite both wanting that they do not collectively perform the set of actions as a whole. The Prisoner's Dilemma is one such case. Each prisoner prefers to defect, no matter what the other one does, but they both prefer that they both cooperate rather than both defect. Indeed, cases of diachronic inconsistency are structurally just like Prisoners Dilemmas, with your different time-slices or temporal selves as the prisoners (Hedden 2015a).[8]

Whether or not Parfit's Appeal to Full Relativity shows that bias toward the near is permissible, what is important for our purposes is that an analogue can be used to support the permissibility of social discounting. Pigou (1932) held that a government ought not only to promote the interests of current citizens but also to safeguard the interests of future citizens as well. He advocated a (pure) social discount of zero.

Marglin (1963) suggests (though it is unclear whether he ultimately endorses) an opposing view, on which government ought to ignore the interests of future citizens, except to the extent that those interests are taken into account by the preferences of current citizens:

> I want the government's social welfare function to reflect only the preferences of present individuals. Whatever else democratic theory may or may not imply, I consider it axiomatic that a democratic government reflects only the preferences of the individuals who are presently members of the body politic.
>
> (p. 97)

One might object to Marglin's suggestion on various grounds. But for present purposes, the important thing is that we have here an analogue of Parfit's Appeal to Full Relativity. Suppose we think that a government may permissibly favor the interests of its own citizens over those of foreigners. This view is in tension with the thought that a government must not favor the interests of current citizens over those of future citizens. As with the individual case, there are two natural views: that a government must be neutral both with respect to its own citizens versus foreigners and also with respect to its own current citizens versus future citizens, and alternatively that a government may permissibly favor its own citizens over foreigners and also may permissibly favor its own current (and perhaps near-future) citizens over future (or far-future) citizens. The intermediate position can be attacked from both sides, by defenders of full neutrality and by defenders of pure social discounting. Insofar as one is sympathetic to the position that governments may permissibly favor their own citizens, one should therefore likewise be sympathetic to the permissibility of social discounting.

3.5. Arguments for Permissibility: Similarity

We turn now to the final argument. As with the previous two, it comes from Parfit in the context of individual time-bias. Parfit (1984) defends reductionism about personal identity over time, the view that facts about whether an earlier person (or time-slice) and a later person (or time-slice) are identical (or part of the same temporally extended person) are not metaphysically deep facts, nor are they what matters to us in thinking about our own survival. Looking closely at Parfit's arguments for reductionism would take us too far afield, but a major role is played by puzzle cases in which the facts about identity over time are murky; that is, cases in which some event occurs, such that it is unclear and controversial whether the person who is around after the event is or is not the same as the person who was around beforehand. Cases include teletransportation, operations that alter many but not all of one's physical and psychological characteristics (and where these changes seem to be near some threshold such that it is a borderline case of whether or not the post-operative person is identical to the preceding person), and cases involving fission, such as where one enters a teletransporter and two, instead of one, perfect duplicates are created (so that it cannot be that both are identical to the pre-fission person).

Parfit thinks that what really matters to us are psychological connections with later time-slices. He proposes that:

> The value to me of my relation to a resulting person depends both (1) on my degree of [psychological] connectedness [i.e. similarity is relevant respects] to this person, and (2) on the value, in my view, of this person's physical and psychological features.
>
> (p. 299)

He argues that this view justifies "a new kind of discount rate" (314) which correlates with, but is not quite identical to, a discount rate with respect to time:

> My concern for my future may correspond to the degree of connectedness between me now and myself in the future. Connectedness is one of the two relations that give me reasons to be specially concerned about my own future. It can be rational to care less, when one of the

grounds for caring will hold to a lesser degree. Since connectedness is nearly always weaker over longer periods, I can rationally care less about my further future.

Again setting aside whether this view is right, my point is that it carries over to the social case. Indeed, Parfit explicates his reductionism about person identity with an analogous reductionism about the identity of nations over time:

> A nation is in many ways unlike a person. Despite these differences, the identity of persons over time is, in its fundamental features, like the identity of nations over time. Both consist in nothing more than the holding over time of various connections, some of which are matters of degree. It is true that in my old age it will be just as much me. But this truth may be fairly compared with the truth that (say) modern Austria is still *just as much* Austria. A descendant of the Habsburg Emperors could justifiably call this truth trivial.

Insofar as Parfit's reductionism about personal identity, and concomitant emphasis on a notion of psychological connectedness that comes in degrees, can justify the permissibility of something very much like individual time-bias, similar views about nationhood can justify the permissibility of something very much like social discounting. In fact, Schelling (2000, 834) suggests (without endorsing) such a view[9]:

> Actually, time may serve as a measure of "distance." The people who are going to be living in 2150 may be considered "further away" than the people who will be living in 2050 . . . In redistributing income via transfer payments—providing foreign aid, contributing to charity, and so forth—people are expected to differentiate, and *do* differentiate, among recipient peoples according to several kinds of distance or proximity. One is geographical . . . Another is political: East Coast Americans are more interested in the people of Los Angeles than in the people of Quebec. Yet another is cultural: Some people are closer in language, religion, and other kinds of heritage . . . Deciding whether one cares more about the people who will be alive in 2150 than the people who will be alive in 2050 is a little like deciding whether one cares more about people in one continent than in another, or about English-speaking people more than people who speak other languages, or about those with whom one shares his- tory and culture more than those who do not.

Insofar as we think it permissible to discount one's own future well-being according to degrees of psychological connectedness (which correlates with time), we should think it likewise permissible for a society to discount future generations' well-being according to degrees of political or cultural similarity (which correlates with time). Once again, the individual and social cases are parallel.

4. Rational Versus Moral Permissibility

We have seen that a number of arguments – in my view, the strongest ones in the literature – for and against the permissibility of individual time-bias have analogues in the case of social discounting, and *vice versa*. This provides inductive grounds for thinking that individual time-bias and social discounting have the same normative status. Being inductive, however, it is not a knock-down argument. Why might individual time-bias and social discounting nonetheless differ in their normative status? First, it could be that there is some other sound argument for or against individual time-bias that doesn't carry over to the case of social discounting, or *vice versa*.

Second, it could be that one or more of the arguments I have surveyed is stronger in one case than in the other. For instance, it could be that it is more clearly impermissible for a country to favor its own citizens over foreigners than it is for an individual to be biased in her own favor. If so, this would mean that Parfit's appeal to full relativity yields a stronger argument for the permissibility of individual time-bias than its analogue does for the permissibility of social discounting. Or it could be that it is more clearly impermissible for a country to proportion concern for future generations according to the degree to which they are culturally or politically similar to the present generation than it is for an individual to proportion concern for future time-slices according to their degrees of psychological connectedness, in which case we would have an argument for the permissibility of individual time-bias that is stronger than its analogue for the case of social discounting. For my part, however, I view the arguments surveyed previously to be equally forceful in both the individual and the social case.

Third, it might be that different flavors of normativity apply in the individual and the social case. I will focus on this possibility in the remainder of this section. So far, I have talked in terms of permissibility *simpliciter*. But it is important to distinguish between rational permissibility and moral permissibility. And many theorists hold that morality only applies to our treatment of other people. One cannot treat oneself immorally (or unjustly). Mill writes in Chapter 4 of *On Liberty* that "self-regarding faults" are "not properly immoralities and, to whatever pitch they may be carried, do not constitute wickedness" except when "they involve a breach of duty to others, for whose sake the individual is bound to have care for himself". Rawls (1999 [1971], 260) endorses this thought with respect to attitudes to time:

> In the case of the individual, pure time preference is irrational: it means that he is not viewing all moments as equally parts of one life.

In the case of society, pure time preference is unjust: it means (in the more common instance when the future is discounted) that the living take advantage of their position in time to favour their own interests.

Indeed, some theorists have argued that the very idea of duties to the self is incoherent. For instance, Singer (1958) argued that whenever you have a duty to someone to perform a given act, that person can release you from that duty. But this means that if you have some duty to yourself to do something, you can release yourself from that duty. But a duty from which you can release yourself at will is no duty at all. Hence, there can be no duties to the self.

But recently, some ethicists have pushed back against Singer's argument for the incoherence of duties to the self and against the broader view that morality does not apply within a single life.

Hills (2003), for instance, argues that everyone has a duty to promote one's own well-being. She appeals to three premises: first, that everyone has a duty to promote others' well-being; second, that this duty is at least sometimes unwaivable; and third, that reasons for action are universal. Thus, "If you have an unwaivable duty to promote the well-being of others, then, since reasons are universal, you must have a counterpart duty to promote your own well-being" (136). She concedes that duties to the self may not be enforceable via blame and punishment but rejects the underlying "juridical" model of duties which treats moral duties like legal duties.

Schofield (2015) endorses Darwall's (2006) view that what distinguishes moral reasons from other kinds of reasons is that they are second-personal. This might initially seem to entail the impossibility of moral reasons to treat oneself in a certain way. But Schofield argues that what is distinctive about relating to someone second-personally is that the two persons have different standpoints or perspectives. It is not crucial that such a second-personal relationship involves two metaphysically distinct relata. And, Schofield notes, a temporally extended individual occupies distinct standpoints or perspectives at different times, and so an agent at one time can relate second-personally to herself at another time. And he argues that in some cases, as when one's younger self smokes and thereby causes serious harm to her later self, or when one's younger self seriously constrains the autonomy of her later self, that later self may justifiably feel resentment – a paradigmatic second-personal attitude – toward her earlier self.

This is of course not the last word on the matter. But I hope to have said enough to cast some doubt on the idea that one cannot treat oneself immorally or unjustly, and so also on the idea that individual time-bias cannot be morally impermissible.

Putting my own cards on the table, I think that individual time-bias and social discounting are both morally impermissible and rationally permissible. I think that the arguments surveyed in the previous section in favor of the permissibility of these attitudes are uncompelling when it is moral permissibility that is at issue. This is because I think it is morally impermissible to weight the interests of future members of society by their degree of cultural or political similarity to current society, and I think that it is likewise morally impermissible for an individual to weight the interests of her future selves by their degree of psychological connectedness. And, in response to the Parfitian appeal to full relativity, I think it is morally impermissible for an individual to weight her own interests more heavily than the interests of others, and it is likewise morally impermissible for a country to weight the interests of its own citizens more heavily than the interests of foreigners. And while I feel the pull of the argument from the permissibility of bias toward the future, I think we should employ *modus tollens* and conclude that bias toward the future is morally impermissible on both a societal and an individual level, while avoiding counterintuitive conclusions about our duties to past selves and past people by adopting a view of well-being (such as hedonism) on which it is impossible to affect past levels of well-being.[10]

By contrast, I think that rationality requires only that preferences be coherent and avoid the most egregious forms of arbitrariness like Parfit's Future Tuesday Indifference (Parfit 1984). Hence, it is rationally permissible for an individual or society to care more about the future than the past, more about those psychologically or culturally connected to it, more about itself than others, and hence also more about its near future than about its far future. And I have argued elsewhere (Hedden 2015b) against the claim that vulnerability to diachronic inconsistency is *ipso facto* irrational.

5. Conclusion

There is a near-consensus among economists and philosophers that individual time-bias and social discounting are largely independent issues. I agree that descriptive facts about how individuals in fact discount their own well-being with respect to time do not entail anything about whether and how society should discount the well-being of future generations. But this does not mean that the normative status of individual time-bias is independent of the normative status of social discounting. And I have suggested that a close look at the arguments that have been leveled for and against the permissibility of each kind of attitude suggests that they should have the same normative status. The arguments for and against individual time-bias yield analogous arguments for and against social discounting, and vice versa. Moreover, I find the arguments equally compelling in the one case as in the other. One might worry, however, that while individual time-bias may be irrational, only social discounting can be immoral or unjust, for morality only applies to our treatment of other people and not to our treatment of ourselves. But I side with a number of ethicists who have recently rejected this common view and argued that morality and justice can apply intrapersonally as well as interpersonally. Thus, far from being independent issues that can be debated and evaluated separately, individual and societal attitudes to time are in fact intimately connected.

Notes

1 Given the fertility of technology, it is often better to receive a given amount of resources sooner rather than later, since those resources can be put to work and yield greater wealth in the meantime. For instance, it is better to receive $1,000 today rather than even $1,000 inflation-adjusted dollars in a year, because if receiving the money now means you can invest it in stocks or start a business and thereby make substantial gains of the course of the year.
2 This quote is alluding to the so-called Ramsey formula, devised in Frank Ramsey's pioneering work on optimal rates of national saving. Ramsey himself endorses a zero rate of pure time preference, though later economists employed a positive rate of social pure time preference derived from evidence about individuals' own rates of pure time preference. Note that one could also endorse a positive rate of social pure time preference that is not derived from, or intended to reflect, individuals' own rates of pure time preference.
3 Rawls holds that the participants in his original position would not consent to the application of any positive pure social discount rate. This is because they are subject to the veil of ignorance and hence will not know their temporal position with respect to other generations. They will therefore "not consent to any principle that weighs nearer periods more or less heavily", since "to acknowledge a principle of time preference is to authorize persons differently situated temporally to assess one another's claims by different weights based solely on this contingency" (1999 [1971], 260). Even given Rawls' framework, I am unconvinced by this argument, for reasons outlined by Broome (1992, 96–98). Broome points out that exponential social discounting, described in Section 3.1, does not "authorize persons differently situated temporally to assess one another's claims by different weights based solely on this contingency". This is because, with exponential discounting, the relative weights assigned to well-being at different times remain constant, and so persons differently situated temporally would be required to agree in the weights they use to assess one another's claims. Moreover, Broome thinks there are positive reasons why those in the original position might accept the use of exponential social discounting, supposing history has no beginning and no end:

> Compared with an impartial principle, exponential discounting treats each generation less favourably relative to its predecessors. But in compensation, it treats each more favourably relative to its successors. And it has the advantage, compared with an impartial principle, of putting less strain on each generation's self-control.
>
> (97–98)

Thus, it is not clear that Rawls' own argument against social discounting works, even granting the background contractualist framework.
4 See Kelleher (2017) for nuanced discussion of debates around incorporating considerations of rights and justice into the social discount rate.
5 In a recent book, Scheffler (2013) explores a possible disanalogy between the individual and the social case which is relevant here. He argues that our sense of meaning and purpose in our lives depends on our belief that our society will continue, at least for the foreseeable future, but that it also depends on our belief in the finitude of our own lives. He considers a doomsday scenario in

which we learn that humanity will become extinct in the near future (but after all presently existing people are dead) and suggests that in such a scenario, we would no longer value most of our projects, or at least not to the degree we currently do (and, moreover, he suggests that this loss of value would be an appropriate response to the anticipated extinction). By contrast, he suggests that if we were to become immortal, this would cause us to no longer value our projects to the same degree that we actually do (see also Williams 1973). If we do have these differing attitudes to human extinction (or the end of society as we know it) and to individual death, this suggests that the overdemandingness arguments for individual time-bias and social discounting may not be equally compelling. Overall, however, the implications for social discounting and individual time-bias of Scheffler's considerations are complex. In particular, they suggest a narrative, or at least non-aggregative, sort of value relevant to the social good and the individual good which is difficult to integrate into the standard welfare maximization framework presupposed in much discussion of these attitudes to time.

6 But see Greene and Sullivan (2015), who argue that the diachronic inconsistency is in fact due to the kind of risk aversion involved, rather than to the future bias as such.
7 Cf. Broome (2004, 46–47).
8 Parfit (1984, 187) makes a related point about predictable regret, imagining the following accusation leveled against an agent who is biased toward the near:

> You do not *now* regret your bias towards the near. But you *will*. When you pay the price-when you suffer the pain that you postponed at the cost of making it worse—you will wish that you did not care more about your nearer future. You will regret that you have this bias. It is irrational to do what you know that you will regret.

But he points out that an analogous objection can be targeted at one who is biased in his own favour:

> he may regret that in the past he had his bias towards the near. But this does not show that he must regret having this bias now. A similar claim applies to those who are self-interested. When a self-interested man pays the price imposed on him by the self-interested acts of others, he regrets the fact that these other people are self-interested. He regrets their bias in their own favour. But this does not lead him to regret this bias in himself.

9 Parfit (1984, 485) also considers such a view, but notes, correctly, that does not involve discounting with respect to time as such, but rather with respect to something that correlates with time.
10 As for the argument from overdemandingness, I am happy to concede that morality is quite demanding. But if you are concerned about morality being overdemanding, this would motivate not the adoption of a rate of pure time preference but rather some non-consequentialist moral theory that permitted agent-centered prerogatives.

References

Adams, Fred. 2008. 'Long-Term Astrophysical Processes.' In Bostrom and Ćirković 2008, pp. 33–47.
Arrow, Kenneth. 1997. 'Discounting, Morality, and Gaming.' Manuscript, Stanford University. Available: www.researchgate.net/publication/23740962_Discounting_Morality_and_Gaming

Bostrom, Nick. 2013. 'Existential Risk Prevention as Global Priority.' *Global Policy* 4(1): 15–31.
Bostrom, Nick, and Milan Ćirković, eds. 2008. *Global Catastrophic Risks*. Oxford: Oxford University Press.
Broome, John. 1992. *Counting the Costs of Global Warming*. Cambridge: The White Horse Press.
Broome, John. 1994. 'Discounting the Future.' *Philosophy and Public Affairs* 23(2): 128–56.
Broome, John. 2004. *Weighing Lives*. Oxford: Oxford University Press.
Broome, John. 2013. *Climate Matters*. New York: W.W. Norton and Co.
Cline, William. 1992. *The Economics of Global Warming*. Washington, DC: Peterson Institute for International Economics.
Cowen, Tyler. ms. 'What is the Correct Intergenerational Discount Rate?' George Mason University. Available: www.gmu.edu/centers/publicchoice/faculty\%20 pages/Tyler/DISCOUNT.pdf
Cowen, Tyler, and Derek Parfit. 1992. 'Against the Social Discount Rate.' In Laslett and Fishkin 1992, pp. 144–161.
Dougherty, Tom. 2011. 'On Whether to Prefer Pain to Pass.' *Ethics* 121 (3): 521–537.
Greaves, Hilary. 2017. 'Discounting for Public Policy: A Survey.' *Economics and Philosophy* 3: 391–439.
Greene, Preston, and Meghan Sullivan. 2015. 'Against Time Bias.' *Ethics* 125 (4): 947–970.
Hare, Caspar. 2015. 'Time: The Emotional Asymmetry.' In Bardon and Dyke 2015, pp. 507–520.
Hedden, Brian. 2015a. *Reasons without Persons: Rationality, Identity, and Time*. Oxford: Oxford University Press.
Hedden, Brian. 2015b. 'Options and Diachronic Tragedy.' *Philosophy and Phenomenological Research* 90 (2): 423–451.
Hills, Alison. 2003. 'Duties and Duties to the Self.' *American Philosophical Quarterly* 40 (2): 131–142.
Kelleher, J. Paul. 2017. 'Pure Time Preference in Intertemporal Welfare Economics.' *Economics and Philosophy* 33: 441–473.
Laslett, Peter, and James Fishkin, eds. 1992. *Justice Between Age Groups and Generations*. New Haven: Yale University Press.
Marglin, Stephen. 1963. 'The Social Rate of Discount and the Optimal Rate of Investment.' *The Quarterly Journal of Economics* 77: 95–111.
Mill, John Stuart. 1859. *On Liberty*. London: J.W. Parker and Sons.
Parfit, Derek. 1984. *Reasons and Persons*. Oxford: Oxford University Press.
Pigou, Arthur. 1932. *The Economics of Welfare*, 4th Edition. London: Macmillan.
Posner, Richard. 2005. *Catastrophe: Risk and Response*. New York: Oxford University Press.
Ramsey, Frank. 1928. 'A Mathematical Theory of Saving.' *The Economic Journal* 38 (152): 543–559.
Rawls, John. 1999 [1971]. *A Theory of Justice*. Cambridge, MA: Harvard University Press.
Scheffler, Samuel. 1982. *The Rejection of Consequentialism*. New York: Oxford University Press.

Scheffler, Samuel. 2013. *Death and the Afterlife*. New York: Oxford University Press.
Schelling, Thomas. 2000. 'Intergenerational and International Discounting.' *Risk Analysis* 20 (6): 833–837.
Schofield, Paul. 2015. 'On the Existence of Duties to the Self (and Their Significance for Moral Philosophy).' *Philosophy and Phenomenological Research* 90 (3): 505–528.
Sidgwick, Henry. 1907. *The Methods of Ethics*, 7th Edition. London: Macmillan and Company. Reprinted by Hackett Publishing Company, 1981.
Singer, Marcus. 1958. 'On Duties to the Self.' *Ethics* 69 (3): 202–205.
Williams, Bernard. 1973. 'The Makropulos Case: Reflections on the Tedium of Immortality.' In *Problems of the Self*. Cambridge: Cambridge University Press, pp. 82–100.

Contributors

Caroline T. Arruda is Associate Professor of Philosophy at the University of Texas at El Paso.

Carla Bagnoli is Professor of Theoretical Philosophy at the University of Modena and Reggio Emilia, and Visiting Fellow at All Souls College, University of Oxford in 2021–22.

Monika Betzler is Professor of Practical Philosophy and Ethics at Ludwig Maximilian University of Munich.

Michael E. Bratman is U. G. and Abbie Birch Durfee Professor of Philosophy in the School of Humanities and Sciences at Stanford University.

Luca Ferrero is Professor of Philosophy at the University of California-Riverside.

Brian Hedden is Associate Professor of Philosophy at Australian National University.

Jennifer Hornsby is Professor of Philosophy at Birkbeck, University of London, and Emeritus Fellow of Corpus Christi College, University of Oxford.

Laurent Jaffro is Professor of Moral Philosophy at Université Paris-1 Panthéon-Sorbonne and Fellow of the Institut Universitaire de France.

Arto Laitinen is Professor of Social Philosophy at Tampere University.

Julia Nefsky is Associate Professor of Philosophy at the University of Toronto.

Abraham Sesshu Roth is Professor of Philosophy at Ohio State University.

Constantine Sandis is Professor of Philosophy at the University of Hertfordshire and a Founding Director of Lex Academic.

Sergio Tenenbaum is Professor of Philosophy at the University of Toronto.

Index

accidie 154, 161, 167, 221
action sentence 18–20, 25, 31
action theory 33, 40, 196, 200, 212
activity 5, 10, 30, 47, 80–81, 102–104, 117, 183, 201; shared 103, 119; temporally extended 75–77, 83–84, 87–89, 92–93, 96, 100, 110–111, 116, 120–121, 124, 139, 169, 202–203, 208, 212, 214, 225
Adams, F. 271
adjustment, normative 7, 120, 196–197, 201, 203, 205–206, 208, 210–212
agency: intentional 5, 80–81, 96–97, 102; planning 75–76, 78–81, 84, 86–88, 90–98, 100–102, 105, 108, 115, 120, 124, 129, 134–136, 145, 193–194, 200, 213, 221, 225, 233, 235, 239, 241; pure momentary agent 108–111, 114; rational 1, 7, 9, 53, 67–69, 196, 200, 203, 206, 208, 210–211, 214, 247, 249, 251–252; shared 4, 79–81, 91–93, 103, 119, 194; temporally extended 4–5, 7, 9, 16, 75–79, 81, 83–84, 87–89, 102–103, 108–109, 180–181, 183, 187, 189, 194, 196–200, 202, 275–276; time-slice 5, 7, 9–10, 102, 114, 180–181, 184, 189–190, 193, 267, 274–275, 277
Ainslie, G. 119, 195, 237
akrasia 8, 9, 185, 213, 221–223, 227–228, 230–231, 234–235, 239, 241; diachronic 227, 229, 231, 239; inverse 9, 243–244, 246–252, 255–256, 259–260, 262–263; as weak memory 230–234; as weakness of the will 8, 160–161, 213, 221–228, 233, 260

alienation 5, 108, 116–119, 121–122, 124, 197, 201, 208–210, 213; temporal 108, 116–119, 121–122
ambivalence 116, 197, 203, 205, 208–212, 215
Andreou, C. 126, 212
Anscombe, G.E.M. 2, 24, 30, 33, 35–37, 46, 48
Arendt, H. 39, 47
Arpaly, N. 8, 243, 245–246, 252, 260–261
Arrow, K. 270–271
Arruda, C. 6, 130, 155–156, 166–167, 170
attitude: change of/shuffling 183, 199, 203; committing/settling 151, 153, 155–156, 183; conflicting 158–159, 244, 257; emotional 61, 89, 200, 204–205, 207–209, 211, 214, 230–231, 236–237, 243–246, 248–251, 254–255, 260–261 (*see also* emotion); judgement sensitive 113–114; plan infused 91, 93; reactive/co-reactive 97, 99, 204, 205, 214; temporally oriented 5, 8–9, 80, 91, 93, 103, 144, 199, 209, 277, 279, 280
Austin, J.L. 48
authority: agential 3, 8, 9, 162, 169, 196, 198, 201–202, 205, 214; normative 54, 67, 197, 208, 210, 248; of prior decision 146, 207–208, 222, 224–225, 229–230, 232, 235, 240; subjective/objective 70, 208–209, 211
autonomy: agential 7, 63–65, 162, 178, 205; diachronic 7, 130, 174–187, 189–192; personal 68, 186, 209, 211, 213, 278

Index

Bagnoli, C. 70, 130, 213, 214, 260
balance of reasons 55, 61–65, 79, 164, 256–257, 270
Beauvoir, S. 47
Betzler, M. 240
Bicchieri, C. 70
Bostrom, N. 270
Bradley, F.H. 29
Brandom, R. 3, 34, 36
Bratman, M.E. 4–6, 8, 16, 26, 28, 29, 57, 68, 95–96, 100–105, 112, 117, 120, 125, 128, 130, 133, 135, 144–146, 149–152, 155–157, 160–161, 166–170, 177, 183–184, 192–195, 200–202, 212–215
Broome, J. 70, 102, 152, 157–158, 213, 260, 264, 269, 280–281
Brunero, J. 158, 261

Callard, A. 102, 128
capacity 2, 206, 254; agential 52, 109, 112, 152, 182, 186, 211, 214, 258; cognitive/meta-cognitive 8, 61, 111, 115, 197, 207; deliberative 1, 120, 176; emotional/affective 61, 205, 207, 208; normative 8, 52–54, 57; of self-governance 96–97, 100, 120, 197, 199, 204, 212, 222 (*see also* control; self-governance; willpower); to settle/commit/retentive 68, 123, 149–150, 153, 155, 157, 166–167, 175–176
care 60, 98, 108–112, 129, 151, 166–167, 237, 264, 267–268, 275–277, 279, 281; for self-governance 98–99
Carr, E.H. 39
causal theory of action 2, 10, 16, 25–26, 28
Chang, R. 53, 66, 69–70
change 3, 7, 9, 15, 25–27, 30, 52; of circumstances 128, 177; descriptive 53–55, 59; of emotion 85, 101, 183; global 201, 203, 205, 210, 212; institutional 53–54, 58; of mind 59, 77, 137, 179, 224, 226, 240; normative 196, 199–201; of plan 77, 84; of preferences *vs.* values 201, 203, 213, 258–259; of reason 257; of will 234, 245
Charles, D. 48
Chartier, G. 149, 155, 170
choice 1, 4, 7–8, 66, 69, 75–77, 88–92, 100, 104, 106, 112, 119, 124–125, 130, 134, 170, 184, 187, 192, 196, 198, 202, 204, 208, 211–212, 221–222, 225, 231, 233, 236–239, 247, 264, 267
Christiano, T. 67, 70
Ćirković, M. 270
Cline, W. 266–268
commitment 4, 26, 59–60, 66, 68, 116, 118, 134, 137–138, 149–155, 170, 174–176, 196, 199, 201, 206–207, 213, 221–224, 226, 229, 231–232, 234–240, 251; pre-commitment 145, 150, 166
comparability 85, 89, 90; *see also* incommensurability; parity
comparison, cross-temporal 141, 201, 207, 265
compensation across time 91, 120, 201, 202, 207, 270, 280
compositionality 23, 29
conflict: of attitudes 158, 244, 246, 256–257, 259; of mind 85, 128, 224; of values 8, 77, 134, 196–197, 201–203, 205, 207, 213; *see also* dissonance
consent 53–54, 58, 60–68, 70; transformative 61–62, 64, 67
consequence 3, 19, 33, 36, 41, 43–46, 63, 143, 227, 233, 236–237, 239
constancy 85, 90, 239–240
constraint: conceptual 121, 125, 208–209, 211, 222; diachronic 143, 161–162, 213; metaphysical 76, 157; rational 223, 227–228, 233–234; self-imposed 237–238 (*see also* control; self-governance); temporal 1, 7–8, 110, 113, 119–120, 129, 196, 198, 202, 206, 208, 238, 247, 249
control: diachronic 8–9, 43, 98, 227–228; distal 111–114, 134, 145, 174, 176–178; emotional 244, 246, 248, 250; evaluative 166–167, 182–184, 194; rational 193, 203–204, 207, 212
coordination: as cross-temporal interconnection 77, 78–79, 81, 83, 86, 90, 93, 96–97; as cross-temporal organization 75, 79, 203; interpersonal 67–68; as inter-selves cooperation 118, 119, 120, 221–222; intrapersonal cross-temporal 68, 76, 87–88, 93; intrapersonal synchronic 87–88
Cowen, T. 266

Dancy, J. 48, 69, 70
Darwall, S. 214, 278
Davidson, D. 3, 10, 15–20, 23–30, 34, 36, 48, 260
decision 4–7, 55, 64, 66–68, 70, 78, 80, 90–91, 95, 101, 133–150, 154, 157–158, 160, 164, 166–167, 169, 173–196, 199, 203–204, 213–215, 221–222, 224, 232, 237–240, 245, 250, 252, 255, 257–258, 264; dilemma about decision 133, 135–136, 138–139, 143; wholehearted 149, 161, 208–209
deed 33–34, 41–48, 63, 68
deliberation 2, 7, 77, 95, 150, 162, 164, 168, 176–179, 182, 185–187, 190–191, 196–198, 200, 203, 206–210, 212, 214, 224–225, 232, 261; re-deliberation 140, 149, 153–154, 159–162, 169; *see also* reasoning, practical
demandingness 269–271, 281
Derrida, J. 39
desire 2, 28, 36, 70, 129, 135–136, 156, 169–170, 187, 191, 198–199, 201, 212–213, 225–226, 236, 238–240, 243–244, 247, 251, 253–254, 273
Dilthey, W. 39
dissonance 7, 197, 205, 209; *see also* conflict
Dodds, E.R. 44
Dorsey, D. 5, 10, 130, 155
Dougherty, T. 10, 272
Dworkin, R. 46, 48

Edmunds, F. 39
Elton, G. 39–40, 47
emotion: countervailing 244, 253, 256, 259; reason-tracking 251, 261; transition 207, 211; *see also* attitude, emotional
enkrasia 244, 247–248, 250, 256–257
Evans, R. 39–40, 47
event 16, 18–20, 22, 24, 26–27, 30–36, 39, 41–43, 45–49, 52, 59, 237, 241, 268, 275; event ontology 15–16, 22–23, 29
evidence 9, 39, 40, 141, 146, 169–170, 175, 205, 227, 245–246, 248–249, 251–253, 256–257, 259, 280
expectation 6, 54–55, 67, 75, 77, 81–84, 102, 111, 113, 123–124, 128, 131, 133, 135, 178–179, 198, 202–203, 207, 221, 237–238, 255, 260, 276

Ferrero, L. 10, 102, 106, 120, 145–146, 157, 165, 170, 174, 176–181, 191–194, 212–213
Ford, A. 30
Frank, R.H. 236
Frankfurt, H. 75, 96, 99, 102, 149, 161, 208, 212–214
freedom 7, 69, 196–197, 207, 210–211
Frege, G. 15, 30, 225
full relativity argument 273–274, 277, 279

Gilbert, M. 68, 155, 214
Greaves, H. 266, 269
Greene, P. 198, 272
grit 150, 169, 196, 201
guidance 75, 88, 95–96, 115, 183, 208–209, 223, 240, 250

Hanslam, N. 237
Hare, C. 272, 198
Hausman, D. 233, 237–239, 241
Hedden, B. 10, 274, 279
Hegel, F.W. 23, 33–36, 39, 43–44, 46
Heidegger, M. 39, 41
Hieronymi, P. 155, 166
Hills, A. 278
Hinchman, E. 149, 155, 261
history 3, 32–33, 38–40, 45, 59, 70, 90, 209, 211, 215; causal history 268, 280
Hobbes, T. 233
Holton, R. 100, 104, 149–150, 155, 160, 167–170, 195, 213, 238
Hornsby, J. 10, 29, 33, 42, 46, 69, 211
Hurtig, K. 53, 60–65, 69–70

identity: as continuity 5, 15, 77–76, 87–88, 104, 108, 110–111, 117–120, 123–125, 127, 129–131, 201, 241; personal 77–78; practical 239–240; temporal 108, 116–118; trans-temporal 5, 114, 123, 128, 129, 131, 185, 193, 201, 205, 209, 211; as unity 81, 111–112, 115, 117–118, 120–121, 123, 125–128, 131, 202, 206, 240, 245; as volitional integrity 197, 206, 208, 211

288 Index

ignorance 36, 228, 234, 247
incentive 145, 181, 187–188, 192, 227–228, 236
incoherence 7, 200, 203–204, 212–213, 215, 227–228
incommensurability 66, 69, 146, 175, 183–184, 264; see also comparability; parity
integration 5, 108, 117–130, 202, 204–206, 210–211, 214, 265
integrity 63–65, 197, 206, 208–209, 211, 213; see also identity; self-governance; unity
intended mutual responsiveness 80–83
intention 3, 5, 6, 16, 19, 21, 24, 28–29, 33–34, 36, 38, 40, 43–46, 68, 70, 77–84, 86, 88, 91–93, 97, 100–104, 113, 120, 129, 131, 133–137, 140–146, 149, 152–159, 164, 167–169, 173, 177, 179, 181–183, 186–188, 190–197, 199–202, 212–213, 215, 224, 231, 240–241, 244, 246, 249–254, 256, 260; future-directed 120, 149, 158, 174–175, 177, 182, 191, 193–194, 196; interlocking 5, 81, 83, 93; past 104, 177, 179, 188, 194, 197, 200; shared 80–83, 91, 96, 103

James, W. 114
judgment 67, 85, 146, 162–165, 173, 189–190, 195, 200, 202, 204, 206, 212–213, 221, 223, 225, 228, 231–232; all-things considered 228, 247–248; best judgment 89, 187, 195, 224, 235, 243, 260; better 243–253, 256–260; evaluative 8, 165, 200, 225, 227–228, 234, 240; moral 8, 44, 149, 223, 229; practical 8, 200, 202, 212; prudential 222, 234, 238–239; unconditional 247–249

Kavka, G. 90, 100, 105
Kelly, T. 87, 104
Kennett, J. 226–227
Killmister, S. 155
Korsgaard, C.M. 118, 130–132, 212, 214

Laitinen, A. 3, 12, 43, 46, 48, 52–53, 66, 70
Lanzmann, C. 40, 47

Leibniz G. 8, 222, 225–232
Levinas, E. 33, 39–40, 47
Liberman, A. 155

Macaulay, T.B. 39
MacCormick, N. 66
Macmurray, J. 2, 42
Marglin, S. 274
McClennen, E. 79, 102–103, 119
memory 38–39, 130, 142, 144, 194, 207, 222, 225–235, 237, 239–241; see also remembering
mereology 33, 45
metaphysics 15–16, 26–28, 30, 76, 114, 124, 135, 275
Michael, J. 155
Millgram, E. 10, 97, 105, 131, 213
Morton, A. 8, 10, 215, 239
Morton, J. 12, 150, 165, 169, 170, 212–213
motive 33, 36, 38, 40, 43, 45, 186–187, 198, 203, 208, 213–214, 234–235, 247–248; motivation 34, 43, 70, 114, 137, 155–156, 162, 221–223, 226, 228, 235–237, 240, 254, 271, 281; motivational force 150, 157, 163, 196–198, 212, 244; motivational stability 153, 201–202, 206, 212

Nagel, T. 10, 48, 200–203, 212–214
Neander, J.A.W. 39
Nefsky, J. 105
norm: rational 95–99, 104, 199–200, 209; social 52, 54–55, 57, 70
normative indeterminacy 197, 212
normative power 3, 52–60, 63, 66–70, 138–139, 207; transformative 53, 60, 61, 69
normativity 52–56, 70, 121, 135, 139, 149, 151, 165–166, 168, 200, 214–215, 277

Pacherie, E. 155
Parfit, D. 10, 46, 48, 55, 70, 126, 199, 202, 212–213, 264, 266, 268, 272–277, 279, 281
parity 66, 164; see also comparability; incommensurability
Paul, S. 98–99, 104, 123, 126, 130, 150, 169–170, 175–176, 181, 191–193, 212–221, 260–261

Index   289

perseverance 6, 150, 153–154, 162; as strength of the will 161–162, 163, 169–170
Pigou, A. 268, 274
plan-theoretic model 76–79, 81, 83–84
Posner, R. 270–271
practical irrationality 8, 208–209, 221–222, 226, 244–247, 256–257, 259
practical rationality 1–2, 4–5, 7, 95, 104, 114, 197–202, 206, 208–210, 221
preference 8, 86, 104, 112, 129, 170, 185, 193, 200–201, 207, 212, 268–269, 274, 279; pure time preference 264–266, 277, 280–281; reversal 127–128; shift 195, 202, 213, 224, 237–238, 240, 245
Prichard, H.E. 42
prisoner's dilemma 4, 133, 236, 274
prudence 201–202, 204, 240
purpose 30, 33–34, 36–40, 43, 46, 61, 66, 173, 280

Rabinowitz, W. 86–87, 104–105
Ramsey, F. 268–269, 280
rationality 1, 4–5, 7–9, 76, 95–97, 98–101, 114, 119, 146, 158, 197–200, 202, 206, 208–210, 213–214, 221–222, 226, 238–240, 244–251, 256–257, 259, 265, 279; rational requirement 152, 154, 157–159, 165, 174, 177–178, 180, 182–183, 193–194, 247, 260
Rawls, J. 211, 265, 267, 277, 280
Raz, J. 67, 69, 70, 104, 105
reason: for action 7, 54, 57, 67, 70, 133, 144–145, 170, 177, 196–198, 201, 205, 207–210, 212; contributory 55, 63–65
reasoning: enkratic 252, 256–257, 259; instrumental 66, 86, 120, 152–153, 200, 202, 206, 209, 214–215, 248; meta-reasoning 244, 252–254, 256–259, 261; practical 1, 3, 5, 8, 9, 52, 57, 123, 134, 200, 206, 208, 214, 221, 226–227; theoretical 84–85; transformative 204, 214
regret 84, 91–92, 105, 196, 200, 202, 204, 206, 213, 224, 254–256, 269, 281

remembering 142, 194, 229–235, 241; see also memory
resolution 84–86, 101, 105, 126, 149, 160–161, 167–169, 186, 195, 200, 213, 221–226, 229–235, 237–240; solemn 221–222, 224, 229
resolve 84, 86–87, 89, 91–92, 134, 222, 226, 231–232, 234–239, 240, 256, 259
Ricoeur, P. 23, 32–33, 35, 39, 40–42, 46–47, 69–70
Ross, J. 155–156, 168
Roth, A.S. 141, 145–146, 155
rule 54, 140, 214, 231–233; personal 222, 233–234, 237–238, 241; see also norm

Sandis, C. 3, 46–48
Sartre J.P. 4, 77, 79, 85, 90, 100–102, 105, 169, 202
Scanlon, T. 68, 261
Schafer-Landau, R. 221
Scheffler, S. 271, 280–281
Schelling, T. 8, 233, 236–238, 266, 276
Schofield, P. 278
Schroeder, M. 155, 260–261
Searle, J. 53, 70
self-command 8, 196, 233; see also self-control
self-governance 4–5, 7–8, 75–81, 83, 104, 115, 130, 146, 183, 192–194, 196–197, 199–203, 206, 208–209, 211, 215, 232, 236; diachronic 75–81, 84, 87–94, 96–102, 104, 130, 146, 183, 192, 194, 196–197, 200, 202–203; dynamic 7–8, 197, 209; as self-control 222, 226–228, 230, 232–233, 235–237, 239, 258, 280 (see also constraint, self-imposed; coordination; self-command; temptation); as self-integration 202, 205, 211 (see also unity); as self-management 8, 76; synchronic 75–76, 80, 85, 88–90, 96, 102, 236
Sen, A. 238
settling 5–6, 76, 78, 121, 133–151, 153, 155, 157, 159, 161, 163, 165, 175, 182, 202, 248; transitive 133–135, 137–140, 142, 144–145
Shoemaker, S. 78, 110
Shpall, S. 105, 155–156, 158–159, 164, 168, 170

shuffling 78, 85, 89–90, 93, 100, 102, 183–184, 194, 203, 211; brute shuffling 4, 8, 90, 102, 183, 202
Sidgwick, H. 265, 267–268
Simon, H. 96, 238–239
Singer, M. 278
Smith, A. 130
Smith, M. 10, 222–223, 225
Smith, T. 103
Sobel, J.H. 86, 104–105
social discounting 9–10, 264–269, 271, 273–280; *see also* temporal bias
stability: agential 150–160, 162–163, 167–168; diachronic 4–6, 75, 84, 88, 95–100, 117–118, 120–124, 129, 146, 149, 200, 203, 207; instability 87, 93 (*see also* incoherence; shuffling); normative 164–166, 195
Strawson, P.F. 48, 97, 99, 105, 119
Sullivan, M. 272, 281
supervenience 3, 53, 59–60, 70
Sverdlik, S. 44–45
Szabò, G.Z. 2, 20–23, 25, 29

Taylor, C. 3, 34, 36, 260
temporal bias 9, 10, 199–200, 209, 212, 265–271, 277–278; in one's favor 273–276; toward the future 271–273, 279, 281; toward the near/present 28, 198, 199, 212, 264–265, 272–274
temporal locality 108–110, 113–116, 119, 121
temporal neutrality 212, 273–275
temporal self 114–118, 120, 122, 125, 127, 130
temptation 4, 84–87, 89–93, 101, 114, 118, 127–129, 149–150, 161–162, 168, 170, 175, 186–187, 193, 197, 199–203, 209, 212–214
Tenenbaum, S. 102, 104, 105, 212
Thompson, M. 2, 30
Townsend, L. 155
trace 3, 27, 32–33, 35, 37–43, 45–48
transformative experience 123, 126, 128, 245
transition 128, 203–204, 207–211; *see also* change
Tuomela, R. 53

unity: diachronic 118, 128, 131, 206, 240; temporal 5, 81, 117; *see also* identity; integrity; self-governance

voluntariness 46, 61, 66–67, 226–227, 233, 237, 239
Von Wright, G. 2, 42, 241

weakness of the will 8, 160–161, 213, 221–228, 233, 260; *see also* akrasia
Williams, B.A.O. 44, 48, 212–213, 281
Williamson, T. 146
willpower 84–92, 94, 100–101, 104, 170, 196, 201, 203, 211–213, 225
Wittgenstein, L. 27, 29, 48

Printed in the United States
by Baker & Taylor Publisher Services